The
1968–2000

CASS SERIES ON POLITICAL VIOLENCE
ISSN 1365-0580

Series Editors: David C. Rapoport, University of California, Los Angeles
Paul Wilkinson, University of St Andrews, Scotland

1. *Terror from the Extreme Right*, edited by Tore Bjørgo

2. *Millennialism and Violence*, edited by Michael Barkun

3. *Religious Radicalism in the Greater Middle East*, edited by Bruce Maddy-Weitzman and Efraim Inbar

4. *The Revival of Right-Wing Extremism in the Nineties*, edited by Peter H. Merkl and Leonard Weinberg

5. *Violence in Southern Africa*, edited by William Gutteridge and J.E. Spence

6. *Aviation Terrorism and Security*, edited by Paul Wilkinson and Brian M. Jenkins

7. *The IRA, 1968–2000: An Analysis of a Secret Army*, J. Bowyer Bell

The IRA
1968–2000

Analysis of a Secret Army

J. Bowyer Bell

FRANK CASS
LONDON • PORTLAND, OR

First published in 2000 in Great Britain by
FRANK CASS PUBLISHERS
Newbury House, 900 Eastern Avenue
London IG2 7HH

and in the United States of America by
FRANK CASS PUBLISHERS
c/o ISBS, 5804 N.E. Hassalo Street
Portland, Oregon 97213-3644

Website: www.frankcass.com

British Library Cataloguing in Publication Data

Bell, J. Bowyer (John Bowyer), 1931–
    The IRA, 1968–2000: An analysis of a secret army. – (Cass series on
    political violence; 7)
    1. Irish Republican Army – History 2. Republicanism – Ireland
    – History – 20th century 3. Political violence – Ireland –
    History – 20th century
    I. Title
    322.4'2'09415'09045

ISBN 0-7146-5070-6 (cloth)
ISBN 0-7146-8119-9 (paper)
ISSN 1365-0580

Library of Congress Cataloging-in-Publication Data

Bell, J. Bowyer, 1931–
    The IRA, 1968–2000: An analysis of a secret army / J. Bowyer Bell.
    p. cm. – (Cass series on political violence, ISSN 1365-0580; 7)
    Includes bibliographical references and index.
    ISBN 0-7146-5070-6 (cloth: alk. paper) – ISBN 0-7146-8119-9 (pbk: alk. paper)
    1. Ireland–History–1922–. 2. Irish Republican Army–History–20th century. 3.
    Political violence–Ireland–History–20th century. 4. Political violence–Northern
    Ireland–History–20th century. 5. Northern Ireland–History. I. Title. II. Series.

DA963.B45 2000
941.5082–dc21
                                                                00-030340

Typeset by Vitaset, Paddock Wood, Kent
Printed in Great Britain by
Creative Print and Design (Wales), Ebbw Vale

Contents

Series Editor's Preface   vii

Preface   xi

Introduction: The Nature of the Armed Struggle   1

1. The Irish Arena   17

2. Analysis and Reality   41

3. Ideology: The Dream Structured   56

4. Recruitment   73

5. Individuals   95

6. Organization   126

7. Command and Control   148

8. Maintenance   168

9. Communications   198

10. Deployment   222

11. Intelligence   240

12. Campaign   265

13. The Enemy   289

14. Endgame   301

Epilogue   317

Sources   329

Index   341

Series Editor's Preface

The editors of the Cass Series on Terrorism and Political Violence are delighted to have this opportunity to add J. Bowyer Bell's new book to our list. Everyone in the field knows Bell as exceptionally prolific. He has published more than 15 well-received, always intriguing, and often controversial books. Beyond this, there is a documentary film, innumerable articles and various short monographs. His books are normally studies of war, and the overwhelming number treat guerrilla and terrorist campaigns, but he has also written a fascinating volume on the art of cheating in war, magic, business, sports, etc.; and there is a second, equally interesting, book on how sports are played.

Bell's first study, his doctoral dissertation, treated the Spanish Civil War. Subsequently, he examined aspects of World War II, and that was followed in rapid succession by various efforts aimed it seemed at covering virtually the entire universe of armed conflicts in the twentieth century, or at least civil ones. No one in this generation has done better work on violent internal conflicts, and no one has produced more work on them either. He has studied most uprisings against colonial powers after World War II, insurrections and wars in Israel, the ANC struggle in South Africa, war in the Horn of Africa and struggles within Saudi Arabia. But most of all, he has been interested in the Irish struggles; indeed, he has devoted six good books to the topic, and Irish matters very often also play a large part in his more general analyses, such as *The Myth of the Guerrilla* and *A Time of Terror: How Democratic Societies Respond to Revolutionary Violence*.

To understand the internal workings of underground organizations, organizations which obviously cannot keep paper records, most of us find the memoirs of participants indispensable. Those who use memoirs in our courses also find that nothing turns students on more. Narratives incite interest and fix events and interpretations in our minds more firmly. Memoir literature is rich, extensive, and can be used for a variety of different academic purposes, for example, Begin, *The Revolt;* Grivas, *Memoirs*; Baumann, *Terror or Love*; Abu Iyad, *My Home My Land*; Mac Stiofáin, *Revolutionary in Ireland*; McGuire, *To Take Up Arms*; Collins, *Killing Rage*. That extraordinarily useful film *Battle of Algiers* was based on Saadi's memoirs.

The problem with these valuable accounts is obvious. Whether written by defectors or those still committed, they intentionally or unintentionally obscure much truth for the sake of the message. But the fact remains that one must find out how participants understand the struggle, how their organization operates, and so there can be no substitute for talking with them.

Journalists favour this approach, political ethnography, much more than academics do; and, indeed, this volume is the only one in the series to rely exclusively on that method. Bell's sources are participants from the various sides of a particular conflict; and, since the primary concern of this analysis is the IRA, most of the contacts are Republicans. For nearly 40 years, Bell has been conversing with IRA and former IRA members, a process he calls 'osmosis'. He has spoken with grandfathers, sons, and grandsons in the IRA, and calculates that he has spent more time writing about that organization than most volunteers have spent in it! This unique experience (can anyone match it?) gives him a rare perspective. Good political ethnography takes time, persistence, and reflection, because the informants, whether they are running or not, are desperately concerned to conceal details as well as reveal them. They are very difficult to decipher, and Bell emphasizes that he needs time and distance to do the job well. He must get out of the island to write about it. He begins always in New York, then goes to the scene, and finally returns to New York to think and write. Republicans may not always recognize themselves in his text, because 'their world is not mine, their world is shaped by a dream I do not share and so any analysis will for the faithful miss the point'.

It is striking, too, that in recent years Bell's authority is such that he has chosen to dispense with footnotes. We who know his credibility continue to read him avidly, perhaps even more so than before. Academics have to be ambivalent about his self-confidence; our eyebrows are raised but our admiration is intense. For the sake of those unfamiliar with his subject, who want other views and more information, he has added a chapter reviewing and assessing what seems to be an endless supply of fresh publications. The Irish fascinate everybody interested in guerrilla and terrorist activity. Academics, politicians, soldiers, police, journalists, and students of all sorts will want to know more about the IRA, who by most accounts, are considered to be the inventors of the protracted national-liberation struggle. Certainly, no other underground element today has persisted for nearly as long. In the modern world, the overwhelming number of rebel groups, despite, or perhaps *because* of, the attention they stimulate, fail and virtually all give up after a few years of struggle. The durable may last a decade or so, but the IRA has been around for nearly a century and understands itself as the heirs of the struggle for an independent republic that began in the aftermath of the French Revolution, and can be interpreted as a continuation of rebellions going all the way back to the twelfth century.

In the early 1960s, everyone thought the IRA to be dead because its campaigns after 1923 had been short, hopeless, and, truth to tell, even pathetic. The Republic's prosperity, moreover, had evaporated much support. Yet in 1968, by taking advantage of vicious Protestant pogrom-like responses to civil rights marches, the IRA revived itself. Its first step was to depose its official leaders, who had decided that bullets were 'out of date'. It then took two more steps, becoming the defenders of the community against Unionist assaults and then finding ways to provoke British troops sent to curb Unionists. Ultimately, the IRA mounted the longest continuous effort in its history. Only the ancient religious groups, the Zealots, Assassins, and Thugs, have displayed such remarkable durability.

Bell is preoccupied with the IRA's properties, namely with its dream, how it is organized and functions, how it recruits, how it makes decisions, internal tensions, communication patterns, intelligence facilities, the ways in which its war is carried on, how it perceives and misperceives the enemy, and how the enemy perceives and misperceives the IRA.

Like everyone else interested in violent underground rebel groups, Bell finds himself most intrigued by the IRA's durability. Throughout this exposition, he utilizes his own vast knowledge of comparable groups to see what is different or what is so special here. He notes, for example, that after its revival the IRA was transformed into the only underground organization composed exclusively of workers – even its leaders were workers. Most comparable entities (including the earlier IRA formations) claim to represent those without property but their members, especially the leaders, come from the middle class. He tells us that the IRA is the most conservative organization of gunmen he knows with respect to tactics, weapons, and strategy. Presumably, though he does not make the claim, that is one reason that it is so durable. Secrecy is very expensive, especially with respect to efficiency; the familiar is the most reliable in such contexts. One might add that the religious terrorists in the past also understood this problem and dealt with it adequately to preserve their durability.

Bell notes the IRA disposition to use the gun for all sorts of unnecessary purposes, and while he does not discuss the issue in other groups, it is a problem for which many memoirs offer solutions, solutions that sometimes work and sometimes do not. Alas, Bell makes his comparisons *en passant* and by implication, for comparison is not his main intention. Still, his description of the IRA is so ample it will provide a series of questions for us to put to other groups and a baseline for a comprehensive comparisons. Over and over again, Bell uses three terms to describe the IRA: faith, sound recruits, and consensus. Faith supplies the energy, and the most famous IRA figure in this generation was not a 'gunman but a prisoner, Bobby Sands', who starved himself to death to protest at prison practices. Recruits are the tools, and they must be 'sound' (i.e. have the faith), reliable, conventional in their habits, and competent. Sound recruits are rarely the brightest or the most talented prospects, and since 1970 the IRA has always had more recruits than it has needed. Surprisingly, the term most used when describing leadership and decision-making is consensus. By 'consensus' Bell does not mean majority rule, because a minority is potentially a schismatic body. To achieve consensus a group must incorporate the various views of its members, modifying them all in the process. Consensus in the IRA, Bell emphasizes, makes changes in any new direction very difficult and very time-consuming.

For the IRA, the British are the problem; the Unionists (Protestants) will come around, once the British leave and the only effective means is the bullet. The ambivalence of the IRA's popular constituency will, so the IRA believes, provide that minimum support needed. The IRA understands that it cannot drive the British out, but it is confident that its endurance capacity is unmatched and that it will win even if it cannot escalate the struggle. But the British capacity to endure, Bell argues, is underestimated; hence, the present deadlock. A settlement eludes participants, partly because recourse to ballots in the past always betrayed the faith or the ultimate objective, so the IRA believes.

Other undergrounds realized that there had to be a point where the gun caused more problems than it solved. The Irgun under Menachem Begin understood that, to persist, it would have to kill Jews and so it accepted less than its original dream mandated. Begin's decision, he said, was inspired by memories of the enormous miscalculation Jewish rebels in a similar situation had made long ago, an act which sealed Israel's greatest historical catastrophe. But the IRA is crippled by a different recollection and faith. Beyond Irish history and intimately related to it, the need for consensus makes any important change in direction excruciatingly difficult and problematic. In the meantime, time works against the IRA, as the minimal community tolerance required weakens and the unused military assets of a secret army constantly erode. Will a true reconciliation emerge? Can the IRA persuade itself that this time, at last, ballots can be substitutes for bullets? Bell concludes on an appropriate but maddening note: 'Perhaps and perhaps not.'

DAVID C. RAPOPORT
Series Co-Editor
May 2000

Preface

For over a generation, for much of my analytical life, in fact for most of my adult life, I have as an observer been engaged in a long march through active and recent undergrounds. I have visited for duty's sake many of the garden spots of internal war: Beirut, Gaza, and Aden, the old battlefields, Cyprus and Ethiopia and the Zambezi valley, and the arenas of the Euroterrorists in Italy and Germany or the separatists of Brittany. These have been way-stations, often visited repeatedly – stops on a terrorist tour, endless hours of boredom, the odd flash of violence, a coup on Cyprus or guerrillas in Eritrea, but mostly questions and answers and discussion.

And no place have I spent more time than in Ireland of the Troubles, the longest running of all low-intensity conflicts with roots that can be traced deep into the past. And in the recent present, there has been an endgame, a peace process without real peace, and for the Irish Republicans more schisms, more problems, and so more questions to be asked about the faithful and their island. There may be all sorts of Ireland, one for those dedicated to the horse or to Yeats, or just the everyday world of getting and spending and sending the children off to school; but more often than not it has been that of the subversives, the gunmen in mufti, the fanatics in three-piece suits. The Irish Republican world is really open only to those of the faith. And what one takes away is not always what the faithful perceive: reviewing one of my books in the *Irish Times* recently, one of the more prominent figures of the last generation, Danny Morrison, fails to recognize my world as his, my perceptions as accurate – but then that is as it should be.

In the course of my Irish investigations, I have not only been criticized by all and sundry for my written word – as, again, might be expected – but also have been an inadvertent target, a suspect, followed by the legitimate and doubted by the dubious, been shot at, gassed, bombed – the usual exposure of many active journalists. I have as well often lived a normal life, written a thriller, gone to the Arts Club, had lunch with the respectable, and shopped at the sales. Ireland is not all troubled and not often, and Dublin is mostly quiet, soft and easy, pleasant for those who can pay the tab, a splendid city if not yet safe from the wreckers and prosperity.

So, much of my Irish life has been conventional even if I have regularly had tea with terror, associated for years with subversives, met all sorts and conditions, some orthodox and some not, at my world headquarters in Bushwell's. I have from time to time reverted to form, published in Irish journals, appeared at seminars. Mostly in Ireland, mostly in Dublin, I have waited for interviews, taken notes, learned by osmosis and then gone back to New York to spend much of my time writing up the results of exposure and contemplation. It has been in many ways a conventional, almost academic, life but for the odd moment and the nature of many of my sources.

The times of exception, the unconventional moments, have hardly been orthodox. Spread over a generation these adventures have with age become rarer. One car-bomb is much like the next, except to those involved, and so one is more than enough. More difficult, if not as spectacular, has been the need to keep a certain distance from sources who have evolved into friends. In theory, to the historian all men are dead; but this is easier quoted than effected. And there are all the other problems of living amid people who cannot go home to New York and are not always delighted to be sources instead of just folks at the pub or in Quinnsworth or for that matter on active service.

I have grown, if not immune, at least resigned to the occasional complexities involved in such research, and the conventional have largely accepted my habits if not the views of my subversive friends. Some, in fact, hardly know that I have such friends, that the car parked at the end of the lane is waiting to see who I visit or that the painter Bow Bell is the American who appears regularly to check on the state of the revolution. Checking on the state of the revolution often involved more than the odd question on Parnell Street.

And, sitting at the side of a ditch in the corner of a far Ulster field waiting for the dubious to appear on matters of most parochial, if seditious, concern eventually brought diminishing analytical returns. One gunman is often like the next. Is one more bit of evidence needed – is this ditch relevant or another tale needed? Do I really want the opinion of a frightened young man in a jumble shop combat jacket with his eyes darting about behind Ray Bans? Am I there because of the charms of the dangerous edge of the politics of the gun or because I need still more data? And after a generation, the answer is, finally, probably 'no'; not because of any risks, rare even in the more violent days of the Troubles but because an addiction to the covert and illicit no longer returns interest on the investment – and playing at the edge of subversion is hardly a mature pastime. Then, too, the arrival of the peace process and its impact on the Republican movement neatly shapes a full generation. There are, or course, still gunmen unrepentant, unhappy with the peace process, and from time to time still lethal acting for the real army of the currents of continuity. And for old times' sake and good analytical purposes, I have kept in touch.

I have noticed on my part a flagging of spirit. The new, the old, the retired, the distant volunteers and gunmen have kept the faith; but as a transient, I have wearied of the explanations of many of those who smell of cordite and possess the absolute truth, not all but many. In time the alien heart tires and the fascination with the raw edges of politics fades. It is thus a good time to sum up, to indicate a special perspective on a world as difficult to describe as it is for a visitor to enter – a world of violence and romance, killing and sacrifice, often visible but inherently secret, shaped as much by perception as reality and with a structure and dynamics unlike those of the everyday world.

So I have mostly, if not entirely, retired from gunmen, if not their doings, and here indicate what seems to me their nature. This text indicates how they function, what the dynamics are of that secret world of Irish Republicans – often seemingly visible but a matter of faith and perception and a dream. It is not the only way of explaining the Republican movement's workings but it is the only one that is shaped to the hidden dynamics that arise from the need to transform the ideal into reality through recourse to an armed struggle. And for well over a century the great strength of the movement has been the legitimacy of the faithful to wage war in the name of a Republic all but established in the hearts of the Irish. There have always been those who denied this legitimacy, never more than now, but there have always been sufficient to tolerate the idealists, the gunmen with a pure heart, to allow the patriot game to be played, to assure that the killing for the cause is an Irish convention.

And in this special area, as in so many others, the Irish experience is long, rich and applicable in far places. Not only are Yeats and Joyce read in African universities and the altiplano but one can still find Bobby Sands a name to conjure with in Cairo or Rome. Gerry Adams is a world figure and Martin McGuinness lectures at Columbia. Times change and stay the same. Ireland's Troubles do not so much trouble analysts as intrigue them – few have to walk over the rubble or past the body bagged on the border. What other secret army could give us an endgame with two ceasefires, two peace strategies for different times and places – and for that matter regularly give us two IRAs, usually the pure and the political, the faithful and the practical. The arena may be a small island on the edge of Europe but the events and the experience are entry into one of the persistent phenomena of our times: the armed struggle that almost always generates violence and horror but also may oversee the transfer of power, a change in history.

My march through what became the killing fields of Ireland began long ago in a pub next to the Spotted Dog in Inistioge. There, with enormous innocence, I began my time with the Irish Republican Army. That story told as a history of the secret army is between pages – over the years the final chapter began to look as elusive as the establishment of the Republic of 1916 has proved to be. In any case the Republican movement has involved more of my life than I could have imagined. I have spent more time on the IRA than most volunteers have spent on active service.

The result has been several books, a documentary film, endless articles, papers and lectures – some to the volunteers involved – and some reticence about publishing a final analysis that might alienate the subject. Much of this story is now readily available in my *Irish Troubles: A Generation of Political Violence, 1967–1992*; but the *Troubles* is conventional, a chronological history, a tale told with a beginning and an uncertain end with the analysis scattered about amid the plot. The work did not intend to explain the dynamics of the Provisional IRA but rather the history of the gun in the politics of the last generation. And my history of the IRA, *The Secret Army*, is history not analysis. I delayed at times in focusing on the Provisionals, for to explain too much might well mean that nothing more would be forthcoming.

As the years passed, my reticence has eroded but not the intensity of concern with a movement that has persisted beyond all reason – my reasons if not theirs. The record of the IRA is so long, so detailed, and so rich that more history is hardly needed. What has not been done, however, is to explain exactly how the underground galaxy of the Republicans works, how a secret army is marshalled, deployed, maintained. The phenomenon is not special to the Irish, who invented the national liberation struggle, or to the Provisional IRA, who have pursued it longer than any other movement, but certainly Ireland offers a case spread over generations – a galaxy that never quite flickers out. And so Ireland presents the observer with an extended example of revolutionary persistence, a galaxy with a very long half-life, a galaxy that has pulsed erratically for nearly two centuries – and one with special dynamics.

All undergrounds, all movements, galaxies of the faithful engaged in an armed struggle, in fact have similar dynamics just as they are special, unique. The Provisionals are part of a genre that includes all sorts; the contemporary Shi'ite Holy Jihad and Menachem Begin's earlier Irgun Zvai Leumi in Palestine, and the Fenians have much in common with the People's Will of Tsarist Russia, just as the Provos do with *Brigate rosse* or the Basque ETA. The differences are obvious but each movement has, beyond the special dream, the particular arena, a general dynamics. And this coherence of each armed struggle, all the same and all different, generated a book on those dynamics found in each, and so did not focus on Ireland in particular. So while I have shaped a more general book *The Dynamics of the Armed Struggle* (1998), I found that a generation of concern with the Provisional IRA warranted special treatment – the movement as a special as well as a general case, a movement that had presented me with far more data than I could fit in one book on the dynamics of the contemporary armed struggle.

As in so many cases, the Irish were archetype, more important than size and sense would indicate. The IRA, in particular the Provisional movement, is a special case that has absorbed me for a generation. In Ireland I have interviewed those out in Easter Week 1916 and those currently active whose fathers and grandfathers I met long ago. Some I have first seen in strollers at Bodenstown as their parents marched to commemorate Wolfe Tone and others met for the first time this year or last. (Giving up gunmen does not mean that gunmen give up on you.) Somehow my presence seems to have validated each new generation, offering the prospect of a place in a book on the secret army as well as in that secret army. And during the delicate manoeuvres of the endgame, much has gone on secretly quite beyond my reach. As an army the IRA was often less than secret but as the military strategy grew less appealing secrecy became more apparent. In the new century the IRA is without a traditional role, without any compelling mission, has become a drag on the thrust of the peace process and increasingly irrelevant to contemporary Ireland. And militant, active republicanism can be found in recollections, sullen aspirations, and the small schismatic undergrounds with eroding assets and limited prospects. Matters may change, they have before, but in the present the IRA is quiescent, and all quarrels deeply hidden waiting on the actions and assumptions of others.

The Irish underground is almost totally sealed except to the faithful – one cannot be underground unless shaped and enhanced by revealed truth, that is what makes the clandestine world of the Republicans real. And real or no, even there in a chamber made cloudy by faith, their vapour trails are difficult to see. It is a world of strangeness and new colours and a certain charm. The underground IRA volunteer lives in an enhanced reality, lives with a new agenda, with new internal virtues and a new way of seeing. In retirement or success, in jail or in power, many remain within the force field of the underground, see matters differently. Others become ordinary. Life is rarely as intense again and so the habits of the underground become vestigial. And in any case those underground often cared as little about the dynamics of the movement as a muon or an electron care of vapour trails. The values of the underground are only crucial underground. The faith, any rebel faith, demands certain responses. These necessary canons of behaviour, patterns of the movement, anatomy of the cause, are little noted by the involved and often misread by the orthodox.

The underground is all unstated, unnoticed premises, all assumptions protected by illusions, on-the-job training in tradecraft, luck, and the failures of the centre. Anyone can see the open face of the Republican movement, attend a Sinn Féin rally or read *An Phoblacht*, but the central core that generates commitment, determines actions, drives the armed struggle is not so readily found. And so the dynamics of the Provisionals are not so readily displayed.

The involved are not concerned with these dynamics, scarcely aware of the real structure of their movement. The volunteers of the Provisional IRA would be amazed to find that they are shaped to the dynamics of a dream. They find the concept alien. On the other hand they will not be at all surprised that their ideal plays such a significant role. The assumption that this ideal makes the movement different from all other movements is mistaken, for the reality of a dream assures the generation of energy and that energy, always the same, drives an armed struggle that inevitably evolves in a limited number of ways. The existence of the faith, not the creed, is what matters.

The rebel's faith, the Provisional IRA volunteer's faith, is so compelling that the dedicated can barely spare the time to wage an armed struggle, learn the rebel craft. They are often consumed by the faith and so pursue the armed campaign in the midst of a secret world created by that faith. It is the faith that matters, the cause, the grievances, and the aspirations, the flow of history. And the faith is unique, relevant, while all the rest arrives because of lack of options and attracts only a few within the crusade: unconventional options are chosen because of lack of tangible assets; much is done without contemplation or planning, without discussion. Why talk about details that will soon be irrelevant when the dream is made real? The only hope of those who would report back on that underground world – even with visa assured – is to undertake research by osmosis. Long contact with those involved can tease out the invisible dynamics.

The IRA volunteer is like anyone else, just as the lover need show no public sign of passion nor the mystic the glow of revelation. The rebel, however, like a mystic or new lover, is not really everyday. The mystic may have a law degree, touch God but once, the lover can make millions or go to war, act like everyone else; but both still are shaped by their special experience, different from all others. Yet they appear normal, orthodox, conventional.

The volunteer in the Provisional IRA then is conventional – not as cover but truly, a law student, the lad down the lane, a railway clerk, or a small farmer. The rebels may appear fanatic in politics but otherwise normal. Even then they may not discuss politics at all, but keep the faith to themselves.

And they do not always stay underground. They may talk to journalists and tourists and the passers-by. They may appear only slightly irregular, reasoned fanatics. The volunteer can often, indeed, be found on assignment sitting in the movement's information offices. There he or she speaks for the rebel, speaks the truth, shapes the dream for public consumption.

In fact the underground is not really about war or danger or risk, the monsters or the atrocities, not about mad-dog murders, gunmen, and the inevitable atrocities, but rather about the organization of reality by the faithful to permit the killing, the war, the armed struggle. Those focused on the spectacular and novel, the violent, the news of the day, the error and turmoil, miss as irrelevant the dynamics of the underground world. The rest, the horror, is not irrelevant but rather a by-product of the dream and so the armed struggle. Many understandably watch only the battle, the war, the low-intensity conflict that generates the horror and the headlines. Much of the Republican world is closed.

Academics often find access difficult, finances difficult, and the promise of real returns faint. Journalists want a story for today, this week, not insight into history or the politics of the gun. Not always, however; some journalists stay on the story, do not enter the galaxy but stand inside the arena and, like Eamonn Mallie and Patrick Bishop in *The Provisional IRA*, or Brendan O'Brien in *The Long War*, produce a valid tale of events founded on contacts and experience.

When in considerable innocence I sought entry into the Republican world in 1965, the movement was in disarray, without prospects and without great need for secrecy. By the time that history began to move in 1968 and 1969, I was a small but acceptable foreign body that appeared from time to time, no apparent threat and a reservoir of the institutional memory. By then I knew that the operational secrets might be important to the movement and to their opponents but were not to me. I did not want to know what was going to happen that evening or who had been involved last week but rather how the system operated – and those who were the system did not care about such matters, hardly recognized them. During the last decade with the focus on the peace process, access to the involved has been rare – there is no reason to reveal the tensions and problems generated by the shifting role and mission of the secret army.

Still, talking to rebels is what I have done, what I still do. 'I learn by going where I have to go.' And I do it among those who no longer seem very exotic. Just as one gets used to the street patterns in Belfast or the rules of rounds in Kerry pubs, so too is the case with the patriot game. These habits and assumptions of the underground are discarded when I come home to the everyday. New York makes all Ireland distant and the Republican world foreign. The gunmen off Riverside Drive in New York are locals, seldom involved in politics, rarely dispatched from abroad. Those within the movement who come to America on business do not consider me even marginally part of that business. Martin McGuinness was taken aback to see me at Columbia to hear his lecture, at my university not his; for he anticipated my presence only in Derry or Dublin.

Many in America and more in Ireland want to hear no more of the 'armed struggle' and must regard my concern with some distaste. For nearly a decade nearly everyone has focused rather on the peace process, the uncertain endgame. The gunman is out of fashion and so too the dynamics of the struggle. The endgame, however, is a crucial part of any struggle and one hardly novel to the Irish, so there is still cause to keep watch on events, return to Ireland, an errant academic on tour.

In Ireland, no longer quite alien but still not Irish, I have had not only the toleration and assistance of those actually involved – for and against – but also the aid of the others, the scholars and experts, the foundations, traditional colleagues and old friends. This book is itself made possible by the accumulated support of a generation of such aid and in particular by five grants from the Harry Guggenheim Foundation, with the oversight of programme officer Karen Colvard, and two grants from the Smith-Richardson Foundation, with as programme officer first William Bodie and then Devon Gaffney Cross. Both foundations, in fact, funded a general study of the Irish Troubles that permitted a final round of questions before I gave up gunmen in the hope that after writing such a history there might be sufficient material for an analysis of the Provisional IRA.

No one foresaw that such an analysis would take the form of a general work – *The Dynamics of the Armed Struggle* – as well as this special focus on the Provisional IRA. Fearful of not finding enough Irish material, I found that a generation's investment has given one more Irish dividend, another book, still more pages to add to all the others. This process rests on the aid and comfort of thousands of people – the hours spent with or about the Provisional IRA have been extensive, usually several months each year including special trips to Britain, to Washington, and through contacts not only within the Irish Diaspora but also in Africa and the Middle East. Graffiti on Irish matters can be found in Rome, Jerusalem, Beirut, and Cairo, not to mention trace elements of the IRA in several far and unanticipated corners, South Africa and Cyprus.

Over the years there has been the assistance of conventional colleagues, the kindness of strangers, the enthusiasm of government officials – many with grave distaste for the subject – and access to the special knowledge of many journalists. There are those who commented over tea or on the ferry, in the midst of a distant war or after a lecture. All the bits and pieces, noted or remembered, have been accumulated, weighed, and filtered into the text.

Some of the most helpful contacts always remain invisible, truly underground. And there are those whose time and talent I have drawn on for years in Ireland, at home, in far places, the subject of repeated visits. Most of these, like most of the involved, are just as pleased not to be listed. It is those not listed – the gunmen and defenders, the volunteers, the pilgrims, old and new, retired, active, unrepentant and persistent, or even in a few cases at ease in office or with a proper career – whom I have most to thank. Those most faithful to the Republican cause will undoubtedly mostly dislike the text with its focus on the details and dynamics of the long march and not the unique banner that the faithful follow or even the grievances that prompt them to persist. And the cause, the ideal, the dream, is for most volunteers the key – and properly so. Yet, albeit at times reluctantly, the devout have over the years discussed the technicalities and so the dynamics of the special IRA armed struggle. These gunmen throw their shadow here.

There are, again, one or two special points for a work made possible largely by the grace of Irish gunmen. Certain words have special meanings to the involved on the island. Ulster, the six-counties not the nine, the Free State, loyalist or Republican, indicate positions and attitudes not simply places or institutions. Words matter and words indicate complex positions and not dictionary meanings. In some cases there is no hope of finding a neutral term in that failure to conform indicates to the critical only ineptitude not disinterest – so my use of 'province' for Northern Ireland to avoid all the linguistic pitfalls has been criticized by a reviewer because it is not common usage – not even used – and, of course, this was why I deployed it, if to no avail. In any case the text tends to make clear the meaning – loyalists or Unionists, where the loyalists are often not loyal and some of the Unionists prefer secession – and no harm is meant, even if taken.

As for cited sources, the reader will find few. Most of the specific data in the text is general knowledge. What is not, the special cases and general conclusions, arise from those thousands and thousands of discussions with all and sundry and the distillation of my previous publications, more thousands of pages, many different. There seems little need but academic pretensions for a more formal apparatus. There is not much disagreement on the 'facts' in many cases, only on the meanings, the intentions of the involved, the later impact on the flow of events. Thus the citations are more likely to be asides than sources. What matters in the armed struggle is not so much the agreed dates and places and fatalities, all on record, but rather interpretations and presumptions.

The interpretation and presumptions are all mine. They rest on those thousands of hours of conversations, time among gunmen, time on politics, time that over time adds up to years. Some of the involved are apt to think them years wasted, since they rarely recognize their world as the one described. In this they are at one with other movements I have written about elsewhere: perception is all. And this is merely one way to consider the Republican movement and is made possible by the kindness of others. Many of these others have not been subversives nor even activists, not responsible for the Troubles, often not even interested in the Troubles. Coupled with all these, co-opted or co-operative, transient or regular, have been my old friends that appear in these prefaces like ghosts of works past: from Oliver Snoddy, one visible facet of the virtual reality of Padraig O Snodaigh, friend, editor, poet, scholar and Gaelgoric, to my Kerry connections, the Browne Group, now sadly depleted with the loss of my sister-in-law Maureen and the keeper of the household Kitty Joy. The Browne family has felt that knitting, good prose, and hot dinners with two kinds of potatoes should play a greater part in my Irish life than the patriot game – and so too my wife Nora Browne and my sister-in-law Denise, both sound on the national issue but, like most of the Irish, with other more pressing matters to hand.

And so I thank all those, the everyday and the subversive, often one and the same, those who were ready to talk and those who were not, those who merely helped me on my way. They were the Irish mostly and so apt to the kind word first. There were those too far off in Whitehall or Cairo or even New York who added bits and pieces. They all, barman and cabinet secretary, constable and professor, supplied, one way or another, foundation for my notions and presumptions. Anecdotal evidence after two generations becomes survey research – more rigorous than the collected opinion of taxi drivers but still less than those suspicious of notions offered without data.

And finally all these notions about the underground, discovered not only in Ireland but also elsewhere, and then detailed in the quiet in New York before my iMac, have often made an easy home-life complex. In this I have been fortunate with Nora, my one Irish connection, my Kerry wife, now doyen of the Ballybunion Brownes, who has made my life less of an armed struggle. Besides gunmen and poets, saints and scholars, the alien have always found on the island warm hearts and blue eyes. And so have I and so grown less alien if no more Irish.

J. B. B.
New York–Dublin–New York

Introduction: The Nature of the Armed Struggle

This century has been an age of anxiety. We live in an era of enormous violence, a time of terror and mass murder. All but the most primitive and isolated have lived under threat of nuclear destruction. If the great, bipolar Cold War with its mutually assured destruction has ended, the legacy is dubious – proliferation of nuclear weapons, proliferation of new states, new ambitions, new rebels, new wars, plague, genocide, and slaughter as convention, Bosnia and Rwanda, the Kurds and the guerrillas of Colombia. At times it seems that the only stability has been the long, long Irish war, seldom enormously costly but to the involved, seldom in the news unless there is a spectacular atrocity. In fact, against the evidence, for Ireland has been mostly at peace for two centuries, the island is listed as one of the staples of modern violence and there is violence even amid the peace process, bombs and suspects maimed or killed.

The other conflicts have been generated by reasons of state and national pride, through blunder and mismanagement, generated by race and class and tribe. There have been national wars and religious wars, civil strife and simple massacre, conflicts that were by-products of the Cold War and a long wave of people's wars, rebel armed struggles, guerrilla insurrections. War has been a growth industry. And the Irish, who invented the war of national liberation, perfected the anti-colonial struggle of protracted war, have persisted in providing the arena for advocates of physical force. Few may have been involved in the various clashes: sectarian clashes, the national wars, the conspiracies and killings; but recourse to unconventional violence is often exaggerated in impact and in perception. And if the Provisionals are at peace their Republican rivals have not been, nor their loyalist opponents.

Ireland, except for a few years between 1916 and 1922, had for two centuries avoided most of the political plagues, occupations, conventional wars, and brutal civil strife that have been the fare not only of much of Europe but much of the world. Elsewhere a variety of governments have slaughtered their own in great internal purges, maintained power through terror, pursued security with gulags of the interned. Once the world wars had destroyed the old structures of state and the great monsters disappeared – Stalin, Hitler, Mussolini – there have been ample replacements: cannibal kings, warlords, bureaucrats of oppression, and lethal idealists imposing fantasy by terror. And after 1969, in a small way, Ireland has been part of the later turmoil, an arena for a low-intensity clash of destinies fed on the grievances of the past, often legitimate, and fears of the future, often well founded. That the Irish butcher's bill on a global scale is small, that much of the island, much of the time is everyday, getting and spending, O-levels and football, does not mean that the renewed Troubles are any less horrid for the involved, for the dead at Omagh or Derry, for the suspect shot dead at the end of a country road or the parents of children murdered by bigots.

Elsewhere these low-intensity horrors continue despite the efforts of the men of good will. If there is hope in South Africa and Palestine and even in Ireland, there are new wars of just grievance and new despots. On the international scene, many leaders seemingly have only the will to power and then in power the will to destroy any perceived threat, at worst simply to seek vengeance and at best to correct perceived grievance by recourse to force. The world is filled as well with real grievances – hunger, misery, disease, humiliation. Neither science nor managerial skill has prevented war or even alleviated natural disaster. The post-modern world is the equal of any dark age in matters of turmoil, chaos, and slaughter. And centralized control and technological triumphs have merely enlarged the capacity to do violence to the many – no longer need armies kill by hand or the news of new taxes arrive on a forked stick. Not that in Rwanda the necessity of killing by hand – the old-fashioned way, one innocent victim at a time – limited genocide or even greatly slowed the pace.

And in Ireland there are seemingly only men of good will, only those who want peace if with justice or on their own terms. Everyone for a generation has advocated peace and yet there has been no real peace; only the long, erratic rise in the death tally as the marching and counter-marching, the speeches and proposals went on. There is a peace process, formal and informal. At the beginning of the new century, the killing is on hold.

For generations everywhere on the international scene, the gunman has played a most visible role in the struggle for political power, casting a cold shadow. Such low-intensity conflict may rarely escalate but does ensure that the terror and confusion is everywhere present: Peru and Croatia, Mozambique and Kashmir, Algeria, and the Basque country of Spain. The volunteers in these asymmetrical conflicts, the weak against the strong, the margins against the centre, are rebels with a cause. Even those without just cause run up banners of liberation over clan ambitions or simple greed. And beneath such banners the IRA finds echo. Still, good cause or bad, most rebels fail. They fail on the streets, die against a wall or at the end of a rope, fail after great slaughter or with almost no harm done; but they fail. In Ireland from 1798, the rebel failed over and over but for the partial success of 1921 that slaked the hungers of all but the idealists.

Usually in frustration, the failed rebel may withdraw to the margins as endemic insurgents, exiles in seedy hotels or bandits with old flags; but most find only exile or shallow graves. Seeking liberty, mostly the bold find death or imprisonment. Rebellion is a high-risk venture, appealing only to the desperate and driven. Occasionally the rebel shapes a protective cover, persists, and the conflict is protracted, can even escalate. Power may accrue over time to the gunman. At times the gunman seeks to transform a secret army into a real one, shape a counter state, make Armenia a nation or free Kosovo. And sometimes the rebel cannot be eradicated and, like the IRA, go on generation after generation. Then the rebel matters.

The uncompromising Irish Republican, even in the least promising years, even when Parnell rode high or De Valera was in power, mattered because none could tell if the dream still had power over the conventional. No one but the faithful wanted to find the answer. The Republicans dedicated to physical force spent generations waiting for the Irish people to tolerate a campaign – and mostly waited in vain. Most of the campaigns after 1923 were short, hapless, and easily ignored.

Sometimes, not often, armed struggles have led in part at least to change. A new image is created or old wrongs avenged if not righted. Armenia issues stamps or Castro takes control of Cuba. The Irish have a Free State. There may be shifts in power, even real revolutions. The end of an imperial age, chaos in fragile states, and even some changes in the West can be traced underground to rebels with a cause. And in Asia there was both an end to empires and the rise of Mao, a new model emperor. At times the tribe may shape a nation or the armed factions achieve recognition as a real army – no longer Palestinian terrorists. Revolt may, as promised – but so rarely delivered – lead to institutional change. And in a few cases, like Ireland, the incomplete struggle may be woven into the fabric of the nation, a secret thread that some feared might, when pulled, unravel the whole. Yet few, barring friends and the police, could even find the secret army in 1969 – but afterwards the IRA, like so many of the covert movements with letters for names and guerrilla texts as guides, imposed change.

There have been all sorts of nasty, small changes in the years following World War II. Airport security is different, the agenda of prime ministers different, the flags over new nations novel, and the backlists of publishers abound with works on violence and terror. China is Red, Lebanon ruined, and Israel exists – as now does the dream of Palestine, even if confined for a time to Gaza and Jericho. And equally important, the rebel with a cause has grown grand in perception. The media, the sponsoring states, the dictates of fashion have often combined to exaggerate the guerrilla role. Bosnia, Kosovo and Somalia, Angola and Lebanon have been focus of the moment, an arena for photogenic violence exaggerated by television news. Everyone knows of Che, but all that most in Tel Aviv or Lima know of Ireland is the IRA, not saints and scholars.

Standing on a jungle hill, clad in beret and combat jacket, bearded and bold, armed with an AK-47, Che the guerrilla became a hero. The freedom fighter appeared to be able to bring liberty and justice, able to topple imperial, even indigenous, despots, and so proved to many that a just cause can devise a strategy to remove the corrupt. Such a hero had charm for those trapped inside conventional Western institutions. Those who felt suffocated by things and requirements and the routines of the regimented world could admire the apparent freedom of the jungle guerrilla or the patriot with a beret and an AK-47 – and no credit cards. Nearly everywhere without risk, the Left – American, German, Western – could assuage private guilt with applause for distant rebels – anti-imperial, elegant. And many who sought justice anyplace saw in guerrilla-revolution a reasoned means to erase grievance. The guerrilla, for good reasons and bad, became a global concept in the post-war world. For a generation there was an era of the glorious guerrilla, defined in posters and ideological exegesis and by the experts of anti-insurgency. And just as the IRA gunman emerged from the shadows of the past in 1970, the fashions changed.

Very swiftly the myth of the guerrilla frayed. Che was dead and despots ruled in the new nations. Soon students had Andy Warhol prints put up in their law offices, not tricontinental posters tacked on the walls of dormitory rooms. And the Marxist-Leninists found guerrillas in their own empire, first abroad and then closer to home. Even the café Left of Europe discovered during the years of lead that their party card did not deter their own gunmen, the Euroterrorists. The new Reds shot the old Reds. And there were new fascists as well to add to the din. The new terrorists like Black September and the Popular Front for the Liberation of Palestine introduced terror as strategy. And amid the turmoil the IRA, Provisional, Official, emerged.

Once gunmen in trench coats had charm, at least in retrospect, but no more. No one loved a terrorist. In the cities no-warning bombs and shoot-outs in the airport eroded the appeal of the gunman, any gunman, any cause. The covers of popular magazines, the television news, the journals and papers and radio presented so many atrocities: dead judges in the gutters of Rome and Milan, the bodies of murdered children covered with blankets lying in airport waiting rooms. Deeply dedicated or hired with a slogan, the cool, urbane, ruthless killers in aviator glasses and Italian tailoring, deploying machine pistols and BMWs became a consumer of Western innocence. And worst, they became a constant, replaced by new killers with different slogans. Their deeds came into every home on television, live and in colour with a push of a button. Click, and there for the viewer in New York or Bombay is the atrocity of the day, the spectacular, the bodies in the street of a city with a strange name.

Even the old rural guerrilla struggles grew more awful. Increasingly, the rebel, urban or rural, has appeared cruel, a new barbarian. Hidden behind those sunglasses the terrorists have the eyes of a gull: cold, feral, opaque. The romantic rebel is dead and gone. No one in Belfast, however, volunteered as a knight errant, or a terrorist. First they wanted to defend their own and to force the British out. Volunteers soon came to an armed struggle, to an Irish armed struggle, hardened to the romantic Irish past and prepared for the new necessities of unconventional war.

Most analysts addressing the phenomenon of the armed struggle have concentrated on the killing and on appropriate responses, on war. The nature and impact of the rebel ideal has not attracted much concern except as a sort of political agenda. Those observers who factor in the power of the rebel dream do so as ideology rather than as the determinate of the dynamics of the struggle. In Ireland, with over 7,000 serious works in print, there is ample explanation for all, for any school or predilection. For most the IRA is considered at best in pursuit of obsolete nationalism spiced with radical slogans, advocated by the simple and self-taught, and at worst a band of killers pursuing base aims, sectarian Catholic vengeance covered in Republican banners and extended out of spite to the authorities. The Irish gunman is a wicked, evil man whose dream is nightmare to the responsible and sensible. So too are all gunman dreams. General acceptance comes only with the end of physical force that transforms the arena in South Africa or Palestine – or Ireland. Then those who dream are assumed dreaming properly.

The revolutionary dream is not only the source of the energy that drives the armed struggle but also largely determines the dynamics of that struggle. Few analysts understand dreams. Much analysis would treat the conversion on the road to Damascus as an event best described by road engineers and tour guides. And so many do not realize how skewed the underground is by perception of the involved, by the power of a dream – any dream. Few have much empathy with the armed struggle, and can rarely imagine life on the run or a life unlike their own, much less the power of an alien dream.

All this is as expected. The armed struggle is by nature a difficult study.

Those involved, once retired, can seldom explain the intensity of the underground. No one, gunman or scholar, sees matters whole. Nearly everyone uses a special methodology and has a private programme, special prejudices. There is often a distaste for the topic or a need to rationalize the past for present consumption. Because of the Troubles, Irish history has been rewritten. The Irish analysts define the problem so that the contemporary Irish gunmen is aberrant – not to mention abhorrent. This, too, is hardly novel, the threatened seldom love a gunman, especially those who assume that the centre monopolizes legitimacy – voted into power by the people or ruled by God's divine providence.

The rebel by definition is a usurper, a killer, a figure who causes trouble by intent. Few Western writers now advocate violence except as last resort. As for recent unconventional war, especially the Irish experience, there is seldom the perspective that time may bring. There is guilt – why us, why the Irish, still and again? – and the shadow of defeat, ruined hopes and all the dead. The whole phenomenon in Ireland and out is elusive.

In the real underground world perception is vital. Analysis is not just a problem of discipline or commitment, not of prejudice but also a problem of clashing perceptions of reality. The involved see matters in strange ways. They must translate them for the curious as well as the dubious. They can seldom explain and seldom can imagine that their reality is not that of others. And those involved within the underground who see reality shaped by the dream are mostly beyond easy access. And when access can be managed by an observer, the rebel vision is often discounted as warped.

No one can come to the contemporary armed struggle innocent. In fact everyone shapes reality: perception is all. In this the scholar and the analyst are no different from the lethal volunteer in an armed struggle; seeing is believing. And one sees as one believes. The rebel is driven by a vision only the faithful can see, and this largely determines his world. The rebel underground is moulded in a special way not readily amenable to the methods of the social scientists or the analysis of the threatened. They, the pragmatists or the scientific scholars, examine the same phenomena and yet see differently from the involved, from the rebel. They, historians and policy analysts and political scientists, often see not through a glass darkly but with great precision and from a special angle. There are many ways to see the rebel. Yet the nature of the rebel world of perception has seldom been seen clearly, least of all by the rebel whose dreams and agendas have adjusted reality, created a special ecosystem that eludes the normal laws of analysis.

Here, then, at the start are the necessary definitions, valid here but perhaps not valid elsewhere, even in the underground. An armed struggle is the means that rebels against the system, transforms a dream into power through recourse to violence. The armed struggle is a *means* to acquire power: power over events, power over history, power over reality. The armed struggle is an act, a procedure – a means of seeing and doing and deploying the dream. Since it is a means, not an end, it is less than compelling to the dreamer who focuses on the content of the aspiration.

For the rebel dreamer in the course of human events all other options except the armed struggle have been found wanting, ineffectual or too slow, lacking in psychic rewards or somehow unrewarding, unpromising. All options have been denied in a long train of abuses and usurpations by the power of the centre. So the only apparent way into an acceptable future is an armed struggle, a right, a duty. Other means can be adapted or sought but the key must be recourse to force.

Once engaged, the rebel must be able to persist, to hide within a protective ecosystem – the underground. This intangible world fashioned by perception, necessity and objective reality, moulded by opposition, permits action by the rebel despite a lack of assets. With cover assured so too is opportunity, but at great cost. The underground assures inefficiency, wastes sacrifice, guarantees schism and disillusion, generates delay and casualties. The innocent, the threatened, the specialists in counter-insurgency are deluded into assuming that secrecy assures competence, that the unconventional means are a first not a last choice, that the underground contains all conventional assets plus those that accrue to the illicit and unrestrained. In reality the underground is a world of scarcity, limitations, and exhaustion.

These are not alternatives to the armed struggle but additions, aspects, and facets. Those rebels too entranced with politics or with non-violence, with the exploitation of injustice or the returns of publicity, often run counter to the central thrust of the struggle, always fixed on the main means. At times, rare times, during an endgame or when protraction has eroded hope that the centre will collapse, politics may offer the only means forward. Then the armed struggle becomes something else, the gunman emerges as an irregular soldier, his organization as a counter-state, his leaders as visible spokesmen, his dream defined as programme.

Even if war is politics by other means, even if the army is controlled by the commissars, war – the armed struggle – remains the dominant task. Yet an armed struggle blends and bleeds all aspects of struggle into the service of the dream. The dream becomes the struggle. It is not that the rebel may talk peace and yet make war but that the necessities of the dream impose different priorities and purposes, bleed away distinctions that are important above ground. And this bleeding out destroys the happy symmetry of the scholars and the skills of special disciplines. The movement underground does not always distinguish between routes forward, between war and peace. Often, in fact, the movement insists that war is simply a way forward, politics by other means, i.e. one aspect of the long march to power. This is unconventional in the field and as subject of analysis. And analysis is further complicated because the reality of the struggle is one determined in large part by rebel perception.

So little rebel attention is given to the dynamics of the struggle but much to the dream and the remainder to tactical operations – the techniques that persistence requires. Persistence made possible by the rebel invisibility allows the struggle to continue: but barely. All rebels, operationally conservative, fear novelty and change that may erode the tiny edge that permits persistence. There is little capital to spend on innovation even when desperately needed. Tactical initiatives are often accepted with reluctance. Even then those underground are criminally optimistic, must hope for the best and ignore the odds. Who would take on an empire with a few revolvers as the Stern Group did in Palestine in 1944? Who would expect that those revolvers could so shake the British empire? And in January 1970 seven other men a generation later sat around a kitchen table and planned to drive the British out of Ireland.

The capacity to pursue the armed struggle must be husbanded. Far from being opportunists eager to strike everywhere, flexible and fluid, rebels are often conservative, static, rigid, fearful of change. Movements may be unwilling to divert assets against perceived vulnerabilities of the centre if it may mean eroding the war effort. Most effort is spent repeating yesterday so as to reach tomorrow. And the means most cherished is the one that has already proven effective.

In an armed struggle the gun, even in the hands of an astute and cunning commander, determines politics; and if not, if the commissar rules without reference to the battle, rebel politics will lose many of the few advantages of the war. When politics subsumes the gun, then the struggle is no longer armed, fits other rubrics, runs to a different dynamic – and the transmutation is as difficult for the involved as it is for the analysts. In Ireland after 1918, there was a hidden struggle between those who sought to discard the gun as soon as possible, fearful that the recourse to violence would unravel the fabric of society or require sacrifices few wanted to make, and those caught up in the movement of history. Every armed struggle contains a potential for legitimacy – and the moment to discard the violent, the unorthodox, the dream ideal is usually a lethal issues, as it was in Ireland in 1921–23.

The struggle may not change the balance of power or the course of history but always transform the rebel. Often the struggle proves more important than the result and most often, usually, the struggle, flawed and futile, fails. Still, at the beginning there are those in the grip of a vision. With limited assets the rebel cannot impose the special vision and so cannot yet determine the end result of history – history as it ought to be. A few from the first argue for war: those caught up with the inevitable success of communism or more particularly the past example of Irish ancestors. In Ireland the decision for physical force has been made over and over, so that there is no first-time-only discussion of the prospects – what is sought is opportunity to deploy arms not discovery of the necessity to do so. Usually, however, the leadership is seized on the moment, often decides by degree, takes risks that force the decision on the centre, delays even when the need is enormous: the dilemma of the beginning. The armed struggle is usually, therefore, the last choice of the weak with aspirations not assets. It offers a means to the only way to power. Few go gladly underground and so put their lives, their fortunes and their honour at risk – except in Ireland where the unreconcilable Republicans are ever eager, often desperate, waiting for the opportunity to deploy.

Those who choose the armed struggle for secondary reasons – romance, fashion, personal gain, or the euphoria of the moment – treat power lightly. At times the armed struggle has had allure and most especially from a distance. Some have been attracted not as last choice but often first. Waves of rebels have sought to emulate the French or Americans, Bakunin or Lenin, Che or Mao, or even the Irish. Some want a gun and others to do harm. Some want to be in fashion as much as power. It is dangerous to lie to oneself and proclaim the armed struggle as not the only way but also the best way.

The struggle is always a means. Power is the goal even if killing and looting and guns are involved. Power to shape the future is crucial. And such power is elusive and the appropriate selection of effective tactics is complex. Those who find easy answers also tend to die beside the road. The real goal is power over the past and most of all power over the nature of the future. The past is disaster, unfair, perhaps necessary for a Marxist; but for all rebels the past should, must, end in future justice. The present is a constant humiliation. Humiliation as grievance is one of the great engines of rebellion.

Most individual rebels go to war because they must. Few go lightly into the underground. Each does so for various personal purposes and under varying immediate pressures. Each volunteer lives at a special time in a particular culture at the end of a long prologue. Every arena is different in place and time, in nature. Each rebel knows the dream is unique, perhaps universal like communism, perhaps very specific like Ibo separatism in Nigeria. Each tends to assume the entire course of the armed struggle is special – it is certainly different from all other experience.

All rebels share this realization that the underground is different. And certainly the dream is different, most special of all, different, very different, often contradictory. In Rome two dreamers by chance at a single café table at Rosati's on Piazza del Popolo may have aspired to a communism beyond Mao or a return to a black fascist Italy. They rise from the table, part, go deeper into the underground and live similar lives. They exist in the same time, at the same table, fear the state and hate each other.

The rebels are not for the easy life, can see no need to compromise the truth or nibble at justice. They are possessed with righteousness. They are keepers of history's legacy, the great ideal. Such an ideal ensures the opposition of the centre, a centre condemned by the rebels and their history to future irrelevance. The separatists would destroy the unity of the nation – Ethiopia or Sri Lanka or Spain. The devout would seize the accomplishments of the secular and impose the past. The messianic would smash the institutions of that past and offer nothing but slogans in exchange. Some murder anyone on their shining path to a garden that has never existed. All say 'No' – no compromise to a state that must not surrender. And the centre responds by arming the present: 'No surrender'.

The armed struggle is always asymmetrical. It is a war between the orthodox centre with conventional assets, and the covert rebel with few military tools but a luminous vision. One can easily count the assets of the centre, the state, the powerful: so many votes or tanks or billions in credit, so many exports or paramilitary police or ambassadors in residence. Visit the capital before the fall, Saigon or Addis Ababa or Managua, where the police in uniform direct traffic and secretaries make ministerial appointments. The rebels are invisible and the orthodox in their offices, uneasy, anxious but on the telephone. Planes come in on schedule and the post is distributed. The state appears to work, the barmen serve drinks at the international hotels and the shoe-shine boys ply their trade. Even at the end of an asymmetrical war, no one can see the gunman at the gate. The journalists exist on rumour and the implications of graffiti. Castro is coming or the army is disintegrating. The Eritreans are in the suburbs or Baby Doc at the airport.

There is no evidence until the guerrillas in make-shift uniforms climb on captured tanks for the photographers. Then the offices are closed, the bureaucrats go home, and the last plane takes out the last orthodox optimist who still has the price of a ticket. Then the underground is inverted and the dream realized, the will made real. Until this moment almost all rebels look like losers or at most distant winners. After all, until the end, the rebel is underground. No matter, the rebel knows. As Giap would say in 1991, 'to the Vietnamese, material strength is not strength; the people are the strength'. The people are out of sight. The dream lives in the hearts of those who cannot be easily counted. The centre can be counted out in ships and planes and men. The centre is organized as state, established, legitimate.

Such conflict between unequals is often protracted. The quick way is a coup, an army take-over with rebel flags, orchestrated riots in the street. The slow way is civil war. And there are still other ways. Gandhi chose non-violence for his followers and dismantled the Raj. The Palestinians in Gaza and the West Bank devised the *intifada*, riotous attack short of irregular war but, as with the fedayeen's terrorist strategy, the gain was in prominence rather than in power. Many colonies achieved independence by concession – often no one in Paris or London wanted another Algeria or Palestine. The will was not there. The winds of change eventually blew through the Portuguese African empire and then over southern Africa. So, too, in Eastern Europe did the will at the centre fail. There freedom came on the instalment plan, haltingly but seemingly irreversible. Poland moved out of communism and so the rest of the Warsaw Pact followed, olives out of the bottle until the bottle broke. Why fire shots? Why choose an armed struggle? Potential rebels – Letts, Slovenes, and Georgians – sensibly seek the easiest road for their dream. Sometimes it is war, unconventional war, often prolonged. In some cases the system can neither repel the challenge nor co-opt the rebel but still remains viable.

Rebels, revolutionaries, ambitions conspirators often come to power in the turmoil of the times. Sometimes they possess, as did the American colonies, sufficient assets, often including an appropriate terrain, to wage nearly conventional war. Few rebels want a protracted armed struggle – all want power.

Some find other means into the future, but the faithful persist. Mostly the centre kills these rebels. The idealists who have misread history are simply rounded up by the strong. The romantics, like the desperate Guevara clones, are the first to go. Even the most pragmatic and shrewd tend to fail. The hard men and the lucky survive, if rarely, and in part because of the contingent and the unforeseen: a dozen escapees from disaster hiding in the outback of Cuba. Since even the most fragile regime can often survive the dangers of a few idealists, the Cuba of Fulgencio Batista did not worry about Castro, Che, and the rest – schoolboy bandits to be rounded up sooner or later.

Mostly small groups appear and disappear, flashes of light not the core of a galaxy. The risks of real rebellion are too high. Revolution, as Mao said, is not a dinner party, certainly not for the rebels. No matter, no matter the risks even if recognized, most rebels expect to win, turn the dream into reality. The world is filled with dreamers. Some dreams are just that, dreams, nostalgia or fantasy; but some are compelling and beyond compromise, incandescent, insistent. And they have appeal to those with grievance, possess then a special life span without a due date.

Some want the dream realized exact, perfect, incandescent. They want not just power but the shimmering ideal turned real. Since this is not possible, the armed struggle at times degenerates into internal war between those who want the possible and those who want everything – the grail. Even if civil war can be avoided, the purges seldom can be. The purists often end in front of a firing squad of their former colleagues as the new regime eliminates those who cannot compromise with history. Revolutions, even rebellions, are apt to eat the most militant, the audacious, the bold and the uncompromising. The assets of the underground are not needed above ground, are often thought dangerous. They may distract the many from the new spectrum of sacrifices and responsibilities that power offers. Some want vengeance. Others want history visibly adjusted or their heart made pure. The Irish Republic is not a matter of voting districts and constitutional amendments. The aspirational Irish Republic is not easily adaptable to the everyday. Even if the peace process led rapidly to a united Ireland the Republic would still shimmer out of sight.

When Peron returned to Argentina in triumph, for example, the Peronist armed struggle went on and on. The dreamers found the reality of the old man insufficient. In the name of the myth, they continued to struggle for Peron the exemplar but against Peron the man. They kept killing. Their armed struggle was unrequited, self-generating, beyond concession or definition. This even after power had been won, history adjusted, the man put in the palace. No longer able to say 'No', the faithful in Argentina persisted. They refused to say 'Yes'. The struggle had become more important than the goal.

Rebellion is a high-risk venture even when directed against the incompetent and ineffectual. The 200 rebel attempts to emulate Castro all failed. And none faced a truly effective, absolutely brutal opponent. No one challenged Stalin or Mao at all: they were too efficient, too brutal. In post-Mao China at the beginning of the new millennium, dissent is a sometimes thing – the tanks and jails cast a long shadow. In the case of democratic countries, most challenges are swiftly snuffed out as irrelevant. Some are merely armed fantasies. Two men bombing a federal building in Oklahoma City, the lone bomber or the revolutionary militia stock-piling arms never to be used, or even school children murdering their class mates. They are examples of the deluded, not threats to civic order. Such echoes of reality generate no energy, attract no recruits, act only as irritant to the authorities and subject for the media eager for the spectacular. Even in the great post-modern era of urban terrorism, there were really very few terrorists in Germany or Japan or France, none in America or Britain or Scandinavia.

Most democracies if not all – Italy in the recent past being an obvious and special case – can absorb demands, especially real demands, however voiced, for radical change. In Italy the radicals wanted justice as promised and found only jobbery as practised. Most of the aggrieved in a democracy have negotiable demands. Adjustment and co-option is possible short of concession to internal nationalists. Then, like the Italian radicals, the rebels want the state dismantled, the nation dissolved. Nationalism is different. Nationalism does not wait on democratic procedures. Those who seek to create a nation do not even poll their own constituency but look into their hearts to find the will, the proper agenda. And always a nation denied generates a lethal challenge to a nation established.

Nations are not easy to make and not prone to self-destruct. So the Kurds, who have never been a nation, who have no friends, seek to dismantle the system – Turkey, Iraq, Syria, and Iran. Nationalism is usually beyond conciliation – a Sweden accepting Norwegian aspirations is as rare as the two Yemens seeking a common destiny. Nationalists present unnegotiable demands. Kosovo is either Serbia or not. At least, the more effective democracies can cope with most radical non-nationalist demands just as the more effective despots can crush those who have any demands.

Demands on the centre are best met by traditional ways, by concession or oppression, by co-option or corruption. Such demands are best pursued by patience or petition, by democratic means where possible and by recourse to the unconventional when all else fails. The armed struggle is attractive only to the driven and desperate. And such rebels are effective only against a centre with uneasy legitimacy but determination to persist despite limited resources. Still, the arena for the armed struggle is quite broad and at times has included even the post-industrial West, broad because it is the rebel who decides on matters of legitimacy and capacity on the necessity to act.

CONCLUSION

An armed struggle arises when the unreconcilable rebel moulds a dream into a means to power. The dream energizes the struggle. Out of weakness the rebel must shape a congenial environment underground and from there wage war even while seeking other vulnerabilities of the centre. This very limited war, waged by various means and out of strength of conviction, tends to be protracted so that the will of the dreamers will have the opportunity to erode the determination and assets of the orthodox centre.

The rebel usually loses, often quickly. At times and for uncertain reasons, the armed struggle may escalate and in fewer cases victory can be achieved in conventional battle as was the case at the end of Mao's Long March and

Ho Chi Minh's war of national liberation in Indochina. More likely victory comes when the centre collapses, as was the case with most anti-imperialist wars after 1945 or in Cuba and Nicaragua in Latin America or in Ethiopia in Africa. The successful rebel wages the armed struggle in the grey area that lies between reactionary and effective coercion by the threatened and assured concession from the centre. Even the local despot and uneasy democracy can usually cope with indigenous rebels. The armed struggle is inevitably a high-risk, low-return option, even if the returns need not be measured in power.

Every armed struggle is different. Some blend into irregular war on one end of the spectrum as the rebel emerges as army or political party, and others are endemic, ethnic clashes, the clan war-lords in traditional pursuits. Each exists in a special time, in a special place, inspired by a particular dream. And success is often in the special details.

Each armed struggle is also the same, covert, illicit, largely structured by rebel capacity and intent and by the powers of the centre structured as state. And so many of the details are not as special as first imagined by the dreamer. The dream must be real, valid, attractive, explain all, predict all, provide a means into the future, supply the energy of the struggle.

There have always been rebels and rebellions, often with a dream, many not unlike the contemporary models. Peasants revolted long before Mao and assassins have been with the West since the beginning. The contemporary armed struggle, however, even when dedicated to the imperatives of ancient ancestors, is a child of the nation-state. These states were founded on dreams not limited by boundary rivers or dynasties but ideas and attitudes. The universals were put to work for the nation. Those first to triumph institutionalized their dreams, staked out the centre, were not averse to empire.

These states often stand in the way of the new dreamers, block history, ensure injustice. The oppressor is almost always a state, the state as alien, as occupier, as symbol: the Great Satan or the Zionist entity. The armed struggle may have universal banners, may have revolutionary alliances and alignments and patrons. And the patron of an international movement is, too, a state – Islam in One Country. And the fundamentalists of Iran once in power, once the Islamic Republic existed, had first to defend the new power in Teheran from the secular rebels who once were allies against the Shah. Being in power meant acting as a state even when deploying terror abroad, especially when using terror abroad.

The modern state as opposition is a major determinant of the nature of the armed struggle. The nature of the opposition greatly defines the dynamics of modern rebels, not their dream or agenda – any dream will do, any state, for the same model underground works for all. Iran proved, as is usually the case, too effective for the secular rebels but no less of a target because the dream was in power – rather more so since the dream was exclusive.

Most new revolutionary states must eliminate those mesmerized by the purity of the dream or another dream and even then new generations of rebels may emerge as in Ireland – unless the state is truly the embodiment of the ideal, truly arises from consensus, or else is both brutal and efficient. Irish history has been troubled if not determined by the persistence of an unrealized dream that cannot be co-opted by the state or quite denied by many on the island – there has for generations been a constituency for the gun. A collateral danger exists: that the demented may shape their mania as armed struggle, establish a killing cult, or shoot the president to get in the history books.

The real armed struggle arises in some part from commitment to an ideal and the acquisition of power. Such struggles are especially cruel because of the wastage assured by likely failure or a protracted campaign that inevitably comes with a butcher's bill. At times rebels cause enormous trouble. They die, their opponents die, vast numbers of those innocent die. The struggle gobbles resources and lives and attention, disrupts the normal and usually to no ultimate purpose. No wonder the orthodox and conventional abhor the pretensions of rebel gunmen, messengers of death, dreadful dreamers rank with cordite and truth.

The importance of the contemporary armed struggle, consequently, lies as much in the added chaos that erodes global order as in the few unexpected triumphs of the weak. Rebellion in the outback, and even in the main streets, is the muzak of contemporary society, ubiquitous noise but noise easily ignored. Such noise made apparent through the tactics of atrocity may evoke indignation and anger at the centre. From time to time power may be deployed – as in Lebanon or Somalia or the Balkans – or the centre responds with greater change – a military government, emergency legislation, or the end of liberty – as in Peru or Egypt or Turkey.

An armed struggle may impose changes no one foresaw and many, even those underground, do not want – a polarized society as tactical goal no longer has many takers after the Latin American revolutionary experience. A generation of violence has given the Palestinians less than any could have imagined. To some, Arafat is a hero and to most so is Mandela; some gunmen are founding fathers even if most are forgotten. The rebels may seldom win but, like Che, they matter. They may seldom plan the changes that occur but the changes may matter. The gunman is a significant figure in our times, a time of personal terror as well as real war.

So there stands the gunman. His cause uncertain and beyond concession, his means intolerable and lethal, his nature elusive. His movement is not easily approached nor readily described. His life is the material of thrillers, inaccurate, romantic, filled with action. His campaign is more dangerous as a spur to counter-violence than as a threat to order. The fact that on occasion the gunman forces change at the centre or at rare times wins as the dream promises is thus fascinating.

Then one special vision may become reality. History may be changed. A mutation survives. Eritreans drink in the Addis Ababa Hilton bar and Castro still talks on for hours elaborating a dream now without lustre. For one bright socialist moment Nicaragua seemed the centre of the world – at least to those on the side of radical angels. Mandela has become a world hero, the dream made manifest. Each underground is special, each dream particular.

One could a few years back walk the drab, dry streets of Teheran under the huge, tattered posters of the old Ayatollah, black and white, great glaring eyes that trace every heretical step, and there find power in strange hands. The same men are still in power. The men at the centre, fundamentalist clerics in brown and grey, scraggly beards and bloody hands, are the past come to rule the present. They now rule as clerks, paper is passed back and forth, violence exported as bankers' drafts and authorized ideas. There is no glow, no trendy admiration of the people's triumph left in Teheran. Between bleak, concrete buildings the streets are dusty, filled with scraps of paper, dry with orthodoxy. And one of those streets, the avenue in front of the British Embassy, is named for hunger striker Bobby Sands, martyred in the H-Blocks at Long Kesh for an Ireland far away. Sands, the Provisional IRA, the whole island is truly a world away – except within the underground.

Iran was a special case. Ireland is a special case; but all the cases are special, some less so – and these have become classics, Vietnam or Algeria, the Italian *Brigate rosse* or the Palestinians. Yet, even when the rebel wins, all is not suddenly revealed; for myths are hurriedly woven by the new residents at the centre – myths to transform the painful odyssey into necessary prologue and myths to adjust history as the prerogative of the newly empowered. The phenomenon of the armed struggle has, in a sense, remained underground.

There have been thousands upon thousands of movements emboldened by a dream, each dream, even the most universal, special. Each has gone underground and opposed the centre, each centre special. Most fail, fail on their own terms, simply fail, the faithful murdered, imprisoned, scattered and in time mostly forgotten. The Irish zealots have also failed repeatedly, failed to achieve the Republic all but established in Irish hearts. But the movement has persisted. Most undergrounds stay underground, fail and are forgotten. Mostly the dream is interned with the dead. Most rebels disappear after harm is done. A few, like Che of the posters and Broadway musicals or Bobby Sands of the Provisional IRA, become martyrs and heroes. The name lingers. The many have neither monument nor impact. It is a cruel trade and long practised in Ireland.

CHAPTER ONE

The Irish Arena

THE IRISH STAGE

The formal arena of any armed struggle is what the military call the battlefield, a matter of terrain and weather, and for the shrewd, especially with the rise of people's wars, includes political and cultural conditions as considerations. In most military campaigns the physical plays a major, often a predominant, role. Battles are fought over civilians, through cities, between big battalions, by those who neither know the local language nor care about the customs of the enemy but rather seek the high ground or a killing box.

In an insurrection or a rebellion the terrain remains but the historical and cultural factors, more elusive, more difficult to chart, matter more. The more unconventional, the more covert the struggle, the more these factors matter. In Ireland at times, it seems that these are all that matter. The lanes off the Falls Road in Belfast or the unapproved roads along the border are always overshadowed by history and dreams. Everyone on the island becomes a player, has a role, displays assumptions and agenda. The Irish terrain is rarely considered as an arena. Ireland is simply there, so that what matters most is not the hills or even the border but the Irish – and all the Irish are not even on the island.

The battle in Ireland and elsewhere involves everyone, even and especially those who do not want to be involved; the English family in Leeds or the old Irish farmer in Cork. There are no innocent people, no one is isolated. An armed struggle involves everyone's assumptions about the intangibles. The arena is shaped by perception more than geography or institutions. The Irish arena is part found and part made and seldom static, hard to map, difficult to assess, different for all those who see the countryside through special spectacles. And everyone wears special prescription lens, has a particular perception of the reality of the arena.

In an armed struggle this perception of the involved is the crucial factor. The battle map is not simply construed from the entire physical and demographic milieu that forms the stage, but from ideas. In Ireland there are ideas about history and reality. There are unstated assumptions. There are the habits and totems of the tribe. There are roles sought and roles found. All this moulds those who fill the stage, may shape the very size of the stage and always imposes on the action.

This is not special to Ireland of the Troubles. In every battle arena each actor has a heritage, a mix of traditions and attitudes, languages and shared or disputed premises and propositions. The physical arena is real enough but history shapes its meaning. History as written by rebels authorizes physical force – from a ditch if need be. And the culture of the times too may authorize such force, even as it generates general outrage at murder from a ditch. Often this strange landscape of legitimacy is hardly noted nor long remembered by the man waiting in ambush or his victim or the audience, but it is far more important than the ditch.

Such a landscape is the really important arena, the one that depends on perception. Such perception, that of the gunman, that of Irish constituency, even that of the victim, provides the setting for conflict, often channels the action. And that action moves. Mountains can seldom be moved but perception is never static. So the Irish arena is a flux but often one with known currents, now strong, now cold, intermittent but tangible.

The stage for an armed struggle is rich with resonances, restrictions, rationalizations, opportunities, contradictions, especially contradictions, as well as implacable reality. Much of this reality is, of course, really real, not imagined by the committed but found on ordinance maps and on the budget's bottom line, and much is not in dispute. Reality is not so easy to adjust. The actors' views cannot change the furniture of the stage, cannot change the historical and cultural factors at will, change the arena simply by desire or in the service of a dream.

In any armed struggle the physical terrain may actually be opened to some tangible adjustment; a new road here and a watch tower there, this forest defoliated and that province brought into the battlefield. What *really* matters – perception of that reality – can be adjusted. The mountains may not be moved by faith but much of the arena is constantly being reflowed by those with varying faiths; now the mountains become irrelevant and later impenetrable. Thus just as the hills must be climbed by the guerrilla, so too must the institutions of man and the legacy of history be considered – the perception of the challenge of each hill.

The family or the tribe is real, imposes bounds and an agenda on all within the arena. What is seen on the television or heard in the pub adds up, changes the total flux. The historian may try to be scientific and the patriot committed but none can deny the events, only explain them. There is always an actual text, often an agreed text, at least a chronology. Few dispute the dates anymore than the mountains are denied as real. There also exists – in theory – an Ireland just beyond touch, an Ireland shaped by past generations, rich in detail, singular and universal, a creation of the mind available to all with the proper tools: some assume these to be scientific, scholarly instruments, precise, amoral, effective, and others art's lyres available only to poets and true believers. Everyone knows that there was once another Ireland that bestows experience, example, rationalization, and access to the concerned. The faithful often deconstruct it and build their own reality, but they must use real bits. Reality can only be remodelled not razed.

In the Irish armed struggle, the key has for generations been a special militant Republican view of reality that has been based on an analysis of history. The volunteers, astute or simple, old or young, look at the arena and come to three vital answers to the crucial questions: What is wrong? What must be done? What is to come? The British are the problem. The armed struggle is the means. The Irish Republic will be the solution. These are the three great insights. For the rebel all arena reality is shaped to these conclusions. Reality becomes an answer to these questions. History becomes grievance, the present latent with promise, the future a certainty. And so is formed the Republican arena with real mountains and conjured meaning.

The other actors have various answers, have their own assumptions about their own roles and rights, their own Ireland: not only Irish Republicans rely on strip mining the past to rationalize present policies. The Irish nationalists are apt to agree that the British must go and that a united nation is the goal, perhaps even a Republic as imagined, but few any longer approve of physical force or the armed struggle – it has cost too much and put too much at risk. All those dedicated to war or politics, all the responsible and concerned, all the ambitious have views that shape the past and look to the future. Those others, the voters, the congregations and marchers, the sometimes participants in events, the watchers and commentators are shaped by perception even as they assume their world is real, history's only heir. Ireland as arena is thus rich, manifold, contradictory. All arenas, not simply Ireland, are conglomerates, layered, various, largely shaped by perception even if ordered by the tangibles.

In Ireland the everyday people, not without importance, seem almost a part of the landscape. They focus on their own rounds, find satisfactory explanation in a private world of jobs sought, matches attended, daily rounds, exams passed, and films seen. Even if they are not replete with ideas or ambitions, they are vital components of the whole, supply constituencies, tolerate or deny, benefit or at times react. For Mao they were the ocean for the guerrilla, but in Ireland they play a different role. These, the people, the

Irish, scattered on the island and in the Diaspora, mostly without great commitment or articulated assumptions, collectively supply the cultural medium for all. A great many of these people are touched by, a few attracted to, the Provisional IRA's struggle, not often or not to any great effect; but they are on the stage, often crowd the stage.

Within the general arena, a composite of individual perceptions and intractable data, the IRA rebel must adapt to this reality of the other Irish, adapt the dream, adjust to effect the form of the underground, the movement's programme and the priorities. The cultural arena composed of everyone's perceptions is recognized as vital. This flux of ideas and attitudes, rationalizations and assumptions, is not neutral; for there is constant adjustment, even by those with little interest in the armed struggle.

Those most involved in the armed struggle, the gunmen and politicians, those responsible for order or for chaos, must read their environment, both the maps and the hearts of the people. For the IRA the reading is crucial – often the movement has had no other assets but the imagined power of that reading. The IRA perception discounts visible assets in contrast to the power of the dream: history and justice will triumph over the orthodox army or the power of sterling. So the tangible is bought at discount while sold by the authorities at a mark-up. And nearly everyone until too late is inclined to believe that history, their Irish history, imperial history, or world history, the times and tides, favour them, not just the bold or the brutal. And in the case of the Republicans, history adjusted to the imperatives of the dream.

Republican reality is thus imposed out of necessity. It is a process not unknown to the loyalist paramilitaries and many Unionists as well, who have long invented for present, largely psychological, purpose their past and even some of their enemies'; but unlike the Republicans their future is to be merely the imagined past made actual. The Unionist looks back to the future. The loyalist kills to prevent not to achieve, to deny, to counter power.

Those in power at the centre need neither vision nor perception, need convince no one. They have books and maps, records and, if need be, the capacity to enforce their interpretation. In Irish matters those in London or Dublin cannot dismiss the reality of Unionist fears or the mortar bombs landing on Heathrow, but they also must take account of the cost of social service and find reasoned accommodations to all the lethal fears and dreams loose in Ireland. Westminster measures out Ireland in minute papers and flow charts, compromises urged and negotiating formulas suggested. Few in London, few in Dublin, can imagine an alternative reality, another legitimacy. The IRA may be more effective and more sophisticated but is as unrealistic as the Ulster Volunteer Force. For the legitimate all such gunmen are the mob, the mob as conspiracy, the mob as threat. Their Ireland, real or proposed, is a nightmare. And so the seeming moderation of Sinn Féin is suspect.

In London, in any case, very few care greatly about Ireland, assume justice is British and history advocate. Ireland is not so much nightmare as inconvenience. Even the charms of a peace process have been lost to old quarrels and new confrontations – interrupted from time to time by sectarian murder and choreographed riots. In Dublin the last generation has been an accelerated course in deconstructing patriot history, advocating new directions, shaping a new Ireland and one not without reality – a tangible Ireland if less than perfect. There is new money, a new young Ireland focused on Europe, a conviction that the peace process must be made to work so that real, everyday life can go forward. Dublin's Ireland is newly minted and still an aspiration but increasingly visible in the Republic, in the 26-counties.

Those deeply involved in Northern Ireland, however, find their assets not in recognition or responsibility but in precedent and presumption. They live within another arena. And so few in those six-counties are free of the dreams, traditions, the power of the past that Dublin and London wish gone. By necessity the everyday in the six-counties must live too amid dreams and fancies, live on a stage filled with irregular armies, exist within an arena not of choice but all too real.

For most nationalists a generation ago the Ireland of Seán Lemass and Captain Terrance O'Neill was well past any armed struggle. There was no need, no prospects, no takers. There was no point in any nationalists North or South saying 'no' to a tolerable reality that only time could adjust. The Unionists might be fearful and certainly the loyalists were – always fearful that the arena *might* still be ripe, that the IRA *might* still be the monster. In 1962, at the end of the IRA's limited border campaign, it appeared that at last reality had sterilized the Irish arena. Romantic Republicanism was dead and in the grave.

Then came the civil rights movement in Northern Ireland and Stormont's hard response that began to erode civil order in the province culminating in the pogroms of August 1969. Dublin GHQ was interested but predicted neither the pogroms nor even then imagined a role for the IRA that would lead to a campaign. The traditionalists and hard men saw the arena differently. They wanted only a change – and suddenly found one a generation early. Ireland was ripe for an armed struggle, a campaign. So the seven men who met around the table to establish a provisional IRA in the winter of 1962 knew, had known since August, that Ireland, unexpectedly, was ready and their traditional reading was valid.

The others, various nationalists, North and South, Dublin GHQ, the radicals and the conventional, were seized on defence, on London's responsibilities, on protest and programmes, on peripheral matters. The Provisional IRA godfathers and their faithful *knew* that objective reality was shaped to allow defence, provocation, and an IRA campaign. They undertook the provisional leadership of the real Republican movement that would surely respond as expected to opportunity. In this the Provos were right enough to begin, to pursue an armed struggle – all that militant Republicans had ever wanted. And the arena *was* ripe. The Official IRA was wrong and the agitators and radicals were wrong and most commentators and nearly all of the responsible were wrong – all wrong, and for the first time in living memory the gunmen were right.

What mattered not at all was the terrain, the size of the battlefield, the reality of the grievances that could be counted out by statistics, or the checklist in counter-insurgency manuals. What mattered was that the Army Council caught the tide while others sought to divert it. The IRA assumptions matched objective reality.

The Provisionals saw the opportunity to turn aspiration into process, the dream into reality. The dream did not lead to victory, not even, not especially after a generation, but rather to a protracted and complex campaign. This was in 1970 all the IRA wanted and this they achieved. In large part the campaign was a result not of the correlation of forces but of the Republican assumptions about the nature of the arena. What mattered was what the Provisional IRA assumed mattered: the mix within the arena favoured Republican aspirations and assets.

THE ARENA ANALYSED

The Mix

The real arena, then, is reflected in the mind of the involved; an image partly physical but mostly shaped by perception. It is an environment descended from history, moulded by present forces, part real, part illusion, partly visible and so tangible. The material stage for any armed struggle holds a special combination of history and culture, a vulnerability, an aura of possibility.

Even in August 1969 not many outside the core of the radical Irish Republicans were so bold or so foolish as to imagine Ireland ripe for an armed struggle. The few potential IRA rebels assumed that since there had been irregular campaigns in the past there could be ones in the future. The crucial factor was not the size of the island, the litany of grievance, the misery of the Northern nationalists but the potential toleration for armed action. Was the arena of the Irish mind ripe? Certainly it was not when 1969 opened but obviously so by the end of the year: obvious that is to the Provisional IRA, who wanted not only an armed defence but also an armed struggle. No map could indicate such considerations. Subsequently, considerable analytical effort has been focused on the nature of the arena during 1970 – after that when the campaign was irreversible the involved have tended to read the flux as authorization for special pleading – rationalizations for compromise or killing or persisting or doing nothing at all. What has intrigued analysts has been a review of the precipitating conditions – and in retrospect how these might have been adjusted.

By 1972 the Provisional IRA had moved from defence to provocation, and on to the campaign – as planned. By then conditions changed, so that in Northern Ireland the arena generated various loyalist paramilitary organizations. With historical precedents but no living tradition, the loyalists found unity of organization more difficult than unity of purpose. Efforts to shape a conventional mass movement foundered and ultimately loyalists who insisted on action chose the gun over politics, the covert over convention. It was the first real loyalist effort from the bottom up so that as in the case of the Provisionals the men of no property came into their own. These loyalists were on stage to stay, for they had found the arena congenial. Splintered, quarrelling, often corrupt, the loyalists without a dream but often with recourse to the gun persisted because their tradition embodied the same fears. The orthodox Unionists, in fact, deployed all manner of means from conventional politics, through a general strike, to armed agitation, not always to advantage. At the same time their arena tolerated, perhaps encouraged, sectarian murder; not an armed struggle but a vigilante campaign.

Most rebels believe that there is room in a specific rebel niche for only one species to survive. *Their* movement is fit to survive; no other. The loyalist paramilitaries quarrelled over spoils and precedents and matters of person, but generally were one on policies: sectarian violence deployed to ease communal anguish. The Provisionals, beneficiary of a revealed truth, had more serious matters to consider. The Provos did not admit that the people were not with them – only that they would not join the armed struggle. As soon as possible, the IRA was provocative by intent thus assuring the support and toleration of their Northern constituency in their role as the defenders of last recourse. It was a role made easier by the policies of the security forces and the limits of practical politics to answer psychological nationalist grievances. As long as fear of renewed pogroms and the resentment at security harassment continued the IRA could wage a campaign indefinitely – and so inspire a loyalist backlash.

The IRA Army Council watched potential nationalist rivals closely, co-opted or intimidated, maintained a consensus. The arena of the Provos – or that of the loyalist paramilitaries – is a matter of perception, assumption, and the real. Few can predict the future exactly – which door will be open to the man on the run – only that mostly doors will be open. That is the real. The orthodox recognize the reality of the armed struggle – the bombs and the bodies – but often not the nature of the arena. Gunmen were often considered criminals or mad, their dream mere rationale to murder, their campaign a refusal to accept reality, compromise, or the good will of others. The conventional and conservative assumed only the demented or the wicked would kill with so little hope of success. The IRA, however, from the first felt success was sure – history vindicated the struggle.

The orthodox depend on the tangibles within the arena, tangibles that can be listed and counted along with the efficacy of compromise and good will. The moderate points to grievances assuaged, the drop in the number unemployed, the rise in housing starts. Just as the soldiers see body bags and the constables number the prison population so do the orthodox number out the Troubles in by-laws and agreements. All are things, indicators, in the almanac. None explains why now and why then the door was opened to the man on the run.

The rebel must always scramble elsewhere for assets – the unseen are easier to amass. The open door must be assumed. The real is another matter. Consequently all rebel analysis, often debased to slogans and graffiti for the simple, seems alien to the conventional. The innocent walk through an arena and see not; nothing but marks on a wall, an expression on a face, a hard word, or a stone thrown: small, outward signs of the great vision. To the conventional the doors along the lane are obviously closed, but to the faithful the doors will be open to need. Not until they are not is IRA analysis invalid. Opponents exist side by side in different worlds.

The arena in 1970 or 2000 follows rebel configurations and reveals a reality that can be found only in rebel hearts. Along with the fields and lanes, the Catholic ghettos and the statistic of the unemployed, the arena has offered to the IRA aid and comfort and legitimacy – offered enough for long enough for the gunmen to move into an endgame – and if that fails to achieve the dream, as has always been the case, it may yet offer hope for a new unknown generation: unless the dream dies.

The Actual

The physical reality of Ireland is easy: an island off the north-west coast of Europe, part of the larger British islands, a small land with a mild climate and perpetual rains. Anyone with an atlas can see the shape and size of the land, read the charts, know the island of green hills, the cliffs of Mohar and the Giant's Causeway. This is Ireland of the map. It is a real Ireland but one Ireland.

Much of the real island hardly looks like poster Ireland; it is urban, suburban, but even then, much looks as expected. The intensively used agricultural land, even if eroded by housing estates and suburbia, is green and pleasant. The wilds tend to be open, barrens and rocks, hardly cover at all, scenery not haven. Ireland is all small and soft. One end to the other is an eight-hour drive in a car; one side to the other takes only four. The Irish, however, do not estimate distance by time or even with a map but by assumption.

All assume that Ireland, their world, is spacious, diverse, wild, and various, part travel poster, part recollection, always spacious filled with distance and diversity. Dublin is a long way from Tipperary, and Tipperary a long way from Dublin. Moving in any direction from any place, the accent changes, the people change, distance is disproportionate to miles travelled. Until recently the country was enormously parochial – the distant was alien and the island huge. This is still much the case despite the automobile and the concentric pull of the media.

The distance within the Republican movement between the Mid-Tyrone Brigade and the battalion on the Short Strand in Belfast is more than two hours drive. To those in the car any drive out of Belfast may seem to be into wilds, into a countryside alien to a city lad who has never touched a cow nor stepped over a stream. And those from Tyrone often find Belfast unappealing, a maze of mean streets and cute tricks, city dirt, and city noise and little to cherish. What is always cherished in Ireland, in the movement, in the IRA is the familiar, the special world that begins to evaporate beyond the catchment of the parish – out there lie wilds and the distance.

Perception

Those who live on the island do not so much see Ireland as live it, seemingly unaware of the peculiarities of their own perspective. They expect nothing novel to be revealed in looking about, feel no shock of recognition at the nature of the island, exist like fish without knowledge of the water. And like the fish they assume water as eternal, shifting, and shimmering but always the same – there, natural beyond comment or notice. And so no great thought need be given to the real world. Ireland as perceived is an accepted universe, place and people, real beyond numbers and beyond analysis.

This is less so for the visitor who mistakes the Ireland described either by Bord Failte and the Northern Ireland Tourist Office or the required reading at the university for the real Ireland. Ireland, in fact, comes in various other packages as well.

who are the alien experts on Ireland, contributors to the
ɔorters on the Troubles, readily find the Ireland that they
ɣ rarely look elsewhere. The National Library is not
ls Road and Crossmaglen, yet these special Irelands are
has come for, what has organized their Irish time.

ɩds the Irish, the Ireland, as expected. It is an Ireland
growing richer and more like every place else. Despite the rush to Europe,
the two weeks on Corfu, the rising sophistication, Ireland is still inhabited
by many who are hardly aware of any other tangible reality. This is their
island, the pub and leaving certs, football, escalating house prices. It is a real
Ireland, the only Ireland most Irish nationalists want and no threat to the
Unionists whose own Ireland – British Ulster – is an imaginary provincial
England. All the Irelands are real but partial and most are special.

Mostly the focus has been on the two Irelands rather than the many
parishes. There has been within the arena for nearly a century an Irish
dispute whether there are two *significant* Irelands, Protestant and Catholic,
Unionist and nationalist, us and them. The two great divisions can readily
be found marked on the British army briefing map or those at the front of
each book on the Troubles. There is then a Protestant Ireland but not
necessarily one that includes all Protestants – those in the Republic have no
interest in the Crown – and certainly not one easy to map. And there is a
Catholic Ireland that subsumes all of the faith, overlaps the nationalist map
which in turn covers Republican Ireland. Such maps are crude but real, for
what matters in an armed struggle is commitment and toleration and service,
all incidental to but shaped by geography and diversity and assumption.

This complexity, real and imagined and perceived, but hardly unique to
Ireland, has a long history even if not the one found in school primers filled
with empire builders or martyr priests. Patriot history is as simple as is
professional revisionist history complex. Yet when the arena comes to be
described, the obvious divisions are both real and vital: religion and politics
and money matter. Which houses are safe and which are not matters to the
gunman. And for the IRA man, member of a non-sectarian secret army,
when on the run down an unfamiliar lane in a mixed neighbourhood just
ahead of the RUC patrol, how better to tell than the red glow of the sacred
heart? *That* division can be a matter of life and death, or years in a cell.

The Culture and the Roles

The illusions and realities aside, the arena in Ireland has for a generation
nourished an armed struggle. The perception of distance and variety may at
times have shaped the direction and pace of the conflict; but Ireland,

Northern Ireland – Ulster in whatever sense – after 1969 proved fertile to
those Republicans who advocated physical force and so too for those who
opposed them with illicit force. Ireland was soon filled with those who had
learned their own patriot history, Orange or Green, possessed real and
imagined grievances, were driven by fears and ambitions generally held and
so sought vengeance or reassurance, and played out their assumption in
secret armies and radical politics. At the beginning of the new millennium
toleration has been seriously eroded but not enough to reassure the uncertain or greatly ease the tensions of a divided society still open to sectarian
murder, paramilitary punishments, and to a degree the military operations
of the most militant Republicans.

In Northern Ireland and so in Ireland, the narrow assumptions, the
specific grievances are easy to detail. There was the miserable housing, the
fear of the IRA as the point of Catholic, Irish nationalism, the humiliation
of the Orange rituals, and the innocent arrogance of the British political
establishment. There were as well the traditional assumptions of the hard
men of whatever persuasion and the political habits, not all savoury and
seldom self-denying, of the orthodox. All of these are familiar. These special
factors, however, produced the proximate conditions for the Provisional's
armed struggle: grievance, enlightened protest, provocation, and response,
with moderation eroded and the gunmen encouraged. And this nexus of
events is generally now recognized, although those who would replay the
match, take back the last three moves and begin again, have different game-
plans for history. In any case what did happen has become clear if no longer
very important in the scrabble for a congenial future often found by rum-
maging in an imaginary past.

The past is not inherited but shaped for current usage: each generation
gets the history not only that it deserves but that it wants and so writes. The
radical protesters addressed real grievance, came at the end of real history,
were different only in that for the first time in 50 years they assumed
that change was possible. Some of the changes desired – one person and one
vote – were easy to articulate if less easy for the establishment to concede;
but others that moved many from vengeance to Catholic triumphalism
were not articulated, not even recognized in many cases. And this hidden
agenda, real or not, was what mattered to most of the Unionist establishment
who assumed not unreasonably that these were primary not secondary considerations. What was not apparent during the heady days of protest and
Unionist intransigence or often not apparent later as well was the part the
long cycles of Irish history played.

All that is perceived as history is precedent. And Irish history was read by
each to special advantage, became rationalization and prophet. So that once

again there is no consensus on the role of this institution or that habit, the peasant mind or the settler mentality, the strictures of late imperialism or the persistence of rural agitation. The Troubles can, in fact, be adequately explained in many ways, each an end-product of a special history – more often product of a special agenda for the future. Many of these descriptions are quite satisfactory without necessarily contradicting quite different approaches: the neo-Marxist treatise can live comfortably with a psychological probe, Gramsci with Freud, and both with patriot history, each adding to an insight of the arena but none having a monopoly. The British often sell the Troubles as a tribal war between Catholics and Protestants and the Irish Republicans assume that they are engaged in a war of national liberation against an alien presence – and there is ample evidence for those who hold either vision. The Irish Troubles you see is the Irish Troubles you get.

The arena of the mind is not quantifiable. In a devoutly Catholic country, for example, even an avowedly non-sectarian movement will be in significant part shaped by the ubiquitous ideas and ideals of the Church. Those who are anti-clerical are anti-clerical in special Irish Catholic ways. The influence of the Roman Church on the mind of the IRA volunteers is accepted but not its intensity. Certainly the Republican movement after 1969 was composed of Catholics, mostly practising Catholics; and certainly that Church opposed, increasingly opposed, Republican policies and pretensions. Not even a plea from a pope standing in a green Irish field could deflect Republicans from a war sanctified by their patriot dead. Still, the values of the Church, service, denial, sacrifice, the nobility of suffering, the assurance of ultimate triumph, need only be adjusted to Republican needs.

The IRA supplied volunteers with a secular vocation, demanded service and sacrifice, offered a compelling and luminous dream, and an ultimate end to history with vengeance as a spin-off benefit. And at the end the just would at last came into their own no matter the earthly cost or the scorn of the powerful. Even the most conventional and conservative recognized the religious implications in the IRA great hunger strikes of 1980–81: those who can suffer the most will triumph. What an ideal prescription for those on hunger strike and one with a Republican sponsor in the martyred Lord Mayor Terence MacSwiney, dead in Brixton Prison in 1920. So surely the ideas of the Church reinforced the needs of the IRA just as the ideas of the Age of Reason and modern nationalism enriched the flux of belief.

Perhaps the ideals of the United Irishmen found less prepared minds for those Republicans in the Ulster countryside. These were more apt to trace their ancestry to night riders defending their own, the poor and the faithful, rather than to the non-sectarian ideals of the French or American deists. The volunteer husbands an amalgamation of ideas and ideals adjusted for the present. Vengeance too can be found, appears more quickly if less openly. Sectarian inclinations may be, often are, subsumed into the ideals of the movement. Each, all, operate with mixed motives, often motives not apparent until queried. No Republican is ever quite sure that shooting the off-duty Protestant RUC reserve sitting on his tractor in a Fermanagh farmyard is not in part an act of sectarian purpose. The Protestants assume so. And for the volunteer who pulled the trigger the answer will come after the deed as expected and no one the wiser.

It is easier to describe the Irish flux at a distance than within the killing zone. And perhaps the confluence of influence can ever be dissected in single examples, each more special than any general Irish model. What does seem clear is that those who advocate physical force have persisted, been tolerated but rarely supported by the Irish nationalists, mostly Catholic but some not, for nearly two centuries. When times are bleak they wait on better times or are divided when some enter politics. In the present peace process the core of the movement has spent years evading a split in order to avoid a split.

Physical force still appeals to the most militant. Their ideas and ideals have not changed. The general ideas loose on Ireland have encouraged or at least not punished the Republicans, and may have – must have – shaped their struggle. Some of these ideas are those of any peasant society, a society still close to the land, suspicious of the elegant or strange, nostalgic for order but opposed to interference, and hard to organize. It is a society often sullen with grievance, indomitable, brutal, and provincial – and persistent. This is not the Irish of Bord Failte or RTE (Irish state television), not everyone's Ireland but certainly one Ireland and one most Irish prefer not to display.

What is clear – at least from a distance – is not that the Irish arena is unique, special, but that the Provisional IRA has consciously benefited from Irish history, Irish assumptions and habits.

The Statistics

The points of the Irish compass have real numbers. A text for the innocent reader would display the details of the population: the numbers of Catholics, the national income, the unemployed, and the votes collected by the Ulster Unionists or Provisional Sinn Féin indicate the direction of data if not the future in detail. There would be maps and charts and graphs, some projection and much to number – the hard data.

The key factors in the Irish arena for many analysts have been the conventional areas that yield numbers. First is the confessional basis of politics, what is Protestant or Catholic, and what the future then holds for a sectarian system erected on patronage. Then the role of money – a factor cherished by the neo-Marxist who finds those of no property intriguing. And finally what do the repeated elections – local elections, Dáil elections, European elections, provincial elections in the North, and Westminster elections and special elections, plebiscites on the border or the new Assembly. – indicate about present motives and future prospects? Numbers can be given to church goers, to incomes earned and spent, and to votes deployed or denied.

Almost all agree that in Ireland religion matters a great deal even if in Antrim or Tyrone tribes are really what is involved. The Republic is over 95 per cent Catholic, and Northern Ireland, with under a million residents, is still Protestant but with a decaying majority population. Each year there are more Catholics but the prospects of a voting majority for nationalists is still distant except to many Protestants fearful of the revenge of the cradle. In Northern Ireland much springs directly from the confessional division. There are sectarian numbers available to predict to a nicety elections in Tyrone or with less certainly advocacy of a united Ireland. Nationalist or Unionist divisions are very real but may be – often are – subsumed for tactical purposes. In the Irish Republic, a Catholic nation of sorts, there is no need for defence, no compelling grievance, little affection for Republican presumptions. Statistics over generations have indicated only a rare and fleeting electoral support for Sinn Féin: one member of the Dáil and a scattering of local success. Often Sinn Féin is seen by Southern Catholics as a Northern phenomenon and the armed struggle ruthless and futile and so those involved, recently if not at present, in a murder campaign. Catholics do not need such defenders nor does Ireland. Religious numbers do not change into religious votes.

What the Republicans can deploy is the energy generated by the dream – the will of the faithful. This fragile but renewable commodity does not assure conventional power, parallels to a degree the conventions of a church, can run with minimal financing, and cannot guarantee anything but the persistence of the struggle. Votes sought, bought, counted, analysed, the means to position, the combination that opens the door to power are beyond the gift of the dream. And so many do not want to transfer allegiance to a political peace process, however futile continued physical force is. In Ireland votes are a means to ensure entitlement and occasionally to punish the presumptuous or inefficient. Only rarely are they deployed to register general protest or for those outside the existing system. Thus despite all the elections that indicate tribal divisions in Down or Derry or the minute adjustments of the steady-state system in Dublin, the election charts and graphs are not effective tools to dissect the IRA much less the capacity and prospects of the Republican movement. No one knows how many are in the IRA – certainly not the IRA. What matters is capacity, what can be done, not how many are numbered on a list. Lift half the list and capacity may be enhanced. This is what matters, not parade strength or votes. If votes matter then the faithful are required to become involved in a painful reappraisal.

And Ireland is changing, far more rapidly than those involved in a clandestine world can easily imagine. Gerry Adams may have been to Dublin and Washington, on the world's television screen, but not the small farmer from Armagh. Tomorrow the rules may change. The British government has promised that the wishes of the majority – solidly Protestant – will be paramount in determining the future; but when the future arrives the promise may not be still valid or the British may decide the guarantee was to the Protestants and not to the majority. So even if the Catholics become a majority, no sure thing, this does not mean a nationalist majority. If such a nationalist majority in time arises demanding Irish unity, this does not mean British acceptance or for that matter a Dublin acceptance. The arena will be different but to no actor's certain advantage. What the Republican advocates in the peace process is a change to his advantage that does not rest on the slow movement of time but rather on pressure, world opinion, Dublin support, and the justice of the cause. Only some of these factors can be given numbers.

If the real data of Ireland tell only a small part of the story, a fulcrum for argument, a partial guide to the terrain, such data are still real, often much of the story and always part of the tangible arena for action. There are Catholics and Protestants and they can largely be numbered and often polled on their opinions. The fact that the strictures of fundamentalist Protestant-ism are still focused on the divisions of the Reformation is both actual and significant. The fact that the Irish Roman Catholic Church remains the predominant factor in the assumptions and attitudes of its flock, if less so than in the past, and has long been enormously conservative in matters of doctrine as well as in matters social, political, and economic, is even more significant. Both nationalist and Unionist traditions have a profound religious content – it is almost entirely what distinguishes the two.

THE IRISH ACTORS

The real Irish, unlike the stage Irish, are more difficult to display to any useful purpose even if their numbers are known or their voting habits detailed. For the purposes of an armed struggle, what matters about the Irish is their own perceptions, aspirations, assumptions, the intangibles that rarely come into view; the Irish nature is elusive. The evidence tends to appear after the fact. Even those who open the door to a man on the run do not know whether they will give haven or not until the moment comes. So many of the Irish appear to run to rules not found in a book, not even admitted – a country filled with those who keep their counsel, say nothing, wait on the crucial issues, know everything – an Irish secret is something you tell one person at a time. Everything else is known if hidden. They talk to you in order that you ask them no questions, reveal a ready tongue to hide the real.

The Involved

The Irish have for long been assumed special, not neat, not tidy, seldom on time but highly creative, garrulous, subject to easy generalization, figures of fun for the foolish, everyday people for their own, wondrously different for their advocates abroad. Their Ireland is still truly an island of saints and scholars, poets and priests – these days let no one speak of the gunman – where the quality of life has not been dimmed by popular taste. The expatriates come home to find their roots – and find nothing changed, all still special – and the specialists come to explore the Irish, each to a discipline and find as expected all special.

Even those on the island are apt to feel that their everyday has special salience. The Irish have seemingly for centuries in a small compass played out, often to no island advantage, many of the major issues of the West. So Ireland still appears more important than numbers would warrant. And the Irish feel themselves special because they have produced saints and scholars and gunmen. The economy is often a shambles, prey to scandal and corruption, crime seemingly on the rise, the green defaced by the jerrybuilt; but the island changes, the population is young, often prosperous and conventional, the successful at ease in London or Brussels and many of the others intimate with a wider world. If there are really few poets and fewer saints, there are some. And the world listens to U2, bets on Irish horses, marches on St Patrick's Day and keeps a watching brief on the gunman.

As far as the armed struggle is concerned the great divide remains; there are two histories in Northern Ireland. Few in Ireland really know anything of the other tradition, assume the others are essentially the same but totally different. The Protestant lives next door to a Catholic but in British Ulster where no Catholic can enter. The Catholic next door harbours the dream of a different Ireland – open in theory to all the Irish but regarded as assimilation and ruin by the Protestant. They exist in a divided society, side by side in different worlds. Both would prefer the other gone in practice whatever theory or the democratic norms may require. These are worlds that do not even reveal obverse sides, mirror images, but rather strange images that are reflected back and forth over time. This wilderness of mirrors imposes on the Irish viewers a strange shifting reality of imagination and exaggeration. Introspection is not common currency in Irish analysis and empathy rarely found.

And this is certainly the case with the British, who act in innocence and arrogance, seldom bother with the Irish they know all too well from comfortable stereotypes. Ireland is not important enough in London to learn new lines, review the role. Britain – England – has provided a remarkable continuity to the Troubles. The responsible have learned little, ignored the history that so convulses the locals, and pursue more important matters: bit part players that own the stage. Those who would end the play or even understand the play find no career in London and so the run continues, the Irish roles complex and elusive and the British intractable as the weather. With the onset of the peace process Downing Street wanted an agreement, a formula, that would allow the United Kingdom to move on. In power Labour finds, as have all the British, Northern Ireland uncongenial, none more so than dedicated Republicans.

For the Irish Republicans, the major island actors in the armed struggle, history is both found in books, in the classroom, and in the recruits class but also in the very nature of the flux. Many in the IRA seek history's roles as much as power or action or prominence. These roles are ready-made, on the shelf, history's bounty. The leadership of the movement has to shape a contemporary conciliatory role that does not reflect the betrayals of the past – those who sold out the movement for political gain that did not lead to the Republic. These are deemed different, mistook the times. And so those who control the past control the future; and those possessed by the past are doomed to repeat it. Sometimes amid the selection of roles and precedents, so many, so various, the difference is not easy to discern, not in the Republican movement, not on the island.

The Irish Republican World

By 1968 at the end of history, however written, the Republican movement inhabited a particular Irish universe integral to Ireland, more past than present. The Ireland of the map, the Ireland perceived by most Irish, was theirs but so too was a particular universe. This was their special, closed Ireland, neglected and forgotten by the many. It was a galaxy united by the force of the old dream and stretched out from the hard core of the activists through the faithful to the fringes of toleration. It supposedly encompassed all the Irish, Catholic and Protestant and dissenter, but only in theory. In fact the galaxy was very small and in the 1960s apparently irrelevant to the new Ireland. It was a relic, a husk, the burnt-out dark star of militant Irish nationalism.

From this narrow, clandestine world, shaped by history real and history as read, shaped by society and special assumptions, kept alive if barely by the faithful, would arise the Provisional IRA. There was no single moment of expansion, no time of singularity. Rather the movement never died, the faith was always there, often everywhere present in some small degree. Nationalism was not dead but irrelevant except within the movement. And there at the core were the true believers. These militant Republicans were all possessed by a dream, were all as one on the crucial issues. They fit no psychological stereotype, were seldom the feckless Irish rebel, but rather fit more easily a sociological pattern: they were apt to be narrow, limited, parochial, and provincial, without property or prospects. Irish Republicans were the dream of the theorists: a movement of workers – often without work – and small farmers – often without enough land. They were, however, possessed of a vision worthy of sacrifice. Few outside the formal faiths – and few there – were as committed, as zealous.

Their adult lives had been given in service to the secret army, to the movement, to the Republic of 1916, to their Ireland. To that secret army came after 1970 thousands upon thousands of volunteers. In many ways these new recruits of all ages were much like the 1970 originals. There were a few with education or time abroad, a few with skills, but most were men and women from housing estates and small towns volunteering first to defend their people and soon caught up in the dream to serve the cause and to secure the Republic. The movement had a role for each, a secular vocation.

The special Republican Ireland that nourished the volunteers and so the armed struggle had and has reality, presents tangibles as well as dreams. There are strongholds, the Ardoyne or Unity Flats, Crossmaglen or the Creggan in Derry, that can be found on the map. There are safe houses and arms dumps that cannot be found on the usual map. There are villages and families to be found in Kerry or Louth or Cork. And there are also ideas and ideals beyond any map. This may be the chart that matters most but the IRA armed struggle takes place in the real world. The conflict zone overlays the largely invisible Republican world and has two major parts determined by the lines on the map, divisions imposed by states and found in the atlas.

There is the Republic of 26 counties where different rules and attitudes determine the people's response to both the Provisional Republicans and the British. These attitudes over time have shifted, eroding the Provisional's freedom of action without a real benefit for the British security forces. The shift against the Republicans often has not apparently shifted basic nationalist assumptions: if this be contradiction it is an Irish one. The Irish seem to want a united Ireland but only as a perfect gift and certainly not at the cost of sacrifice or the price of change. After a generation they have made it clear that they abhor root and branch the IRA's campaign but somehow not enough to deny it absolutely. If such ambivalence is eroding, if the IRA has wasting assets in the Republic, that part of the arena remains more congenial than the six-counties. Even the conversion of the Republicans to negotiations has not generated enthusiasm, only support. Such support is tentative, conditional, and quite unrelated to the legitimacy of physical force.

In Northern Ireland, the majority Protestants may be at one with their Catholic neighbours in some social and economic matters but have always differed in the crucial and so often lethal matters of loyalty, the national issue, for they live in British Ulster. The IRA is anathema, the volunteers criminals, their political leaders recent terrorists, almost always with criminal records. Thus the IRA during the armed struggle most often had to operate in very hostile territory. There is none of the ambivalence of the 26-counties. The IRA can only find a welcome – often only as defender and at times not at all – in the nationalist areas. And this welcome is tempered by the proximity of the security forces.

There is no easy IRA field of operations. Beyond the island, in Britain, the Irish Diaspora is mostly anti-nationalist and under close watch by the Special Branch, hardly an asset at all. The IRA have increasingly used England as battleground – taking the war to the British establishment – but only by operating in isolation from the local Irish community. During the past 20 years the IRA has also found friends and opportunities elsewhere, in Europe and the Middle East, in Africa. Each time it is easier to operate in a novel extensions of the battlefield, easier in Holland than Holland Park, easier in Lebanon than Leitrim. Thus, if in a small way, the armed struggle has spread out beyond the island, beyond Britain to Tripoli and Gibraltar and Germany. Such action that is exported relies on raids and delegations not residents. When the struggle began the endgame, a crucial arena was not Ireland but international opinion.

Where residents always and still counted most outside Ireland is, has been, in North America. The Irish-American communities in Chicago or Baltimore, friends in Toronto, all these matter, mean money and gear and influence. And all of these assets have eroded over a generation as both Dublin and London have competed effectively for converts. The emergence of Adams, McGuinness, and the peace process tapped new sources but few that could imagine the necessity of a renewed armed struggle, so most were alienated, some for good, when the IRA broke the first ceasefire. The new friends are peace-process friends. Thus the Republican galaxy extends great distances but thinly, sometimes no more than a single agent and at times thousands of Americans cheering the arrival in New York of the president of Sinn Féin.

For the Provisional IRA the Ireland that matters is first and foremost their own. The Republican structure stretches over the two parts of Ireland and beyond. It must adjust to the nature of that arena even if the tangible aspects – time and distance and things – are almost incidental to the armed struggle. Distance can be made good, Derry is not too far from Beirut or Kerry from Belfast. Time is an Irish asset. Gear or money is always short and always found. And so the new adjustment to politics has been difficult, time does matter, frustration erodes support for the new IRA role. What always matters within the galaxy is the intensity of the faith and that is unevenly distributed.

A map of the galaxy is quite different from any supplied by Bord Failte or Esso. For Republicans some small villages, certain town lands, this parish or that loom large, large today but perhaps not tomorrow. There are huge blank areas. Many parts of the island lay fallow, the faithful never present, long gone, or died off. Who do we know now in Mallow or Sligo? Some parts are dominated by those outside the faith: dragons of coercion or repression or betrayal rule there. In East Belfast the IRA gunman uses a real map, operates in alien fields, patrolled by real enemies. Actually for the IRA the most secure zones have been at the heart of the struggle along the Falls or within the parish lands west of the Bann, in the estates of Derry or Newry or Strabane. There the nationalists are under siege. There defence is needed. There the faith is tangible, and haven found. There trust is more nearly absolute. Peace as prospect has made little difference.

The Republican galaxy while an invisible ecosystem, rarely open to tourists or the alien, does have tangible aspects. There are open rituals and rites. There are signs and symbols that can at times be seen out the window – wall murals and painted kerbstones and lads selling *An Phoblacht*. Mostly, only the initiated can tell that this crossroads is at the heart of a secret army unit or those houses, raided each week by rote, hold the next generation of volunteers. Mostly, the galaxy is a matter of the mind, of the faith where the true recognize each other, find comfort without need of display, are at ease within a special world. No place is more congenial, safer, than ground zero in West Belfast or on the square at Crossmaglen in the Republic of South Armagh.

In the Irish Republic the Republican world has gradually been circumscribed. While only a few places are dangerous, much is barren, no haven, no support, except for a few areas along the border. Nowhere is physical geography very relevant. The country used is the country that holds the faithful. The IRA operations along the border occur not simply because there is a border but because there are faithful along that border – because of that border. So the operations move into and out of the North, rely on local toleration and conditions rather than heavy cover, find beginning and end in Louth or Donegal, especially in Monaghan, exist because the Republican world and reality converge. Here those dedicated only to physical force found sanctuary for persisting in a campaign that led to the Omagh bomb – but not to betrayal by their own.

The IRA have made historic Ulster – with the addition of a few border areas – the real, physical arena of the armed struggle. And the operations take place at the edges of the tangible galaxy whether in the city centre of Belfast or the hills of mid-Tyrone. It is, in fact, probably easier to bomb in the City of London than off the Shankill. Mostly the IRA penetrates an alien zone of control, risks both the security forces and a hostile local population and then withdraws into safe havens. Such operations have been constant in the six-counties for a generation.

Operations wholly within the Republic are rare and seldom even para-military: armed robberies, occasional kidnapping, theft, extortion, smuggling, the dark side of the struggle. In Adare a failed attempt to seize £500,000 from a post office lorry on 7 June 1996 collapsed into a shooting that caused the death of Detective Gárdá Jerry McCabe. The murder during a foolish operation, feckless but authorized, did vast harm to the movement. Operations are authorized, like the great Sallins train robbery in March 1976, and others not. There is always the assumption that success will make everything right and so no one plans for failure. Only a few IRA operations have been truly significant or spectacular, like the assassination in Dublin of the British Ambassador Christopher Ewart-Briggs on 21 July 1976 or of Lord Mountbatten on the last day of his vacation in Sligo on 27 August 1979. There is some training in the Republic, some rest for those on the run. Actually, for the volunteer on the run a house off the Falls feels safer than a farm in Clare. The key in the Irish Republic is maintenance of the campaign under the Southern Command and agents of GHQ that remains easier in the somewhat more congenial setting.

In the Republic if there are no loyalists – although there are Catholic Unionists, some no longer in closets – more important are those who detest the Provisionals. Among them are an increasing number who will act against the IRA instead of tolerating their presence – a fluctuating number beyond the polls that has grown as the armed struggle has eroded Southern nationalist patience. The Omagh bomb in August 1999 engendered horror and fierce public opposition to those remaining Republicans still dedicated to physical force. Toleration in the Republic has always been beyond easy measurement despite the polls, election statistics, editorials, television reports, conversations, and conferences. All these indicate little support for the Provisional IRA or for Sinn Féin. Toleration, however, involves either doing nothing or doing nothing yet. It is easy, comfortable, cost free, traditional and widespread. Informing still has a bad repute. Extradition is not generally popular. The old ways have left a residue. And so even those who detest the Provos, and even more so the radical splinters, may hesitate to deny those still, somehow, perceived as their own – that fewer hesitate is a most telling sign of the times. So the Provos do not have a free run but more so than across the border.

This north–south border is both tangible and beyond easy reach. The border itself is a largely unmarked, twisting line that coils and doubles back, follows natural features and cuts through houses and across villages, visible when a road is bisected and a fence erected. Traffic in and out can be monitored by patrols and informers, by the giant British army watch towers looming above the fields or by aerial reconnaissance; by all sorts of means and machines. Some have been dismantled during peace negotiations and some have not. In any case, the border cannot be closed or even totally monitored except at a financial cost far beyond British capacity and a political cost not worth paying. Cross-border operations can be made very difficult – in 1998–99 schismatic Republican groups were regularly thwarted – and still managed to move over the border to bomb.

The closer to the centre the harder is penetration – and a journalist may stand next to the Chief of Staff and be at the very margins of the world. The Republican world has few entry markers. Within Northern Ireland, the main battle arena, there are a few signs that the visitor has entered a different country: graffiti, tricolours, tattered Sinn Féin election posters – who would tear them down? – and often a heavy security presence. The IRA spokesman comes into the outside world not the reverse. Most contacts are as far from the core as the soldiers and police, the armoured cars and block-houses of the cities, or the armed patrols plodding across green fields who indicate the edge of the invisible Republican world.

This IRA universe, the militant Republican world, is found in the heads of organizers and in the associations of generations, found in the rebel heart and through practice. Few could follow an Army Council meeting filled with allusions and assumptions, nods and obscure references. So little need be said. So much is taken as granted, as given, arises from shared lives and the binding power of the dream that holds the Republican world in place. That world is still limited, has always been limited, even in 1916 or 1920 it was a small world.

In no place is the IRA very strong and in many places it is very weak. Over a generation the Republican universe has exploded and collapsed in a series of pulses, each usually less impressive, less bright than the last. The edges are what often determine efficiency. Out there far from the Army Council and those on active service are Republicans whose convictions are uncertain: Who will help? Who will hinder?

At the best of times the galaxy can deploy only a few so numbers are even less important than might be imagined. Often the problem is that there are too many who want action – the prisons are filled with the overload. Released, many are offered no new mission, have a lesser role The active are inactive but must appear to be conventional. Thus the arena imposes on the rebel the necessity of artificial cover: the necessity to be above ground on appointed rounds if only to collect the dole and visit the pub. On the other hand, with a new mission, new power within the structure, Sinn Féin does offer such a role and one that attracts a somewhat different kind of pilgrim.

Ireland as a combat arena geographically cannot long hide the operational; only a few hours, a few days. Thus, whether or not Ireland seems grand in Irish perception, the Provisional IRA must operate on a very narrow stage and mostly in full view of all actors and the entire audience. Much of that audience is violently opposed to the IRA – all the Unionists, many Northern nationalists, much of Irish opinion in the Republic. Many of these are active opponents when in theory they should be part of the IRA's constituency. Few in that constituency – the Irish people – are part of the galaxy, few even can imagine that it exists; rather they are apt to imagine a tiny band of fanatics beyond logic or hope of victory, bombing and killing without wit or reason. In fact, as elsewhere, the vast majority on the island want no part of politics at all – a vote in an election is politics enough. Politics may colour life, but after a generation of Troubles most of the Irish are tired, long for neutral hues and peace and quiet. True believers, whatever the faith, cause trouble, always cause trouble. In the case of the IRA, the Republican faith generates general horror and righteous indignation. Such indignation is short-lived for most of the island returns swiftly to the everyday: even in West Belfast there are classes to attend, bets to be made, milk to be taken in from the door, and jobs to seek.

The result on a very small island has been that a very small part is open to free play by the Provos and even there active support is not assured. Even then Republican Ireland, even ground-zero in West Belfast or South Armagh, is still divided and diverse, still seems part of the main, even if organized by the Republican movement. And that movement is made up of those who live within the invisible Republican universe. It is this incandescent, unseen world created by special perceptions generated by the commitment to the ultimate Republic that matters most of all. The galaxy is the present product of the dream that in turn is the most significant engine of the armed struggle, the most crucial part of the general arena.

There are other dreams abroad in Ireland: that of the Unionist for past comfort and security that never existed; that of the British for assurance that their long Irish adventure was truly based on just principles and the right; that of the nationalist that unity was inevitable and not necessarily at the cost of turmoil or at any cost. Not one of these has the power of the incandescent Republic that moulds a special universe, has powered a special armed struggle to reach an endgame.

The Republican dream is best detailed in similes and denials, by poets and in rituals. With the incandescent dream, comes the very tangible butcher's bill. The Irish flux open to many meanings, many roles, real and imagined; but above all else it is a flux congenial to the IRA gunman smelling of cordite who moves out of the past toward a special future engaged now in an end-game but not unmindful of the power of the gun in Irish politics.

CHAPTER TWO

Analysis and Reality

As is the case with all valid revolutionary movements, the Provisional Republican analysis was shaped by the dream. Ideology is essentially the tangible, intellectual structure of the dream. All such dreams provided as well the medium through which the arena, the actors, the armed struggle are perceived. And each supplies the energy that powers an armed struggle, thus is both medium and message, engine and effect.

In the case of the Provisionals in 1969–70, the dream was old, comfortable and pure. Modern class-based analysis played little part in Republican consideration nor did the radical trends of the times. In any case, the ideals of the movement appealed mainly to those of no property, limited capacity and prospects, those with little to lose. Elsewhere radical ideas tended to appeal to the middle class not the workers and peasants, more apt to be bemused by consumer durables.

In Ireland these volunteers without property could be trusted for they had only their lives and honour to sacrifice: and they were unlikely to question the articles of faith on analytical grounds, be swayed by current fashions or intellectual trends. Certainly those clustered around the new Army Council in that first winter of 1969–70 had no property, provincial experience, little to offer but life and honour – and that long pledged.

For a modern nationalist dream the Irish aspiration hardly differed from many comparable movements, movements that had created an Italian or a Bulgarian nation or failed to do so in Macedonia or Palestine. There was a touch of European irredentism, a reflection on colonial experience, intimacy with national liberation struggles, mostly in the Third World but mainly the basis was solidly bedded in Irish experience. For the Irish much came from the eighteenth-century age of revolution as shaped by those who rose for liberty in 1848. These new national ideals were later draped in the language of the Left in much of Europe: socialism and nationalism. This was not the case in Ireland for the heirs to 1848 were the Fenians who focused on the means and legitimacy of physical force rather than dialectic analysis. In Ireland the socialists' vision had only a marginal attraction despite the reality of economic grievance. And again each nationalist dream would be special.

Some were more special like that of the Zionists, some classical like that of the Basques, some captured by the radical Right as in Italy or Poland, and some the property of the Left as in much of Latin America. Some dreams were specious, illusory like those that would be summoned up on proclamations by the new African states, and others warped by poverty as in Haiti or rewarded by external intervention as had been the case with the Baltic states or denied by such intervention as had also been the case with the Baltic states. The Irish case was special and general.

After 1848, in Fenian hands Irish nationalism matured, defined means and aim, and seldom grew more elaborate or less appealing. The Irish Republican dream was mostly typical, diverged only in the matter of Marx and the persistence of a single movement. Unlike other movements the dream tended to become institutionalized in opposition rather than in power. The Republican movement – the Fenians, the IRB (Irish Republican Brotherhood), the old IRA, or the new Provisional manifestation – shared the usual nationalist dynamics, transformed the devout and offered a secular faith, adjusted history to advantage, unearthed old symbols and institutions, revived the language and invented what was necessary. And this was done generation after generation. Most important, as always, was the incandescent power of the ultimate goal: a risen people in a free nation.

The Irish Republican dream had been configured not only by the avowed ideas of the Age of Reason and the rise of modern nationalism but also by the existing institutions and customs on the island. Of most importance was the overwhelming reality of British – English – power: for centuries to be Irish was not to be English. Even as the Irish ways, the Irish language, the Irish differences were eroded, being Irish, not being English, remained a hidden national goal, hidden by masks, by cunning, by adjusting reality. These means of resistance, conscious and unconscious, articulated and soon natural, were various: sullen resentment, passive truculence, public faces and private faith, covert conspiracy, foreign alliances, and night riders. All of these were facets of a people denied, who must in part invent themselves as different. The great institutions of the island were largely alien: law and order, the mores of the middle class, the wonders of success.

And all the Irish nationalists, Catholic, Protestant, or dissenter, were exposed to the grievances of the margins, the denials, the perceive oppression and the reality of British power for British purposes – none more so than Catholics but at times Protestants and dissenters as well. As time passed, and for varying reasons, Catholicism and nationalism became converging parallels, there were fewer Protestants attracted to the ideal; but always even in the narrow years there were a few just as there are a few within the Provos. Whatever the creed or origin, all were agreed on the seat of all ills.

The movement, in fact the inchoate Irish nation, often defined itself by recourse to an English opposite. This, too, was not unique for small nations next to the grand, but special because the Irish had resisted for so long being absorbed, becoming provincials, as did the Bavarians in Germany, the Virginians in America, or the Cornish in Britain. The Scots gave up national aspirations and before them the Welsh, but never the Irish. Simultaneously with the rise of the Republican movement the role of the Roman Church shifted. The great difference for nationalists had been the Roman Church as increasingly the faithful were also loyal to their different church. Loyalty to the workers or to the ideas of secular nationalism could for many be adjusted to their religious commitment. The people and so the nation might increasingly identify Catholicism and nationalism but the movement was capable of adjusting so as to attract Protestants – and Jews – and then socialists because nationalism on the island was inclusive. Those in Ireland whose loyalties were elsewhere, looked to London and the Crown, tended to be Protestants, often outside Ulster recent arrivals, and those co-opted by opportunity, Castle Catholics. Those who found first loyalty in the Crown were for the Republicans West Britons, not Irish, mostly not Catholics, certainly not nationalists. Those who would deny their own, their heritage, their nation on sectarian grounds were simply misguided, Irish but misguided. And as misguided they could be left to later. As militant Zionists in Palestine tended to concentrate on the imperial foe – the British – and ignore the others, the Arabs, as peripheral to the armed struggle, so too the Irish Republicans who felt that the conversion of the Irish Protestants, mostly in Ulster, was a matter of timing, was assured, was not a major analytical factor. And even less important were those in Ireland who were loyal to the Crown for practical purpose or as transients. These were irrelevant to the march of history while the Irish Protestants would in time march to the same tune: A Nation Once Again.

The complexities of religion and nationalism, socialism and nationalism, the hard questions had long before 1969 became the subject of formula and denial. There had been for generations explanations for Irish loyalists, for Catholic practice, for class considerations that satisfied the volunteers if not the logician. The Provisional Republicans almost all shared the heritage of the Church despite its disapproval and all opposed, root and branch, the English, the British entity, the never-failing sources of all Irish political ills, despite the fact that Irish Unionists on the island supported the British presence just as the loyalists had supported the island's integration into the United Kingdom.

Irish Republicans, unlike most Irish nationalists, did not in theory identify Catholicism as Irish or accept the validity of the Unionists' conviction. In primary matters, they did not believe that power, longevity, and reality, and the changing times should alter the urgency of responding to Britain's usurpations on the island. They did not see that such a proposition should alarm the Roman Church or threaten the Unionists or alienate other Irish nationalists who had often been satisfied with concessions – especially those who claimed to rule an Irish Republic of 26 counties from the Dáil in Leinster House. Thus the dream was often in opposition to the policies of the Irish Church, enormously conservative in social and economic affairs, in all matters of doctrine, in opposition to the avowed interests of the Irish Unionists and to the legitimacy of the governments in Dublin and London.

The Irish Church recognized the compelling power of Irish nationalism and had over the generations adjusted, co-opted, and co-operated rather than opposed the faith: not always with good grace, for the astute recognized a competitor, a secular faith. In the nineteenth century, the Church, if puritanically suspicious of secular attractions and conservative by wont, was eager for a modern, disciplined flock that would be immune on the one hand to the sloth and fecklessness of the Celtic heritage, and on the other to the materialism of the West and in particular the British example. Unlike the Republicans, however, existing reality after 1921 favoured the aims and intentions of the Church, gave special position in the Catholic Free State and a special provenance in the nationalist community isolated in the six-counties of Northern Ireland. In 1969 the Church needed no change, had seemingly successfully weathered the Irish nationalist storms and certainly wanted no revived Republican movement exploiting a role as defender. The Dublin government and establishment now responsible for governance not dreams had increasingly since 1922 opposed Republican pretensions and rigidity. Leinster House, the Irish establishment, those who still spoke as if Irish nationalism in their hands was on the eve of final triumph abhorred the militant Republicans, claimants to history legacy. Both Church and state were satisfied institutions even if a satisfactory Ireland had yet to emerge. The Unionists feared what the nationalists assumed inevitable and satisfactory. Isolated in the six-counties, a minority on the island and part of the greater British majority of the United Kingdom, the Protestants had always claimed that the IRA was the shock force of Irish nationalism that in turn was rooted in Irish Catholicism. Irish Catholic nationalism was the enemy. They chose to perceive the IRA as a truly secret army, a constant threat to the Unionist tradition. Some believed and some so chose to believe in this threat.

In Ireland the past was never far gone, certainly not for the faithful with the nation unredeemed. With their conversion to a secular ideal with transcendental resonances, the Republicans had had created after 1921 in the Irish Republican Army a secular order filled by those who advocated physical force as a means to establish a pluralist Republic. They were one with the Fenians, had forgotten nothing and each generation learned lessons best shelved. Increasingly these crusaders were often as narrow and conservative as their parish priests, often shared the same assumptions not just about salvation but also about the dangers of the English Sunday newspapers or salacious prose sold as literature. Their view on faith and morality was the same as those who opposed them in Leinster House and not as different from the Unionists in non-political matters as the Protestants imagined. Irish Republicans grew increasingly parochial, isolated from great events, their parish perceptions filtering the world beyond the island. The movement eroded, the faithful grew few, their world was confined if intense, a fading galaxy centred on a molten core of dreamers denied.

What made them very different than the conventional in Dublin or their parish friends, from the Unionists with another church and a different tradition and certainly from the British was a dream. Dreams erode in power. In London those who thought at all about Ireland wanted merely peace and quiet, and in Ireland the powerful wanted prosperity. Dreams to generate power must be more than defence of privilege, often as in Northern Ireland privilege imagined or recalled rather than tangible, for the poor in Belfast or Colraine were still poor even as they marched in Orange triumph past the miserable Catholics, equally poor but without banners. Dreams, too, must require more than service for returns. And Dublin offered only the everyday and the promise of better times to come. And the years passed and there was neither riches in the South nor contentment in the North.

Those who clustered at the centre of the Republican galaxy in the winter of 1969–70 were provincials, everyday people transformed by the patriotic ideal but otherwise parish bound. In a new Ireland that sought prosperity, international standards, the universal not the particular, the wonders of consumption not the narrow patriotism of the 1916 patriot game, the IRA, Sinn Féin, the rest were historical anomalies. The nation was on the march toward Europe, out of the bog and needed no ghost at the banquet reading old promises. Times had changed: romantic Ireland was dead and gone and the international investors boarding jets for Shannon. The entire Republican movement, Official or Provisional, gunmen or orators, were assumed irrelevant.

In 1969–70 institutionalized optimism in London, Belfast, and Dublin opposed the real and tangible to the ethereal and the few. Irish optimism is almost a contradiction in terms. Even tomorrow would not be like yesterday. And London, Belfast, and Dublin began to pay the cost of their conventional and comfortable analysis. There were no easy answers and in fact there were not even any hard answers. And those responsible could not deny the allure of old ideals or even old hatreds. And so they could not reward the nationalists and still appease the Unionists nor could they kill the Republican dream with kindness or force.

The compelling IRA dream of a Republic all but established in the hearts of the Irish, has existed, complex, rich, evocative, shaped by reality and romance, poets and politicians and the common people for 200 years. The dream itself arose from a long and special history, a transmuted past, enhanced and transformed over generations into a powerful, luminous reality that was available for the taking in various editions and texts. The past was not over; it was not even past.

Republican history was actually a motley of alternative visions, constant battle, repeated failures, and indomitable persistence, a tale of martyrs and prison escapes, conspiracy, and always the disaster of alternative strategies. Irish history by Republicans, by generations of historians, Irish history out of the Christian Brothers' schools and the national school primers, Irish history as accepted in 1969–70, was a dialectic between the native and the alien, the Irish and the British, them and us. After 1916 the dream produced a satisfactory consensus founded on the long chronicle of sacrifice and combat that lasted until 1921. After that for the new state in Dublin, the dream was over but for the details. For the militant Republicans this was a betrayal. The war was unfinished, the mission of the IRA incomplete.

This glittering Republican history, not so different from that produced by professionals focused on war, politics, and nation building, was a battle saga. It was also the orthodox history of the new Irish state, the Irish Free State, Éire–Ireland, the Republic. History was shaped to finish with a united, free Irish-Ireland, the language saved, the people risen, justice done. Dublin said, assumed, this would come in time, without violence, naturally, and without sacrifice; if need be through the influence or capacity of others, but if not because history so ordained. The Republican underground disagreed, advocated, if rarely deployed, physical force as the only effective means.

History was prologue and then as time passed history had been left to look after itself. The state's history ended in 1916, in triumph – martyrs and the old IRA, Irish postage stamps, solicitors in power and judges in wigs. There was no need for physical force. A united Ireland would come without violence. At first unity was delayed because appropriate power did not exist and increasingly because the will did not. The Irish establishment was willing to wait on the last act, the end of history, for someone else to act, to sacrifice, to force the six-counties into the 26 as justice and the political agenda demanded. And the IRA found no general Irish support, no rush to sacrifice, no effective means to deploy the dwindling force available, no real role in modern Ireland but as witness to the past. Even those in Dublin IRA GHQ grew tired and decided to play within the system, opted for politics, for the practical not the absolute.

The Dublin IRA GHQ was even attracted to the non-violent demonstrations in Northern Ireland. This was the future – the past was the old men in the parish who showed up once a year at Bodenstown and failed to subscribe to the *United Irishman*: the faithful and futile. The real struggle was not armed but adjusted to the perceived class realities of the island. Politics offered a way forward not the gun. Then came August 1969. The gun had returned to Irish politics and the IRA found itself without any and without the will at the top to use the few that could be found. GHQ was blamed for the lack of arms – fairly or not and often by those long inactive. Yet, to many Republicans it seemed that the GHQ persisted in their political agenda, tolerated action at a distance in the North but increasingly moved towards a conventional 26-county destiny. And in time, indeed, the Official IRA evolved into one more Free State party, one more splinter under various titles – Sinn Féin, Sinn Féin–the Workers' Party, the Workers' Party, the New Democratic Left – that seemed to the purists no different from the old tired Labour Party, where Lenin had long been discarded and politics was alliance and alignment not revolution, and where the officials finally came to ground.

The Republican dreamers who controlled the Provisionals had kept the faith inviolate. The key was force, revolution, recourse to violence. The Irish Republican rebel has always found most strategies of liberation – parliamentary politics, boycotts, and general strikes, passive resistance and public protest, sit-ins and elections – and all efforts at accommodation – concessions and liberal legislation, self-rule, Home Rule, Dominion status, and the Commonwealth – potentially futile and dangerous. They might be of use in association with physical force but when deployed alone had always eroded militancy, split the movement. Regularly the dream has been deserted for immediate advantage, political advantage. In this the Official IRA GHQ was little different than those who had settled for less than all in the past: formed parties, entered politics, accepted concessions. And in 1970 there was still no Ireland. The only hope was physical force.

The faithful believed, not without reason, that Ireland could not be a nation while the British in form and in fact ruled any of the island. They were not unduly worried that a physically united Ireland would remain disunited if the Protestants, the Unionists, rejected such an imposition. Republicans were willing to offer the loyalists guarantees but denied them a veto on the march of the nation. The dream insists that the source of

Ireland's ills is the British connection not the Protestant minority. That minority will sooner or later realize that a Republic can contain two traditions, that to be Irish is more important than to be protected uneasily by London.

The movement believed that the Republic might remain sealed in the hearts of the loyalists until the connection with the greater island was at last broken. In this there can be no accommodation. The loyalists should recognize that the triumph of the Republican may break their hearts but from the trauma a united Ireland will grown. The loyalists should not be loyal to a foreign monarch nor the Unionists seek to maintain a connection with the alien British. In time they will not. The problem is Britain. Whatever they say, the Protestant opposition is a secondary matter deployed by the British to hide their self-interest in Ireland.

All liberation strategies that foresee British concessions as assured, that require gradual change, that promise tomorrow what cannot be offered today are suspect. The Provisionals saw politics as entangling and dangerous. The British will only give way to Irish will deployed as physical force by the IRA. Without the reality or threat of physical force there is no reason for the British to deny themselves, to accept their long Irish presence as wrong, not disinterested, as injustice imposed by power, not a benign presence at all. Without arms Britain will shape the compromises offered; with the Irish in arms the British will concede as much as the Irish can win. Those in Ireland who imagine otherwise simply do not want to pay the cost of liberation. In the 1990s many of the militant still believed this during the peace process; the armed struggle had made negotiations possible and possession of arms would make them fruitful. And all were united only if negotiation and concessions led toward a Republic.

Again and again, in part because the evidence on the ground often appeared otherwise, the Republicans stressed their perception of Irish realities. Once liberated, the Protestants will make their peace, participate, become truly Irish. All the threats of confusion and strife, civil war, blood in the streets that would follow a British withdrawal are products of the wishful thinking of the establishments avid for no change. All the demands for a loyalist Protestant veto arise from British self-interest and a failure of nerve by the Irish establishment. Any assumption that the British have any interest but their own in Ireland is foolish. London does not want to leave. And so the Protestants, who want no change, tomorrow like yesterday, can refuse even to contemplate the inevitable integration. They have sought repeatedly to avoid even a serious dialogue – postponing in the peace process previous concessions, doubting Republican good will, putting off tomorrow. Since Dublin does not want a state full of Protestants achieved by Republican gunmen – or for that matter those gunmen in the state, the governments of the day, the propertied and powerful, those with something to lose, can always find reasons not to act as the dream would require. Unity would produce not one Ireland but a civil war: accept our analysis or accept chaos. The present is better than any Republican future and even the past was not so awful in retrospect: the present killing is tolerable and were not there 50 years of peace? Those not in harm's way or with assets at risk are apt to opt for doing nothing, defending the present by fine tuning. They support Northern Republicans in any pan-national front because conciliation and compromise assures tranquillity if not the Republic.

The Provisionals, of course, have to explain the reluctance to act; not only those of property and propriety but also that of their avowed constituency – the people. The Irish people have never been especially keen to sacrifice for the Republic supposedly all but established in their hearts. After 1970 as the defenders' role diminished, the Irish electorate made clear that there was almost no support for Sinn Féin, for the dreams of the past, for the means of the IRA. As is always the case for the faithful – and not only the Irish faithful – the people had no right to do wrong and so the IRA soldiered on. Those who oppose the armed struggle are fools or knaves, avowed enemies or the misguided.

Catholicism as much as the Enlightenment has a major part to play in the movement but, unlike the aspirations of the men of reason, the part is ignored by those who controlled an avowedly secular movement. It is the Church that gives example of vocation, sacrifice, temptation, and salvation through a meld of good works and the faith, just as it is the village that teaches persistence, conspiracy, recourse to evasion, as well as violence. The lessons taught in recruits class are not as important as those absorbed outside on the street, during matches, at the pub or mass. Many of the ideas and ideals of Ireland make for effective rebels – to be Irish is to descend from those whose very nature was shaped by rebelling against being English.

The movement has all sorts of ancestors and exemplars: the rural night riders, the eighteenth-century conspirators, the religious orders, and the habits of the humiliated and the hunted transformed into tradecraft. All are merged into a core labelled physical force: ends and means, sources and resource, the last, best hope for the Irish Republic. This Irish Republican dream as catalyst to action relies, as do most rebel dreams, on will to balance power, faith to move history. It is a faith that requires adult conversion although some are raised within Republican families and so often within the faith.

In the case of the Provisionals, as with each previous Republican generation, the new recruits had to be shaped to the dream. Then they, too, would perceive reality as did their colleagues. What was novel after 1970 was the number of the new recruits eager to serve: even in the glory years of 1919–21 there had not been as many volunteering for service. In contrast, the Provisionals after 1970 made every effort to see that their army was devout, that the faith was propagated – a process made easier because of the nature of the covert armed struggle.

A band of the hunted becomes close, bonded, and the ideals have enormous power to meld and to protect, to give reason and meaning. Nowhere was this to be more apparent than in the Irish prisons where life was stripped to the basics, where the struggle could only continue by recourse to denial and sacrifice, where will was all, and trust in the few absolute. Thus, during the H-Block campaigns of 1979–81, the volunteers in prison refused to be coerced, refused to wear prison clothing, refused to be clean, to be tractable, refused to obey, ultimately refused to live – and so died on hunger strike.

As the present Troubles have stretched on and on, there has been a concentration of minds. Those potential recruits in Northern Ireland have grown up with the IRA, know the limitations and risks and the prospects. In the terraces of the Ardoyne and Creggan or the hills of South Armagh and Mid-Tyrone, romantic Ireland is dead and gone and the Provisional IRA institutionalized.

The volunteer can be promised almost certainly that service will endanger life, ensure a brief career in harm's way, time in prison, and at the end a broken heart. For most there is no end of the dream even when service is denied or time served. The dream turns the recruit into a volunteer, a member of the IRA and a believer. And all about is thus evidence that those beliefs are valid.

A volunteer comes into the movement as to a vocation, a conversion in time to a secular church long part of a personal and Irish political landscape. In bad times the prospective volunteer may have to hunt down the few – knock on the door. Some undergrounds, like the Italian *Brigate rosse*, have been so sealed from penetration, so hidden that not even those desperate to serve could find them. In 1970 after the Northern Ireland pogroms of August 1969, those nationalists eager to serve, to defend, knew no more than romantic rumour and a few names of old volunteers. This was sufficient. In good times the secret army is hardly secret at all. In 1921 and 1972, the IRA was a major force, an irregular army, a defence militia that paraded to pipes, easy to find, an orthodox option for the dedicated and adventurous. None stayed long unless touched by the dream and so the IRA and the movement remained a single universe of believers, a galaxy expanding rapidly after 1971.

The novelty of the Irish dream is not its compelling power over generations, nor the richness of experience regularly reinterpreted for contemporary purpose, but the persistence of the analysis. A Fenian awoken from the grave or a man from Easter Week would fit easily into a Provisional Army Council meeting, not know the names of those about the table or the slang of the day but be comfortable with the arguments. The core has always argued over war and peace, politics and the gun. It is not only first principles but even tactical options that remain generation after generation. It sometimes appears that all the arguments concerning the ramifications of the dream are re-runs in a dry season, the Republican chaos played over at half-speed while the volunteers on active service seek only to avoid yesterday's errors. Moving on is not easy when all options have been pre-played in the past.

The dream is rich, evocative, powerful; it appeals to the elegant and sophisticated as to the stolid and limited. Flawed, tarnished, often irrelevant, the dream is the one great asset for an Irish rebel, for it proffers legitimacy, hope, and a glimpse of the Republic, a grail and a goad. The clever, like Conor Cruise O'Brien or the mandarins of the intellectual Left, may devastate the Provisionals with argument; but you cannot kill a dream with arrogance or logic or the weight of reason. The moderates may urge democracy, fair shares, the wisdom of peace now, and the rewards of compromise; but again dreams are as immune to decency as to tangible returns.

Perception

The recruit walks into the shadow and harm's way when the dream moves within; a dream inherited, a dream chosen always. For whatever reasons the pilgrims come to the dream, each takes away the same thing, an intense burning conviction, a love of the Republic, a will to sacrifice and, most of all, perhaps, a special grasp of the reality of the times. Recent history simply extends back from the present to merge in the long struggle. Recent events have old explanations that still seem valid. In fact so valid is much of Republican theology that few bother with recounting the axioms of the faith – some may not even recognize that these convictions are not universal among nationalists.

All the aspects of denied nationalism are present in Ireland – the assumption about the legitimacy of the risen people, a golden past, the nation-state as ideal and the volunteers as proper repositories of the faith supposedly held by all. The nation has been denied both by external power – the English, the British – and by betrayal. Once the external power is destroyed, coerced into leaving, then Ireland will be a nation and its problems if not solved will at least be amenable to intervention by the new governors. In its most reductive form: the Brits must be driven out. The efforts to ease the terms for such a transition – contemplate a phased withdrawal – despite the logic and the changed reality apparent to all – still engenders doubt. In a sense, for so long history has been merely a prelude to the ultimate British withdrawal, and the discussion of the reality of that withdrawal makes the faithful uneasy. In theory, if the British were to go and the Republic was to emerge – any endgame was suspect since the Irish had so often been split and denied in such negotiations. Negotiations, the politics of concessions, meant that the faithful had been co-opted, the people had been seduced with promises, the nation had been lost and the advent of the Republic postponed. None of these dangers was apparent during an armed struggle where politics was a secondary matter and compromise a technical consideration. War, and especially war without end, did not endanger the ultimate Republican; only the prospect of triumph, the offer of concession, the signs of victory could do that.

Most internal Republican arguments are at best primitive or vestigial ideological quarrels over degrees of purity and means into the future. The focus has always been on the nature of the armed struggle and the purity of commitment rather than the details of belief. What analysis has appeared has been above ground and hardly in a century produced sufficient items to make up a Republican reader. What has always mattered has been the gun in politics, not politics, not programmes, not the subtleties of Document No. 2, the agenda of the Republican Congress or an Éire Nua manifesto. The major questions are decided. Only the proper and effective use of physical force is open to discussion. Politics is a means to enhance the armed struggle or to accept victory – thus victory in pieces is an enormous obstacle to those who are inclined to analyse in absolutes. With the peace process the role of the IRA changed, as did the mission for the movement leadership. How does one make a dream tangible? So for many the matter is best left for tomorrow, to the Army Council, to those concerned about such matters, left for others as long as the integrity of the armed struggle is untouched. The very existence of hidden arms offers the faithful evidence that the dream is not up for barter.

What is particular about the Irish dream has been its staying power, still a factor on the island even when the converts dribbled away to the very few. The ideal has persisted. Elsewhere the myth of the guerrilla has assumed that a protracted struggle is needed to shape the new nation, the new citizens and thus present failure will have future benefits. Opposed to this the IRA has not sought to tease virtue out of defeat. Defeat has been a concomitant of the Irish armed struggle, not a necessary stage. What Wolfe Tone wanted at the end of the eighteenth century is still desirable at the beginning of the twenty-first century. The struggle has been long because the Irish lack power not because they need defeat to steel their soul.

Rebel Reality

For the Provisional leaders in 1969–70, the dream provided inspiration and, seemingly incidentally, an explanation of visible events. The Army Council could see that a window of opportunity had opened. They knew their own. Their reading of history, however limited, indicated how the British would act and the British army in particular. There was almost no need for analysis – and there was none in any conventional sense – no need for discussion – and there was relatively little. For generations the movement has spent most years waiting, hoping, plotting for an opportunity and the emerging leadership had no problem in grasping that one had suddenly, unexpectedly arrived, a surprise only in the matter of timing.

The Republic required action, not contemplation and consideration, not continued recourse to civil disobedience or a new emphasis on the politics of protest. What had emerged after August 1969 was a role for the gun in Irish politics that could be expanded into a campaign. No one else in Ireland saw this as swiftly or as clearly – the others still sought compromise or protection or assurance. The IRA sought guns. They would deceive everyone by playing the defender while the volunteers provoked the British into actions that would justify a campaign. The old and faithful would convert the new defenders to Republican principles in the process. And no longer deceived about their role and mission, the new generation would as the old pursue physical force.

Few of those involved in the Provisional movement believed that their reality was a special view or shaped by ideological glasses or divorced from the events of the street. They knew what they knew – and like all revolutionaries were almost criminally optimistic about their capacity to act on events, but act they would. The Official IRA might try to fit the three stages of revolution to events. The more orthodox Marxist-Leninists might have class explanations. The establishment in Dublin might try to deny the direction of history or at least seek to attach their future to the aspirations of the real Republicans. The Northern nationalist might want protection and concession but would tolerate, perhaps support, the IRA. What choice had they? Who else would defend them? What other aspiration could complete with an Irish Republic. Even the Protestant Unionists could be ignored as opponents, for they were Irish used as pawns by the British. And the British might pretend that the game was not the same as it had always been – but not the Provisional IRA Army Council.

For them all that need be done was to respond as history demanded and the dream would reward the acolytes first with toleration and support and campaign and finally the Republic. The key was toleration and all on the

Army Council recognized that could be achieved by defending the interests of Northern nationalists. This would allow what was the great goal of each generation of Republicans: recourse to the armed struggle. By 1970 few of the faithful thought beyond this, the first great hurdle. Once this fence was taken, once the shooting started and the IRA went over to the offensive it would only be a matter of time. And so the dream presented the Provisionals with an explanation of the past that might not convince all but proved a powerful and effective reading of the present and immediate future.

In fact the opportunity – the reality – created the Provisionals rather than the reverse, as is often the case with rebels. This time the gunmen saw through the glass – no mirror, not even shadowed, but crystalline. They saw a role, a window of opportunity, the way into the future and more clearly than anyone else: their reality was real and their dream operative. When the galaxy reached a maximum size and influence in 1972, there had been no shift in assumptions. When the IRA's day did not come, the movement sought not a review of basic assumptions but means to escalate the struggle and under severe pressure to persist. A variety of conventional and unconventional avenues were discovered, explored or rejected; but the basics of Anglo-Irish history remained those of the Fenians. And again reality might be adjusted to Provo perception if the proposal appeared congenial – hunger strikes were a means that presented all sorts of options at last taken as obvious, and negotiations with all and sundry could over the years be pursued as long as the IRA was comfortable.

So those who would not talk to terrorists found themselves talking to Sinn Féin on Sinn Féin's terms, and those who would deny the prisons as a proper battlefield found the IRA's hunger strikers had won by dying; the will was stronger in Ireland than tangible assets. That Republican perception is special and available ordinarily only to the faithful does not necessarily mean that it is unrelated to reality, especially Irish reality. It is not wise to assume that rationality belongs to the state or that reality cannot be shaped by a dream.

The IRA in general – and in 1918 or 1922 or 1938 – and the Provisional IRA in 1969, simply inherited whole and without difficulty the long heritage of the past that answered the crucial questions of any armed struggle. What was the matter? The British presence. What was the aim? The Republic. And the means? Physical force. The answers of others might have changed, been updated, shaped to new considerations, be complex, and might well be intellectually compelling, or simply the rationalizations of those in power who wanted no sacrifice. For the IRA the questions were the same and so too the answers. And so they are at the end of the century for the most militant, the few and faithful, Republican Sinn Féin, the Real IRA, and many volunteers sullen if unorganized.

For nearly a century the primary problem for militant Republicans had not been the shaping of reality with ideas but the search for an opportunity to deploy the chosen means. In 1970 what the Provisionals wanted was not explanation and exegesis but the opportunity to wage war. This was especially true, for time had eroded both the commitment of the intelligentsia and the highly literate, leaving the movement to the men of no property whose ideas arose from an immediate grasp of the dream and a reading of patriot history. This in 1970 was sufficient to grasp that an opportunity to act – to begin as defenders – existed and so to generate the momentum for a full campaign. For those still faithful to physical force at the end of the century, the same problem existed – toleration for the use of the gun. When the bomb went off at Omagh for most nationalists the end had truly come – Republicans are apt to make use of even the slightest opportunity so that there are still those waiting on events, waiting to use the gun, waiting in sure and certain knowledge that their analysis is valid.

CHAPTER THREE

Ideology: The Dream Structured

No Republican has trouble with the basic principle that there is an Irish nation, that its appropriate arena is the whole island, that this arena has been denied and divided by British interests. This is almost reality. The conclusions drawn from the basics are, however, unacceptable to those of the other tradition who accept the island as Irish, even mostly accept themselves as Irish but to do not take as axiomatic that there should then be a single state, a Republic. This would mean that their tradition, as valid as the nation, would be subsumed. The Irish nationalists, however, believe that this is not the case and that no tradition has the right to draw a bound to the march of the nation. There is no doubt that the Irish people who would be nationalists recognize that the Protestants have had the power and the support of London to impose their desires on history. This does not make Ulster British but the Irish Protestants misguided, unable to accept the benign aspirations of the other Irish who – certainly in recent years – have no wish to impose unity or sacrifice for a united Ireland or allow others to do so in the name of all. There are then three basic structures erected on nationalist ideas: that of the purists within the Republican movement, that of the Irish state, and those who would deny the assumptions of both.

The Republican acceptance of a basic reality has rarely been challenged on ideological grounds: the split with the Officials and their introduction of class analysis indicated how little appeal any such alternative has in the marketplace of ideas. The lethal disputes have been on the means to achieve the unrealized, and again recently a reconsideration if that ideal is – for the foreseeable, imaginable – desirable. It has certainly been accepted as not viable by the establishment in Dublin, by the Unionists, by the British government: six will not go into 26 especially since the 26, whatever the Unionists may think, do not want such a merger except at some future date of judgement and redemption. Thus the Unionists deny the Republican ideological assumptions root and branch while accepting the same vision as the Republicans: that the Irish people are engaged in a long war to achieve a Republic. They assume any 'peace process' to be a wile but one accepted by the British government and so to be taken seriously. They remain convinced that all the Catholics are nationalists and all nationalists are those Republicans in tooth and claw. The real Irish Republic and most of the other Irish now deny this root and branch, deny the Provisionals or Republican Sinn Féin or any of the other advocates of traditional aims and means.

THE PERCEIVED ECOSYSTEM

What the recruit to the IRA, if not all the converts to the movement, sees once transformed is not especially different from what any observer on the Irish scene finds. The volunteer need not understand the labour theory of value, seek evidence of the international multinational conspiracy or even look far from the malevolent impact of the British – Irish reality is easily, effectively explained. The volunteer does, indeed, as do all volunteers in an armed crusade, enter a special world made luminous by explanation, but in the Irish case that explanation is pragmatic and tangible, reflects reality, if only one reality.

The appeal of the movement is not in the articulation of ideas but rather the luminosity of the ideal, the opportunity offered to serve and serve in a cause that is grounded in ideas. Those ideas are just sufficiently different from the conventions of the times to require consideration and so conviction: not vengeance but an armed struggle, not black Protestants but misguided Irish of other traditions as well as their own. To be a Republican one must deny the easy emotions, anger, hatred, the worldly emotions – and so enter a secular order where the dangers are tangible, the sacrifice all too real, and the personal returns rare. The appeal is in a way the obverse of the Roman Church, as the Republic is of the Crown. In both cases the movement's offer is closer to immediate reality, within the grasp of those of no property and limited education but not without appeal to the more comfortable and more sophisticated who can adjust the fashions of the time to the rocks of Republican faith. So far, the offer of political power, progress measured in compromise, has not had the same appeal, has been sold to the movement but not to many others. Who would join an IRA denied the opportunity of a military mission?

What unwittingly the movement had achieved was an appeal that focused the aspirations and assumptions of their constituency, an appeal intensified by the more traditional and general rebel attraction for the young: excitement, danger, service, novelty, and sensation, pride and even prospects. What the Republican volunteer has is a dream not a truculent commitment to inherent superiority as in the case of the loyalist paramilitary. The IRA knows what is to be gained and so need not invest in analysis. All are agreed and all that is needed is to reinforce capacity, not to fine-tune concepts, not to be reassured by a leader or any leader, not to learn more but rather to feel the faith in the everyday. What the leadership had to do in the 1990s was to make the faithful feel momentum in negotiations, feel history at work.

What many saw as a 'split' in 1969 was for the Provisionals merely the faithful drawing back from the wrong road. Dublin GHQ had chosen seeming advantage over principle, were in the process of discarding the ideal for lesser gain. Many suspected they were about to offer the movement to false gods, give up the gun, provide unsound answers to questions long decided. The arguments in 1969 at the Army Convention, at the Sinn Féin Ard Fheis, were perfunctorily presented, for the movement had actually divided. The same arguments occurred again a generation later when the question of abstention divided the movement – but this time the majority of the IRA and those with the guns accepted the new direction for it did not hamper the armed struggle. The same arguments were secretly deployed and maintained the consensus once the endgame had begun. In 1969 the Provos had the dream.

In 1986 the majority stayed in place for they had the guns, the authorization of the IRA, and the same dream. And once the peace process began and the arguments, the leadership offered neither dream nor gun but practicalities arising from the long war. Validation could not come from majorities or minorities. Majorities could not deny past generations nor the transcendental Republic – they had never done so for the faithful – but are needed within the movement if consensus is to be maintained.

ORGANIZATION

For much of its long history, the Irish Republican movement has been structured as a covert conspiracy seeking legitimacy in part through the forms of the resistance. While only briefly in fact has the movement had realistic aspirations to rule, by the time of the Irish Republican Brotherhood, founded in 1859, the conspirators felt that not only was the Republic all but established in the hearts of all the Irish – not the same thing as a realistic claim to rule, rather an assertion of legitimacy – but also the movement had the capacity to wage war against the British to achieve their ideals. This right to resort to physical force in the name of the Irish people became the core of the movement – not necessarily the right to govern the Irish people – so that no matter what the ideals and ideas of the movement the volunteers were structured as an army. The modern army, the IRA, was founded with the creation of *Oglaigh na h-Éireann*, the Irish Volunteers, in Dublin at the

Rotunda Rink on 25 November 1913. Founded by the IRB, the volunteers could look back over a century of struggle and so a long institutional as well as ideological heritage.

The gun implied enormous risks and the Irish, as a people, were more apt to resist by less compelling means. The IRA's adventures always meant risks and often undesirable risks. If the Republican crusade became too risky, was too foolish, endangered what had been won or challenged the legitimate, that toleration eroded. And so much had been won and at the same time once the Troubles began again in 1969 the ideal became dubious, not a simple matter of righting history's error. Who wanted all those Unionists whose presence would not only disturb present arrangement but would not achieve any sort of unity? A united Ireland filled with disloyal Unionists and bitter Northern nationalists held few charms.

So the IRA's ideal gradually become a bad dream for many in the Republic for much of the establishment. The old nationalist ideal, while not quite discarded, was shaped to new priorities, new assumptions, a new reality that had arisen from the IRA campaign and the loyalist resort to terror. The IRA largely ignored their denial by the people supposedly their real constituency. The Irish people as a whole, the Irish establishment, had always proven all too fallible, all to often, for any new betrayal to undermine Republican conviction. Their faith and their institutions remain credible.

The ideas and ideals of Irish Republicanism are not complex, hardly alien to the times, easy to grasp, and comforting to possess. The result has long been that the movement is remarkably free from the detailed internal analysis of reality and response found in those undergrounds using Marxist-Leninist scientific socialism as a tool and rationalization on the one hand and those driven by the charisma of an individual that need to disguise this factor by recourse to complex reasoning on the other. The IRA as nationalist army representing the nation runs mainly by consensus, needs no intellectual explanations and is often uncongenial to intellectuals. Those involved, especially in publicity or Sinn Féin may in their own terms deal with ideas and ideology, but in contrast to truly ideological movements are innocent of analysis. The IRA *Green Book* is not an ideological primer like Mao's *Red Book* but rather operating instructions for the involved. Even discussion within the movement has focused not on ends but on tactical means, not on explanation for events but opportunities to act. This is often as true during the endgame as when the gun was deployed. There has always been detailed internal political analysis, ideological argument, the printed word in party documents: the Republicans are not, as their opponents contend, mindless, but are focused on reality rather than more fashionable academic theory or the ideas of the political marketplace.

The Republican ideas are easily organized, easily taught. The volunteers, as always, live in a closed ecosystem that reinforces the ideals and ideas and that of the Provisional IRA does not require exceptional commitment of resources for that end – in this a special case, more so than many nationalist movements filled with the fashionable ideas of the times, staffed by middle-class strategists, eager not only to do right but to appear justified. For the Provos, visible reality provides justification, a justification made historic and relevant by the original conversion to the movement.

The movement has shaped commemoration to honour the dead. No such commemoration is more intense than the annual march on Bodenstown to the grave of the founding ideologue Wolfe Tone, Protestant, martyr, exemplar, rebel. There on a June afternoon the secret army emerges before the eyes of the faithful – and the police. There many of the core in everyday clothes mingle with the little old men, the lads down from the Falls Road in Belfast, the men of no property and their wives and daughters, the true believers, the mute, the inarticulate. There the sometimes soldier in crumpled suit and dusty shoes with a tricolour pin and an easy heart hears the message from the Army Council, sees his own clear each year, finds in bad years reassurance and in the glory years vindication. Bodenstown is not merely commemoration but the visible sign of the faith, an idea as institution. So too are the marches on Easter, the collections around the graves of the fallen whether Seán South in Limerick or the hunger strikers in the North. The patriot dead matter, matter more as patriots than as martyrs, matter because all the movement can offer is a piper and a march, for the secret army is not only without banners but without uniforms or promotion or mostly prospects. What the movement has done is shape institutions that give visual reality and virtual participation to the faith: ideas and ideals as acts rather than ideology. The shift to ideas in action during negotiation of an endgame does not offer the same rich diet – so the leadership is still to be found at the rites, their rites too, for often the patriot dead were friends and always colleagues.

The great ritual of Ireland is not in possession of church or state but rather occurs, appropriately, in a graveyard when an IRA volunteer is buried. Volunteers have been buried in state and within the confines of the mystical Republic for centuries. The first Orr, a Protestant, a United Irishman, a rebel hanged in 1796, and the last volunteer, the last lost for the Republic, is yet to come. Each of the patriot dead is asset and loss, each grave a monument. The ritual is played out, each time the same, each time special.

There need be no detailed planning or preparation even if the process must be through a riot or come under fire or take place despite a reluctant church or an angry family. It has all been done before, grand process and a few straggling after the coffin, thousands hurling stones, baton charges, helicopters, and gunfire at the cemetery – it has all been done before. For Republicans nearly everything has been done before, offers precedent and guide. There may not be easy answers or a single manual but the procedures are sound. It is the ritual of the simple and the soldier, history made to live and the Republic to appear.

The procession begins at the beginning, in an Irish front room, the volunteer displayed, at home for the last time. And there the honour guide waits and the process begins – a straggling procession led by a piper, men of no property, women and children stretched out behind, the coffin draped in a tricolour, black beret, and gloves, carried by the family and fellows. It is often accompanied by an IRA escort, young men freshly shaved, hard eyed in dark glasses, dressed if possible in paramilitary costume – camouflage jackets and black berets, polished boots and white belts. If the security forces are aggressive, symbolic uniforms may appeal, the young men in a way more awesome in identical jackets and ties and dark glasses with their black leather gloves and military bearing, stepping out in time toward the cemetery followed by everyone, friends and neighbours and the locals who dare subversion as a social duty. Led by a piper the procession in Belfast on the way to Milltown may be enormous, a great train of the faithful and curious, straggling up the Falls far behind the pipes and cortege. In the country the walk is shorter, the same one to mass, a walk through the lanes to the bright green graveyard.

Always there is a square of mud and bright green grass, a great heap of flowers, yellow, white, red, tangles of ribbons and cards, the mourners and the neighbours, the faithful and curious. Teeming rain and a slate grey sky, a cold winter day, an autumn day or rarely a lovely blue June day, a long march or a plod through puddles and mud; the weather, the location, the time, or the company do not greatly matter. What matters is that over a fresh grave and a dead volunteer, the Republic for a moment is manifest, lives. Those who know, know that they have, however briefly, lived within the cherished Republic, stand not just by the grave of the patriot dead but within the Republic of their dreams: a Republic made real for a moment by another's sacrifice, by another death for Ireland. They stand, they all stand, all the faithful, within a secular miracle on an island that cherishes the miraculous and rewards the devout with gifts beyond price. Those gifts have been dearly bought for Republicans but are real – the graveyard is a platform of hope not an end at all but a beginning made possible by sacrifice.

As ritual there is nothing quite like it in Ireland. In any other place, during all those other armed struggles, a Nasser or a Khomeini is buried amid national turmoil, crowds of millions, a nation weeping and is dead and gone and the faith institutionalized by others. Some rebels win and get tombs in the central square, commemorative postage stamps, a mention in texts, some lose and are forgotten; a few find fame like Che – a myth written out on bumper stickers and T-shirts and into Broadway musicals. In Ireland each volunteer is buried within the Republic, is part of a beginning as well as an end, services in death as in life.

The long march from the front room to the grave brings all who believe to the moment of truth when the writ of the Republic will run, made visible to the perceptive, made tangible at the end of life and at the moment of renewal. The moment is sealed off and ringed by the others, occurs inside a ring of uniformed police. The constables are often sullen, talking to be overheard, bitter, always at risk, seeing a criminal dead not a martyr honoured. With them are the men in cheap suits with cold eyes and secret credentials – this one with camera and that one with the harsh word. Beyond them is the watching British army. The officers close-shaven, stern, regulation, trim, and polished, and so perceived as arrogant, and the men watchful in an alien field. Overhead is the clatter and drone of a helicopter, sky spy and harassment, a hi-tech option for any Irish crowd. The crowd, often a huddle under a teeming wet sky, sometimes a mass meeting, like the security forces know that this moment is not like any other.

There at the graveside the Republic lives. And out beyond in the disputed territory, the rows of council houses, the small farms, the disputed territory in an undeclared ancient war, the everyday rules. There is no Republic, no visible dream, no transcendental moment, only the milk float on its rounds, the children off to school, the police in pairs and armed vests at the corner and the traffic stalled. For many, most, of those beyond the circle the funeral is merely a funeral, the Irish Republic of 1916 a fantasy, the Provos criminals, best buried, the ritual irrelevant. For the faithful the dream is made manifest, the nexus of ideals and ideals becomes tangible. And these ideas and ideals are what any Republican endgame must cherish, ignore for political gain at risk. And at the end of the century the leadership sees the risk worth taking to make further funerals unnecessary.

Thus the ideology of the Provisional IRA is not about logic or reason or the correlation of forces, not about political structures or British capacity, not a matter of analysis, not a display of ideas but about the perception assured by the dream. And this perception has been transmuted into reality through ritual. Some of the rites are spectacular and effective, the great marches up the Falls Road, the riots that begin as scheduled, the funerals. Some rituals are more special and often more impressive that others, some, hardly seem rite at all: the painting of the great wall murals in Belfast begun in the 1980s, the sound of the pipes, the cluster at the back of the hall during a protest meeting – nothing said. There are always signs and ceremonies to be found 'Seán South of Garryowen' sung late at night by the side of the road, the tattered black flags tied on line poles of an Armagh village, the expression on children's faces when the police come into the Ardoyne, a lark in a buttonhole. There is here nothing that a Marxist would recognize – little that the Official IRA wanted to keep. These signs and rites are not aspects of ideology at all but only outward and visible evidence of the faith.

For Republicans their ideology has no need of elaboration, exposition or sacred texts: fundamentalists need only the revealed word and that the Republicans possess, not an ideology but a faith. The literate may read, prisoners may go to class in Tone and Pearse, *An Phoblacht* may publish the late word but the true believer is most often content with less. Each is empowered by history, made bold by experience, shaped by the dream to persist.

COMPETITION: HERESY, BETRAYAL, SCHISM

The fact that the nexus of ideas central to the Provisional movement is neither tangled nor complex does not mean that disputation is absent. What is on offer is the revealed truth – not even a text open for interpretation. Essentially the conviction of the volunteer is based on revelation, reinforced by the movement, and so also open to interpretation. The basics are, however, so basic that the disputes tend to focus on tactical matters raised to principles. As always the key moments of concern come with the efforts to escalate the armed struggle and with the options offered by declining capacity – the problem of persistence. And persistence during the long war led to the question of whether gains could be made without use of the gun.

The major strain inherent within the movement has always been between those focused on the Irish Republican Army as army and those who seek a broader means forward with the army still as balance and ballast. The Officials, like the Republican Congress before them, did not simply discard 'the army' in the name of politics or ideological purity. That for the Officials came later, much later. For the Provos there was little dispute over the nature of the Irish or the goal of the Republic or even the need for physical force. Other ways forward were acceptable as long as the army was not deprived. Thus disputation was and is often secondary – how much force and what else?

Anything else has traditionally been defined as 'politics' and all non-military options as lesser. It is recognized that any move into politics – however necessary and vital – erodes not only the assets of the movement but also the purity of the military task. The IRA in the decade before the end of the border campaign in 1962 reduced 'politics' to the support of the small Sinn Féin party that acted as claque and vehicle to support symbolic candidates in elections. These elections were used as stage not as a power base, used to indicate support for physical force, the campaign, the Republic. And in Ireland such electoral support on the national issue has always been transitory: Irish elections are in large part held to designate agents of influence who will ensure entitlement. The party Sinn Féin has always been a limited if necessary force, far more important after the flexibility intro-duced after the hunger strikes, but still a means to establish movement consensus, a pressure group, a platform not a real party nor a volcano of ideas. When the major thrust of the movement became the peace process the role of the party changed – and so too that of the IRA: but not easily or at once or completely.

Even with the new prominence given Provisional Sinn Féin after the hunger strikes, the faithful were faithful to the Army Council, to history, to the faith, not to the needs or ideas of the party. Still, the movement, cored in the military, recognized the need to inspire, direct, and support non-military activities – especially since they were advocated by colleagues on the Council or in military positions. There were for most Republicans fears about the implications of the need. There was a concern that 'politics' was not necessarily about escalating the pressure that the IRA could exert but often about changing the fulcrum of the campaign. In the past, those who became involved in politics, almost always parliamentary politics, had been corrupted by the lure of power, moved away from physical force, recognized the legitimacy of those who would rule Ireland without the Republic, and abandoned the reliance on force. During the entire course of the move-ment's history, certainly from the founding of the IRB, the great alternative to the physical was conventional politics. Such politics required compro-mise, recognition of present reality, and habits and assumptions uncongenial to those necessary for an armed conspiracy, for a secret army, for a military campaign.

The Irish people more often than not accepted compromise and con-cession as the means forward: home rule or reforms, a Free State or an Irish Republic for 26 counties. Always the militants hived off, left or right, into politics: those who accepted the Anglo-Irish Treaty in 1921, those who followed De Valera and Fianna Fáil, dumped arms and went into the Free State Dáil and power, those who sought revolution with the Republican Congress or the hard Left, those with Seán McBride who created *Clann na Phoblachta*, and finally those in the official Dublin GHQ of Cathal Goulding, Seán Garland, and Roy Johnston who traded Tone for Lenin. In time each initiative was tamed, drawn into the system, became dedicated to means not ends, part of the problem not the solution. This was what Republican Sinn Féin feared in 1986 and opponents of the peace process a decade later.

Yet for most of Republican history the Irish would only tolerate political initiatives. In fact a basic always unstated assumption of the Republican movement dedicated to the freedom of the Irish people was that the Irish people had always been loathe to sacrifice for freedom, were apt to deny, even betray, those who did so. The avowed constituency of the movement was often unworthy of sacrifice. The Irish people seemingly would not support a rising, would not come into the streets even with knives and forks to assure victory, were more apt to inform than contribute.

Thus in 1970 the great obstacle to a campaign that would have to rely largely on the ideologically committed, the Republicans, the faithful, was to shape conditions that would permit the toleration of the Irish people, a condition that had existed only once and briefly during the Tan War. The people should, perhaps would, participate; but the past indicated that they had not. They would not be English but the vast majority had not gone the final step to risk being only Irish. What the movement had won over time was the right to wage war in their name but only at very special moments. Most of Republican history was waiting for those moments: organizing, persisting, probing to hurry along history. The events from 1954 to 1962 indicated just how intransigent history and elusive popular support could be, how little the Irish nation admired the gun when introduced into politics.

Yet for the Republicans, the Provisionals, the key was the gun and the right to use it for the Republic was a principle all but established in Irish hearts. The voter might deny Sinn Féin, the media decry the campaign, the proper and those with prospects scorn the IRA, but all Irish nationalists accepted the motives, recognized the legacy of the IRA even as the validity was publicly denied.

The Provisional movement from the first felt that any non-military effort would have to be circumscribed. There was suspicion of the civil rights tactics of civil disobedience – unlike the Official IRA's fascination, suspicion of co-operation with non-Republican groups even toward agreed aims, suspicion of the aid and comfort offered by those outside the faith. The great danger was not on first principles but on using improper means that might postpone indefinitely the struggle for those principles. Those who – sensibly, logically – insisted that *some* means forward had to be adopted, that waiting for the ideal moment to begin shooting was futile, risked the wrath of the purists who wanted only to shoot because only by so doing could the Republic be achieved. And once the shooting started those purists only reluctantly agreed that many means forward might be acceptable as long as physical force remained the prime focus. Pearse knew. 'Ireland unarmed will attain just as much freedom as it is convenient for England to give her; Ireland armed will attain ultimately just as much freedom as she wants.'

All Republicans agreed to this proposition, to the armed struggle, to the lessons of history and the shape of the future. Yet there were always splits, the traditional splits of a revealed religion rather than an ideological faction. There was in fact always some difficulty in defining Republican heresy, at least in the beginning, for there was no single sacred text to defy. Arguments were not over words but ways and means. Everyone still claimed to be a Republican: Michael Collins and De Valera and Seán McBride, Republicans all. Dublin IRA GHQ in 1969 claimed to be Republican. After 1970 these Official IRA units, especially in the North, not only claimed to be Republican but even pursued an armed struggle.

The real difference, as far as the Provos were concerned, lay in the primacy of military deeds over ideological explanation. McBride had given up the gun and despite leading a slightly constitutional part in Fianna Fáil so had De Valera. In the years after the rise of the Provos, the Officials tried for a time to have it both ways, to keep the gun and enter politics as a conventional party. And this did not work and so a generation later there were those who feared the same fate for the IRA if physical force was discarded. The impact of the long war, the endless funerals, the persistence of British nationalism only convinced some that there was another way – not a better way but another way that would work.

Those within the movement who sought other means forward had always claimed their dedication to the Republic. Heresy thus tended to mean the reduction of physical force's primacy. Such erosion was in the details. These details were often matters of programmes and the allocation of resources not ideas. No one wants to be quite without ideas. No one, not even those in Pomeroy or Andersonstown, wants to be considered obsolete in the marketplace of analysis. Much more important, however, that pretensions of analytical capacity, the Provisional leadership, did not want to dilute the war effort or even to compete with the Officials in a free marketplace of ideas. The Provos soldier on with only an occasional armed clash with the Officials – the Stickies – as evidence of disagreement increasingly over ends as well as means. The Officials were heretics discarded. On the other hand, Republican Sinn Féin was isolated and denied as the futile persisting in reliance on old options in a new situation.

There was novel danger for the Provos in responding to concessions if concessions were to be offered. For Republicans endgames historically had been as fatal as co-option into conventional politics. In 1972, when a truce was declared and the Provisionals sent a delegation to London, Seán Mac

Stiofáin left Ruairí O Brádaigh, the President of Sinn Féin, in Ireland and took the military leadership in the North, Séamus Twomey, Martin McGuinness, Ivor Bell, and Gerry Adams with Myles Shevlin of Dublin for legal advice. There was a determination within the delegation to stand fast, not to discuss but to declare Republican intentions.

The British, seeking only respite and perhaps a useful exposure to the IRA leadership, found the Irish rigid, unsophisticated, ignorant in matters of negotiation, and so irrelevant to any future politics. The delegation was not really ignorant but quite innocent of the forms and opportunities of such negotiations. They saw the meeting as a replay of the crucial London discussions that led to the Anglo-Irish Treaty of 1921, while the British in 1972 saw the meeting as a low-level exploratory probe into the radical edge of provincial Irish politics. Even if the Provos had realized this rather than, as was the case, assume a symmetrical dialogue between campaign opponents, fear of 'politics' would have dominated any discourse. Republican ideas were more apt to be attitudes and unarticulated assumptions just as Republican ideology was most apt to be rituals and ceremonies, not concepts.

This self-denying strain, generally accepted, largely prevented the appearance of heresy. The Officials, where ideas and definitions mattered, were split by the withdrawal of Séamus Costello, who felt there was still a place for the gun. The Officials, still run as a conspiracy by those trained in Republican practice, divided on means rather than ideas even as all the concerned offered highly detailed analysis to disguise a largely traditional split, a matter of personality and tactical priority. Costello formed the Irish Republican Socialist Party and the Irish National Liberation Front that without him decayed and splintered. The Officials moved on beyond Republican habit, the Official IRA reduced to theft and the core conspiracy to Lenin. The Provisionals had no such split. They managed subsequent negotiations if not well at least without division. As long as the IRA was sound, dissidents could only resign, not become heretics. O Brádaigh and O Conaill were simply obsolete purists. Those who criticized tactics and pace were either discarded or kept as a minority on the Army Council.

There would be dissent over policy steps, over the truce of 1975–76, especially after the lack of useful results, over Ivor Bell's criticism of the campaign as a failure in 1983, over priorities and details but not until 1984 and the O Brádaigh–O Conaill withdrawal over anything that mattered. Then opposition coalesced around the need to expand the political option by making Sinn Féin more attractive, especially in elections in the Republic of Ireland. Was this a matter of principle as the purists felt or merely a shift in tactics as the majority – and those who controlled the IRA – contended?

The former could not define the latter as heretics without the support of the secret army and this was not forthcoming.

Everyone agreed that politics could be useful, that the experience gained during the wide protests and symbolic elections of the 1980–81 hunger strikes indicated means to broaden the struggle. The intention of the majority, those on the Army Council and those from the North who increasingly dominated the movement, was to take any seats won. Abstention on the part of the Republicans – especially in the Irish Republic – meant a voter would not have the conventional friend at the centre. The purists felt that the centre was illegitimate, should not exist, could not in any way be recognized. Without this denial, the Republicans would lose some of their legitimacy which was the invisible mantle that protected the armed struggle in the first place. The existing leadership denied that abstention was a matter of principle, marshalled all the resources necessary for a vote, and in particular kept control of the army and the new arms imported from Libya.

After a first formal attempt in 1985, the result first at a General Army Convention on 15 October 1986, and then at the Sinn Féin Ard Fheis on 2 November 1986, was a foregone conclusion. Abstentionism was out. The IRA and the arms stayed with the new Army Council as did many of those who would have preferred that the old ways continued. The new Republican Sinn Féin competed for members and for control of the assets in the Irish-American Diaspora but did not attempt to organize their own secret army for a decade. The group could not run effectively in elections and so evolved into a voice for tradition most often crying in the wilderness and events moved on, the campaign continued and the Provisional movement weathered the 26-county electoral disasters. Even with the advent of the peace process Republican Sinn Féin remained isolated, for the Provisionals from the first had agreed that a consensus would operate – even to the extent that negotiations collapsed when the Army Council returned if ineffectually to the armed struggle. What those who sought a way forward that did not rely primarily on the gun had agreed was that such a way could not be attained except if agreeable to all. And so the purists, with whom many sympathized, remained isolated: the mandate of heaven did not pass to them.

Heresy in the movement is an argument over possession of the gun, the control of the IRA and so the means to act on the future. The Officials inspired a lethal response only as a result of quarrels focused on arms dumps. Costello was tolerated but not absorbed – a parallel subsidiary. The Republican Sinn Féin movement without guns was no threat – unless there was a renewed division over the tactics of any endgame. Ideas within the movement have always been about the gun, for the legitimacy of physical force is the great asset.

If the movement still holds a monopoly on the dream, then dissent, withdrawal, opposition is not a zero-sum game but good riddance. Those who leave the faith do not threaten the faith – it is those who betray the faith from within that are the great danger. It is not simply that an informer is operationally a danger but that the movement must assume that such people exist. As any campaign is protracted, the reality of the informer is obvious: the security forces seek them, suborn the likely, seduce the innocent, coerce the vulnerable, and in time reveal publicly in courts or through traps and ambushes their presence: captured pawns. Any secret army knows that within there may, almost surely will, be someone who betrays the organization, a poisoned pawn that may ruin the finest gambit, set back the gameplan, endanger the true believers.

First, the betrayal is obvious in campaign terms – the army as an army is damaged. Second, equally dreadful is the betrayal of the others, the volunteers, the band of brothers who trust unto death, who have not power but each other, not heavy weapons but their own. In a secret army, living under cover, under threat, each must rely on the other, trust implicitly all of the faithful. Some commanders accept that torture will reveal all, but some do not – demand loyalty through pain to the grave. To be betrayed by one dilutes the trust of all. When such a betrayal is revealed, everyone is lessened, everyone becomes suspicious of further betrayal.

The usual free-floating anxiety is particularly acute in the IRA because it relates not so much to ideologically appropriate responses to reality but to operational reality. This anxiety, an anxiety with long historical roots, has been increased during the Provisional campaign by the use of informers – 'supergrasses' – within the Diplock courts judicial system and by the deception operations of the security forces, operations often intended to sow operational doubt. The informer endangers the life and freedom of all. Such an informer as a beast known to all has long been part of the Republican demonology. And such informers are now sufficiently visible that they have written a series of bomb-and-tell books, some merely everyday volunteers but one or two more important individuals. One, of course, is one too many.

Each hidden traitor, no matter how marginal or minor, once found indicates that the faith has been betrayed as well – if the faith will not hold him, will it hold us? True, the answer is usually yes. Yes, the movement has always gone on. Informers can disrupt operations, destroy units, hamper the campaign, but not ruin the movement. Informers cannot break the great chain of faith but can impose stress and anxiety and doubt. Still, there are practical steps to prevent betrayal, to exploit through awe and cunning the existing betrayals to IRA advantage. Most of all the intensity of concern arises in the movement not so much before the deed as at its revelation. Then the free-flowing fear engendered by the revealed truth coalesces on the deed. And such deeds must be expunged. Then the investigation, trial, and if need be execution eases anxiety and controls the damage done. The body bound, bagged, and deposited on a country road is lesson and marker, a message to the weak, to the strong, to the enemy, and one's own. It, too, is a ritual not an articulated idea, a practice, a process, brutal, cruel, hateful, and effective.

Schism

The betrayal of the ideal that produces ideological options rarely comes from the informer, the operational traitor, but from within the faithful and usually after the most intense debate. Schism may disappoint, may shock, but in a sense does not surprise. The movement has long assumed that some will not stay the course but will seek less than all. The Provisionals felt in 1969–70 that Dublin GHQ was going 'political', being seduced with alien ideas, letting the army run down. All of which was true if not always apparent to Dublin GHQ or not without remedy by those who became Provisionals. Once organized the Provisional IRA focused for a decade on the military options disputed, the means of tactical escalation, and in particular on the potential of diplomatic options. The truce of 1972 resulted in almost no internal discussion, but that of 1975–76 was accepted by some reluctantly and so subsequently was considered the most divisive event of the decade. After 1980–81 the shaping of the political option, the needs of Sinn Féin, produced the split that led to the formation of Republican Sinn Féin in 1984–86. Only in 1998 did opposition to the peace process generate a splinter group: the Real IRA, which offered operations as much as sound practice and to keep up militant spirits as in any hope of actual gain. The bombs were to symbolize the old role and mission, maintain the faith, embarrass the new leadership but not expel the British.

Thus the schism that occurred in a generation of violence tended to be individually and ideologically unpleasant but was pragmatically useful to those who stayed behind. The Officials had gone their Marxist way and become irrelevant to the Provisionals. The Officials had discarded the indigestible Costello and the radicals – the Provisionals thought to their own advantage. And Republican Sinn Féin had taken away the old generation of critics without producing any real defections from the IRA – rather the reverse in that now all recognized the movement to be indivisible. The Real IRA with the Omagh bomb merely made the peace process more valid.

Schism then produced for Republicans personal anxiety and yet very considerable tactical and strategic advantage, at least in the short run. Revolutionaries can seldom take long views except to assume they know the end of history. The Republican splits represented in a real sense divisions of attitudes and assumptions within a movement notoriously inarticulate in such matters. The great chain was unbroken. The movement was never seriously challenged, and so the future was not without prospects.

CONCLUSION

Ideology in Ireland has been special because of the lack of concern with the formalities, which was rather proffered as patriot history and explanation. The nationalist assumptions coupled with the Fenian legitimacy and the priority of physical force became Republican 'ideology' – an ideology not easy to code, not found in a text but ample for usage on the island. Those articulate, lettered, focused on reason and form, intellectuals of various sorts, ideologues and apparatchiks of doctrine assume no revolution can exist with text, without index and logic. Such rebels are comfortable with words and formulas so pursue the armed struggle in print and pamphlet. Their ideas shaped as ideology inevitably play a larger part in explanation than in the campaign, for they appeal to those who must explain, who write history, produce television programmes, find comfort in logic and events that fit expectation and experience. They know the map not the terrain, the three stages of revolution not the smell of cordite.

The Republicans of Ireland rarely seek comfort from orthodoxy or authorization from the printed page. Ideology for the Irish Republican is most apt to be found in process, in acts rather than declarations, in demonstrations not proofs. The Republican ideology, such as it is, has largely been in place for a century. The attitudes and assumptions have been reinforced during that period by a reading of objective reality. This reality is skewed only in that the dream overpowers any obstacles, even when the dreamers are reduced to penury. The dream itself is little different from that of most nationalist movement except that Irish history can be read and need not be created whole. The organization may invest considerable time in detailing the history of the dream, the litany of grievances and failures, but not much in probing the nature of that dream.

In Ireland the organization need only be sure that the recruit recognizes the implication of conversion to the ideal and is conversant with the history of the movement as repository of the nation and its secret army. This conviction is not elaborated with ideas but is strengthened through ritual and rite and repetition of first principles absorbed as history. A volunteer does not so much learn right thinking as perform rites, acts of doctrine, visual litanies hallowed by usage, that shape and deepen the faith. There is,

however, for those so inclined a massive body of analytical political interpretation – especially generated over the last decade as the Republicans
became deeply involved in political process.

The true danger to the faith in Ireland has always been with those who
would make accommodation to reality, take the freedom to pursue freedom
as ample gain. This would be the great betrayal – the people doing wrong
not the weak man selling the brave. Thus the one real schism of the
Provisional movement came over fear of a general betrayal. Those who left
for Republican Sinn Féin did so not to pursue conventional politics but to
oppose it. And those left behind who might have been so tempted, especially
within the IRA, were for a time dissuaded by the results of their new
operational freedom that saw Provisional Sinn Féin fail electorally. When
the opening occurred that led to the peace process, the Downing Street
Declarations, and the difficult road to a Northern Ireland Assembly the
leadership of the movement had to wait not on events or tangibles but the
consensus. And this after 1993 produced stress if not schism as the problems
of an endgame were compounded by persuading many to play at all. The
question had arisen: When not to use the gun? And none of history's
ideological answers had heretofore been found in favour of politics by the
pure in heart. Thus ideology had to be adjusted, the faith widened, the new
direction offered as convincing as well as profitable – and certainly the costs
of the long war, the endless, endless funerals, played as great a role as did
ideas about tactics.

In a real sense structured ideology is a crucial component but has played
only a limited role in the Provisionals' armed struggle, in the evolving history
of the movement. The basic questions of Irish nationalism have been solved
long ago to the satisfaction of the converted. All that need be discovered is
the operational means into the future through the armed struggle. When the
future intrudes as practical, when the patriot game may have an end, tactical
options may again be seen as principles about to be betrayed. Those who
seek the play of ideas and the challenge of concepts, the academics, the
ideologues, the thinkers and conventional, find the commemorations and
processions, the murals and the meetings, the visible litany of the faith,
provincial and parochial. They miss the reality of living history, ideas as
process, ritual as concept, and they hardly understand the obstacles to
moving the faithful into the future without the necessity of physical force.

CHAPTER FOUR

Recruitment

Before there could be volunteers for a reconstituted IRA, such a structure had to emerge. The events of 1969 formed the mould for that structure. Before the winter of 1969–70, and the withdrawal of the dissenting minority from the official Army Convention over the abstention issue, there had formally been but one IRA. That one IRA, as always, was umbrella over quarrels, a central magnet that did not always attract all the faithful. Even when only a few of the faithful are left, unity of means if not unity of purpose is rare. Revealed truth, the costs of secrecy, the perceived differences on an island assumed grand and diverse all tended to encourage dissent and division that only the reality of action dispersed.

By 1969 for some time many Republicans, many previously inactive, had been preparing provisionally for what seemed the inevitable: a break by dissenters with the Dublin GHQ. Many throughout the movement hoped there would be no overt break. Some in Dublin GHQ, on the other hand, sought such a break as a release from ancient error. These, the more politically concerned, felt that the loss of the old guard, the traditionalists, would be no real loss, just as many of that old guard felt the only way to husband the Republican dream would be to expel those who had already discarded the ideals in exchange for tactics long proven invalid. Most of the GHQ saw a struggle between the old and the new, the way forward and the way back; those who opposed the new, the means proposed, felt that Dublin was discarding the essence of the movement, the rock on which all else rose: the dream made manifest by recourse to physical force.

The slow division of the IRA had begun soon after the end of the campaign in 1962 when the focus of GHQ in Dublin shifted away from the failures of the immediate past that had embittered many, alienated others from the movement, and produced the usual splits and schisms. The movement never grew too small to split. At the time many volunteers had simply withdrawn, despondent or bitter and without hope for the immediate future. Generally, those who left in 1962 would never again be active or very active.

There had always been, however, many who were not very active, still

Republicans but often very still, who might help under other circumstances. Some had served one way or another years before and others had not been asked to serve at all. The IRA for a generation had been too small and too ineffectual to involve many. The campaign that had ended in 1962 had recruited only a small generation of the young. After all, the campaign had been quite limited and had deployed few resources because little was available. GHQ had made no use of many Republicans because there was little that could be done and often in Northern Ireland concern that anything done might lead to pogroms. Thus after 1962 the movement was reduced, first to the few activists, especially in Dublin; second, those untouched but Republican still; and third, the estranged and despondent, some still eager to serve and others permanently alienated. Not since 1945–46 had the galaxy been so small. And external observers were inclined to suspect that this time the militant Republican universe had collapsed into a dead, dark core without the capacity to expand. The IRA was an historical anomaly, an artefact, irrelevant to the new Ireland touched by the first rays of a rising economic boom.

Those volunteers who stayed began to shift priorities and prospects. With no prospect of a military campaign, the campaign generation still wanted to act. Essentially, those who wanted to act felt that only more conventional politics offered an immediate way ahead. Others felt political action unwise and inadequate, preferring to wait for a better day to begin once more a military campaign. The latter, many radical in politics or belief, were often singularly dedicated to physical force. All other activities, publicity, politics, commemoration of the past, agitation, and analysis were lesser means, useful in conjuncture with force but irrelevant and perhaps dangerous deployed alone.

The issue that appeared to divide the movement after 1962 was the question of continuing abstention. Abstaining from the three parliaments – Leinster House, Stormont, and Westminster – was not only for some a matter of principle but also relevant to the movement's priorities. The abstentionists opposed channelling resources away from the military into politics even when there were no resources, no real military wing, and no congenial political options. There were always those who were cool to any GHQ, especially sited in Dublin, and cool to recent and fashionable postures: the centre of the circle, no matter where, always had critics.

There were also those who deeply suspected involvement not just with political people but with socialist politics. Generations of propaganda had convinced many of those with no property that socialism was little more than communism, a Godless, futile, evil, totalitarian system, alien to Ireland. Many within the Republican movement felt as well that 'communism' was also alien to Irish Republican aspirations. The leadership after 1946 had made every effort, whatever individual private political views, to keep the movement clean of radicalism: the pious had to be kept content, the conservative American Diaspora content, the Irish people unprovoked. Previous radical Republican initiatives had led to splits and to the opposition of the deeply conservative Irish constituency.

For many Republicans, especially in the countryside, away from Dublin in miles and back in time, the only ideology necessary was faith in the nation. One joined the IRA to achieve the Republic through force of arms not to pursue revolution and certainly not to dabble in political action. The national issues was the issue, the grievance was the British, not class oppression. Even James Connolly, the Leninist socialist, had come around in 1916. After 1962 GHQ had taken a wrong turn, a left turn. The Dublin radicals had enlisted strange volunteers, especially Roy Johnston, an Englishman with university degrees and alien ideas who was suddenly welcome where old faithful from the country were ignored. Johnston might be a revolutionary but he was not a Republican and the Chief of Staff Cathal Goulding might be a Republican but was prey to enthusiasm unshared by much of the galaxy.

The result was a slow division. Those too conservative to be attracted to GHQ's new course and those who wanted the focus on the military and so felt any widening of the movement would dilute purpose and principle all, one by one, privately and in small groups, recruited themselves as an alternative to GHQ if the need arose. Until 1969 no one really saw the prospect of such a need. There was hardly enough left of the movement to warrant such a quarrel. There was hardly sufficient at issue to engender a split only a failure of the centre to hold the galaxy intact. The resistance to the centre led on 6 July 1969 to a public speech by the Belfast Republican Jimmy Steele at a commemoration platform that Goulding had sought to deny him. The new direction was attacked: it was too political, too radical, too uncongenial to the traditionalists. The dissenters felt that Steele had spoken for the real movement and the radicals assumed it was the last hurrah of those on their way out to pasture.

No one but a few from Northern Ireland or along the border felt that neither set of concerns should top any agenda. There was within the Northern nationalist community growing concern that the civil rights campaign could provoke Unionist violence that might be tolerated by the Stormont authorities. Dublin GHQ was complacent. When the North exploded in August 1969, the IRA had no response, no gear, no volunteers to deploy, nothing but an absence that exposed the secret army to be ineffectual and irrelevant to events. Nothing had been done and after August 1969 many felt much must be done.

In the summer of 1969, some of those volunteers who doubted Dublin began to see that a defensive but military mission might evolve from Northern events: a campaign might be possible, not simply a defence of the nationalists. Dublin GHQ still gave first priority to political options and to moving forward – defending the nationalists might be necessary but was a diversion. Although the movement remained seized on the 'abstentionism' issue this subsumed the two attitudes that had emerged after 1962 – each with roots – into a specific quarrel.

The need in Northern Ireland for a military tasking for the movement to defend the nationalist population later was offered as rationale for the split. All sort of rationales were to be offered: that the Dublin government engineered the split; that those who argued for a military approach had been represented on the Army Council that they attacked as unready; that the dissenters were pious anti-communist bigots. Their opponents stressed not only the failures of August 1969 but also the refusal of GHQ to seize the opportunities offered by Northern events. The issue – abstentionism – that came to a vote in 1969 was and to some degree had always been irrelevant. Dublin GHQ had increasingly been attracted to radical politics and found the traditionalist opposition on one hand to be the obduracy of the parochial and on the other the needs of the nationalists of the North for defence a diversion rather than an opportunity. The riots and chaos of August 1969 had revealed that GHQ had neither plans nor arms to distribute. At the end of the year GHQ still had little gear and no master plan – something had to be done. But with a GHQ dominated by the new priorities, the volunteers in the six-counties were largely on their own. The critics of the GHQ were accurate in matters of priority: the turmoil in Northern Ireland was resented rather than welcomed.

Those opposed to GHQ saw a military mission that would unite all real Republicans and recruit in Ireland those who wanted to move forward to the Republic. Since someone in the movement had to be blamed for the incapacities of the IRA in 1969, those at the top in GHQ were the obvious targets. The internal opposition to GHQ within the movement – some expelled from the IRA, some long inactive, some of the active as responsible for the incapacities as their colleagues – found that events had rescued them, rescued the IRA from politics, and with luck and daring might well rescue the new Ireland from the advocates of compromise and concession.

Visible dissent had begun in Belfast, Steele's home territory, long suspicious of Dublin, radical initiatives, and soft southern ways. The Republican dissenters acted against the local Belfast IRA unit under O/C Billy McMillen, forcing him to accept or appear to accept changes in the local structure and to isolate his assets from Dublin. In effect an alternative

Belfast unit had emerged dominated by life-long Republicans, especially from the 1940s and 1950s, with immediate local needs that GHQ could not – would not, many suspected – meet. McMillen had managed to evade the full take-over but the dissenters were in place.

Even before the Belfast volunteers had acted, those in opposition to GHQ policies had withheld not only their hearts but also certain assets. Sound men began seeking each other out in muted discussions over kitchen tables. Money was not donated. Contact was made with the like-minded in America where arms and money might be found. There was no organizational break but many had long lost faith in GHQ. Some, perhaps many, hoped that an accommodation could be reached, but as the weeks of autumn passed GHQ seemed to lack any sense of urgency about Northern defence and continued seeking a way forward politically. In August, having done nothing for years, the outraged veterans showed up at GHQ on Gardiner Place in Dublin seeking arms and a mission. There was neither; only resentment that the request should be made, and be made by those who had contributed nothing for years to maintaining the movement. GHQ was not going to shift priorities but only to add defence to the movement's agenda. This was not enough for many activists: everything had changed utterly but not GHQ.

Sooner rather than later that autumn, many accepted that GHQ had become irrelevant. In the North, recruits who wanted to defend, not to march in protests, were dribbling into the IRA. Thus the first recruits to the Provisional IRA were self-selected on attitudes and assumptions – some of these had already led to action, as in Belfast, and in more cases to contacts and promises in the country. It was easily possible to determine within the movement, within the ranks of the IRA, nearly all who would stay with GHQ and most of those who would go. Some of these had already left. The latter had drifted away to private life as had those alienated by the campaign years. The troubles in the North concentrated minds, indicated that not only were the nationalists in need of defence but also that the Stormont system might be vulnerable. GHQ did not read events this way. The prospects of military action tended to irritate others at the GHQ centre more concerned with conventional political options for the movement, newly dependent on class means of analysis.

The first recruits to the dissenters, often not recruited and at times not even in touch with the organizers, were a cross-section of the movement sharing not age or location, social background or past history but rather a single priority: the need to act militarily rather than continue to dilute the IRA with a political agenda. The Provisional IRA on the night of the split was thus more than those who had prepared for such an eventuality, 40 or 50 volunteers, mostly from the North. These volunteers who voted against abstention voted against the GHQ concept of the movement, but most importantly voted for a more traditional movement that provisionally would be structured immediately – and later authorized by a special Army Convention open to the like-minded. The voters, however, were surrounded by a vast nimbus of potential support. Thus the movement was composed of a few dozen who provisionally chose seven men as an Army Council.

The Provisional IRA purported to represent the faithful within an existing organization that was dedicated to the liberation of all the Irish. They were self-selected but selection was restricted at first to those within the core of the galaxy. Beyond that core was assumed to wait a large number of unassigned volunteers awaiting word from a proper Army Council. It was also assumed that once the word had been given others – new volunteers – would be attracted. What distinguished the first Provisionals from most revolutionaries was the organizational and ideological legacy of the movement: they came first but not without assets. Fatah or *Brigate rosse* or EOKA had to begin at the beginning even if there were assets and precedents to claim, currents to divert. The Provisional IRA simply was a title given to existing reality.

What distinguished the Provisionals from the Official rivals was not to be found in social or economic statistics nor even in psychological profiles. In the autumn of 1969, the movement was the residue of a truly national movement, but erosion of the successful and skilled was easily noted: the middle class was thin on Republican ground and the wealthy and successful rare indeed; the Protestants had gone and those Catholic nationalists with no property had stayed. Those who stayed with GHQ tended to be less provincial and more political but many stayed from lethargy or personal loyalty just as those who departed to establish a provisional movement were apt to be more conventional, more disgruntled with policies, more traditional in attitudes but also went for reasons unrelated to events – old favours, family ties, habit. What really distinguished those who stayed and those who did not was the weight given to the power and potential of the dream. The attraction was not one that isolated age or education, ethnic consideration or geographic factors. There were sullen and dour, shrewd and taciturn to be found in either camp, just as there were those from Dublin, those with decades of service, those with no interest in abstentionism. What each group shared was an attitude toward reality that all the involved could recognize: there were few surprises, for most of the involved knew their own all too well. So those who doubted the assets of the old dream kept the title deeds to the movement, and those who never doubted provisionally established themselves under familiar banners.

To these banners came the first wave of new recruits often without any

Republican credentials, often without any aspiration other than to defend the nationalist people of Northern Ireland. Unlike each previous generation the new volunteers did not aspire to establish the Republic, were not moved by history or traditional grievance, often in fact saw the British army as a necessary presence in the defence against loyalist mobs. They sought arms for what appeared a clearly defined responsibility, assumed the IRA – any IRA, Official or Provisional – would so supply them. So after 1970, with the situation volatile and the British military presence no assurance of nationalist security, all sorts and conditions appeared at the Provisionals' door – when the door could be found at all.

The immediate task of recruitment was to touch, encourage, shape, and direct this pool of willing and unassigned volunteers. The unstated basic assumption was that exposed to the Republican dream such recruits would be converted – a natural process, an inevitable process. For the faithful the dream was so compelling few could imagine the new generation could not be moved – many of the old generation still could not imagine the failure of the Dublin GHQ to be moved by traditional verities. How could they be so foolish?

All the forms of the 'new' Provisional organization began to fill with old Republicans dedicated to the new direction – Sinn Féin and a newspaper, a woman's movement, the Scouts, IRA units to parallel the old ones or new ones to incorporate those long inactive. In a very real sense none of these people, old or young, male or female, radical or conservative, felt in any way 'recruited' but rather comfortable with a long-sought opportunity to serve the Republic as it should be served. They had for greater or shorter periods been provisional in their support and loyalty to IRA GHQ and now had found in an official movement means to act. No matter that it was labelled Provisional and the unworthy rump in Dublin Official; all real Republicans knew the difference.

In the midst of organizing this existing support, the new GHQ had on offer what the movement had always proffered to the idealist: a means to achieve the Republic. In the winter of 1969–70 this had very little attraction to most of the concerned outside the movement, but remained the lodestone for those who came into the Provisionals. Nearly all those who wanted to act, old or young, North or South, had focused on the need to defend the nationalist from future loyalist pogroms. Many – including old-line Republicans – often saw the British army sent into the province in 1969 to maintain order as temporary saviour. For many of the vulnerable the British army was welcome; not an alien occupier but the soldier with a rifle at the bottom of the lane who would keep the mobs away. During the worst moments in August in Belfast, Republicans, fearful of the Orange mobs, had found it necessary to request British troops for their particular neighbourhoods: pragmatism over ideology. Of course once the army was in place other opportunities were available to transform the protector into an occupier, but that came much later. Most Northern nationalists, relieved with the arrival of the British army, still felt defenceless. It was *an* army not their army. And 'their army', the IRA, since no one anticipated the arrival of the Free State regulars, had been thin on the ground in August. Northern nationalists had assumed there really was a secret army, an illusion shared with the Unionists. What the Provisionals wanted was to make the illusion reality as quickly as possible.

The graffiti on the Belfast walls after the August turmoil read – '**I R**an **A**way' indicating the nationalist assumption that the IRA did exist. For two generations the Orange establishment had trumpeted the threat of the IRA even if the real IRA consisted of old felons and a few of the faithful. The nationalists as well as the loyalists believed in the IRA. So, the young and militant began to seek out the members of the secret army to volunteer for defence, to get a gun, to act.

The Provisional Army Council had assumed from the first that the new people would want to defend – perhaps even seek vengeance against loyalists. So first would come defence while the recruits were converted to the ideals of the Republic. Then would come IRA provocation against a British army that the volunteers saw as the primary opponent – the loyalists being Irish if misguided and so dangerous. And almost certainly that British army acting like an army would engender nationalist suspicion – especially when provoked by the IRA. Finally, given the nature of reality and the arena and especially the British, would come at last the campaign waged by volunteers dedicated to the Republic and shaped by the period of provocation. First, however, the way had to be cleared for the expected wave of recruits.

In order to defend, the existing and potential assets had to be organized. All the recruits were welcome regardless of their motivation. None, however, could remain long without being exposed to the Republican dream. Those who sought only adventure, violence, prestige, or the main chance were eased out as discovered. Since few arms were available and since defenders without ideals or gunmen driven by hatred would not be assets for the long haul, the new people were passed into recruits classes. There the winnowing continued. As in the past, the recruits were often bored by long lectures and movement texts. To serve, one began by sacrificing; even and especially the long, futile hours in a dull class intended to discourage as well as convert.

The Provisionals made their most immediate impact in Belfast and Dublin and then in towns and cities as long as the local leadership was effective. Thus in Derry there were rivalries, lack of empathy between the old and the new, not enough military gear to appeal to the bellicose recruits and so uncertain organization well into 1971. Some of the country areas, long untouched and without fear of pogrom, remained beyond reach unless, again, a local with drive and charisma surfaced. Some existing units remained with the Officials because of personal contact or lack of options. Increasingly, however, the Provisional galaxy expanded as their spokesmen got out the word that for them the gun was more important than the stages of revolution.

For the Provisionals the greatest difficulty in absorbing the new occurred in the traditional catchment basins, especially where there seemed the greatest need to act – to defend, to provoke, to use force. There were too many potential defenders. In the nationalist areas of Belfast, the few old Republicans were not enough to go around. Each recruit could not be firmly ground in Republican theology, even carefully tested for character and potential. Friends and neighbours and unknowns increasingly arrived, some with good recommendations, some who proved ill-suited. The old guard plus a few young people, usually from Republican families, were not enough to shape the brigade. The new, almost at the moment of conversion, had to be given responsibilities. The best were soon in positions of responsibility and often teaching lessons that they had barely learned. These were the first new generation, the children of the past like Gerry Adams, a barman who had grown up within an old Republican family on the Bone and simply took on greater and great responsibilities – capacity meant not so much promotion as more assignments.

In a sense until mid-1972, the situation did not change for as the number of convinced and dedicated Republicans increased so did the number of recruits. With the growth in size, the IRA increased the intensity of the campaign and so the need for more recruits than could be easily Republican-ized. This was true not only in Belfast, the core of the Provisionals for much of the armed struggle, but in Dublin and Derry and to a degree even in the country. Some recruits had all but to create their own units. In Derry, Martin McGuinness, a young butcher's assistant, sought out the Officials first in an effort to be a defender and there disappointed found that the Provisionals if more militant in theory were in practice in disarray. There were few Republicans in Derry, no one like Adams to bridge the generations, so that by 1972 McGuinness found that he was in charge. Between 1969 and 1972 three generations emerged within the Provisionals: the old Republicans, some young, most middle aged or older; the transitional people, few and previously inactive; and the rising new generation, not all young, that McGuinness represented – those who volunteered to defend, converted to the ideals of the movement, and shaped the campaign foreseen by the Provisional Army Council in 1970.

To absorb the new generation the movement had to rely on traditional values adjusted for the crisis – much easier in the country, especially in the six-counties where memories were long and grievances historic. There in the Northern Ireland townlands the Republic might have become the ideal of the movement, but the tactical means evolved out of the night riders and ribbon men of the eighteenth century. In South Armagh or Tyrone the new recruit was like the old recruit, and the effective tactics of the past were for some time effective. The new generation was a mix of traditional Republicans and those arriving within the movement for the first time, no Republican family, no exposure to Republican conviction. In Belfast, with the escalating campaign, the thud of bombs, the shooting, amid the first wave of missions and operations, many of the new volunteers learned not only how to conduct an armed struggle on the job but also why they were doing so.

These recruits from outside the movement were not unlike those who had been attracted during the previous generation: young men and now women of limited formal education, without property or profession, eager, enthusiastic, determined to serve, to act for the greater good. These recruits were mostly in their late teens or early twenties. A few were older but these were seldom deployed on active service. Those younger, if used at all, were incorporated in youth organizations like Fianna Éireann or told to wait. Few attracted to the Provisionals had formal training or great skills, in part because few nationalists, i.e. Catholics, did in Northern Ireland, and in part because those with training and skills were elsewhere employed, at work at the university, in a law office, or in front of a class. Many of the working class in the six-counties did not work and so were available for assignment. The Provisionals were thus largely composed of underutilized young people, parochial, marginal, badly educated but often capable of far more than society had on offer. In a sense the Provisionals offered everything – a vocation.

Those within the secret army attracted their own – an Irish solicitor or teacher does not readily appear at the door of a notorious working-class gunman looking for a weapon to defend the threatened people of the ghetto although a student may. Even the students, especially the university students, so prominent in other European radical movements and in the civil rights demonstrations, were rare in the Provisionals. Students were involved in words and politics and parades; they were not apt to spent hours in a recruit class with those without O levels. The IRA, unlike many nationalist movements because it was organized as an army, because such an army recruits from the bottom up, because there was no conventional means to use professional skills full time, was composed of the threatened in the ghetto, the recalcitrant in the countryside, and in the South the idealists who would sit through classes and wait on unlikely assignments – easier to do if there were no other prospects pending.

For a generation the secret army had grave doubts about the staying power of university students with other priorities, questing instead of obedient minds, prone to stunts and independent action and so schism. Radical ideas had ruined the Dublin GHQ and the rhetoric of the civil rights people had alienated many nationalists – Bernadette Devlin might be sound on the national issue but won the seat at Westminster despite, not because of, her socialist ideas. The Irish were conservative and so too the Provisionals, suspicious of the trendy and the elegant. The clever were too clever by half and the professional had other priorities. And both the professionals and those with necessary skills had traditionally been co-opted, used for special purpose not melded into units or often even into the organization. A chemist would help out sometimes and a banker lend money; there were doctors on call but not needed at parade. Many of the most important individuals could not even be found on membership rolls, could not be found at all if their one contact with GHQ was not available. Thus, as a national movement, the Republicans like colleagues elsewhere could draw on many talents – if fewer than most other colleagues; but unlike most others kept these contacts at one remove from the volunteers.

Beyond the secret army is, then, a thin ring of assets, stretching out to the edge of the galaxy and even beyond the power of the dream. These are often even more secret than the active service people and so can perform all sorts of tasks. Some at times even become involved in operational assignment: not all who carry a gun have made a declaration, belong to a unit, are a paid-up volunteer in a secret army. Mostly, however, these unlisted in the rolls are involved in maintenance, communications and intelligence and supply, not in the killing by the secret army.

The volunteer in that secret army, however, was and is very much a type. The recruits reflected the existing Provisional membership except for age and experience. Being young, filled with pure ideals, enormous energy, eager to contribute 24 hours a day, desperate to play a role however slight, the recruit was easily attracted to Republican ideas, discipline, and insight. There were initial ideological problems. The concept that the Orange mobs were *not* the enemy was eased by the rationale that even if deluded they were still a dangerous pawn in the British game: the real game. To give up a desire for vengeance, to eschew hate had a positive side: one chose justice. Those who could not, who sought to avenge wrongs, to kill loyalists, to use a gun for the sake of power, were discarded. So the successful recruit accepted the Republican vision and became a volunteer in an armed struggle that they had not previously imagined.

What the Provisional IRA offered over the years was an opportunity to serve in harm's way, the chance of jail, a ruined conventional life – the movement could be honest if for no other reason than it had a surfeit of recruits but also because what was needed was faith not skill or ambition. So few enlisted underground without knowing the terms and most found the exhilaration of the Republican faith ample reward. Once within the IRA the volunteer found his or her own, the same background and accent, the same ambitions and skills. Increasingly the IRA drew from Republican families, not all ancient, Republican enclaves, some new, Republican resources renewed by security behaviour and local conditions. The movement also drew in those with no previous connection for much the same reasons – many Republican families had apolitical children, many off the Falls or in Crossmaglen wanted nothing to do with the Provos. Those who did came not to their heritage, except in rare cases, but to serve. And they found more than simple opportunity but haven.

The movement was comfortable as well as inspiring, familiar, and demanding. The other volunteers were those known from the same parish or the same school, from down the lane. The few with real credentials were often shunted into political tasks, appeared at Sinn Féin offices where the president, Ruairí O Brádaigh was eager for middle-class recruits, partly to exploit their skills, partly to indicate that the Provisionals could attract all kinds of Irish idealists not just 'defenders' at Northern barricades. Thousands of these defenders appeared in the Republic as well as Northern Ireland and most reflected the same economic-social profile. In the South the draw was more various, the pool of recruits larger, but those with an interest in armed defence were likely there too to be working class, often with no job or a poor one. Dublin was still a long way from Tipperary or Tyrone but the IRA profile was the same.

Once the transformation of recruit into volunteer had occurred, there were few differences visible, North or South, urban or rural, less than before for now all shared a single vision of contemporary society. All were now members of a special Irish galaxy. The Provisional volunteer had enlisted in a national crusade, in an army, and so unwittingly had entered a new world, an ecosystem invisible to the everyday but one that gave meaning to life, enhanced the conventional, turned the unused, the unwanted, the marginal into crusaders, some with bit parts, some with a gun, all with a role.

The influx of volunteers peaked in 1972. In Northern Ireland British coercion began to narrow the battle arena, deny operational opportunities to the many, require the formal IRA structure to be adjusted and downsized. There were fewer opportunities to serve and so fewer recruits: the secret army became more secret, more skilled, less open to volunteers too young to have served in the first influx.

By then the potential recruit in the Republic recognized that the chance to serve as a soldier in the secret army was slight – there was no need for service in the South and almost no one could be sent to Northern Ireland where there already was a gunman overload. In any case the man from Tipperary would be too obvious standing in Pomeroy. The IRA in the Irish Republic began to erode. Overt membership in Republican activities, the first knock by the Special Branch at the door, often meant that assignment to England or the continent was foreclosed. The eager volunteer usually wanted to serve and not to attend classes and training camps and certainly not to become involved in Sinn Féin action. Some were content with Sinn Féin or training but the lure was gone. Fewer recruits appeared, fewer than even this were needed. The heady early days were gone and the cost of both subversion and an armed struggle had become apparent. The Provisionals were not trendy; rather the reverse: not only the proper were horrified but also parents and friends and neighbours were apt to be as well. And so bit by bit the army was run down in the South – only along the border was the prospect of military action real and so patterns of recruitment remained similar to those in Northern Ireland. In a sense the Provisional IRA in the Republic contracted not because of the general distaste – to be so dissuaded would not have lasted in any case – but because the recruit could not be promised an opportunity to act in ways the general public found distasteful. Those who would volunteer for sedition want at least the prospect of subverting the system.

The same recruits still came, knowing all. In a very real sense the socioeconomic profile never changed and the psychological desires never changed and the ideals never changed: what had altered was the recruits' perception of the future. And this pragmatic perception did not so much weed out the idealists as steel them – produced volunteers with ideals but without qualms or illusions. The process did not need to produce many because after the 1975–76 truce there was an erosion of opportunity. Only the few could be used and even the most promising often had to wait until operational attrition of special conditions opened an opportunity to serve as a soldier. A grand sweep of all the active, the introduction of internment, all the panaceas to destroy the Provos would only have opened the way for the generation in waiting to become operational.

THE CRITERIA OF THE MOVEMENT

Neither the Provisional Army Council nor the training and recruits officer, has to hand a file on what is wanted in a volunteer. Everyone knows what they want and who is to be avoided. There may be some dispute on the need for certain talents or the risks of the capable but none as to the nature of the volunteer. For a generation the IRA has wanted those committed to the Republic, motivated by patriotism and a disinterested desire to serve. It is assumed that each recruit accepts the necessity and dangers of physical force and recognizes the cunning and capacity of the imperialist enemy. Those who want service are offered not a gun but risk, those who seek to act are offered not adventure but opportunity. What the IRA had done is institutionalize sacrifice, created a lay order bound as one in a historic effort to move history.

The IRA wants someone sound. This means that the volunteer maintains an internal guidance system that is capable of interpreting all events; the past of course, the present certainly but most importantly any future prospect. Away from others, solitary or in exile, out of touch with the hive, far from the galaxy core, the sound Republican is not isolated but sound, faithful, and true. There is a tendency to extend this conformity down through the major issues – the national issue is always supreme – so that every technique and tactic is considered carved in stone. After a century the degree of dissent is narrow, the Republican is narrow – but sound. And never so rigid that under pressure, especially operational pressure, the desperate will not opt for originality, the unconventional.

It was possible in 1972 to sit in an IRA recruits class and find a typical sprinkling from any working-class neighbourhood: young people, rising adults, some tall, some short, mostly dressed garish and cheaply, a few girls in Belfast, seldom elsewhere, all of a time and age and inclination but each different. They had come to contribute, to act, to be part of history. They were unlike others elsewhere in Europe with educational credentials who chose the armed struggle from guilt at privilege or from the revelation that the state and society were fallible. The Irish had no need to emulate the rebel of the Third World or expunge Western sins suddenly discovered. They had no luxuries to discard and only the probable anguish of their parents and, as time went on, the disapproval of the many to consider. The appeal was seemingly to simple nationalism arising from patriot history, a simple motive for the innocent, who sought access to a secret army dedicated to a risen people. The later recruits had lost the early innocence but was as little interested in texts and manuals. The recruit was innocent of the dialectic, the complexities of analysis or academia but often quite familiar with Irish history, with Irish grievance, and with the evidence of the streets. Many came experienced in deprivation that was not perceived but everyday. The six-counties was often closer to the Third World than to London, the murals for the ANC or the Palestinians less related to the fashions of the time than perceived similarities. In any case, the recruit came to be part of something that had a special lure for the young, for the avid, for those who need challenge and danger. And the attraction was natural, an aspect of reality not learned in class but part of the flux. Those who did not seek out the IRA knew exactly why others had; headmasters knew that some in each class would go, not who, only that the lure would again prove effective.

Gradually in Derry or Belfast the units were filled with recent converts. Elsewhere the mix was more complex. The cunning lasted longer even in the cities and towns. The need for new volunteers was not great. Only a few of the new volunteers stayed long or moved up in the leadership if they could not convince their own that they were sound. Thus the unit in Derry was led by Martin McGuinness, an exemplar for his generation, sound, dedicated, careful, ruthless, and, often rare in Ireland, painstaking in detail. At the beginning his example dominated the unit and those eager for action or a gun; those without ideals, not fully touched by the dream, found no place in the Derry Provisional IRA. The military talents, the professional or technical skills of the volunteers were no different, but discipline was internal and dedication great. The Derry unit was sound, dependable, and so overused and overextended. As the years passed, the profile of the volunteers remained much the same; a bit older, the new recruits entered not a door to the unknown – a door opening on nothing much as McGuinness had done – but an institution.

The purpose of the sound volunteer is to be deployed and even if other skills are needed conviction dominates selection. Thus the movement continues to recruit novices for a lay order, not to find the best and brightest, not to attract those with connections or talent or conventional resources but to accept those who are touched by the dream. In an arena where a religious vocation is cherished – and beyond the capacities of most of those of no property – where ideals in church and out are not matters of text but example, where denial and pleasure postponed is admirable, those who sought and those sought recognized the nature of recruitment. One can be recruited for a crusade but only those are accepted as volunteer who are transformed.

One cannot shape an exam for a vocation but one can surely eliminate those without interest in the ideal. So the Provisional IRA, like the generation before and the one before that, was different only in that there were more recruits, a greater pressure of time, the impact of events – history moving – to hasten the process. Whatever the obstacles, however, it became evident that the movement had recruited in the first levies largely those desired. Some came easily through family and tradition, some came with the blinding intensity of conversion, but most came through the recruits classes to conviction and service, sound and persistent, Irish Republicans, soldiers of a special destiny. This conviction bonded by risk and association, by hardship and danger shared, by prison time and in the end by rejection and retirement seldom wavered. The leadership, the movement could do wrong but the appeal of the transcendental Republic remained. The attraction was still there a generation later despite all, because of all. Most Republicans once convinced keep their faith; and this is what the movement seeks – those who can be faithful. All else will follow.

THE RECRUIT'S ASPIRATIONS INSTITUTIONALIZED

Very few recruits arrive at the door of the secret army anticipating conversion to a secular faith. A few from the right background come with an inherited conviction and are moved through with dispatch. Most, however, come burdened by mixed and often contradictory desires. Some of these are little different from those possessed by the volunteer in a conventional army, by those who want to be commandos or paratroopers – and now even women want to leap from airplanes or serve at the front. The recruits in a normal everyday world seek adventure, excitement, danger, and the reality of films and television. They want to serve with the best, test and try themselves, go to war and possess the prestige that a uniform brings. They are patriotic and idealistic and innocent of violence. This is not quite the case in Ireland for those attracted to the Provisional IRA

In Northern Ireland over time, this innocence has eroded – the young knew that the IRA is not a crusade for the pure, that an armed struggle is brutal and vicious and often skewed to less than savoury aims. For a generation, however, the recruit arrived most eager to take part, to take risks for good cause, to sacrifice if need be but to play a real part if at all possible.

Some, as always in armed struggle, came in order to possess a gun and the power that flows from possession, or to be someone special or to gain through the movement what could not be achieved alone. They stood before the door seeking advantage, not service; opportunity, not responsibility. And they often seemed no different from the others until tested and found wanting. A few, as always, came attracted to violence, the chance to kill or to harm with legitimacy, came in turmoil to seek a private career denied in peaceful times by law and convention. Those who enjoyed their work were even more deadly than those who sought profit from it, and were discarded with haste and at times with violence. The enemies of the IRA were apt to stress the presence of criminals – after all, the IRA was illegal – the illogic of operations – undeniably the IRA was often ruthless, brutal, and unconventional but then so are most armies. But, like most armies, the IRA had little place for criminals or the mad, who seldom are sound and never make very good soldiers.

Any army, every war, attracts the criminal and the unbalanced; but in an armed struggle access to the front is easier, entry into a secret army apparently less difficult. Thus the unsavoury always appear; but in a small, closed, homogeneous society some are known previously and usually all are discovered. Those who steal in the movement's name, kill for their own pleasure in the movement's name are a clear and present danger – they tarnish the ideal that already must weather the operational errors, the innocents killed, the informers murdered, all the brutal evidence of a dirty war. No one needs madmen and thieves. The psychopathic recruit, like the criminally inclined, soon finds no identity of purpose with a secret army. In the IRA advantage comes only through service; power is a burden, sacrifice is the only opportunity, murder is no joy nor a gun an icon. Operational thrills are short-lived and the main chance unappealing to real pilgrims.

The average recruit with appropriate motives, declared and inherent, is in almost all ways that can be quantified quite normal for time and place: not criminal, not mad, not much different from the lad who shows up to join the navy or the police, not even very different from the loyalist paramilitary. And the desires and immediate ambitions of the IRA recruit are within the gift of the movement. In this – service, perhaps action, even sacrifice – he or she gets what is sought. What a volunteer unexpectedly finds is that conversion to the dream empowers, that a transcendental ideal transforms reality. The new soldier or the professional paratrooper unless member of a revolutionary army is seldom so touched any more than the loyalist paramilitary abroad for vigilante purpose. In a real sense the IRA volunteer is born again – some are born into the galaxy and others are converted to the dream. That dream is not easily defined, not in recruits class or in patriot history. It is available to all and nearly all are touched by it – or so pretend and pretence under pressure seldom lasts for long.

Seeking to serve, the recruit as volunteer discovers what is to be served – not his own, not his parish or the people, not even the nation, but the ideal. This realization comes over time, is made indelible by example and association and for the inarticulate is difficult to explain. He may be a simple soldier in the service of the Republic but somehow that Republic is more than governance, more than 32 counties, more than history would allow.

The recruit becomes part of the dream, part of history, part of a movement that is within the galaxy of the faithful. The volunteer is there immune to reason, the appeal of priest or parent or often to common sense, there becomes sound, an asset in the armed struggle.

From this conversion all sorts of benefits flow that the volunteer had really not imagined. Just as the people sought defenders in 1970 and were led to support provocateurs and then the Provisional armed struggle, so too is the recruit led into the galaxy, given what was sought and rewarded with what could not have been imagined: conviction.

THE VOLUNTEER INDOCTRINATED

The conviction of the volunteers is the single greatest asset of the movement, of any movement engaged in an armed struggle. The complex nexus of beliefs that make up the faith ensure persistence and a determination to contribute, to sacrifice, and so to read reality to rebel advantage. The volunteer seeks risk, danger, hardship sacrifice, and even death as indication of loyalty to the dream. It is thus far better to have sound volunteers than talented specialists with uncertain convictions. It is far, far better to have the faithful than the tangible assets of the conventional.

In Cyprus Colonel George Grivas wanted young Greek idealists for EOKA, Orthodox in religion, conservative in politics, filled with patriotism. He would turn them into guerrillas and gunmen. Those who led Latin American *focos* took into the wilds those who wanted to go, not those most fitted to do so – Che, an aging asthmatic without experience in Bolivia, was an example of the faith trusted over capacity and the fate of such value judgements. In Ireland those without property are assumed to be more amenable to the gifts of the Republican movement which have little currency in conventional society. And thus the volunteers supply unexpected capital unleashed by the dream.

The will of the secret army, the faith made engine of the armed struggle, is the great asset. This makes a secret army possible. Any movement needs to persist, but the Irish Republican movement, repeatedly thwarted in operational matters, feels a greater need to ensure continuation than most. As long as the dream is valid, attracts and shapes sound volunteers, there is hope; and in the meantime there is service and suffering and the rewards of sacrifice for those whose lives otherwise would lack purpose, be everyday, never touched by the incandescent promise of the Republic.

During the past generation, the IRA has been able not only to maintain the dream, and recruit for deployment, but also to continue the armed struggle at a considerable but not unacceptable level of violence: mostly before operations floundered and the campaign aborted. Not this time, however. This time the involved have recruited during a continuing armed struggle, kept the faith and the war going. As a result recruitment, still about the dream, has become more pragmatic, more focused on persistence in the existing armed struggle than in an unavowed determination to keep faith with the past. This time the gunmen are not witness, not gesture, but all too real even for Britain to put back into the bottle. The level of violence may be tolerable in London, even in Belfast and Dublin, but it is real violence arising from a real campaign – one of the world's premier armed struggles. This time no one involved in the IRA sees a pause before a new campaign: after 25 years either it is war or peace with justice at last if not necessarily through military victory. This time the struggle cannot be put on hold so that the IRA must soldier on until the will confounds the assets of the conventional – and for many the conventional is a greater danger than the British army, than the police or the informers, than the monster at the end of the lane. Knowing this, the recruits still arrive seeking a role in the slow crusade into an uncertain future.

Such recruitment for the Provisionals in the midst of downsizing the army rather than maintaining an escalating campaign has generated problems. Some want to serve operationally but not become involved in other routes forward. Thus the recruits officer often hews down the prospects to the few that show promise, to the needs of the moment. While the same rules apply within the recruits class, within the entire process, the IRA as a result of events has been transformed several times in size, in structure, in capacity and focus since 1970; but the recruit has not.

Very few of the young appear in the Republic. There are few opportunities to serve and few attractions. The campaign has gone on too long. Everyone is tired, even the young. All the errors and blunders and brutality have long been visible. The Provos are not pure in deed if they are still in heart. Irish society in general and the institutions of the establishment in particular oppose the Provisionals root and branch. Those involved are harassed, their careers circumscribed, their conventional ambitions thwarted – only those who draw significance from being 'subversive' are so attracted. And those so attracted and deemed subversive cannot be used operationally. So most importantly there is no need to serve in the South and little hope of service elsewhere. A few persist, stay in the shadows to appear only as wanted for questioning by the Sussex police or arrested in Holland for transporting arms. A few operate the units that maintain the struggle from the Republic. The appeal is limited.

Even those all but convinced of the validity of the dream are aware that enlistment in the crusade may bring nothing but horror and dismay, the interest of the Special Branch, the ruin of any conventional prospects, the dismay of parents and family, and at the end nothing asked but to attend meetings, write editorials, put up posters. These are often not seen as tasks for the dedicated. Still, at times they are the entry-level post for ultimate use as a gunman, for only the truly sound would so serve.

In the North, establishment disapproval and the attention of the security forces may even be recruiting assets for the potential Irish rebel, not barriers. Most have no prospect of conventional careers even if the parents and the family are just as horrified to find a child within the Provisionals. It is the lack of operational opportunity that is apt to limit the size of the recruits class as much as the erosion of purity or the costs of the crusade. The young who can most easily serve generally mature in the countryside in Republican areas and are deployed not only, of course, because they are faithful but also because they are intimate with the arena and the unit. Those in the towns and cities must wait their turn and so many who might also serve by waiting do not: patience is not a common virtue of the young and determined.

For a generation the IRA has sought to find the faithful by winnowing away those unsound. The process has generally produced more rather than fewer volunteers and always the sound. Despite all, despite the opposition of an entire spectrum of the decent and conventional, of much of the electorate in the South, of Church and state and even many in the Diaspora, the appeal of the dream continues to attract recruits, produce volunteers, present assets to the leadership.

IN SUM

While the underground is engaged in an armed struggle, one of the constants is the process of recruitment. Those who come to the movement are often given other than they seek – for some much more and for others a whole new life shaped by a new vision. They may also receive what was sought – adventure, risk, a gun but in a novel context. And if what was sought is in violation of the ideal, it will be rare for the movement to tolerate their services for long – the IRA wants sound volunteers, those touched by the dream.

The differences over time in social profile, in age or skill, in class or caste, has been, in the case of the Provisional IRA and as is usually the case, slight. The Provisionals are novel in that within the secret army responsibility is almost entirely rewarded to emerging capacity – there is no mid-level entry and the required skills and talents not found in the working class – and there is more to be found than the middle class imagines – are sought beyond the centre of the galaxy, among veterans, among the faithful, among the sympathetic, and if need be from those who can be purchased or wooed.

Recruitment to real armies reflects similar needs and aspirations, and produces similar profiles. Some real armies rely on peasants but so does the government which supplies the leadership for the masses in military matters as in politics and society. Most armies, one way or another, reflect the nature of their origin, their constituency, their nation. The IRA, on the other hand, has recruited almost entirely from the working class, augmented by those who could help in more complex matters. In 1970–72 some recruits who arrived as defenders were older but the major differences were expectations differing from those of the self-selected at the core in 1969–71. These, the leaders, were traditional Republicans – they wanted an armed struggle. Most but not all of the next levy wanted to be defenders but became volunteers in the armed struggle. And after 1971–72 there was a decline in innocence, a decline in those from the Republic of Ireland, and over the course of the long war a decline in those who sought entry and those who could be deployed. As a result the age of the volunteers tended to increase but the rising capacity of the security forces neither let the IRA age or grow isolated from new recruits.

Within the Irish Republican movement many are not really concerned with what tangible is offered but rather with entry into a living tradition. Even if not well understood, the IRA is part of history, part of real life, a constant and so a partly known part of the flux. Recruits come for all sorts of reasons, good and bad, but stay because of the lustre of the dream. As time passed this was increasingly true. At first and even now, recruits certainly come because of the perceived need to defend the nationalist people; but increasingly they are allowed to participate only if they are sound – and opportunity occurs.

All undergrounds during the armed struggle do not stay the same, even if the size is static and the arena stable, but most do – beginning and end filled with the same types. This has been largely true with the IRA. The new recruits were and are more pragmatic than those who came to defend in the 1970s, but their profile is still the same. Most movements, of course, never attract the many but make do with their own. In Ireland a generation of tolerable violence has filled the jails but also the ranks of the Provos. Most movements fail and a very few escalate to victory absorbing the more conventional imperatives as the irregular is left behind – follow Mao's route to power. Those who persist without escalation repeat themselves. And so too have the Provos. Without losing and unable to win, the Provisionals have never had to worry about novel recruits; each new levy is remarkably like the last but with hearts grown cold. And such recruits bring dedication but few talents; however, the armed struggle can be pursued with the talents they bring since what matters to the movement is the dedication, the will, the faith. All else can be made good and much has been.

So the new have not diluted the faith; rather the reverse, the new if fewer – fewer for all sorts of reasons – are evidence of the persistence of the dream despite the times, despite failure, despite the cold hearts and innocent victims, despite all. Each volunteer – once a recruit then pilgrim – is the ideal made manifest. This has always been the purpose of the movement and is the gift offered to each recruit: not service and sacrifice alone, not just a role in history, a position bonded with a band of the dedicated, but the dream. And it remains a dream worth the price, worth the dying and more telling in Ireland, island of saints and scholars, worth the killing.

CHAPTER FIVE

Individuals

In national movements the spectrum of individual rebels is apt to be sufficiently wide to include all types and professions. Even those who have something to lose if the cause succeeds – privilege or power – are often represented, certainly by their children. Those movements driven by an ethnic dream or a religious vision may also involve all sorts – but not always; some ethnic loyalists exclude their own on varying grounds, place or class or habit, and some fundamentalist aspirations appeal only to those denied more opportunity in more established denominations or societies or systems. Some individuals are denied places not as representative of a group but because of personal animosities, character flaws, special reasons. What all share who enter a classical underground is a sense of grievance, a feeling that history is askew, and that the only way into a satisfactory future is by means of an armed struggle.

In Ireland the Provisionals – like all others a special case – are at odds with most national resistance movements in that the volunteers represent far less than the whole in economic and social terms for the island at large, if less so for Northern Ireland. Much of the nation is excluded because the Provisionals lack general appeal, appeal to many nationalists, appeal to the other tradition, appeal even in the core areas of support. Militant Republicans have always been in a small minority and only rarely supported by those nominally nationalists. Radical change, a real Republic, would have severe and unpleasant consequences for a substantial number of people and most institutions on the island. Power, position, ease of place, a part, even if small, of the action would be in jeopardy. Protestants almost all, would be forced to adjust to an unimaginable situation – and the nationalists, Catholics mostly, would find that the parochial habits of the existing Republic and the aspirations of those in Northern Ireland could not easily be fitted into the Provisionals' aspiration of a pluralistic, secular Republic. The churches would have to adjust and the banks and the bureaucrats. The nationalist ideal might remain for most of the Irish in part because prospects remained dim even at the beginning of the new century. The reality of a united Ireland was simply too difficult to imagine. In any case if there were to be unity, none wanted it as a gift of the IRA. Few after the first hectic days in 1970–71 wanted any IRA at all and almost no one not within the movement wanted an armed struggle. So in the general population few perceive themselves sufficiently deprived or intolerably humiliated by existing reality – rather the reverse. And so the pool of potential support is small, shallow, and uniform, a mix of militant, largely Northern, Catholic working class, a residue of the traditionalists on the island and the odd radical.

Since nearly everyone else would have something to lose in a united Ireland even if these would be secondary benefits, so nearly everyone, nationalist or no, opposes – more or less, usually more – the Provo's pure dedication to the Republic. Those with most to lose, those with property, with power, those who are Protestant or profess alternative ideologies, actively oppose the Provisionals. Thus the IRA is left with those who have little to lose: the denied, deprived, the wretched and humiliated, the ghetto Catholics and country people of the North and the border and a scattering of idealists and traditionalists. The result is that the Provisional movement is composed of those that most revolutionary movements claim as constituents: those of no property denied their nation. Most in Ireland feel neither grievance.

Most revolutionary movements not grounded in national resistance must depend first upon the idealists, usually middle class, and then tutor the beneficiaries, the poor, the peasants, the Indians, or the tribes. Movements that rely on existing faiths and ethnic loyalties need not tutor on basics, only reveal the necessity for an armed struggle. The Provisionals are one with their core constituency but are denied by much of their proclaimed constituency, the Irish. Again this is often the case: Menachem Begin's Irgun Zvai Leumi arose from a minority strain of Zionism, and even in occupied France many opposed the resistance. Mostly rebels are apt to speak for all when visibly denied by many who want no part of an Islamic Republic or an end to the Italian Republic. Most in the Irish Republic, many in Northern Ireland and much of the Irish Diaspora are content with an unattainable ideal of Irish unity. Those opposed to unity, all Protestant Unionists and some pragmatic or self-interested Catholics, favour martial means to prevent such an eventuality. Thus the individual that appears as convert to the ideal of the Provos is different in the acceptance of the armed struggle as appropriate and *effective* means to create a nation once again. Once the peace process began such recruits were rare, since the movement's secret army was no longer focused on the most effective way forward.

The recruit to the Irish armed struggle fits a very special socioeconomic profile; unrepresentative of the nation as composed but at one with some of those that Wolfe Tone assumed would be faithful to the dream, those of no property; but also a few, the learned or skilled found in other national movements. Castro and Begin were lawyers, George Habash in Palestine and Che in Latin America doctors, Guzmán in Peru a professor like Tony Negri in Italy, Arafat an engineer, Grivas an officer, the *Brigate rosse* and German Euroterrorists university students. Peasant revolts are often in the hands of those who have spent years in seminars, and the first on the barricades often come directly from the university or organized labour. In a real nationalist movement they represent everyone and every category is apt to be represented. This is not true in Ireland.

In their solely working-class base and therefore leadership the Provos are all but unique. The faithful are truly those most oppressed by existing national structures – not merely those conscious of that oppression and too guilty that their class or the colleagues or their family benefits from injustice. Moreover and more important, the entire movement is so shaped that unlike many nationalist movements the IRA leadership arises from the ranks, not from the skills and capacities available to the few with education or property or privilege. No Chief of Staff of the Provisional IRA had had a university education and few had experience within the middle class before their tenure. Several have had no career but the Republican movement. The IRA 1913 to 1923, the secret army represented an inchoate nation and was an army of all-talents. Anyone could and did join. The erosion after Eamon De Valera took his Republicans into the Dáil – into the system – was rapid so that by the end of the depression and the arrival of the wartime emergency devastated not only the movement but also the recruitment base. By 1945 the middle class had largely gone, exhausted, retired, alienated. Reorganized in 1946, the IRA retained the sympathy of many with professions and property but was working class – often in Ireland a class without work. By 1969–70 the unassigned IRA volunteers that flocked to the Provisional banner were nearly all working class.

For a time under the threat of Orange pogroms the Provisionals, especially in the South, attracted more varied recruits: students and teachers, a few from the middle class, but more from stable working-class backgrounds. Only a few in the leadership were comfortable with the middle class, preferring those, like them, of no property. For immediate purposes defenders did not need university degrees and no one until much later imagined a long war, a generation of violence, or the elaboration of the struggle by political means. By 1972 with the armed struggle underway and the cost of the dream more apparent, recruitment turned up the odd idealist with credentials – some were kept out of the normal intake routes to be used covertly, and others were shunted into non-military roles where their skills were needed – publicity, finance, organization. There were not many of these to deploy and many of the necessary skills did not require a degree but were open to conviction and experience. None felt a great need for the talents of the middle class. In the Republic recruiting dried up and co-option of talent, even the use of the barn, at times became more difficult. This did not matter greatly for the movement had the skills and resources to persist and lacked the talent and vision to escalate in more complex ways. When such ways began to appear after the visible advantages available and the impact of the hunger strikes in 1980–81, the involved simply coped, learned to manipulate the press, digest complex political texts, run election campaigns, make do nicely without recruiting accredited talent.

In Northern Ireland most individuals still fit a single socioeconomic profile, not unlike that in the Republic. North or South all came as recruits of their own volition whatever their aspirations for themselves or the island; but most had only service to offer – they would do anything but were trained for nothing. And the Provos were more interested that they become sound than skilled – idealists could learn on the job, usually had to learn unconventional war on the job and almost always at great cost.

THE CHOSEN

When an armed struggle grows grand, becomes more conventional, fields armies and requires ambassadors, the leadership may well draft in those needed, just as do states. The gunman may make the talented offers that for various reasons they cannot refuse. No movement follows an ideal text, is pure in thought and deed. Those engaged in dirty wars become smeared as well so that not every recruit arrives voluntarily aglow with idealism. Some are dragged in to fill the levy, to post the letters, to carry messengers, to become part of the crusade, come to serve for fear of worse. Some are kept on salary and some are kept in line. Everyone might read in unison Mao's *Red Book* but some did so out of fear not faith. In the case of the Provisionals – and in many movements that have not grown grand like the Chinese or Vietnamese did and the Palestinians have – all recruits arrive as volunteers, self-selected, idealists of one sort or another. The movement does not want nor will keep the reluctant, those not sound.

The IRA recruit may come seeking vengeance for perceived grievances or the power of the gun, seeking romance or comrades or excitement. They stay as volunteers only if touched by the faith. Thus for a generation the individual volunteer in the IRA has first chosen to be a recruit, then becomes a volunteer on accepting the ideology, the dream of the Republic. Most of the recruits to the armed struggle come from Northern Ireland and share not only a homogeneous background but also certainly other characteristics.

These are hardly novel in time and place. Most recruits had personal contact not only with the Republican movement but also with friends or relatives who are involved. Most have personal grievances: harassment at a roadblock, a friend lost or the sight of the dead bodies on Bloody Sunday in Derry or on a Strabane Street. The security forces did not change their habits once over a generation, only grew more discreet. Most recruits as well have had evidence of more general grievance: the most obvious being the presence of the British army and RUC constables on the streets and country roads. Time has not eroded the reality of their presence within nationalist ghettos, only made it conventional, not acceptable. For the British the paradox has been that an effective security presence assures IRA recruitment and so persistence of the armed struggle and the need for the effective security presence. The ceasefires only put such matters on hold.

All the IRA recruits have the idealism of youth – a desire for service and sacrifice and a belief that change is desirable and even feasible. There is as well the lure of the covert, the romance of the armed struggle even after years of a dirty war. There are, in fact, ample reasons to volunteer; but few recruits know far in advance that they will step over the line, seek entry into a movement damned by all the conventional, by the parish priest, and often by anguished parents fearful of the obvious cost of commitment. Even the hereditary Republican youth has anxious parents. No matter the flaws of the movement and the appropriation of society, the appeal of the secret army persists. Mystics do not choose to be transported nor lovers to become involved, nor do most of the young men or women expect one year to be a volunteer the next. As in the case of mystics during a time of piety and the young in the spring, the possibility exists and so influences the future. An IRA vocation is always an option in the Short Strand or Fermanagh or the Bogside. This one or that one will volunteer this year and next. They always have.

The variety of the volunteers simply reflect the conventional variations of the nationalist population. There are differences in temperament and in personality. Some are glib and articulate, others glum, sullen, often arrogant, rarely sprightly. Each comes to the armed struggle with special motives and special talents, each comes from a similar background and experience and each is shaped by the movement to the dream and to purpose.

PROBATIONERS

A few volunteers are swept into the crusade without entry exams. These are hereditary Republicans. Cathal Goulding from Dublin, who led the Officials away from the Provisionals, had an IRA father in the glory days of the Tan War, and in turn his father a Fenian, while Goulding's own son was in the movement and married a woman who went with Seámus Costello's IRSP dissenters. Gerry Adams had a father in the movement and a famous IRA uncle, a clan of Republican relatives, and at 16 was involved – family and crusade all one. And in the Ulster countryside some townlands have long been pure Republican and each parish has its own. In the Republic there are villages and townlands where that family has long been known as Sinn Féin. With the onset of the Troubles in 1969–70, many without formal Republican connections appeared just as they had each decade. Everyone knew who they were – everyone always does in Ireland. It is almost impossible in the closed Irish world of parish and townland to remain anonymous – even emigrants to Dublin or Belfast are known with a question or two and the questions are inevitably asked. Thus a recruit came as known, recommended by his place if not his neighbours or the movement. A recruit, however, remained on probation until those in authority within the movement could be assured that his convictions were sound – difficult in 1972, far easier later. This was determined not only within the recruits class and the formal winnowing of a secret army but also within his daily rounds, determined subliminally by his associates, by his own, all apt to note unsavoury motives or unwanted ambitions.

Many volunteers who were accepted were not especially delightful, not charming nor kind, not shy and proper, but all were assumed to be sound. Even those volunteers who proved skilled and cunning in operations, could kill personal and close up, could kill on request without qualm and get away, a talent beyond training and vital to any underground army, might be discarded once the realization came that the ideal was not at work in them but less appetizing imperatives.

Always the novice remains probationer until the movement is assured that the recruit, even the volunteer, is sound. No one expects each volunteer to be able to make similar sacrifices, keep the faith under unimaginable pressures. Those most sound will, however, do so, suffer beyond reason, resist to the end, accept the agony of force feeding week after week, stay sound even isolated in bleak English cells, beyond comfort of the movement, some will die on hunger strike. Some remain faithful to the dream even when discarded by new directions, unwanted and worse often unrecognized in prison or in exile, left behind as the crusade moves on. It is this faith that transforms the individual into an asset and this is what the movement seeks in each individual: not talent, not education, not professed loyalty, not any special personality, not charm or Republican parents or fame or the capacity to kill, but rather conviction. All else can be taught or must be learned. And conviction is what transforms the individual into a volunteer in the secret army and it is a transformation that must be sensed not seen. And it is a transformation that can be reversed: the apostate denies the revealed truth, the weak become informers, the faithful are vulnerable to weakness. And so all movements founded on conviction offer haven and exhilaration and the prospect of betrayal, absolute security amid free-floating suspicion.

Once the individual has the faith, is transformed from recruit to volunteer, there is little visible transformation in personality: perhaps a certain maturity, but that might be natural, perhaps a greater ease, but that could be maturity. Just as there was no indication in the classroom or at home that this one or that would enlist in the Provos, once enlisted there is no way in general conversation, across a table or in a pub, to tell that the faith has touched the man or woman. And so those who keep the faith seem little different from those who have hidden doubts. No one can tell simply by looking. The wary habits of the underground may in time show but only to those exposed to such conditions. The only revelation of conviction comes in an open discussion of politics where the convinced speak with the surety of the faith – a faith deep and narrow.

Followers and Faithful

The volunteer in the secret army, if fortunate, serves as a soldier, touches a gun, pursues the military option but only because of the support, the aid and comfort, the assurance of maintenance of many within the galaxy whose only reward is service given not recognized. These Republicans are at times the most faithful of all, operating at a distance without the reinforcement of shared acts, late news, the smell of cordite; they must keep the faith alone. Some were once volunteers but many were not.

Most recognized at the time of commitment, when it was too late to draw back, that the movement could only offer limited opportunities of service – attendance at meetings, the sale of newspapers, the defence of the indefensible before conventional wrath. To do *something*, however, appeared sufficient – and at times that something is more vital than active service and more dangerous, but not often. Mostly the faithful must operate above ground, circulating in paths hardly illicit and rarely covert, collecting and proselytizing and crying to the deaf and sullen. They mostly become the visible facet of the secret army – those whose service is more delicate remain, like the active service units, beyond view.

Like all movements the Provisionals have organized their own. The secret army, the core, is scattered across the island and at times abroad. Most volunteers are clumped in nationalists areas in Northern Ireland and along the borders, but no county is without the faithful and no area without some organization. The obvious vehicle for most individuals is the Provisional Sinn Féin party, everywhere legal in Ireland and Great Britain if everywhere suspected as subversive. It is an actual force in Northern Ireland but marginal in the Republic; one member elected to the Dáil. The party gives the many an opportunity to participate, to act as well as to forward funds and support. From time to time the party appears the most effective means to move the struggle forward, at least to those not absolutely dedicated to the gun. Mostly, the role of the party – the outward and visible institution of the movement – has been overemphasized by observers. Historically, all Republican institutions rest on the consensus of the IRA not the pro-grammes and policies of the moment. Mostly, the party and the newspapers, the posters and pamphlets and meetings, the whole spectrum of the conventional preach to the converted, keep rather than spread the faith. Local political power is possible, even regional gains, and often the overt representatives may negotiate and elaborate movement policy; but the driving if unstated purpose has always been first to maintain the faith and then augment the power of the movement. With an unarmed strategy the party's role has become central but that role is legitimized by the majority on the Army Council at the core of the movement: there may be no war but neither is there peace, there may be a limited role and an unclear mission for the secret army but the Mandate of Heaven remains intact. This means that there is more room in the movement for recruits to politics but almost none for the traditional recruit for an army.

The Provisional IRA is special in that the Republican ecosystem is ancient; generation after generation renewed, replaced, adjusted but always persist-ing. There have been other long wars but none as long as that of the Irish and none that can display a single, persistent organization. For two centuries the Irish Republican movement has been present but without sufficient countervailing power to impose the dream on reality. In a sense despite all the movement could do, their world has been institutionalized and marginalized: kept alive on the island but often sealed in Irish amber. Tolerated as defenders, aided by the conventional, filled with the traditional, the Provos became a major player but arose from a narrow base of activists. These have been ample to persist but after 1972 have not managed either to escalate the struggle or to attract the diverse, no more so at the end of the century with the movement focused on concessions, the Republic on the instalment plan.

For the hard-core Republicans much necessary support is generated by latecomers; the new and eager are always late. Yet some are always attracted, move in closer to the centre and replace the old faithful. This has been true generation after generation and continues to be the case even as those who

arrived in 1970–72, the Adams–McGuinness leadership, continue to dominate the movement. Thus like all revolutionary ecosystems that persist, the
Irish Republican movement is self-sustaining, maintained by commitment,
crisis, occasional military success, the errors of those in authority, and always
the power of the dream. What is different is the age of the ecosystem and
the profile of the faithful.

The Rebel

Perhaps no character out of the island is more generally known than the Irish
rebel: boisterous, feckless, brave, and indomitable, a man with a gun, a man
for one season, irresistible and futile and larger than life. In literature if not
in life, the Irish rebel stands tall, a drink taken, a fight relished, a boyo with
a ballad for an epitaph, and a death as martyr for Ireland. For many this was
Brendan Behan, who in real life did his prison time, appeared at parades,
wrote as well as drank and made an enthusiastic but undisciplined volunteer.
For many the Irish rebel remains a stereotype unrelated to the pious, lethal
pilgrims of Belfast and Crossmaglen. Such an imagined rebel is also a figure
of fun, a perpetual loser, doomed and jocular, irrelevant to the real world, a
sometimes thing.

All the imagined IRA volunteers are as fodder for thrillers and film
scenarios – the Troubles as Trash – as were their ancestors: the Fenian
bombers, the gunman in a trench coat, the informer – and Behan as a Borstal
Boy. Mostly the novels and films simply tack the IRA tag to stock figures:
mad dogs or cankered old men, monster villains or the young misguided,
perhaps saved by the love of a woman or more likely dead in the final reel.
They are bits of a formula played out to commercial advantage. The serious
novels seldom have as author those with underground experience – and
those with underground experience often produce not serious work but the
flip side of the monster, the guerrilla without fear or reproach.

The real rebel is rarely the caricature, awful or splendid, created by an
author. Often the gunman is a frightened and ill-trained boy sent out on a
hopeless mission or a stolid lad waiting at the bottom of the lane with a
shotgun and the closed mind of the countryman. There are few rebels that
fit the form of the patriot ballad, few that are as feckless and vicious as the
British media is apt to think, and few who would serve as characters in a
complex novel. Like most everyday soldiers the gunman and the guerrilla
are everyday. Few Irish rebels are as skilled as the professional soldier –
although the protraction of the struggle has meant a rise in standards,
standards constantly eroded by losses, lack of training, the needs of the
moment, and the failure of corporate memory. A professional gunman is a

contradiction in terms: what is sought is not competence, a vocation, but power, an end to the clandestine world not the pleasure of the underground. The individual relies on natural talent, experience, and luck. The volunteer even in craft is everyday except in rare cases.

Few Irish rebels are natural gunmen. Few are feckless or vicious, although some are both; but others, most in fact, are badly trained for their trade. All armed struggles impose incompetence, rely on faith over talent, must rely on luck, the contingent, the unconventional not by choice but because of lack of options. The volunteer must in the end as in the beginning rely on the dream. Many in the IRA, even the feckless and vicious and the incompetent, are idealists making do, ordinary people who have moved into harm's way.

The traditional Irish rebel who brought his own pike at the rising of the moon only to find the insurrection ruined by informers or doomed by incompetence had disappeared even before 1916. The open rising gave way to conspiracy, another Fenian gift that required special talents and assumptions. Even then most rebels wanted to be an Irish Volunteer, a real soldier not a gunman in the city shooting the unprotected or a rural brigand murdering from a ditch. The volunteer even in the years underground was treated as a soldier, went on parade, waited not as conspirator but as volunteer. There had been columns and guerrillas living in hides during the border campaign. Even after 1971 the species did not really die out completely although almost no one could last long in Northern Ireland on full-time service with paramilitary costume and arms at the ready. Mostly the volunteer, who had enlisted to serve in an army became a soldier only briefly, for a few minutes, firing and disappearing, arriving and bombing and gone again into the everyday.

THE PROVISIONAL PROTOTYPE

Amid the films and academic analysis, the television documentaries, the comment and the popular assumptions about the Provos, several variants have emerged as types. And even when these contradict each other (cunning and craft however vicious is rarely found among the feckless) the new caricatures of the Provo remain. A generation of the armed struggle has also produced the Provo as stereotype. The opposites are the idealist volunteer buried with military honours, admired in *An Phoblacht* and offered to recruits as exemplar, and the mad-dog killer who kills the innocent, pursuing no rational strategy. Those more observant are apt to find the Provo a highly skilled professional rebel, prone it is true to Celtic error, but a survivor who has persisted and must be taken seriously whether or not amenable to accommodation. The opposite is that the Provo is merely one more levy of misguided, incompetent Irishman eager for violence, savage, thoughtless, cruel, often brutal, whose persistence is remarkable. The latter's efforts are restricted by the Paddy Factor, inherent, perhaps ethnic-based, Irish incompetence, and the former are admired not for their cause but their horrid but effective means that kept the campaign going for a generation. In neither case is there much feel for the volunteer as person or type.

For a generation the elucidation on the terrorist mind had been a prevalent analytical delusion. Those who have managed to question the activists in Italy or Ireland are apt to find the everyday – no strange quirks, no great difference from the average, communists and fascists, orange and green, quite conventional – neither mad nor criminal nor unbalanced. In any case today nearly all true believers any place, those who opt for violence and those who do not, share certain characteristics with the Provisional volunteer. Mostly what is not easily explained is the gunman's vocation in an Irish context. How is the Provisional volunteer on active service like other rebels, like any soldier? How is a Provisional volunteer different and special and Irish?

The most famous Irish rebel of the last generation, the most famous Provo of all, is Bobby Sands, a volunteer without a gun but illuminated by the faith who found his vocation in prison not in the lanes and back gardens of Belfast. Sands starved to death on his 66-day hunger strike as the IRA prisoners refused to accept the criminalization policies of the British administration. Such an acceptance would have meant they were not soldiers, not volunteers in a crusade, not faithful to the cause but simple criminals. With no assets remaining but the capacity to say 'no', Sands and the others generated a long and violent crisis, a net loss for the British and, which is not always the case, a concomitant gain for the Republican movement.

Sands was in most ways the epitome of the ideal rebel and in all ways most ordinary and most Irish. He had a limited career on active service but one that gave him a role and time in prison. In the H-Block prisons absolute commitment meant confrontation with superior power 24 hours a day. Sands was effective mostly within prison. Outside he had played football. Inside he wrote poems and convinced his own that none were more faithful. One in any case cannot be trained to denial, trained to die by suffering self-inflicted. Once committed the action depends completely on the individual emboldened by societal norms and movement commitment. This is true in any rebel career.

For an individual there are seldom promising prospects, none can look ahead with confidence to promotion or pension, none has a government for succour. There is no one to intervene in hard times, no legitimacy but one's own conviction. Isolated in prison the rebel can draw support from only the very few but, as with Sands, it is often ample to maintain conviction. In fact it is that conviction that makes the rebel, and especially as Irish conviction that admires a vocation, sacrifice, service, even the monastic life. One cannot pay a man to starve or to go years without wearing clothing living in filth when food and decency and comfort are but a nod away. It is a conviction that is enhanced by generations of example and authorization. Other societies have similar values and others resort to the hunger strike but Sands was acting within a very limited context shaped by old but narrow considerations.

In Sands the faith led to his death, to the giant Belfast funeral, his name scrawled on walls in Rome and Rio and poems written, ballads sung. His death also led to the Provisionals opening a new front with Sinn Féin, exploiting a death they would have preferred to avoid. And Sands was in a way the archetypal Irish rebel, very Irish, who pursued a vocation, found suffering effective, built a prison life and death shaped and sanctified by the dream. And, also typical, was still used by the movement when his aspirations had to be adjusted to the reality of an unarmed strategy – during the hunger strike the IRA had escalated operations, persisted in the armed struggle as well as exploiting the deaths in the H-Blocks.

Like Sands, all rebels are so shaped by conviction – or else are no more than stragglers in an alien crusade. Most rebels, however, do not find their names written on walls but on markers over shallow graves or in court records. And most rebels, Irish included, pursue more conventional careers. Most of the time is spent waiting and hiding interrupted by the few brilliant moments of tension or terror during operations: weeks in preparations, days in waiting, and a single moment blurred with quick violence, danger, and the smell of cordite. If lucky, if clever, then the waiting again. And only the very lucky live to see the dream in power.

The Provisional Guerrilla

For much of this century, one variant of the Irish rebel has been the IRA man in the country. The texts and orations remembered those old Irish heroes, Tom Barry and Daniel Breen and Ernie O'Malley, back in the Tan War who ambushed the British and confounded their pursuers. In time these guerrillas provided through their own books examples for national liberation movements elsewhere. In an era of anti-imperialist national liberation struggles, many angry young men read Tom Barry in bedsitters and back rooms to learn how it was done and how it would be done.

The Provisionals, even with a post-industrial opponent, even within the United Kingdom that lacked jungles and wild places, produced if only at first just such guerrillas. In time, the active-service units adjusted to the narrow Northern Ireland arena and the British hi-tech responses that made real guerrillas obsolete. The IRA relied not on full-time guerrillas – neither did the commanders in the Tan War – but on volunteers who operated under cover, often at night, always in secret. Even then, IRA volunteers in camouflage appeared from time to time, ghosts from campaigns past, romantic, elusive, transitory, totemic. In fact, at the beginning for a time, the Provos found there was still room, if barely, for the classic countryman.

In Bellaghy, Derry, a small, divided farming village, one of the new breed of rural guerrillas was Francis Hughes. A success in the field, Hughes, rose to O/C of South Derry and then had to give up command because he was on the run, continually seeking targets while pursued. He could run and he could hide but he could not at the same time command others. The RUC and British credited him, like another local, Dominic McGlinchey of the INLA, with a string of killings. There was no doubt that Hughes operated as a lone guerrilla within an environment too hostile to permit columns or even permanent units – the last of a dying breed who avoided dying.

The conflict in the area was particularly bitter in that the RUC and the RUC reserve, the Ulster Defence Regiment, the local security forces, were made up of his neighbours. He was not striking at anonymous imperial soldiers but those next door – hardly a novel experience for a guerrilla but unpleasant still, especially since each such victim was Irish, and should not in theory have been a target at all. Everyone knew everyone if perhaps not very well. A divided society divides intimacy and faith, not presence: the man next door is well known but not at all.

Casualties touched everyone. In the Maghera UDR barracks, five men were killed during Hughes' time. The Protestants suspected all Catholics of complicity in such murder. Killing the police and militia only tinged Republican purity with the taste of vengeance, sectarian murder denied by every volunteer and assumed by every vulnerable Protestant. Volunteers like Hughes and their leaders on the Army Council denied any sectarian intent and went on attacking those inevitably Protestant. The result was a bitter and unforgiving civil war that first divided the community along sectarian lines and then increasingly divided the Catholic community into those tolerant of the IRA and those violently opposed to violence used in their name. Hatred, hidden but real, festered. No one knew whom to trust, who was the real enemy. Many felt the IRA gunmen a Catholic killer.

Hughes saw himself, as did his associates, in a quite different light; not sectarian killer but an Irish rebel guerrilla. He admired the heroes of the Tan War, Tom Barry and Dan Breen, sought a romantic career, not to murder from a ditch. His enemy was the Crown and those who favoured the British presence: the hereditary enemy. 'I don't want to be shooting them. I want them to bloody go home in the morning. But what other way do I have to protest, can you tell me? … I hate what I'm doing. I really hate it. But I'm going to keep doing it – that's the funny thing about it.' His career as a guerrilla had dash. He spoke to his RUC opponents on the phone, walked through road blocks, became a legend as the Boy from Tamlaghtduff, intimate with the countryside, sleeping rough in a potato field, escaping army patrols, hitting and running and dropping by home for Christmas dinner. His was a military style soon out of fashion; the long odds favoured the security forces. The times, the arena, could not support a career as a full-time guerrilla.

On a moonless night, 16 March 1978, at a quarter past nine, Hughes and one other volunteer moved up through Barney Cassidy's field near Ranaghan Road, Fallylea, two miles north-west of Maghera. In the same field was a two-man British SAS surveillance post – a Security Forces Observer Point – hidden near a manure pile. There had been information that Hughes would be in the neighbourhood. The British intelligence net, fashioned from informers, bits and pieces filtered out by monitors, gossip and rumours weighted and balanced, produced not for the first time seemingly firm word on Hughes.

The two IRA men were in paramilitary uniform. Hughes wore an IRA black beret, a green army combat jacket with an Ireland patch on the sleeve, olive green army trousers and carried a Garand M-14. The SAS men thought he was British army – he looked like a soldier. He was a soldier by intent. Even in a trap ambush the SAS blundered, broke standard operating procedure and challenged the IRA men as the two came up to within 12 feet of the hide. They assumed them British. They did not want to shoot their own. It was a fatal mistake. The two IRA men immediately opened fire. Their slugs tore into Corporal David Jones knocking his SLR out of his hand and fatally wounding him in the stomach, lungs, and liver. The second SAS man was hit, knocked on his back, but not disabled. With Jones screaming and the IRA men firing, he managed to open up with his sub-machine gun, firing one long automatic burst of 26 rounds, hitting both IRA men, smashing Hughes' thigh.

Sending away the other volunteer, Hughes, much of the time crawling, got across the Ranaghan Road and up into the fields, struggled into a tiny culvert screened with gorse and shielded with thorn bushes and whin. He could hear the arrival of an ambulance and the Quick Reaction Force of Gloucestershires from Kilrea, both radioed in by the surviving SAS man. The British were looking for three IRA men. In the dark no one found him. The dogs lost the scent. Hughes lay in his ditch covered with moss and bramble bleeding and waiting through the night and into the daylight. Eventually at about noon on Saint Patrick's morning, 17 March 1978, the soldiers discovered him. Badly wounded, he should have been dead but was still defiant. This was a classic engagement in country warfare, a cameo from old guerrilla wars.

After a couple of hours waiting for the ambulance, Hughes was moved to Magherafelt hospital. Later he was questioned. He would eat nothing during the four days in hospital, in January 1979. He was tried in February, convicted, and sentenced to five counts including the SAS shooting and a bomb at Coagh, County Tyrone, in January 1977. He received a life sentence for killing the SAS man and 83 years on the other counts. He had told the authorities nothing, had no regrets. He was a soldier.

He was moved to Long Kesh in February 1980 where he joined the IRA prison community. One leg was nearly two inches shorter than the other and his Republican convictions unchanged. He went on the blanket refusing to wear prison clothing – he was a volunteer, a soldier, not a criminal. He joined the dirty protest when the prisoners refused to wash. He had by then become a legend in an organization ever mindful of history. Solid, taciturn, and enduring, he was a real guerrilla from the hillsides of Derry. Even in prison, especially in prison, if not like Sands, he was an asset and in time subject of the inevitable poem that ended 'I'll never see the likes again of my brave Francis Hughes.' He was by then a martyr, dead on hunger strike, but in his last gunfight in Cassidy's field, he was an expiring breed.

The war no longer had room for the columns in the hills but for a generation deployed rural active-service units composed of locals with cover. They made use of sound young men, volunteers, many were from Republican families, from strongly Republican townlands or parishes. Some were new to the cause. Some were not young and others had only secret Republican connections.

These volunteers had the mind of an Irish countryman, slow, suspicious, at times sly, often truculent, unvarying of conviction, inarticulate in expression, parochial, and proud. In distress and danger they, like the hedgehog, closed down and withdrew. Under questioning, Hughes had refused to eat or drink for fear of drugs, refused to answer questions for fear of tricks, sat mute out of malice for days and days. In prison he refused the state's coercion and ultimately refused to eat and died.

The Provisional Gunman

Over a generation the films and thrillers have tended to focus on the new model IRA volunteer, the urban guerrilla, the gunman, the terrorist replete with trench coat and smart bomb, intense, implacable, usually evil. The media has noted the spectacular horror of no-warning bombs planted by young men and women, planted without remorse, without great skills, with dreadful results. Everyone has read of the assassin moving through exotic cities at night – for much of the world Belfast is exotic, alien, a backdrop for thrillers. Yet the gunman's career is mostly mystery; for the real volunteer is seldom depicted but cast as mad or feral unless misguided. When brought into court in Belfast or London, such killers are seldom awesome; young, working class, unfashionable in dress and accent, defiant as sentenced to long terms. Whatever makes an effective gunman is not apparent on sight, in court, and rarely through conversation – and certainly seldom apparent to the involved. Some, a few, given luck, inherent talent, and practice have become that rarest of rare in an underground professional, not just sound but also effective. One of the Belfast premier gunmen was Bobby Storey; not mad, not feral, certainly deadly and ruthless and, most of all, a survivor in a hard trade.

Storey had come under police notice in Belfast even before his 17th birthday, been arrested as soon as he had come of age. He was constantly monitored after that, for the authorities early recognized him as a potential danger. At six feet four inches with a ruined complexion, he was easy to spot. No matter, he was sound and soon on active service. Arrested and despite two honest eye-witnesses Storey still managed to be acquitted of a charge of causing a huge explosion that destroyed the Skyways Hotel at Belfast's Aldergrove Airport on 31 January 1976. Similar identification failed to convict him of a kidnapping and murder on 11 March 1976, in Andersontown, Belfast, for the judge doubted if he were, indeed, the gunman. The police were outraged. They had no doubts.

Storey was suspected of various crimes including a series of vicious murders. For their purposes the police had ample indication that Storey was a gunman, good at his trade, without mercy, compunction, or moderation. He killed on order, was a valuable IRA asset in Belfast. He was arrested again in December 1977, but the charges were again dropped. He was almost immediately rearrested on murder charges; but in May 1979 the judge failed to convict him because of dubious police procedure. The security forces were even more incensed. Storey was a most wanted IRA gunmen, violent, ruthless, cunning, and incredibly lucky – and, of course, at six-four most visible.

An IRA gunmen does not learn to operate in training but on the job. If fortunate he has time to watch others, learn on the job. Luck in the gunman's trade is a matter of sensitivity to the operational arena, meticulous planning – not always an Irish or revolutionary trait – and an assurance arising from success. Two contradictory traits are required – audacity and cunning caution. The bold are caught and those too cautious fail to act. An effective gunman must risk all but in the service of operational craft. Some pay for success with anxiety, live on their nerves, grow not cautious but pessimistic. Some find a natural vocation in a life led on the dangerous edge. Storey had the arrogant assurance that he could not be touched and that made it difficult to touch him – certainly made it difficult to convict him. As a GHQ asset he was deployed again and again: sound, effective, send Storey. He proved both effective and durable – and always sound.

In 1979 for a complex helicopter escape from an English prison to free a key IRA commander, Brian Keenan, IRA GHQ dispatched a team composed of Gerard Tuite, who had taken part in a British bombing campaign the previous year, two senior IRA men, Bobby Campbell and a middle-aged Republican Dickie Glenholmes – and Bobby Storey. No matter that he was famous, monitored, most wanted, six feet four and easy to recognize by features and accent, he was still chosen for the English escape. GHQ depended on a sound volunteer for this crucial operation – not someone intimate with the London arena, not someone unknown to the authorities, not anyone with the proper accent or habits, but someone sound, not perfect by any means but available, eager, dependable. This was Bobby Storey, surely one of the most visible IRA men in Belfast, a man who could hardly be missed by the most inept of constables, even missed by the public. He was sent anyway. He was sound, experienced, a proven commodity. He would, somehow, cope, manage. Who else would be better?

The operation was a failure from the first. There had been a leak in Belfast, and British intelligence from dribs and drabs had tracked the operation. The IRA team in London was under police observation. Finally, when the British felt there was no point in more delay, on 14 December 1979, the Anti-Terrorist Squad of Scotland Yard arrested the four in a luxury flat in Holland Park. It was a clean swoop, a security triumph built on information received, sound police practice, and the limitations of the IRA. And the authorities had Storey at last.

Storey pleaded not guilty and although the other three were convicted he was not – the jury did not know his record and accepted his explanation. Not lucky again but free because he had been audacious, convincing, assured.

A gunman's effectiveness continues beyond the moment of the kill. No one plans for failure, but someone like Storey never plans to be caught, if caught to be tried and sentenced, and if sentenced to stay in prison. Audacious and resilient in adversity, he was not just lucky, he was, indeed, gawky, unattractive, provincial, ill-educated, crude; but he glowed with assurance, was a survivor. He was tried again and the second jury again accepted his explanation and he was released from the Old Bailey in April 1981.

His gunman's career continued. GHQ was hardly going to retire him. He was an asset in hand. Arrested again in August 1981, this time he ended in the Maze prison. There he was a prime leader in a mass escape of 38 IRA prisoners in September 1983 – the largest peacetime prison escape in Europe. He was recaptured almost immediately – within an hour – and returned to the Maze. He was hard to replace, a patent example of an exemplary gunman.

IRA commanders have always relied on the sound gunman, proven volunteer dispatched again and again. Not all have the survival skills necessary to persist. Some have spent years engaged in active service, deliver milk by day and operate at night; but the mix of caution and audacity is still necessary, not simply a willingness to plant the bomb or kill from a ditch. Such qualities cannot easily be taught any more than can such practice be grasped from a book, from a lesson plan? Certainly the IRA had no time nor inclination to run classes for gunmen – a training game offered weapons and target practice, bonding but no assurance of survival. Assurance, grace in adversity, brutality coupled with a sensitivity to the arena are virtues not found in guerrilla texts. One has or acquires a sense of the arena, feels when operations are at risk, senses oddity and threat – a capacity part natural and part practice. Those who must will learn on their own if given the opportunity and those who don't are replaced. The attrition rate for the maturing guerrilla is high, there are seldom re-examinations and no one to tutor the slow of wit or the hesitant. No one quite knows what blend of habits and inclinations produce a survivor but the mix is rare.

Storey fashioned in the lanes and council estates of Belfast a career without the historical precedents of Hughes in the Derry countryside but one that rose from the wisdom of the streets, the dedication of the faith, the power of the gun, and confidence. He found operations natural, killing as a trade not a pleasure but a culmination of capacity. His career in a sense was not different from that of Hughes in the capacity to survive, to survive this operation and this court and this prison, to survive and operate despite all. And no gunman survives forever but is used up by GHQ, by the shifts in the arena, by the odds and by a change in luck. One mistake is one more than is allowed in the gunman game.

There were also those not famous, often not even wanted who had been active volunteers, appeared on parade this decade or that, stayed with the faith and then came to serve the Provisionals. Many volunteers drifted away when there was no action, when the recruits classes bored or political activity was suggested. Others had stayed. Some had stayed for generations. In County Kildare, hardly ground zero of the Republican movement, since the 1930s Frank Driver had been a well known Sinn Féin figure in Ballymore Eustace. The locals knew him as slightly eccentric, the Kildare Gárdá as one of their few Republican subversives, and the Special Branch in Dublin had him on their list. In his long coat and black beret, he collected money, appeared at commemorations, made his views known, lent a fiver, carried messages and made friends on his way – many in the countryside cared little of politics and a great deal for Frank Driver. He had money of his own that went to the movement as did his life. He was, then, one of the old faithful that Dublin GHQ found distasteful: fighting old quarrels, uninterested in present reality, decent but obsolete, not worth the trouble to keep, no loss. And so too assumed the authorities, not worth the trouble to monitor closely, no threat.

The Provisionals, however, found his contacts, his friends, and his services made possible after 1970 an extensive net that absorbed, stored, and distributed most of the imported IRA arms. Driver was too notorious for anyone to take seriously but all those still touched by the faith are, if nothing, more serious. Driver did not show up for parades, carry a gun, fit on a chart but was more important than some who attended Army Council meetings because he was willing to exploit his life, to serve without notice. In this, if nothing more, he was typical.

THE LEADERS

In the IRA those who survive long enough may find not rewards but responsibilities. If sound and available and useful, they will be used. Some stay hidden like Frank Driver. Others discover useful talents unimagined on parade, join to be a soldier and end as an accountant. Some who become leaders have no talent as a gunman but other skills, other contacts, other virtues and some may simply have kept the faith, be sound and available. Where most covert movements arise from the self-selected, the leaders without followers, IRA rank is shaped by necessity. The long history of the Irish meant that there was an appropriate means to select the leadership. The secret army mostly recruited from bottom to top, only rarely co-opting talent. The Provisional IRA was in theory and usually in practice a democratic army, selecting its leaders from the available talent.

The structure of the IRA had been maintained without discussion in 1969–70; the rules, regulations, and procedures as well as the assumptions. Thus an Army Convention, a provisional Army Convention, would have to meet to legitimize the reorganized IRA. And so it did, hastily collected and voted on an Executive that chose a seven-man Army Council which in turn secretly appointed the Chief of Staff Seán Mac Stiofáin – no real secret there and no real convention, only a provisional one. Mac Stiofáin chose his own GHQ staff to manage specific areas – an Adjutant-General, the Quarter-master for arms and explosives and dumps, officers for intelligence and publicity and finance, and those attached to the centre for varying purposes. Thus almost at once those involved took action to establish their credentials as legitimate leaders of the IRA. All had long Republican careers, represented the various surviving IRA generations, were legitimate, recognized. And voted on as was proper.

In the very beginning, then, the Republican dissenters in Belfast and those who prepared the break with the Official GHQ felt an urgency to confirm a provisional leadership, then organize all else: tradition demanded this. In effect not so differently from the Italians of *Brigate rosse* or Fatah, those involved in the split chose themselves, mostly the choices were obvious. Some did not or soon made clear that they would not be candidates and others were selected as obvious choices. Thus a small Army Convention chose an Army Council that represented the existing trends and desirable options, some from the North and others from the South, included different generations, recognized both past service and present need. As usual there were no surprises.

The first Chief of Staff was the key position for the new Army Council. As GHQ Intelligence Officer Seán Mac Stiofáin was the only one on the Dublin GHQ to come with the Provisionals. And he was also chosen C/S for obvious reasons related to career and character. Besides the Dublin connection, he had a singleness of purpose, absolute and determined convictions tested in prison in England and in service in difficult times in Ireland. He had learned Irish and invested his time in the movement. He had not been involved in the squabbles of the recent campaign. And he had recognizable leadership qualities, was precise, painstaking, solid, sound, often dour, but with a sense for the galaxy long lost by his colleagues on Dublin GHQ. He was also quite atypical as a classic Irish rebel, as a typical Irish Republican, even as an Irishman having been born John Stephenson in London in 1928 into an English family with no Irish connections – not even a Catholic family. He had chosen to be Irish, an intellectual and emotional decision that in many ways enhanced rather than complicated his service within the secret Republican galaxy. His active service had been in

England when with Cathal Goulding he had been arrested after an arms raid. As he learned Irish he became Seán Stephenson and then Mac Stiofáin. Finally in 1970, he was Seán Mac, Chief of Staff of the Provisional IRA and until his arrest the dominant figure in the military campaign. He was a generation older than the new volunteers but not one with the older people inherited from the 1930s and 1940s like Frank Driver. From England, he favoured no special Irish area; was in the South but not from the South. Not especially genial, serious, more conscious of efficiency and detail than many, he seemed an obvious choice, even over the former campaign leaders.

The two most prominent of these who came with the Provisionals were Ruairí O Brádaigh (b. 1932) and Daithi O Conaill (b. 1937) as one on most Republican issues if not the closest of friends – in the movement association was a matter of faith not friendship for within the galaxy the nature of the commitment not the congeniality of the mix was crucial. Before the obligatory public use of Irish, they had been known as Rory Brady and Dave O'Connell. Both had matured during the campaign of 1956–62 replacing the older generation in a time of great bitterness. They stayed until the end of the campaign in 1962, Brady finished as Chief of Staff and was already well known as an elected abstentionist member of the Dáil. O'Connell was one of the last released from Crumlin Road Prison by the authorities in Belfast.

Once the IRA loose ends were tied up in 1962, they largely retired to private life, their active service apparently over as the movement entered the doldrums. O Brádaigh remained active in Sinn Féin; but O Conaill, doubtful of the intentions of the GHQ, took little active part in Republican activities. They, like many others, assumed that their generation had kept the faith and time would produce another campaign. In the meantime the faith could be maintained without radical departures.

The two, so often linked, were quite different and, like Mac Stiofáin, not at all the perfect profile of the Irish rebel. O Conaill had left his job in Cork as a telephone lineman to join the IRA full time when the campaign began in 1956. He served in the North, participated in several engagements, was badly wounded, captured, sentenced to eight years in prison, and so had ended his campaign years in Crumlin Road Prison. Along with Seán Garland, who became a dominant figure in the Official IRA, he was the most prominent volunteer at the end of the campaign. With no armed struggle in view, he felt he had no real role. He then acquired credentials as a woodworking teacher and accepted a position in Ballyshannon, County Donegal, no small achievement for a felon with no real education in a conservative and class-bound society where advancement was limited and often achieved through connections. Married and with a family, a position in Donegal, a real life, his ideas had not changed. His position on physical force and his dislike of GHQ policies had made him a natural for those who sought a military alternative to Dublin GHQ.

For some in and out of the movement O Conaill was pretentious, a strategist without grounding, possessed at times of ideological airs and graces; but none could deny his service or his commitment, or as spokesman for the Provisionals his value. Tall, lank, sanguine, a chain-smoker, ready with both a reasoned explanation or the hard word, he fitted the innocent assumptions about the Irish rebel. He looked like a gunman and when he talked policy few doubted he spoke for gunmen.

His contemporary, Ruairí O Brádaigh, was quite different, another kind of Irishman altogether. He came from Longford and taught in Roscommon, an Ireland largely without romance, often neglected by those interested in scenery or charm. His family had Swiss Protestant connections and was clearly middle class. Brady had graduated from University College Dublin – amid service in the IRA – and without intellectual pretensions was still far better educated than the Republicans of his generation or most of those who came after 1970. Short, cheerful, kind, considerate, in his way as recognizable as O Conaill, he was married with a growing family. He was in all ways but one just as he seemed, a devout, provincial school teacher with neither great ambitions nor special attributes. In conversation he was reasonable and open, his political convictions were always easier to see than his commitment to physical force. The media sought out O Conaill for his aura and the hard word; but O Brádaigh always had the time for explanations and details, the kind word from a decent man.

The two were soon highly visible at Sinn Féin headquarters on Kevin Street in Dublin, a crucial media stop as the Troubles escalated. In a sense what was most remarkable about the two was that despite their Republican convictions, the long campaign years, the anger of the establishment, they had managed by 1970 such outwardly normal lives, married with families, teaching, had everyday friends and simple ambitions – and were linked only by their faith. After 1970 all but the faith came second, teaching was abandoned, everyday life disappeared, and families seen rarely and at times while on the run.

In a sense the Provisionals' rejection of Dublin GHQ proved at first largely a rejection of Dublin itself long the centre of the Republican universe – even Mac Stiofáin did not live in Dublin but in Navan in the Irish-speaking Galteach of County Meath. Those from the Republic on the Army Council were not from Dublin. Many of the key figures in 1970, of course, were from the North, especially from Belfast where the danger of disaster had been greatest, where the closed Republican society had been most distressed that their movement had been taken over down in Dublin by politics. Most in the North had been all but born into the movement, did not have to seek it out as did Mac Stiofáin or O Conaill. All had lived deprived, narrow lives, harassed by the police, discriminated against by a Protestant state, getting by with menial jobs. In Belfast Republicans had always been at war and after the campaign ended in 1962 wanted no novel directions out of Dublin that would erode the IRA – their IRA.

Jimmy Steele, who would be first editor of the new newspaper *Republican News*, issued to replace the official *United Irishman*, was a truly sound Republican, a Belfast Republican. And so he was a man of no property, no education, devout, pious, absolutely dedicated, and a man who had spent 17 Christmas days in prison for his faith. He had chosen to speak for all, all true Republicans, from the platform over the grave of martyrs in Mullingar in 1968. There he warned the movement that the leadership in Dublin had taken a wrong course, was leading the faithful down the garden path of politics in the name of false gods. Those who became the Provisionals began to come together to contemplate options that did not become truly pressing until August 1969.

Billy McKee, a former O/C of the small Belfast unit, was deeply pious, deeply conservative on all matters of moment, unwavering in his dedication to the Republican movement and very doubtful about the new directions and the new IRA O/C Billy McMillen, a decent man but one with Dublin. McKee's generation was represented in the Provisionals by those very different in personality but almost identical in attitude and profile. Joe Cahill (b. 1920) was born on Divis Street off the Falls Road into a Republican family, had at the last moment escaped hanging in 1942 after he had been convicted with five other IRA men of shooting a policeman. He was another conservative Republican, parochial, working man – not averse to a pint and often less sombre than his Belfast colleagues who in turn were often less sombre among their own. Few Belfast Republicans had complex skills, much education, and none had property. Hugh McAteer had a travel agency but most of the others simple jobs. Steele had delivered milk as had Joe Cahill's brother Tom. Joe Cahill, who would be Provisional O/C of Belfast after McKee and then briefly Chief of Staff in Dublin, worked as a carpenter and foreman on construction sites until the Troubles. After that his life was the movement. Seámus Twomey (b. 1919), who replaced Cahill as O/C of Belfast and then became Chief of Staff, had worked as shop manager in a bookmaker's establishment. There were others, famous among their own, well known in Belfast as Republican. None looked much like a gunman: Steele aging and gentle; Cahill short, somewhat reminiscent of a garden gnome, once seen never forgotten in his pork pie hat; Twomey with dark glasses in a dark climate, bookie's suit, not one for the easy word in public but a convivial man with friends. There was from the next generation John Kelly, involved in the construction business, a man with a family, had organized Republican resistance to Dublin, organized resistance to the loyalist mobs, and had come to Dublin seeking guns from Southern politicians, an endeavour that led to the Arms Trial crisis involving members of Fianna Fáil – all found not guilty. Kelly became finance officer under Mac Stiofáin and continued to seek both money and arms, the twin basics for any campaign, for all campaigns.

Later there was Ivor Bell, like John Kelly of the 1950s generation, a hard man who would become O/C Northern Command, then rejected by his own, ended retired as a plasterer, and Brian Keenan, shrewd and haphazard, who was Twomey's adjutant and ended in an English prison that even Storey could not open. There were others as well – at the beginning more leaders than followers and then all leaders as too many recruits appeared.

The Belfast Republicans were not necessarily immune to new ideas, even at times to radical ideas, ideas often circulating in Belfast where imperialism and capitalism had demonstrably failed to produce an adequate life for those of no property; but they all believed as had the Fenians, that the core of the movement was the IRA and that concentration on physical force was vital. Obviously their faith could not be read on their face or often in their words. They looked rather like what they were, a mix off the Falls to be found in any pub, at church on Sunday and then the GAA matches. Almost without exception unlike many in their city, they were employed, often hard working but rarely in a position to do better. They were also conservative socially, pious, with close families and short views.

Most of all they were dedicated. The dream of the Republic was the single incandescent engine of their lives – they had spent individually years in prison, years being harassed, a lifetime of service without great expectations. At the very least they wanted fair shares. Like those in the countryside vengeance had charm. Like the city they were often dour and dark. Their accent was grating, unintelligible to many, their wit sly and local, a few wore the twin pins of identity – a *Fainne*, the gold ring that designated an Irish speaker, not easy to acquire in the six-counties, and a Pioneer pin that identified a total abstainer. Some spoke only in the accents of the local tribe and could be found in the pub on Friday. Most had families, often Republican wives who, too, on occasion ended in prison, and Republican children who would provide volunteers in the next generation.

If O Conaill and O Brádaigh were enormously different from each other, to the Belfast people they like most Republicans in the 26-counties seemed as one: soft of accent, genial on acquaintance, easy and for the dedicated, flexible in contrast to the Northerners, good people but innocent, without exposure to humiliation and deprivation and threat that came in a province run from Stormont. Even those who lived in the Republic, sound men like Charlie McGlade or Harry White, felt different, shared much with those still in Belfast. They, the Belfast people, the old generation and the next, would dominate the movement for a generation rather than those from the South or even volunteers from the traditional Republican areas of the countryside.

The third stream that came to the Provisionals sprang from the Ulster countryside of the North including the border counties. This was an area of secondary agricultural importance, often marginal land reached by narrow roads, a green land pocked with small market towns and tiny villages – a pub and post office, a school, a row of houses, a church, or two if there were Protestants as well. While the Belfast man was cute and cunning, sly with an urban arrogance, the countryman chose to be taciturn, seemingly slow, slow in friendship, slow in speech, and slow to change. Some was patina to confound those suspected, to defend against inquiry, but the man from Pomeroy in Tyrone or Crossmaglen in south Armagh had a Republican faith that was immune to time and disappointment. There was a determination to resist perceived oppression that stretched back beyond Wolfe Tone and the United Irishmen of 1798.

One of the early recruits to the Provisionals was J. B. O'Hagan who had business interests including a chicken-processing plant in Lurgan that would in theory have made him a conventional nationalist, have placed him in the small group of Catholics who did not exist on part-time work, miserable land, or the dole. He was a solid man not inclined to explanation or doubt. O'Hagan, however, was sound, uncompromising, all too familiar to the RUC. Another Northerner, Kevin Mallon, was in many ways the typical country Republican, intimate with his area, his family was involved with stock and horse trading, but from early on he had been concerned with the movement and was dedicated to physical force. He had participated in the campaign and been charged with serious crimes. He, like O'Hagan and the others, saw no point in the political direction taken in Dublin, a centre that seemed an enormous distance from Tyrone, even from Lurgan. Mallon was a physical force man not a strategist, not a manager. At a different time he would have led a column, been a ribbon man, moved from pub to ambush and on to the hills. Often less sophisticated, less exposed to the world beyond the parish than O'Hagan and Mallon, the Northern countrymen found the distance to Belfast and Dublin vast, a matter of years not miles, a matter of attitudes and loyalties. And Tipperary was far, far away. They, like all the Irish, were parish bound, saw differences invisible to most alien eyes, suspected the distant, the clever men from Belfast, the organizers up from the Free State, those who came from the far side of the hill.

Those who were Republicans before 1970, those who chose the Provisionals not the Officials were easy to pick out: their commitment was traditional, conservative, but most of all to the IRA – to the use and necessity of physical force. When O Brádaigh and O Conaill took the most faithful out of the movement to form Republican Sinn Féin, those who persisted with the Provisionals, despite doubts, despite the appeal of purity, did so because the secret army remained Provisional. The army came first even over tradition and the risks of politics. And when the peace process began, the ceasefires and the decline of capacity, they stayed on not only to provide an armed alternative to an unarmed strategy but also to protect the army, to maintain its power to continue, to effect the future if, as many suspected, the Republican would be no closer no matter how successful the Adams–McGuinness leadership. So there was Joe Cahill of one generation sent to America as authenticator and Brian Keenan of the next preaching militancy – both still operating under the Mandate of Heaven that did not yet extend to Republican Sinn Féin or a Real IRA.

From the generation that came into the movement after 1970 – mostly in the six-counties – a new tier of leaders had emerged. They did so swiftly because of the enormous escalation in the intensity of the campaign and so the size of the IRA. And the new generation of leaders differed in some ways from the old – but not in matters of faith. The two most famous were in a sense typical of the attraction and variety of the Provisionals in the 1970s. The first, Gerry Adams (b. 1949) came from a Republican family, became a barman on leaving school, and emerged from the Bone in Ballymurphy off the Falls Road into visible action by the time he was 16. He differed in two ways from many of his own: first he had radical social ideas and ideals, and second he had personal virtues that fit political success. He had a probing mind, a faith in consensus, no airs and graces and no doubt about the value of physical force. The second was Martin McGuinness (b. 1950) from the Bogside of Derry, who had first sought to defend the nationalist people by appearing at the door of the Officials in 1969. When he eventually arrived as a Provisional recruit, he found in the Derry unit only uncertain direction and divided counsels. Derry was nationalist by tradition while Belfast was Republican. In Derry for years there had been Seán Keenan of the 1940s generation to keep the faith but few others. Without the support mechanism of Adams' family and neighbours, McGuinness, without education or exposure to more than Derry City, emerged as a natural leader, idealistic, shrewd, ruthless when need be, cautious in operations and totally committed as a Republican with all the conviction usually reserved for late vocations. Mac

Stiofáin was delighted to have him in place in Derry. By June 1972 McGuinness had become a key Provisional commander taken with the other key IRA men, including Adams brought out of prison, to a conference in London with the British.

Adams would grow a beard, smoke a pipe, later have ambitions as a writer, could prove genial, was a natural world-class politician but in 1970 was on active service. Very early his talents were recognized. He had an inquiring mind and a hard core. He was given responsibility and pursued, as did so many Belfast volunteers, the armed struggle and a regular life. He married, had a family, moved swiftly within the movement, assuming greater responsibility, finally moving almost wholly into politics in the 1980s. In 1983 he won election to Westminster and would dominate the politics of the Falls by edging the old Republican-Labour man Gerry Fitt aside. He was famous, notorious in Britain where his entry was barred as soon as he lost the Westminster seat, still famous in America, where the government finally permitted him entry to New York for a weekend in March 1994 when he was media flavour of the week – a long way for a barman from the Bone. For the Unionists he was a terrorist, once and still, and to many nationalists in the Republic most uncongenial – the Provos unpopular with the conservative, the conventional, many everyday people, and always the radical Left often shaped by descendants of the Official movement. For his own his active service, his prison time, his commitment to the common ideal reassured all that any new agenda, any political programme or peace process would not be a betrayal as it had so often in the past.

Adams was in a sense the next and logical step for Belfast Republicans. In an era of radical language – 1968 was the year of the guerrilla – Adams saw no conflict between Irish physical force and global directions. The civil rights demonstrations echoed Paris and the United States, the Vietnamese war internationalized even Irish issues for many of the young – through television Belfast was part of the whole flux, not just a backwater. The media made the city, the IRA, the Troubles famous, a stop on everyone's terrorist tour, and the Sinn Féin office on the Falls Road and Adams a crucial attraction.

Adams never felt reason to jettison conventional Republican assumptions about the nature of reality. This is what the Officials had done – chosen models over reality, the map over the terrain. Adams was a physical-force man and also a radical, a true believer but one willing to convince others. As he aged his grasp of the content of politics and the means to organize policy grew but the commitment to the armed struggle remained – no conflict apparent.

Quiet, sincere in conversation, he was also articulate on a platform. He could make even the most horrid, bloody blunder reasoned, turn aside questions about his IRA membership without offending, move the discussion in his direction. Adams as a spokesman possessed both the desire and the capacity to explain, felt explanation necessary and so did not rely on the traditional responses of the faith, reiteration of historic grievance, adamant on policy and expressed doubts about all but the true believers. The Republicans traditionally had neither explained nor apologized, resented the need to conciliate those who should be avid supporters. In fact they were reluctant to associate with anyone outside the movement; even those eager to be allies.

Adams recognized early on that the legitimacy of the gun was insufficient asset to maintain the struggle. In prison he planned the restructuring of the IRA in response to the rising effectiveness of British counter-insurgency tactics. It was, however, his more visible political leadership of Provisional Sinn Féin that after the hunger strikes in 1980–81 transformed the party from claque into political asset that proved most notable. As a member of the Army Council, Chief of Staff and visible Sinn Féin leader of the North, he came to dominate the Provisionals along with his ally McGuinness. McGuinness, in fact, become synonymous with the IRA, for over a decade the dominant figure in the armed struggle, Chief of Staff, Director of Northern Command, exemplar, a cheerful and conventional exterior that masked a fierce dedication and a ruthless determination to deploy force effectively. And in time he, too, became involved in political options when force no longer offered prospects. In 1986 they had replaced O Brádaigh and O Conaill without a major split and with a considerable display of political cunning as the new generation came fully into power – but only after 15 years. The lessons learned then proved useful in carrying the movement and the IRA with them in the new directions of the 1990s.

McGuinness was in many ways less articulate but more visible, more sincere in Republican matters. Tall, handsome, married with a growing family, a full-time politician when in Derry, he was patently an idealist, a doer not an ideologue nor really a politician. He was exemplar and manager and most of all faithful to his own, to the IRA, to the ideals of the movement. Like Adams he was a physical-force man, a gunman who unlike most of the others looked exactly as an Irishman should, red hair and freckles and roughly handsome, growing a bit bald as the years passed. He conducted himself as any parent would want – honest, honourable, accepting responsibility rather than seeking promotion, He was increasingly the visible face of the secret army. Certainly McGuinness was concerned with the ultimate Republic, with the ideas of radical change, with negotiations and politics but always as an army man which gave the new direction great credibility.

In a sense Adams and McGuinness continued to dominate the movement even when they were replaced formally by Kevin McKenna from Tyrone as

Chief of Staff. The others served their time and departed into retirement or prison or sullen exile. Mac Stiofáin was arrested and eased out on his release. Joe Cahill spent his tenure in Libya. Eamon O'Doherty, a former British paratrooper from Tipperary who was more concerned with active service than movement management, had lasted just over a year. Seámus Twomey served twice before and after O'Doherty but ended up in Portlaoise, an Irish prison, while his right-hand man, Belfast man Brian Keenan, ended up in an English prison and ultimately on his release back at the centre of the IRA circle, representing the hawks who stayed within the movement instead of seeking to form a 'real' IRA. After this Adams–McGuinness and their generation controlled the movement, weak in the South, strong on the border and in certain Republican areas, and always cored in Belfast. The turnover in the Belfast brigade was constant but with the advent of Adams and McGuinness the leadership was stable. The old timers were going.

Jimmy Steele, the milkman, had died early in the campaign and tens of thousands went to his funeral. McKee had a job in a hotel in the Republic and John Kelly in Dublin had been edged out by Mac Stiofáin who in turn came out of prison to find no role. The movement had moved North, did not want a return to his dominant hand, so he retired to Irish and scrabbling for a living, He recovered from a severe stroke in 1992. O Brádaigh, badly injured in a car accident and hampered by illness, was back in Roscommon, came weekly to Dublin to run Republican Sinn Féin. O Conaill, who died unexpectedly at the age of 50 on New Year's Day 1990, had returned to teaching in Dublin and remained active in Republican Sinn Féin. Eamon O'Doherty went to New York and then for awhile opened a book shop back in Ireland, and died in 1999. Twomey until his death lived in a council flat in Dublin. Bell was in internal exile, O'Hagan was back in Lurgan, and Mallon lived in Dublin. Joe Cahill served Sinn Féin at headquarters on Parnell Square in Dublin. The others served, if at all, quietly.

The new generation was out of sight within the galaxy ready to move into the Army Council into Sinn Féin, a different but similar generation, harder, more flexible, no more inclined to compromise and conciliation, Republicans all, still. They would be joined in Sinn Féin by still another generation, mostly in Northern Ireland, of the young eager for radical Republican politics – and some of these would rise rapidly on service and talent but not within the IRA, which attracted only a few – and most of those for clandestine operational purpose. The IRA grew static and Sinn Féin vibrant but both still shared the ultimate agenda and so the revealed truth.

These Republicans, obscure or notorious, were hardly typical of a pollster cross-section of Ireland, even perhaps of the Irish of no property. The faith inherited or discovered was unevenly distributed, more to be found where grievance was real and where example existed. Within the movement, the competent often found opportunity that Irish society denied them. They lacked credentials, lacked realization that ambition was spur not waste. Irish society, Irish Catholic society especially in Northern Ireland does not abound with optimism, encouragement to excel or institutionalized opportunity. Every American child is told he or she might be president and some so believe, believe that they will be star basketball players, doctors, or rock stars. Most are content with the everyday but the prospect exists where it does not in Ireland.

Thus for some the Republicans supplied not only service but skill – and not always in subversive matters. For example, Gerry Adams proved, given the opportunity, a world-class political leader: in Manchester he would have risen in the Labour Party or in the Bronx found a broader stage than as barman. Others, like Rita O'Hare, a Belfast woman who was severely wounded on active service, found a career in the movement, became editor of *An Phoblacht* and then Director of Publicity, had opportunities that would not have existed in a normal Northern Ireland. This was true of many even if the career had risks often only found on active service: Maire Drumm from the previous generation (b. 1920) was a Vice President of Sinn Féin when she was murdered in October 1976 by Protestant paramilitary while in the Mater Hospital. Some Republican careers had no civilian equivalent: volunteers who succeeded in the import–export business by transporting arms or entered the movement's diplomatic service and negotiated arms deals abroad or the new volunteers who learned to structure complex operations or deploy scant resources against a professional army. And when the agenda changed and Sinn Féin offered a way forward, there was a new wave of younger and more sophisticated talent. These often were joined by those who had used their long prison terms to get credentials – Belfast often seemed filled with former gunmen holding degrees, often advanced degrees, in the social sciences.

Prominence and opportunity often came to those who would never have found another route to achievement of any significant sort. Those who remained gunmen might have done well only in the secret army, lacked the appropriate skills for a formal military career and certainly for a conventional civilian life. Many without prospects found that their services had a taker in the movement, learned on the job, demonstrated that credentials are often overrated – the authorities could never decide whether the IRA was a collection of incompetents or a ruthless, skilled underground. Often, the volunteer demonstrated either case, often simultaneously. And politics proved amenable to raw talent, dedication, and commitment: a different sort of crusade could be organized by those long denied.

As for the IRA the leaders were in profile, in background, in expectations no different from the followers only capable of more responsibility. They had almost all started as followers, as recruits. Most had limited education, no great conventional skills, no focus of ambition, all were Catholics, most were men but not all, especially in Belfast. Increasingly they were younger and more radical in their views. This was especially true of those serving in Sinn Féin. Thus, unlike most other movements, those at the top were no different from those they led, but were rather survivors, unrepentant and persistent. They were in matters of faith deep and narrow, true believers; but in all else, composure and personality, mien and attitude, they varied, as did the Irish. Some were tall and some short. Some had odd accents or short tempers. All were more similar to an alien eye than in their own but in no way especially remarkable. An innocent introduced to the Provisional Army Council would be baffled to find their communality beyond the socio-economic similarity – at their meetings the seven could be organizing a county football match, raising money for a child's hospital bill, attending a session of a local political party instead of directing an armed struggle against the British. The IRA leaders are then ordinary in most matters, are various and often uncongenial, men of no property and often little conventional talent. They tend to take their conspiratorial background with them into conventional politics – although Sinn Féin is not really a conventional party but an aspect of a movement that holds the truth. The Republican leaders are not monsters but merely gunmen grown old but not too old and, survivors with some skills, those lumbered with administration. Others without careers in active service serve with them and are no different. What they all share in common is the faith and that shapes all else to pattern, not the other way around.

CHAPTER SIX

Organization

The Provisional IRA has always been special because of the longevity of the movement structure – an armed conspiracy with generations of organizational history. This inheritance was never seen as a matter of choice, sometimes as a responsibility, but mostly as desirable. With it came the legitimacy to wage war, even to claim the right to govern in the name of the Irish people. No militant Republican ever gave very serious thought to the particulars of the organization. When a rare change had been introduced – when Goulding had increased the size of the Army Council from seven to 20 for example – it was usually an indication that those in control sought to achieve specific policies through an adjustment rather than an expression of interest in structure. Only from time to time did the suggestion arise that the form of the movement – an army with outriders – might be reconsidered, might not be appropriate for the proposed Republican agenda.

For most within the movement, there seemed really no need for changes – although often GHQ recognized that in some ways the IRA form did not fit either the reality of the movement or the intentions of the leadership. When special tasks or novel directions became imperative, new forms might be co-opted or adjustments made; but the IRA as matrix remained as always. Thus in the 1950s the Sinn Féin party was co-opted as a political vehicle and the Wolfe Tone Society encouraged; but the IRA remained the core. Those attracted to Republican ideas found that unless they were a member of the IRA they were not fully accepted, not at the core of the movement. The organizational structure of the movement remained much the same decade after decade.

Thus the Provisionals did not carry another form into the armed struggle in 1970, did not rely on theory for guidance in establishing an organization or apply the fashions of the day. The Army Council did not even contemplate the organization's needs. Everyone knew what was needed: fill in the open slots, open up new units, get underway. The leadership assumed, not inaccurately, that what was needed was not time spent on new directions. The Provisionals considered themselves the real movement – provisional only in that a real Army Convention had to be called to authorize events. The faithful had been denied possession of the titles of an organization by those who had left the true faith – or were leaving – to pursue strange means and perhaps strange goals, but the organization was theirs, provisionally until the Army Convention made it formal. So organizing was directed toward the campaign as well as to controlling the system: much the same thing.

In a sense the IRA was always at war, always involved in an armed struggle even during periods of quiescence, always waiting to deploy as the legitimate agent of the nation as soon as the nation would tolerate a campaign. Thus those who left the Army Convention and later the Sinn Féin Ard Fheis in 1969 felt that they *were* the IRA. All that was needed was to give the old titles to the new reality. This was done – provisionally – in December 1969. A more inclusive Army Convention could be called once the faithful had been scooped up by the old nets, after communication within the movement was established. There would be an enormous job revitalizing and expanding the movement but none in reorganizing the structure. That structure existed in theory and soon in fact and was the advantage and curse of the movement's historical legacy.

THE ORGANIZATIONAL FOCUS

The core of the traditionalists from the first were outraged that they were described as a schismatic group or that their IRA was somehow 'new'. They were the traditional IRA with all its legitimacy, all its legacy, with the over-whelming responsibility to seek war against Britain – in this case through defending the nationalist people of Northern Ireland. The only thing provisional about those involved was that the first Army Convention did not truly represent the strength of the movement but only those available who could symbolize the potential. By the time that potential was adequately structured on conventional lines their IRA had long been labelled the Provisionals, the Provos, by all including many of their own. The same was true for those left behind who moved on with a new name. They were called the Officials formally and informally became the Stickies because in another new direction they affixed glue instead of the usual pin to the back of their Easter Lily paper rosettes sold to commemorate 1916. Gradually the Officials became less official and the Provisionals less provisional.

Within the Provisional IRA, the idea of organization was simply to fill out the familiar. This meant an IRA based on the constitution drawn up for the huge secret army that had dumped arms in 1923. This form had granted subsequent legitimacy over the decades to an organization that often bore little resemblance to the IRA of the 1920s. The form lasted as the organization declined. For some years after the introduction of internment in 1939–40, the IRA seldom had more than a few volunteers active – most were in prison or detention camps North and South and others inactive. Large segments of the movement were usually out of touch with any central direction command and tended to erode. The Republican movement emerged from the war years as a small, ghost of past glory. Growth and change was slow. The IRA form was enhanced by the co-option of Sinn Féin in the early 1950s as a political option to the planned military campaign, a campaign that showed no organization change in the traditional form. In the years after 1962 and the failure of that Northern campaign, the military structure again was unrelated to movement reality. In Dublin Cathal Goulding and others instead of discarding the IRA form as they moved toward conventional politics adjusted their agenda to it.

The Provisionals kept to tradition, organized as an army, elected representatives to a general Army Convention. By then the form was set for a decade – and because of the campaign no Army Convention need be held. With the establishment first of a Northern Command, long an aspiration of Northern IRA volunteers, and later a Southern Command, GHQ and the C/S grew less important. The Army Council monthly meeting was largely dedicated to oversight and GHQ to servicing the active service units. In any case, as in the past, the inner circle tended to be dominated by one or two individuals and their immediate colleagues. Turnover tended to be the result of arrests: one loses rank in prison.

Beneath the leadership are the military units with the Northern units again dominating consideration and their commanders often found on the Army Council. Belfast, Derry, and the border dominated the leadership not just because of the influence of Adams and McGuinness but because the active supplied those most likely to be given responsibility. Thus a typical Army Council represents the island as a whole, the active in particular, the Republican constituency in general, and is composed of both the responsible and symbolic – all managed with very little planning by the allocation of the seven places by the Executive. During the campaign when Sinn Féin appeared to move into a more visible and dominant role the hard men who had been attracted to politics served on the Army Council to reassure those suspicious of the political option. Once the unarmed strategy was accepted there was a balance of those fully committed – often four, often active and visible members – and three more dedicated to the priority of physical force.

All of this is the formal structure and the more formal treat it formally, using titles, dispatching memos properly titled, giving the secret army a patina to assure legitimacy. The adjustments, Northern and Southern Command or IRA conferences, were simply that – adjustments. The basic form remained the structure of the IRA from the Tan War. And with the new millennium it was still the structure of the secret army. The role and mission of the IRA might have shifted but not the structure.

No one in GHQ before 1969 wanted to jettison the existing structure. Goulding might foresee a movement not an army but he had matured within that army and saw no need to close it down. To do so would have caused a split with the traditionalists on a minor issue. Organization was a minor issue. The split came, as always, on the argument over principles and tactics, extending the mission of the faithful, over the implications of the revealed truth. Two very similar secret armies emerged. After 1969 the Officials were inclined to keep names and forms no longer needed in part to deny them to the Provisionals who were increasingly seen as neo-fascist, sectarian, conservative, green nationalists. As the years passed and a ceasefire was declared on 29 May 1972, the Officials kept the IRA as a parallel and eventually secret secondary form. The IRA became adjunct to the secret leadership rather than the core. The core of the Officials still ran as a covert conspiracy even as the movement changed to party, dominated by individuals who had recanted the old faith but still operated under its rules and habits. The IRA finally supplied useful services, the returns of armed robberies, mostly in the Republic, and minders and enforcers in Northern Ireland: there was for a long time a Chief of Staff and a Dublin unit but this was the last residue of a military past discarded. None of this bothered the Provisionals who watched the Officials' military capacity disappear along with the last traces of Republican legitimacy – a legitimacy that the Provos made sure was theirs.

For the Provisionals the structure of the whole movement was not simply the structure of the IRA. The movement was overlapping, often blending parts and cored within the secret army. This essentially military core was then deployed by the army leadership while the rest of the movement structures were subordinated to the demands of the ensuing campaign. For over a decade the role of Sinn Féin was to explain and to encourage, to offer opportunity for those not in the IRA and at times contest elections. The centre of the Republican movement was the Army Council that oversaw the campaign and the Chief of Staff who directed the daily activities. The purists felt that the Army Council could be considered the legitimate government of Ireland since the surviving members of the Second Dáil – the only legitimate Dáil – had transferred their powers to the IRA in 1938. All agreed that the IRA had the right to pursue the armed struggle and such pursuit had always been directed by the Army Council. Authorization came from the patriot dead, from history, not from votes or even the Second Dáil.

The Army Council tended to be dominated by two or three figures who in turn dominated the Executive and the selection of major commanders.

All the other groups beyond the military followed Army Council directions. These other groups, often with a life of their own, Sinn Féin, Cumann na mBan, the Boy and Girl Scouts, the welfare groups, were deployed as out-riders for the covert core. Some Republicans, some volunteers, had places in more than one organization, but all functions were Republican, blended into a single movement with different responsibilities and so often varying priorities. Everyone was comfortable with the results. And so the Provisional leadership had organized in 1970 without any serious consideration of the relation of the new events of 1968–70 to the old forms. The old forms were hallowed and comfortable and served. If someone had to go to America, someone, a sound man, was sent without need of a new form – unassigned volunteers were assigned, those needed were attached formally or informally to GHQ. Everyone knew everyone, at least at first. There were no problems with the familiar forms.

These forms often produced a certain Irish ambiguity. Observers often wanted to know specifics. What had been rendered to Sinn Féin and what to the IRA? How many members were on the books? Who was in charge of strategy? Who, in fact, was in charge? And in the 1990s the crucial questions remained – was Sinn Féin the IRA or a front, a dominant factor; what was what? None of these questions had an easy answer for they were con-siderations that did not trouble the Republicans for years – everyone in the movement was in charge, if some more than others. Thus Ruairí O Brádaigh was a member of the Army Council, governing body of not only the secret army, the IRA, but also of the Republican movement with all its parts, and he was also president of Sinn Féin. He thus spoke from beneath two hats but rarely felt uncomfortable. The Army Council did not feel the need for membership rolls – those who were volunteers knew that they were volun-teers; those that were not knew their role anyway. In theory the movement was a garment without seams – and more often that not the consensus held. When Sinn Féin became more important, more independent, division between IRA military concerns and those of the political wing were often exaggerated. The movement ran on consensus made articulate within by the Army Council and without by Sinn Féin. Disagreement, in any case, was almost always on details not direction. If there was tension between political and military needs, this would have been true no matter what the form. And in a war the military must predominate as it did in the Republican move-ment. When the consensus agreed to a ceasefire in that war, the movement made every effort for tactical reasons to separate Sinn Féin from the IRA: old service went unmentioned by the candidates and organizers, the party had to consult with the IRA, the visible spokesmen increasingly distanced their party from their past associations. And in fact the role of the IRA had changed but at the Army Council core the balance of the movement's mission was still determined.

The secret army had always had other than military tasks even if the form was that of a real army with brigades and sections and each volunteer was a soldier. A unit might be a covert armed cell, a neighbourhood action committee, an intelligence asset, a branch of a political party, a distribution network – all manner of things, all necessary to wage war. As O/C of Derry Martin McGuinness could be found pasting up a poster, visiting families, organizing operations – all aspects of a campaign. Thus O Brádaigh with a generation of service felt no confusion about role or responsibilities – nor did his successor Gerry Adams. In any case the leadership seldom had time to worry about the structure of the movement – unless and only when the campaign was hampered militarily by the existing IRA form. This did not occur for some years, in fact rather the reverse was the case as the old IRA structure proved ideal for an escalating campaign, a growing secret army. What the threatened nationalists needed was a secret militia army and this was what the IRA form offered.

What the nationalists wanted, what the Republicans could provide, was an armed, defensive militia maintained by an underground support mechanism beyond easy reach of the authorities. This was just what the Republicans had in place in theory and increasingly in fact after 1971. Thus Belfast was a brigade area with a central GHQ and the city was divided geographically into three battalion areas covering the nationalist areas. Within these three areas the units were sited at points of particular strength and enthusiasm. The maintenance of this militia proved a congenial and traditional task – if one enormously difficult: arms to be found, training to be given, leaders to be discovered, Stickies to be isolated, dumps established and communications maintained. The enthusiastic who could not be harnessed as a specific military asset were given a supporting role. Someone, everyone for a time, had to be involved in all aspects of the campaign: Sinn Féin duties, commemorations and parades and demonstrations, fund raising and publicity, tutoring the boys in Fianna and controlling the agents sent abroad to structure support in the Diaspora.

The only great difference, when the period of provocation faded into a conventional campaign, was that more of the structure became covert – and the numbers were larger. Everyone no longer knew everyone for the first time since the 1930s. Specialization had occurred by 1972–73, for the army was too large for each to be involved in everything. Then as the impetus shifted from defence to offence the security forces escalated pressure again transforming the Northern Ireland arena. At this point in 1973, the active army began to be reduced in size by circumstances so that the new specialization at times remained more as title than accurate description: the intelligence officer again had other duties and the local volunteer was also involved in intelligence.

When security pressure increased the size of the IRA, active service decreased, the units were isolated – the cell structure real but more a sign of the times than a means to keep the organization impenetrable. By the late 1970s the army was mostly secret – the authorities assumed that they knew the crucial 400 volunteers – key in arenas of strength where the units were often traditional names. Neither the hunger strikes, the politicalization of the 1980s, nor the new strategies of the 1990s greatly changed the size and structure that had emerged at the end of the 1970s.

THE STRUCTURE SOUGHT

What the leadership of the Provisionals wanted in 1970 was exactly what they got – a clone of the classical IRA. It was their ideal. Getting what you want is often no great challenge nor even advantage: Che got his Bolivian *foco* but such an ideal in practice did not work as promised in theory. In Che's case the theory might well have been an inarticulate screen to disguise his commitment to a course of action that could hardly have a militarily or politically successful end. In Malaya the Chinese communists shaped a communist army but the ensuing centralized control, politically proper, handicapped the guerrilla campaign. Often the form, however labelled, is determined by existing arena conditions: Grivas or Begin could only deploy the very few. In 1936–39 the mufti in the Palestine Mandate simply encouraged the natural bent of his Arab followers to ambush, arson, and riot, and thus needed no real organization, needed only issue explanations for the violence.

In the case of the Provisional IRA, not only did the leaders manage to fashion the ideal form in 1970 but also discovered without surprise that this ideal form fitted the arena, the objective conditions, worked in practice in 1971–72. What an IRA campaign needed was an underground militia cored in nationalist areas supported by militancy on the island and in the Diaspora. All this should be structured so as to make the involved participants into a great, historic crusade – first defenders and then Republicans – legitimized in purpose, form, and ideals. And all of this went without saying.

In fact the greatest difficulty for the movement was absorbing the huge number of volunteers, who had to be tutored in Republicanism as well as haltingly trained in military matters. The difficulty, however, that confronted the leadership was not the glut of volunteers but the problem of arming them. Even in the best of all possible worlds with lots of arms, most of the volunteers could not be deployed in Northern Ireland against the security forces. And almost none of those who lived in the Republic could be given a military mission. As an all-Ireland 32-county covert militia the movement had too many volunteers. And so many left only to be replaced by new recruits inspired by the events to the North. Over the years this revolving door gradually let most recruits out as the IRA, especially in the Republic, was run down in response to reality on the ground.

The IRA could only use a few hundred volunteers without a gunman overload. And no security pressure for long could reduce the small active units who had ample arms and materiel in hand and in stock and a second tier of volunteers eager to act. If all the active – all the 400 the authorities claim to know – had been removed at one sweep, there were ample replacements.

Thus the Provisionals had used a form in 1969–70 that fitted the strategic needs of the movement, worked objectively, satisfied the involved and reflected the social structures of the combat arena – and could evolve over time. Not only had the leadership got what they wanted as an organization but also that organization worked, worked in a particularly effective Irish way.

STRUCTURE ORGANIZED

What the Provisional movement had as structure was exactly what was needed to launch an armed struggle against the British, the never-failing source of all Ireland's political evils. Some other form might have served as well but none appeared, none was even considered by the Republicans. The Officials increasingly focused on what seemed lesser priorities but many in Northern Ireland still kept most of the old forms but could not compete as a secret army. When Seámus Costello split off from the Officials in 1975 in order to deploy the gun for something more than a means to raise money or intimidate local dissent, he set up a secret army – Chief of Staff, Army Council, the usual. Even the most transitory nationalist groups like the Trotskyite Saor Éire appeared in form more military than political. In Ireland the natural and declared form for revolutionary politics was a secret army – as the Protestant loyalists also demonstrated.

In any case the major thrust for the Provisionals was always the armed struggle enhanced by political action that would predominate only during an endgame when terms of success would have to be negotiated. Until then the Army Council focused on military options. If sufficient numbers of the

Irish refused to tolerate the campaign, then the IRA could not persist – thus nationalist competition mattered a great deal although the struggle could not be weighted by election results but only by the intangibles, the open door, the nod on the street, the barn offered, or the word given.

The greatest change in agenda and structure made by the Provisional leadership came with the recognition that the armed struggle alone had grown too narrow, circumscribed by the capacity of British counter-insurgency policy and isolated by the opposition of the establishments in Ireland and Britain. The British might not be able to close down the IRA but the campaign could never be sufficiently intense to win militarily. The first attempt to pursue an endgame during the truce of 1975–76 failed – the British sought not an endgame but to erode IRA militancy in hopes of a temporary accommodation. By 1976–77, the result for the new model IRA was pursuing an endless war with wasting assets. The IRA was smaller and likely to be further restricted. Even to maintain a respectable level of violence, every effort had to be made to escalate the campaign. The Army council realized that not all of these stratagems had to be military. To leave nationalist 'politics' to the conventional was not only to abandon part of the battlefield but also to risk an erosion of the legitimacy of the present campaign.

The way out was found when the movement and the Army Council reluctantly became involved from 1979 in the protests of IRA prisoners in the H-Blocks. It was necessary to adjust to an association with radical groups, with conventional political norms, with the requirements of elections and even parliamentary politics. The hunger strikes in the H-Blocks of the Maze prison plunged a reluctant movement, even a flexible Army Council, into active politics where power, not simply protest, mattered. By 1981 this involvement had produced a far more active political front on the battle-ground, a shift in priorities for the Army Council. The forms would stay the same but many of the new generation wanted the opportunities of action to be increased – and this could only be done politically.

To escalate the potential of Sinn Féin those who had come to the move-ment after 1970 wanted to enhance its political appeal by accepting seats in Westminster and especially in Dublin. The traditionalists, many of the founding fathers, felt that such a move would erode Republican legitimacy, deny first principles – and produce no compensating electoral results since the Irish voters seldom expressed concern on national matters but rather focused on entitlements and parish loyalties. The result within the move-ment was the split as the traditionalists hived off into Republican Sinn Féin.

The Irish voter refused to vote for Provisional Sinn Féin, just as predicted, but by then, especially in local politics in nationalist areas in Northern

Ireland, the Provisionals had become a major player in a game that some of the physical-force people felt might – or in some cases was – hampering the military campaign. There had always been some tension between politics and the military but even after the rise of Sinn Féin under Adams as a major Republican asset this tension was less pressing than observers imagined. Local power in nationalist areas, the evolving black economy, the publicity that followed Adams to Westminster, the option of service that politics offered, meant that there was no either/or struggle within the movement.

Over the years the movement had found forms to fit the new opportunities – and if all the opportunities foreseen had not been forthcoming the Provisionals had still found means to enhance the campaign. Sinn Féin with Gerry Adams as President and Martin McGuinness as one Vice-President could play a continuing and public role in the Northern Ireland arena – a role often misunderstood by those who saw Provisional Sinn Féin as merely or largely a conventional political party rather than as an aspect of a movement maintained by faith not structure. Public dispute between Sinn Féin and the IRA was rare indeed, since the central leadership was the same, but it did surface from time to time.

Internal disputes concerning the balance of politics and war were, as might be expected, continuous but not aggravated or contained by the nature of Republican organization. In the end the Army Council as well as Sinn Féin and all other Republican structures rested on a consensus – the same consensus that had reluctantly allowed those in Republican Sinn Féin to go, the same consensus that would decide the terms of any endgame. The long and often tedious discussions of the 1990s were neither hampered nor contained by existing structures. A consensus permeated the movement but did not arise from forms or agendas or votes – or often debates and conferences, all outward signs of the adjustment of revealed truth to reality.

The structure of the Provisional secret army had over the years changed for technical and tactical purposes. The IRA could not move upward and onward, escalate, transform their military campaign into conventional guerrilla operations much less the mobile warfare foreseen by the Vietnamese. Some in the Provos had begun to hope by June 1972 that IRA operational pressure would actually coerce British concession, that the British losses which surpassed those at Aden would not be tolerated in London. In fact the losses were tolerated and after July 1972 the British security response began to reduce the intensity of IRA operations. Hope, an endless revolutionary asset, within the IRA for operational success – not so much victory in the field as managing an unacceptable level of violence faded slowly. The truce in 1975 was the first real evidence that the thrust for escalation had failed, a most unpalatable conclusion. And so organizational matters after

1976 were adjusted to new and largely unpleasant conditions. This narrowing of the battlefield was a major factor leading first to the shift in IRA form and then in 1980–81 the commitment to Sinn Féin politics.

While the formal IRA military structure had existed from the beginning, operations had often determined the nature of the deployed rather than form. Many formal units were names given to neighbourhoods or a townland, many titles indicated only that procedures were being followed rather than actions performed. This did not change. The IRA became more concentrated, more covert, and often more efficient as time passed and on-the-job training improved skills. The creation of a Northern Command simply recognized the necessities of the campaign – and the Southern Command the marginalization of those areas away from the conflict.

Again by the 1980s everyone was often simultaneously intelligence officer and quartermaster, took part in an action, and sat on an IRA court-martial. The local units coped. The C/S and the GHQ were less important in Northern operations but did not really add a layer of bureaucracy since the primary mission was to assure that military missions were undertaken – and in the case of English and continental missions this meant direct oversight. Always what was needed overrode formality – everyone became involved if a bomb was needed in London, arms purchased in Holland, or volunteers to go to Gibraltar – and formality was often given to what existed. After the 1975–76 truce, the basic structure of the army was formally changed to recognize reality but not exactly according to the charts and graphs and programmes, and the same was true when Northern Command was established. The IRA had to fit the times not the organizational chart. In the late 1970s the new cell structure did exist – Belfast was no longer one big brigade – but secrecy was not really possible given the nature of the Republican movement. There were sleepers and quiet volunteers but in the core areas many knew or suspected who was operational. This was only less true in the countryside. This shift was as much imposed as fashioned by applying the new GHQ directives. The most effective means of action was reliance on locals, all known to each other – and at times to the security authorities. These men but rarely women embedded into their communities could be shaped to specific operations. Gradually the IRA outside Belfast assumed the major role in the campaign. And no change in form – no Northern Command – nor in mission – the endgame – greatly changed habit or increased capacity.

The countryside arena simply permitted more operations than Belfast where after a generation the nationalist segments were as much like a low-security prison as housing estates. In the country when new volunteers were needed, a few well-known lads could be trained. Some could even be dispatched on foreign missions by GHQ. When explosives were wanted, they could be moved from safe dumps elsewhere. Arms were shipped in, used, stored, and at times shipped further into Northern Ireland, ultimately to reach units in Belfast – the core. Some favourite weapons were kept in local dumps along with supplies needed for pending operations. The big dumps were often over the border as well as many of the full-time active-service people, for in the Republic security was more lax, and there were no Unionist eyes at every crossroads.

Direction and organization of the country units were often in the hands of full-time active-service people on the staff of either Northern Command or GHQ centred over the border. Thus operations were both local – planned and organized in South Armagh or mid-Tyrone. They were perhaps in line with general GHQ directives, perhaps not – or they were directly under staff control sited over the border. The mix was often difficult to categorize but full-time people were rare, local initiative high, operational secrecy vital even for those suspected of IRA activities. Efficiency improved only slowly, hampered by arrests, old habits, and a slow learning curve; but it did improve. Strong nationalist areas became bandit country and stayed bandit country no matter what went on elsewhere.

No soldier, no police constable was safe beyond the barricades, all the reserves were at risk all the time, no bunker beyond reach or vehicle assured free passage. The countryside might appear green and pleasant, the newspapers might seldom report incident but no place was secure and some very dangerous indeed for the security forces – and so too for the IRA.

The result was an operational mix determined by the shifting capacity of the security forces, the vulnerabilities of the chosen IRA targets, the skills and cover of the volunteers, and the luck of the arena. Operations in Belfast and Derry were more closely held by Northern Command and more restricted by security arrangements. The IRA on organizational matters had simply shaped their volunteers to the task in comfortable and so effective ways and kept all the old airs and graces that military titles gave to those from the countryside who old-soldiered for a few minutes a month.

In the towns the operational units having even more difficult logistic problems for the volunteers were usually clumped in easily observed nationalist council estates and the targets were fewer and better protected. The size and capacity of the units was determined by enthusiasm, opportunities, a few keen volunteers, and the coercion of the authorities – and the nature of the target. Some targets open to both rural and urban volunteers are easy of access but limited in significance. One or two volunteers can place small bombs on the Belfast–Dublin railway, but even major targets must be attempted by small units. In Northern Ireland any operation that requires more than three or four volunteers becomes complex, does not feel small at all to the involved. In fact considerable results can be attained by even two volunteers in a car loaded with explosives or one or two snipers, although in both cases the chain up to the action includes a great many more activists. One shot fired on a country lane may involve dozens of Republicans, some not on active service.

In Belfast the city is cut by barriers, traffic flows through choke points, even then unmarked cars and hidden army observation posts make any target difficult to approach and all targets safe from major assault. The IRA adjusts by scaling down operational size and so scaling down opportunities for active service. Much active service no longer consisted of an ambush or car-bomb but intelligence, preparing entry, protecting withdrawal, planning and maintenance and security. These became sufficiently dangerous and difficult that they constituted the service many volunteers seek where once in the days of large-scale operations they were thought subordinate tasks.

Over the course of the campaign, most IRA operations abort, more often than not in the city, too often for most commanders in the country. Most units plan and wait and cancel and plan again. All of this has imposed a structure not unlike the cells proposed and announced in the past. The major purpose of the small unit, even one drawn from outside the target location, is to permit operations in hostile conditions. And rarely have conditions been so hostile as in Belfast where a vast monitoring machine, computer-linked, technologically elegant, is fed by the military, the police, and the loyalists. Suspects are under constant observation – the whole nationalist population in hard-core areas is under constant observation. Arbitrary and random checks are routine, computer-generated investigation and searches are the norm. There are surprise road blocks, listeners in pubs, tapped phones, automatic photographs, long interrogations of the detained or arrested, searches of records, and debriefing of patrols. All this means that the IRA's urban organizations must be cunning, deceptive in their patterns, small, and experienced. And this they are, with the newer volunteers working their way into more responsible positions as attrition slowly provides operational opportunities. Such opportunities are sufficiently rare that the urban campaign by the 1990s was as much symbol and threat as reality. And once the ceasefire was negotiated on-the-job training ended and so capacity declined – as the renewed campaign revealed.

Operations in England where an Irish accent creates suspicion and the authorities have invested a generation of concern, great technological capacity, and considerable cunning, still take place. The IRA units are not resident, are sent for a specific operation or series of operations and each faces a variety of obstacles, some hardly recognized. The result, however, has been spectacular: Downing Street mortared, truckbombs in the city that did billions of pounds of damage, Prime Minister Thatcher – and much of the Conservative government – nearly wiped out with a bomb in Brighton. In many cases the units were organized as they had been from the first: a small group dispatched from Ireland to find their own way around the obstacles and pursue operations as long as possible or planned. In many cases capture was the result of luck not cunning, but as far as the IRA has been concerned in England, if less so on the European continent, the organizational means used in the bombing campaign of 1938–40 with all its advantages and risks proved as valid in 1974 or 1994.

The organization is thus shaped not by the IRA constitution, the chart on the wall, nor by the formalities and titles that the commanders will relate if asked, not by the cell plan or any plan at all, but by the nature of the arena, operational needs and possibilities, the personal links between the activists, and the practices learned on the job.

TYPOLOGIES AND UNDERGROUND REALITY

The structure of the Provisional IRA no longer fits any real pattern. There are only so many ways to organize covert, illicit gunmen and fewer if the gunmen must operate in the countryside. If all rural radical guerrillas in the 1960s in Latin America were not clones of Castro, most of the *focos* were just that, to fit the pattern. On the other hand, most of the clone *focos* never matured or like Che's merely persisted until destroyed. The other rural guerrilla movements, no matter how radical in theory, if they persisted, evolved into rural columns defeated by the centre, usually by recourse to terror, or into institutionalized guerrillas isolated in the wilds but secure because the centre does not want to invest the resources necessary to impose order at the margins. Those who sought action in the city were often spectacular but seldom attracted a second generation or eroded the capacity of the military. There were only so many guerrilla options in Latin America although often more than most, more tradition, more cover, more historical grievances but no more success – one Cuba and one Nicaragua.

The Provisionals are in many ways an organizational mix typical of most national liberation struggles. These armed struggles are usually a combination of responses to particular tasks. Many campaigns are often dominated by rural guerrillas – the wilds provide cover, allow the movement to persist but only at the margins. So many armed struggles have had the guerrillas as hero that the man in the black beret with the AK-47 has become a universal symbol if not always a military asset. Thus Colonel Grivas consciously organized some EOKA guerrillas in the mountains as much as gesture as tactical asset. Mostly, the classical guerrilla campaign that begins with a focus in the countryside seeks to move to the city. Most fail, but not all – China is the great example and there is Cuba and Nicaragua. So, failures or no, the heroic guerrilla concept is maintained – even the IRA volunteer who appears in view for only a few moments in a country ambush may do so wearing a black beret and a purchased paramilitary coat. Such images, however, seldom impose order on an armed struggle – if so they tend to do so at great cost to the rebel. In Rhodesia African guerrillas dressed in paramilitary costumes were inevitably victims of their own desire to be recognizably legitimate and so leave boot prints on the trail and present uniforms as target points.

What does tend to impose organizational form regardless of the location of the armed struggle is a specific idea about ideologically or strategically appropriate configurations. Communist rebels want appropriate communist forms – usually take them underground, for most communist organization is focused on purely 'political' matters. The forms, of course, may determine the strategy or like that of the Provisional IRA be amenable to shifting tactical options. The IRA simply preferred legitimacy and habit but found that the movement and the secret army could expand and contract, be made to work in the hills of south Derry or the lanes off the Falls in Belfast. What had been an alternative, orthodox army of national liberation in 1921 and fought a conventional if irregular war the following year before going underground in 1923 was simply adjusted as the years passed to effect as the needs of the movement shifted. At times in the hard years, there were hardly enough volunteers to make up an Army Council and yet in 1971–72 the form was adjusted to permit escalation and after 1976 adjusted again to permit persistence in difficult times. Further adjustments came with opportunity, pressure, and a shift in mission but none that transformed the legacy of the past. The inherited system works.

The IRA as secret army then is neither urban nor rural, ideologically neutral, an organization shaped by historical accident and the inarticulate realization that the greatest asset of the movement was the legitimacy to use physical force to secure the Republic. Thus a movement driven by an army was natural – and a comfort in difficult times. That the IRA was never really an army after 1923 but rather a nationalist revolutionary movement with command centred in the military was accepted but ignored. The major and special purpose of the movement was to deploy force. Pretensions of legitimacy, the right to rule, were voiced, but the key was physical force. The Fenians had won the right to use force and the volunteers of 1916 had deployed it in the name of past generations as well as the Irish people and this was what the IRA had for generations sought, sought so that the secret army would perform its allotted mission.

This IRA structure was seldom replicated elsewhere beyond the island because other movements came later, had more fashionable models, chose ideological sound forms. Those without interest in the radical fashions in structure who wanted to be a military organization chose different forms – the Irgun Zvai Leumi in Palestine or EOKA in Cyprus may have entitled themselves military organizations but were a small group of gunmen isolated from their political power centres. They were not the core of a great move- ment, although they claimed a grand constituency, and they were not a secret army whatever their title. The Provisionals claimed to act for all Ireland. In a sense they were not a national liberation movement but a legitimate institution representing a Republic. The volunteer was a Republican soldier not an Irish rebel. So politics was largely incidental to the Provisional organization until the opportunity to escalate the general struggle by political means during the hunger strike occurred. Even then, in Ireland the core was military and the armed struggle is *the* means to power. All else will follow the gun. Elsewhere, whatever the claims along the way, legitimacy could really only come with victory. Power for the IRA truly flows not from the barrel of a gun but from its use and the Provisionals' structure reflects that assumption adjusted to arena conditions. Only when those conditions were perceived to have changed radically in the 1990s was a way perceived that would offer the Republic on the instalment plan and not by recourse to force: it was an option that did not appeal to all but could be debated within the existing forms and procedures.

COMMAND CENTRE

The IRA Army Council is the core command and yet the Army Council is largely a validating organization, seldom meeting more than once a month during the campaign, reviewing options and prospects, dealing with matters of finance and discipline. During the peace process it was a key arena of balance but not always the core of the debate. It almost never votes formally, rather authorizing and recognizing the initiatives that arise from the independent units or from the staffs. And if there is to be a vote, it is largely a formality to allow dissent a statement. It is mainly concerned with moni- toring IRA GHQ and Northern Command, where there is more overlap than might be apparent and less conflict than would be assumed.

When Northern Command was established, the control of the armed struggle was largely in the hands of Adams and McGuinness in any case, so they and the structure worked in tandem. Since consensus and local initiative play a very large role in IRA tactics and for all intents there are no strategic decisions to be made except to persist, control at the top is seldom exercised and so seldom a contentious matter. The debates over the ceasefires and the progress of negotiation have been essentially a search for consensus.

In the past, even with a very strong Chief of Staff, as with Mac Stiofáin, local units had considerable operational freedom. With less control at the top, this freedom often allowed tactics and so the pace of events to be determined for the most narrow operational reasons. As long as these reasons related to escalation and then persistence, there was little complaint. Bungled operations or those considered sectarian caused problems – especially for those who must answer public questions, face public complaint; but again GHQ found it hard to complain about audacity or to question Republican principles in sound volunteers, even those killing innocents or Protestants.

In any case, no one was going to be able with any effect to tell the Republicans of South Armagh to restrain themselves. Commanders of a secret army rarely give orders unless they are going to be obeyed and even more rarely punish zeal. The involved usually insisted that the innocents were an accident not intended and the Protestants members of the opposition were not innocent or the man punished by kneecapping a danger. And dirty unconventional wars were always filled with mistakes and the Provos struggle at the mercy of those who controlled the media. And the media, as far as Republicans were concerned, always blamed the IRA volunteer but never the victim – a part-time reserve constable but a full-time spy, or a retired UDR man but still at work, Protestants only incidentally.

So the form that allowed tactical freedom had costs and benefits, but most of all no organizational adjustment seemed likely to increase the latter and reduce the former. The war would still be dirty, mistakes made, the media hostile. Why tinker? Those who supported the armed struggle did not believe the media in any case. And so a secret army worked as well as any form and worked as intended and so ground zero remained first the Army Council and then the two or three important operational commanders – the C/S, Officer Northern Command – and others.

Thus the organization of the IRA: Army Convention, Army Executive, Army Council, Chief of Staff, Northern Command, Southern Command, and other units is real enough; orders go out from the top – again no order sent that will be disobeyed – but relate more to pace than to direction. The command structure is focused on marshalling resources to maintain the campaign, to respond to competing priorities within the movement, and if possible to seek tactical ways to escalate. Those involved, whatever their titles, have long and intimate contacts with most of the senior people in the movement, many of whom have no title and no formal place on any chart. They often offer means of action outside the formalities of the structure. Much of IRA armament for years arrived without formal direction and increasingly outside the control of the Quartermaster. With the re-establishment of the Libyan connection control came back to the GHQ – hardly anyone noticed the difference, only that there was new gear, AK-47s instead of Armalites, and Semtex to boot.

All undergrounds have a real central command, one man or a single committee; and the IRA is generally dominated by a few at the centre, usually on the Army Council, who are advised by those with titles and those without. Most of these men, always men, have known their colleagues much of their lives, may not be friends but are truly one of the same congregation. They have moved into authority not so much out of ambition as necessity, their position more necessary service, not a reward. They, like all, may be prey to ambition, to personal faults, may be limited in talent or vision but all inevitably are sound. The Provisionals have gone through several periods of command, but for well over a decade have been directed largely by the Northern generation of 1969–71, a mix of Belfast and Derry and the countryside with a few lesser, often token, individuals involved. The debate over the peace process has not generated much change at the top, only a balance of attitudes, a new consensus among the largely like-minded.

Even continuity is conserved. In the years since 1968 there have been only two serious command splits. The departure in 1986 of those who formed Republican Sinn Féin as a result of a mix of principle, generational conflict, and Northern direction, and the withdrawal of Ivor Bell, an O/C of Belfast, O/C Northern Command, and for a time Chief of Staff, who resigned from the Army Council because the armed struggle was not sufficiently intense. He had felt, and was not alone, that the leadership – the command centre – was not fully focused on the major purpose but sidetracked by other fronts. He carried almost no one into opposition. Bell was court-martialed, discarded, isolated. The militant were momentarily rewarded by increased campaign operations and command central moved on still dominated by those Bell had called a failed Army Council. Other divisions, even those over the ceasefires in the 1990s did not lead to resignation and withdrawal: in considerable part because all had agreed at the beginning that the foundation for the future would be an agreement not to split: all began with a consensus to continue. And so the leadership led the movement in and out of war and back and forth to the bargaining table.

What remains curious and special about the IRA is how few commands

Command Central gives. The faith tends to supply almost all the answers, even the tactical and technical answers. The commanders do not as much command as oversee and build a consensus, engage in the diplomacy of control. It is an army with remarkably few orders. The IRA Army Council devotes a substantial amount of time checking that those operations are possible rather than determining what they should be. All aspects of armed struggle come under the provenance of the leadership and so the leaders have to see not only to the maintenance of the armed struggle – the arms and money and comfort – but also to the morale of the movement, the support of the people, to the details of administering not a party but rather a movement: and with the changing in role and mission after 1993 oversight of the endgame strategy.

The IRA fits neatly on a chart from Army Convention to the local unit but the chart is not of the real world. The Republican movement is even more difficult to chart, for it is composed not only of sound individuals, some few on active service or within the IRA, but the many fitted into visible roles as voter or subscriber as well as those individuals who contribute not just secretly but rarely. An effective chart of the movement is a chart of degree of faith and sacrifice not of formal organizations. A member of the Army Council may be less significant than someone quite out of sight who handles the money or controls intelligence. The real structure arises from capacity and responsibility and faith. Who is who in this movement, what is the real shape of the Republican movement is knowledge acquired over time by those who will or do lead. It is for this reason that formal credentials are of less significance in the covert world than the conventional might assume. The Irish Republican movement as a galaxy is filled with the dust of the faithful that lights up only on rare contact or when a spectacular occurs at the core. It is also made complex by the invisible force fields of past service and present commitment.

In reality the Republican universe is organized by the intensity of the fire at the centre of the faith, the engine of the movement and so the armed struggle, that attracts those who can be measured by their service, the risks taken, the returns guaranteed, the faith displayed. The O/C of a brigade may be a transient parochial figure, bold, ruthless, effective for a time; but the old farmer living at the top of the lane with 50 years of service in the faith is the never-failing source of local strength, a voice of wisdom as well as a safe house, a man who has spent the coins of his life on the Republic. The latter belongs to no party, subscribes to no journal, appears at no commemoration, nor has money for the dependants of the prisoners, but is far closer to the centre of the movement, far more important, and forms the very foundation that has allowed the Republicans to persist.

ASSETS ARRAYED

Because the Republican movement depends for persistence on the invisible assets of the faith of individuals, a conviction passed on by example and proximity, often the visible structures are not what matters. The crucial organization is not an Army Council or even a secret army but the arrangement and disposition of the faithful that allows the involved to act. At the very beginning with the Provisional IRA, numbers do not matter nor equipment but rather capacity. What can the IRA do and how often and under what conditions? The IRA may have thousands of members but not be able to organize a raid on a barracks or car-bombs in London. The IRA during the 1975–76 truce was not the same as the IRA when the truce dribbled away, but was not greatly different. The departure of Republican Sinn Féin changed nothing. Yet, the endgame meant readjustments in operational matters: capacity had declined and recruiting and commitment.

Again with a core of the dedicated who possess appropriate skills, the IRA might devastate London if there were to be a decision to return to the military options – but not to organize the extensive campaign of disorder and persistent operations that once existed. Capacity changes with both the intensity of the faith and the arena. It took only a mix of access and a long-term timer, a few not especially competent volunteers and determination to bring the Grand Hotel in Brighton down on the British Conservative Party on 12 October 1985, nearly wiping out the government and almost killing Prime Minister Thatcher. A very few determined volunteers can cause havoc even if they are not formally organized, formally educated, adequately trained. Of course, the IRA, like all organizations, is inclined to want more, more arms and more volunteers, to be a grander organization replete with titles.

It is, however, possible for convention's sake, like the police and security forces, to estimate size, weaponry, funds, and capacity – if not intention and certainly not the hidden assets. The formal map is not wrong, need not even be misleading but is very limited. The formalities, the IRA and Sinn Féin, the Americans in NORAID who gave money and the subscribers to *An Phoblacht*, can be weighed, measured, and charted. The informal organization of the movement is not as amenable to charts and graphs, works secretly in the hearts of the faithful, and so is rarely visible. Even those within the movement often have as little idea how to structure such a secular faith as analysts have in depicting it. In effect, when examining the Republican movement what you see you get but you also get far more that cannot be seen. And what is not seen often does not exist but may soon, rather like an electron that may appear but only at an unpredictable location. In Ireland the faithful are scattered, devout in varying degrees, real but not readily weighted. They are the crucial black matter of the movement, the invisible dust that provides the necessary bonding and the required matter so that the faith can be sustained.

The commitment to Republican ideals is the most important asset of the movement. The Army Council must then organize in ways to encourage the commitment, to offer opportunities to sacrifice and to serve. With the endgame and the shift to political priorities the assets were shifted as well: Sinn Féin became the cutting edge, the means of service. Both have often had more problems than solutions for faith is elusive and existing structures not ideal – functional, mostly effective but halting.

ACTION AND FORM

It is most difficult to describe a dream working. This, however, is what an armed struggle is in fact. Certainly it is what the Provisional IRA is – a dream working. The faithful have for generations accepted that only through recourse to force will the ideal be achieved and during the present endgame have to accept that while this for the foreseeable future is not possible, much can be gained on the instalment plan. The commitment to the Republic is stable but the means engenders varied individual responses: to rely solely on physical force was always a comfort, assured for each Republican generation an argument over ends and means, principles and tactics, that also was a comfort. The form that survived was the one inherited – and so too most of the disputes.

During the years 1980–81, when the Republican movement and much of Irish opinion was seized on the struggle in the prisons, the dirty protest, the hunger strikes, the confrontation between Irish aspirations and British assumptions, the nature of the form was almost irrelevant to the action. The action that mattered was in the perception of the involved, first those in the prison, then those touched by their dedication or opposed to their campaign, and gradually out to most observers. What mattered, even what was happening, was what was perceived by the involved from those dying on hunger strike to a news commentator in Los Angeles or Berlin.

There was very little visible organization – obviously the IRA men and women in the cells had a traditional organization and obviously the Republican institutions outside prison – the newspapers and the active service units and the friends abroad – were involved. Clearly the impact of the strikes and the Republican response produced a still greater broadening of the battle front with the arrival of Provisional Sinn Féin as a vehicle for action, as a means of acting on events rather than explaining policy and reassuring the committed. The impact of the hunger strikes was shaped by a simple reality that the Republicans shrewdly exaggerated and transmitted by recourse to traditional institutions and practices. The Provisionals organized monster demonstrations or great parades, and posters, and the single great gift of the movement at the ceremony when the dead is transmuted into martyr at an IRA funeral. They did not organize the black rags fluttering from telephone poles all over the island, the arm bands worn by those who the year before abhorred the Provos. They did not organize the public graffiti or the private anguish – that was structured by the reality of the faith so many had thought irrelevant, denied, obsolete.

In a sense the exploitation of the hunger strikes was not so much a rush to organize the novel but rather an exploitation of what was always claimed – the nation. The hunger strike, a matter of shame and sacrifice and the power of the powerless, could easily be explained by recourse to the values that Republicans understood – and so in time did the others, the Irish. The Republicans could organize outward and visible rites of this faith: a funeral march or a gable-end painting. What happened indicated that the movement was driven by rules and assumptions that were only haltingly reflected in formal structures. What is there is not all that is there. And what cannot be seen is the force that drives the movement and the armed struggle and the endgame.

CHAPTER SEVEN

Command and Control

More than almost any other underground movement, the Irish Republicans are structured as an army with all the other agencies in one way or another controlled by the elected representatives of the military. The leaders emerge from the ranks. In theory, on form, the lines of command and control are obvious and real. The General Army Convention meets to decide major matters, allow an exchange of views from all-Ireland, and engender enthusiasm. If there are logistic or occasionally internal problems an Army conference performs the same function. In practice, excluding the first meeting after the withdrawal from the Official Army Convention, the Provisional Army Convention has almost never met because of the times. The Army Convention did formally convene in 1970 to legitimize the organization of the still provisional IRA – an IRA that became known as Provisional even as it evolved, as the leadership planned, into the official IRA. Another Army Convention met to support the end of abstentionism, long the cutting edge of orthodoxy and which had been the formal breaking point in 1969 when the Official controlled the votes just as the non-traditionalists did in 1985. The prospects of an endgame in 1993 meant times had changed and so the role of all-IRA institutes. Conventions and conferences were used to achieve a consensus.

The General Army Convention does not meet more often in theory because of war conditions, but in practice the Army Council has felt that there is no need and some risk at bringing together so many of the faithful in one place. For the much smaller Real IRA after the Omagh bomb in August 1998, the Army Council could not even meet to declare a ceasefire because security surveillance was so tight. The risk for any Army Convention is only in part security, for discussion and contact might lead to dissent as well as consensus. And dissent is throttled as swiftly and as quietly as possible: Ivor Bell's grievances in Belfast were smothered in a quick reaction that left him in exile and his allies quiescent. Minority dissent on the new direction in the endgame has not been welcomed. As has almost always been the case, an Army Convention organized by the existing Army Council is congenial to the existing leadership so the security reason is not simply self-serving.

There is in Republican history exception to any rule, so that the 1938 Army Convention permitted the campaign people of Seán Russell to take over the IRA but largely because the moderates felt that they had no compelling alternative to hand; a generation had exhausted the practical and the possible and left only the desperation of the implausible and impractical. So the IRA embarked on a futile, low-level campaign. Any Army Convention risks dissent unless consensus is assured before the meeting just as was the case in 1969: a majority, real or contrived, is not consensus. Thus the endgame conferences and conventions have been part of an erratic, occasionally reversible process toward a full commitment – not necessarily an enthusiastic commitment – to the new course. The power of the argument is that no one has an alternative that offers more than risk and sacrifice for no gain.

The endgame meetings were thus somewhat atypical of IRA experience but not in matters of control. The General Army Convention meetings like the 1969 last joint session, the provisional organizational meetings, and the 1986 abstention vote that led to a split and the withdrawal of Republican Sinn Féin were controlled, democratically perhaps, by the leadership. In IRA history this has nearly always been the case, delegates carefully chosen, some not invited. There may, indeed be opposition to the direction of the leadership but always minority opposition. The General Army Convention is a means of validating a direction and inspiring enthusiasm – and at times a stage for schism that in theory leaves legitimacy and the dream behind when the dissenters depart. In the discussions of the new direction during the 1990s, the crucial purpose of IRA meetings was to avoid a split even if a consensus could not yet be found. New volunteers came on the Army Council from time to time for new purpose.

Over the years losses on the Council and the Executive were replaced by co-option as the IRA Constitution authorized. Prisoners lose all rank if not always all influence. Individuals lost by arrest or resignation were replaced either from the members of the Executive or by obvious candidates – often those who had served before. In 1986 at the Army Convention, the majority leadership was re-elected, their policies were validated, and a decade of leadership recognized. The dissenters thus departed as schismatics who would not accept majority rule nor recognize that times had changed. Their arguments that the argument was a replay of 1969 and that no leadership had the right to violate principle – they had no right to do wrong – could be discounted because the Army Council had made sure that their own policies were supported by a consensus – as well as by a majority. And having learned this lesson the leaders of the new direction in the 1990s were determined that there would be no split: if the movement and the IRA could not move on to another strategy then they would wait and argue, use conferences and logic until the volunteers and the faithful accepted the reality of the peace strategy.

In sum, then, the IRA has been run by a closely held centre that has co-opted congenial talent and regional barons, kith and kin and those with a singleness of purpose. The individuals bring with them certain talents and experience but also represent certain constituencies within the IRA and within the movement, not always the same thing. In the 1990s the new direction generated new alliances and alignments, new strains; but the old command structure worked quite effectively. The leaders used what was to hand to address the most serious Republican questions.

Those who did so, those who had arrived at the centre of the circle, were often not the best and brightest, but the most faithful and representative – and sometimes too the most talented. Too much talent can generate suspicion in a conservative, working-class movement suspicious of airs and graces and well aware of the contempt expressed by most of Ireland's educated concerning their own pretensions and limitations. Formal talents, certificates and degrees, are rarely offered by the recruits – even in the great influx of 1971–72. The articulated and certified Republicans often found a more effective role above ground, the first sacrifice being access to a military career. The movement as a whole offered those with great talent and little scope opportunity. The result by the end of century was a pool of highly competent, deeply dedicated, increasingly experienced political talent. The opportunity for raw talent, for the clever, was often more readily found in Sinn Féin than in the IRA but not always. Still, the Army Council, more than the political leadership of Sinn Féin, has been composed of leaders no different from the shrewdest and most competent of the volunteers. And at the centre these few, largely the same few, made the decisions for all.

When the break came on abstentionism in 1986, the movement had long 'decided' that the old leadership would have to go, but peacefully and without leave to pursue their own armed struggle. The Army Council felt that to persist, to find new ways forward, old postures – even old moral fortifications – had to be discarded. So those who would be Republican Sinn Féin withdrew from a consensus that was cored in an IRA convinced that the political option was valid as the armed struggle continued. Many sympathetic to the dissenters simply stayed with the IRA – the more who stayed, the less appealing the old traditions. And many in the new generation had come to accept – not for the first time in Republican history – that the old traditions were handicap not advantage. So few walked out of either the IRA or Sinn Féin.

To command, as is done, through consensus, the leaders, especially at the central core, must represent properly the movement. If Belfast is too dominant, then Tyrone must be represented. If the tone is too radical, a conservative must be co-opted. If too many volunteers prove too opposed to the unarmed strategy, then they must have representation on the Army Council. Some of those chosen are present mainly as symbol, for the armed struggle can in the end be directed at the top by only a very few. And these few, absolutely dedicated, generally represent not merely their generation, their priorities and agenda, but everyone, no matter how special their statistics. Mac Stiofáin was an Englishman from Leytonstone, north-east London. He had no Irish connections and was not a Catholic. On the other hand, from the previous Republican generation Seámus Twomey, twice Chief of Staff, was a hereditary Belfast Republican – and so too were his wife, neighbours, and colleagues. And from a completely different generation, so too was Gerry Adams. None who has been at the centre of the circle conforms to any special personality type: some are amusing, some glum. During a Northern campaign more have been from the North, most are in mid-career – a career, a lifetime, dedicated to the movement.

The first Provisional IRA generation consisted of those elders who had been active as young men during the 1940s reinforced by a few 1950s volunteers. These were generally thought to be 'Belfast men' – Seámus Twomey, Joe Cahill, Jimmy Steele, Billy McKee, and John Kelly – but also included many scattered throughout the island from John Joe McGirl in Leitrim to Paddy Mulcahy in Limerick. They shared failure, persistence, schism, and scepticism, were limited, parochial, narrow, and sound. They knew each other, if not well, for the campaign years 1954–62 had not deeply involved all of the Republican faithful, especially in Belfast where the 1940s generation was supportive but seldom asked to be active.

The next generation, those who had been out in the 1950s campaign, formed a smaller pool; some, some of those thought best, went with the Officials. Others had found careers elsewhere or were not even in Ireland, and in any case the IRA in the 1950s had attracted only a few new volunteers.

In a sense those of the 1940s who had been tempted by politics or practicality did not re-emerge in 1968–69. Some of those in the 1950s who had given up hope reappeared – John Kelly and then Ivor Bell of Belfast or O Conaill in Donegal – and some had stayed the course like Ruairí O Brádaigh and Seán Mac Stiofáin who moved away from GHQ. The leadership pool was small and often out of date. Of course, the Provisionals in 1969–70 were also small and many thought out of date. No matter, those immediately available selected each other for the first Army Council. They would represent the army to come as they represented the sound Republicans of the army that GHQ had led astray.

This Army Council was typical of the subsequent mix of talent and representation often with individuals known only to their own: Mac Stiofáin was Chief of Staff, O Brádaigh became President of Provisional Sinn Féin, Daithi O Conaill, who was a campaign hero, Paddy Mulcahy, the sound man from Limerick and Seán Tracy from Leix – and Joe Cahill and Leo Martin of Belfast. This was a mix of the convenient, the representative, and the available from two generations.

The strength of the early Provisional movement arose from the vulnerable in Belfast. The sound men had emerged, Steele, Billy McKee, a pious, narrow, physical force man – everything the Officials wanted to discard, their old campaign friends in Dublin like Harry White and Charlie McGlade, and the rest – more leaders than followers. These were not only the godfathers, the first generation leaders, but also at first hewed the wood, carried the water, did the work – and were delighted for the chance to do so.

The next generation of commanders, the first career Provos, arose from the recruits who were at first largely inspired not as much by the mobilization of the civil rights movement as by what followed: the pogroms of 1969 and so service in the emerging Provisional IRA. Only a few saw civil disobedience, largely in the hands of the educated Catholics and a few Protestant friends, university students, political activists, not the unemployed from the estates or the small farmer's son in Fermanagh. What moved the potential volunteer was the threat to the nationalist community and so the desire to defend. And the only prospect was the IRA. Once a volunteer the new recruit was also a Republican. Some of the new men, hurriedly recruited, hurriedly trained, improperly motivated did not work out – were not sound and so were discarded. Those who stayed generated leaders as well as volunteers for the active-service units. Escalation, internment, the hurried organization of units, the necessity for effective on-the-job-training in command and deployment had all produced momentary heroes, spectacular and undisciplined gunmen, neighbourhood legends, adventurers and opportunists as well as the sound men for the future. These recruits became devout Republicans. Along the way many dropped out. Some were killed or forced to flee south. Many ended in jail, often to emerge still in the movement, disciplined, determined, self-educated in theory and practice, in tactics and techniques. All told, over 2,000 young men and women, and some not so young, passed through the movement in the early years, some very quickly indeed. They provided the pool of talent that by 1972 saw the new generation accepted as leaders with places on the Army Council.

Because there was a formal military command structure and most volunteers wanted to be soldiers not gunmen and had been converted to Republican aspirations, they took comfortably to the traditions of command, found control congenial. The IRA's consensus represented them as much and soon more than the faithful in Cork or Dublin. Such a consensus was hardly noticed; in fact the dynamics of underground command simply made sense, went unnoticed by the new volunteers: this was the obvious way matters were arranged, a mix of formal order, unarticulated consensus, small group rewards and penalties, the power of the faith and the intimacy of the neighbourhood. It was also how Ireland beyond parliament and the law worked. Ordering the Irish about is not productive and command within the IRA fit the habits of the tribe.

At the same time as the new were being absorbed the balance in the IRA shifted, became more representative of the emerging Provisional IRA rather than of the organizing fathers. The profile of those at the central core of the movement, those on the Army Council or soon to be co-opted and those in significant operational positions – who directed rather than acted – shifted in composition. The leadership became younger and those from Northern Ireland grew in importance. The shift at the very top was slow but inevitable because of the focus of the campaign. Further down as the Provisionals expanded rapidly local leadership went directly to the competent volunteer. And increasingly the Northern units became central to the focus of the movement. Belfast was ground zero even if the C/S was in Dublin and the Army Council met south of the border. It would be a decade before GHQ moved to the border, Northern Command dominated operations, and those within the Irish Republic beyond the border were marginalized. In the 1990s Southern Command often had a Northerner in charge and the Army Council five or six Northern-border members.

Not everyone might be happy with this, with Belfast as command centre not on paper but through campaign focus; but there it was. Those in the North were the ones engaged in pursuing the war. It was in Belfast that the struggle was most violent and then along the border. Those who took the risks by right should make the rules. So when Mac Stiofáin was arrested he was replaced as Chief of Staff by Joe Cahill, one of the inner circle of Belfast Republicans, and then Seámus Twomey would serve twice before and after Eamon O'Doherty from Tipperary, the last significant leader beyond the active-service arenas. The new Northern generation of Adams-and-McGuinness took over by the 1980s with only Ivor Bell of the 1950s as a hold-over. In the countryside along the border the IRA leadership was represented on the Council, but except for the odd Kerry man for 20 years a small circle of those from the north led the IRA.

For the new generation the war tapered off at the border while for Dublin that is where it began. Soon Dublin was a way station, a day trip for the leadership looking for money and comfort. The border counties continued to grow in importance, first as an operational as basis and then in time also as the only area of political support in the Republic. As the IRA campaign continued on and on, many new people emerged as well as some forgotten ones who added continuity but still created a different active universe and so different command imperatives.

The creation of a Northern Command in 1976 was in part an exercise in nostalgia that gave Northern units something that within the movement they had long wanted. Leo Martin had been the proposed O/C of all Northern units in 1969–70 when those units were notional, but Northern Command under O/Cs like Ivor Bell or Martin McGuinness was a reality not because the IRA had been reorganized but because those individuals were dominant figures. As always, the IRA was commanded by the few. One more overlapping command centre would have clogged conventional command, but for the Provos it provided necessary linkage, reduced the needs for GHQ to be involved in many Northern details – worked well enough since the appointed O/C was a dominate leader in any case

Northern Command was really an unnecessary formality in that the six-counties by the time it was established already dominated the movement. GHQ became more closely associated with maintenance. And the Army Council dominated by Adams and McGuinness oversaw the campaign – a process that required a full-time commitment, travel, and internal negotiations so that the organizational chart was confused on paper but simple in practice. Those at the centre did everything to maintain momentum, ease dissent, and further the cause.

The rise of several new Belfast commanders, Ivor Bell, Gerry Adams, Bernard Hughes, Seán Convery and a constant stream of first-rate local operators like McGuinness in Derry and the activation of new units in the countryside changed the face of the campaign. By 1973 the third generation was in place and the first declining. The Provisionals were increasingly campaign-heavy in command and so no longer all-Ireland in orientation: the leaders were focused on the war not Ireland. Still, a balance was achieved that recognized the new and the old, history and the campaign, and included three generations – the Belfast people, others in Northern Ireland and the border counties, and then the units from the South, those active in Sinn Féin and those whose capacities or personality imposed them regardless of the need for representation.

The Southerners forced into maintaining the army and political agitation became a subsidiary command factor in Republican terms. After O'Doherty was arrested, Twomey returned with Brian Keenan, also of Belfast, as operations officer. Then came the establishment of Northern Command and the rise of Adams and McGuinness. There was, still, resentment especially at Northern parochialism; but this was an island matter not a

Republican one. To a Kerry fisherman in Fenit the Belfast man is from Mars, accepted because of his Republican record despite his accent, habits, or appearance. In Belfast there were Brigade officers who had never touched a cow, walked in a field, been away from the city.

In Ireland these differences appear enormous – the distance one travels before being among foreigners is short; the distance across the country in time and in perception enormous. This meant the command structure had constantly to be regionally balanced, at least in concern if not personnel as well as cope with the inevitable disputes on the means to broaden the struggle beyond the Armalite.

What caused problems was the necessity to respond to novelty, to do today something different so that tomorrow would not prove disastrous. Much of the Republican universe on matters both great and small was as one – no need to adjust the ideals and assumptions of all were the same. This remained the case for a generation: the armed struggle was to be maintained and escalated. When the prospect of an endgame arose the old came under question. And there was a new generation involved – the political-Sinn Féin people, some with IRA experience, some without, some younger, and the rest colleagues of Adams and McGuinness. This generation differed in aspirations and analysis, in Republican careers – but rarely in basic matters.

The great truths had been unquestioned until the time came to discuss details. Could a united Ireland be more than a geographical expression? Could Ireland be united if the Protestants refused to participate? If the British were on the way out, was the armed struggle still justified? And if not was a ceasefire justified when there were so few returns? Those who discussed such matters were those in charge, the IRA of the armed struggle and the Sinn Féin people, a different mix.

Unlike an army with firm command-and-control based on education, class, seniority, and national purpose, the IRA Army Council had to represent as well as lead a movement. Control came through consensus. Command came after control was assured. Orders cannot be issued to a secret army unless they will be obeyed. The popular view that a disobedient IRA man will be hunted down and shot is romance: the IRA with an enormous enemy's list has generally eschewed revenge. One can resign as long as no information about the movement is divulged. The IRA does not want reluctant volunteers. And so any order, every order, may risk control. There is always room for schism and dissent but because of the power of the faith and the pressure of their enemies this room was narrowed. The endgame simply complicated all of these problems: in fact the 'problem' became one of avoiding failure signified by a split as much as deciding on a new direction.

There had been no schism until 1984–85 and very little dissent. The loss of those who favour abstention merely meant a loss of traditionalists, many in the South, from Sinn Féin. Ivor Bell's complaint that the Army Council was not sufficiently militant was stifled by the existing consensus carefully nurtured by Adams. With the first ceasefire, potential dissent by militants was very real. Those who had organized Republican Sinn Féin also were involved in organizing a military alternative under the aegis of the Continuity Army Council, limited in capacity but a magnet for the militant. Then at the end of the second ceasefire, the militant in South Armagh and the border decided to continue the armed struggle – emerging as the Real IRA under the aegis of well-known local figures. Neither new army troubled the IRA central command unduly for long because the Continuity Army Council lacked assets and the Real IRA collapsed after the Omagh bomb in August 1998. The two splinters, however, indicated to all the need to make haste slowly – increasingly difficult in 1998–99 when no progress was visible at all but the release of prisoners.

The IRA ran as always on consensus, took inordinately long to make a move that would engender dissent, ran without great conflict because the faithful need only look into their hearts to know what was right, acceptable, and thus were seldom in need of coercion. Bell had not prepared the way and the way that Brádaigh and O Conaill chose attracted few since the IRA would not split over an issue that no longer seemed vital. Nearly everyone, certainly those active before 1970, had been comfortable with abstention; but being comfortable was insufficient: risks had to be taken if the campaign was to continue and comforts had to be weighted carefully. Nearly everyone had agreed with Bell that more could be done but few believed that the armed struggle was a failure. And many understood why volunteers persisted in the armed struggle in the 1990s. But their time – for the moment – was past. Even the hard men of South Armagh accepted this, however reluctantly. The new direction offered prospects, bombs none. Most Republicans accepted existing reality – a struggle over consensus, a struggle to pursue advantage during the endgame, a new way to achieving the Republic on the instalment plan – especially appealing to those in the North who had always wanted fair shares first and thus the Republic.

For a generation the capacity to operate without direct control because the consensus remains valid at a distance can and regularly does mean that such operations are apt to go wrong – and that those at the margins may violate Republican principles for parochial purpose. The latter case – sectarian murder – is often difficult to punish since the act is usually aggressive and visible, and since authorization was by those difficult to replace as they are to discipline. The former, operational incompetence, is not novel in war nor easy to correct: talent is limited. As for sectarian murder the involved are in theory targeting British agents – loyalist paramilitaries or Unionist bigots – not Irish Protestants, if in practice this is patently not the case.

The typical response to a flawed military operation arising more often than not from inherent incompetence that results in the slaughter of the innocent or the murder of Protestants is an internal investigation. Audacity is difficult to punish. Accidents happen. The loyalist gunmen are acting against Irish and for British interests. The investigation has little impact on the future conduct of operations. There is a limit to what commanders of a secret army can control.

Those who rose to the top tend to understand their limits, the limits of control, the gap between the dream and anger, the ideal and ineptitude. Most of the Provisional leaders were cautious, both devout and slow to decision, cunning, careful with limited assets, eager to act but not to risk. Novelty was always a risk, for consensus ruled – tomorrow was like yesterday and no orders needed. Orders generate problems. And the IRA had ample problems keeping the volunteers attuned to the ideal and fit to operate. The first priority being by far the most dominant for the sound volunteer is more to be desired than a skilled recruit untouched by the dream. When the focus switched slowly to the political option after 1993 every care was taken by the leadership to hold to the power of revealed truth.

Striking initiatives, strange technologies, and insight into British psychology or the politics of others, all these are rarely displayed. They have been ignored in large part because the impact of a few determined individuals can have a disproportionate effect on the established order – and repeated efforts no matter how unimaginative will from time to time prove effective. The two great bombs in the City in London used 20-year-old technology and techniques – a South Armagh export item. The City operation did not need micro-management, many orders; fit tactical practice and strategic intentions worked.

Some revolutionary organizations are far more stringent, fearing resignation is defection, fearing an example will be set for further defection, fearing the denial of the faith. Such a secret army eliminates those who would drop out along the way – not the IRA. Everywhere, Ireland included, informers are shot if found, for this is the nature of a dirty war. In Ireland, informers who go public, fleeing to the authorities trailing their immediate family, are successfully protected by the British as long as they follow the rules. The IRA does not have the resources to hunt down such enemies – the desire exists but not the assets. If such individuals are foolish enough to reappear in Ireland they are targets. The danger from informers is only in small part the information supplied to the enemy. What counts is not control but the failure of the ideal to make an individual immune to temptation:

heresy is revealed. And to maintain command and control through the faith is crucial so that within the security of the Republican underground the apostate lies outside command and control.

A rebel army that has to convince each volunteer of every order will not last long. What is needed – and what as a result of a long heritage, previous campaigns, and a tactical ideology, the IRA had – was basic agreement on almost everything at the top as well as at the bottom. The Army Council almost never had a formal vote over a 20-year period. Mac Stiofáin, benefiting from a rising tide, a movement reacting naturally to opportunity, and an enormous sense of momentum, hardly found consultation necessary or congenial, nor overt dissent present. The interregnums under Cahill, followed by Twomey and then O'Doherty reinforced the need for a stable and effective command centre. This was managed for some time when Twomey returned. He was not authoritarian by nature, open to suggestion and new ideas despite his orthodox background and parochial career. The only real dispute was over the 1975 truce which he opposed but accepted, but for much of his tenure the IRA ran without need of great managerial skills.

On Twomey's arrest the IRA was dominated by Gerry Adams and Martin McGuinness with the aid of operational commanders like Ivor Bell in Belfast and those less visible in the country. There seemed no need of a General Army Convention. The Executive continued to represent the movement over time and the Army Council the existing balance. The campaign had been disorganized by the 1975–76 truce and then narrowed by the growing effectiveness of the British counter-insurgency campaign. The IRA accepted with reluctance that there was to be a long war but all the involved remained convinced that the will of the faithful would in the end win out.

Ulsterization was an attempt to shift the defence of the province from the British army to the civilian if paramilitary police, a policy that indicated IRA difficulties in engendering chaos and the British desire to lower the intensity level of violence. In fact the growing counter-insurgency skills and technology of the security forces, coupled with the exhaustion of the nationalist community, did establish what was an acceptable level of violence – as seen from London where the government seldom was distracted by Irish matters. There was thus, less for the IRA leaders to command, fewer to control, and a more challenging operational climate.

For over a decade the McGuinness–Adams tandem would dominate the command structure. The first generation had retired or died off, were inactive or withdrew. All were known, all watched, few able to help. Some, especially those always invisible, remained important, but all the early, public names went. Twomey was first in prison until released in ill health to drift from his council flat in Dublin until sent on tour and then dead. McKee retired disgruntled to Dublin. Joe Cahill, assigned to Sinn Féin duties in Dublin, often in poor health, served where he could. The Republican Sinn Féin people – Brádaigh, back in Roscommon, O Conaill, who died on New Year's Eve 1990, and some not so famous, had gone, and many of the old Belfast people were dying off. Jimmy Steele had gone early and Harry White gone along with Charlie McGlade. Some of the 1950s men soldiered on. Some went into Republican Sinn Féin. Others dropped out of sight, unassigned like Mac Stiofáin or uninvolved for years like John Kelly. A few remained in prison like Twomey's operational specialist Brian Keenan, until on his release he moved back to the centre of the circle and became a spokesman for those with grave doubts about the advantages to be gained from an endgame. The new Adams–McGuinness generation had weathered both Ivor Bell, Republican Sinn Féin, and the Real IRA, and for the new direction had represented militancy on the Army Council not in a new underground.

Politics before the ceasefires caused less IRA command problems than observers were apt to imagine since their sources were most likely to be within those whose service was through Sinn Féin and so political. No one spends all the waking hours and all one's hopes and fears on Republican actions that have no importance. The Army Council might well consider much done in politics and publications peripheral but those out there with a meeting to chair or a poster to design do not. And in the full glare of the media, when an election is won or lost, when there is visible excitement, when Adams wins or loses his seat at Westminster, there is a tendency to forget that the invisible Republican world is like the base of the iceberg. Sinn Féin is a part of the whole, an important part and not all visible, but not the centre of balance. The growing importance of the political focus meant real but slow changes. So the natural antagonism between war and peace, the general hope for an accommodation, the accessibility of the new Provisional Sinn Féin regularly lead to the assumption that the Army Council and so the IRA is seized on some political issue: the army wants this and the party that. Command is seen to be disputed or imposed. Even during the seemingly endless discussions during the endgame this is not really the case.

Since consensus dominates command, the Army Executive does little but act as a formal oversight board and a holding pen for potential Army Council replacements. It may even offer a seat as a reward for service and more often to give balance to the various factions. The Army Council is not a dynamic institution. The movement and certainly the IRA are not ruled by committee; in fact at times the movement seems barely ruled at all. Much is discussed but little needs to be decided. This appears to be the case after

1993, but increasingly the Army Council, the Army leadership, has been the arena for the strategic shift within the movement. Not since the 1930s has there been such a shift.

Within the IRA the rare crucial decisions are talked over and over until action is neither needed nor sought. The decisions are not so much made as moulded. This does not seem the case to the harried and often desperate men attending such meetings at some risk and facing enormous problems that are almost always without solution: no money, no momentum, no arms, no operations, always pressure and often failure, still no money, no votes, nothing big on the horizon. Each meeting every several weeks in someone's front room over cold tea and scribbled notes finds the same agenda, this year remarkably like last year. After 1993 the items on the agenda changed but the process did not.

The Army Council works by overseeing the general direction, by forming the central consensus to match the model, by inspecting the new and protecting the old. Each meeting's agenda contains both major concerns and minor matters, would provide no text for efficient management of most orthodox organization. Some very minor matters are simply seen as large at a given moment, this disaster or that operation, and others mean more than they seem, a funeral or an agent sent abroad. What is important within the movement, within the IRA at any given moment rarely has to do with long-range views, with strategy, often not with tactics, but with the pressing needs of the moment. With the new directions this became less the case although there are always basics. What is needed is more; more money, more gear, more reassurance, more action, more votes, more concessions, and always there seems to be less. The seven, assuming all could make the meeting, focus on the immediate responses, on morale and on details – no one can affect the direction of events in any case.

Military operations once completed had to be explained and rationalized by the visible leadership, often publicly by Sinn Féin. The experience was then incorporated into the wisdom of the moment by the Army Council. Many operations were so obvious to all concerned that orders are not necessary – certain targets were always on the list, others seem appropriate to the involved – and who in command wants to punish enthusiasm and initiative? Mostly no one needed ask. Saying no to South Armagh or the Third Battalion was no way to run a war. And when things went wrong, as was often the case, it was too late – the members of the Army Council learn about the operation on the television.

In disaster no one is at fault or rather those at fault meant to do better, meant no harm, may do better next time. War is war, mistakes are made, the innocent die everywhere. So innocent people were dead – in Omagh or

Enniskillen, next to Harrods, or down the lane. From time to time commanders exert very direct, very exacting control over operations – this was done in Derry City during the Provos' city-centre bombing campaign. At other times operations were worth setting up a special command, as was the case with the assassination of the British Ambassador in Dublin, Christopher Ewart-Briggs. Sometimes commanders were told to look in certain directions – toward Thatcher or to raise the pressure by bombing over the week-end. Sometimes the locals do what they choose, close down the Dublin–Belfast railway over and over – hardly a move to unite the island – because they can. Mostly, in fact, the local commanders are left to command as best they can.

What was not apparent during the campaign was that the price of unity and conformity within the Republican movement, a consensus on direction and control, was paid for with these operational blunders. The odds that initiative will bring operational success, an article of faith with commanders who must risk too much, in any case, are really very long. In the underground, in every underground, in Ireland, the favourite, the safe choice is still often disaster, even the long-shot often shoots the wrong man. The daring and the bold often open fire too soon, kill the little old lady or the nun on a bike. The cautious sent as replacement in turn fire too late and kill ineptly once again, unlucky too. Irish luck is notoriously bad. And the problem again is there is no solution to control at the margins. Commands won't change enthusiasm or instil discipline, make the inept effective or the feckless thoughtful.

It is not wise to rule operational matters by fiat, not in any case the Irish way where authority generates resistance and the ranks do not reflect real power. Among their own, the Irish can be truculent if driven. So it is 'natural' to structure on paper a firm and abiding command-and-control structure but 'unnatural' to impose that military structure on the real Irish. The instruments of command are used, instead, to control through shaping a consensus that influences the margins, does not determine or deter as much as suggest and encourage. What the volunteer wants is to sacrifice and, at first, the danger of risks, and always to serve, not discipline by rote and operations by the book.

Strategic and even tactical dissent often means schism – an end to consensus, a fragmentation of the imperatives of the dream. Like all revealed religions and many revolutionary faiths, Republicanism generates constant division as well as general consensus. Most change, most suggestion can be seen as a challenge to the faith, as apostasy. Consequently, most of the involved seek to raise or lower the level of dispute, tactical or strategic, principle or no. The majority wants to maintain the rules of consensus and the others, citing the faith, to seek a vote on the basics. A command can be refuted if it is a matter of consensus, if the faith has been violated.

Divisive tactical decisions unrelated to principles are so rare that they are readily remembered – the exaggerated role of the truce of 1975, cited by those from the next generation as the failure of the previous leadership, is the exception that proves the rule. The IRA is structured to assure control without command. There was actually a vote on the truce – and most in the army accepted easily the majority decision until a specific complaint was needed to harry the old guard. The vote, however, was special. The General Army Conventional almost never meets. The Army Executive almost never acts. The Army Council almost never votes, never has to vote, the whole purpose of avoiding a split is to avoid division. Everyone knows how the vote would go since the seven represented the state of the consensus. For a generation no one could remember more than one or two shows of hands in the Army Council that was more than a cursory bob to democratic procedures. The point of consensus is that votes are not necessary, thinking about votes is not necessary. Consensus means for the Provisional IRA a unity of purpose, seldom questioned, rarely noted nor remembered. Everyone knows what needs to be known, can command or obey without need of reflection or fear of contradiction.

PERCEPTION AND ANALYSIS OF CORE COMMAND

The key to the IRA's command has always been a few men, the Chief of Staff until the establishment of Northern Command and the dominant figures on the Army Council. This core expands when the campaign does and contracts, as was the case in the 1950s, to two or three commanders. The Army Council is as much concerned with oversight as initiative. The result is that the Chief of Staff and the Northern Commander, their one or two close friends on the Council, have tended to dominate the centre. It is the individual – Mac Stiofáin or McGuinness or Adams – that dominates, whatever the titles. In the extended endgame a careful balance of those enthusiastic about the new directions and those less so must be maintained. The number of those in and out of view who are important in policy matters and in campaign affairs over 32 years runs to about a dozen. The endgame allowed several political figures a new mission as their role expanded but the core remained small. The debates are often widespread, again especially during the decade of the endgame, but this is to shape a consensus not a matter of command. In fact during one or two periods in the campaign control was largely exercised as consensus when the centre did not operate properly for various reasons.

The centre of the circle is small and, given the risks and pressures, very stable. The view from the top then is narrow and consistent, arises from the dream, the Republican analysis of history, the legends and experience of the past, individual predilection, and the intrusion of reality. Those who have inherited the Republican dream are not by nature introspective, not concerned with models and ideas but with men and ideals. They are possessed by a special truth, valid for Ireland and for them. The implication of the truth is so obvious that none can easily imagine it is a special perception rather than obvious revelation. The Republican assumptions arise not from a universal or complex ideology but the parochial reading of Irish history. During the long campaign years, most commanders have lived so long within the Republican ecosystem that even the outside Ireland of the normal is a place to visit. Once there was a need to visit Ireland, to transform the scope of the arena, to circulate in sophisticated political circles, to negotiate in London and Washington as well as run for elections in Northern Ireland, the leadership, as always, coped using old forms and building on previous assumptions that the Irish Republican acts as everyone, everyone Irish, like his own.

Not only did the Republican leaders during the campaign not contemplate the nature of the faith at length but also the commanders of the armed struggle rarely focus on matters dear to strategists or conventional analysts. The concerns of the IRA command are operational and technical. The academic pursuit of strategic thinking is alien – the statistics of deadly quarrels, psychological strategies, even propaganda of the deed evoked little Irish interest. There was almost no strategic discussion – everyone knew, knows, the rules. And after a generation the campaign may have been broadened, other options explored, new techniques and tactics introduced, even many non-military priorities accepted, but the key strategic decision remained. Even the intense discussions about the new direction, the new strategy of the endgame has not greatly shifted military thinking in the IRA or operational commander's priorities. Once all are agreed on the basic matter – the armed struggle will continue until the British are gone or say they are going for in the end they will go because they do not have the will to fight forever. The hope of the command was to escalate and their fate has been to persist.

In fact, as the British increased the pressure with growing skills, advanced technology, and resort to counter-violence, they maintained an acceptable level of violence. Escalation has been beyond the IRA. So time and British skill has prevented an unacceptable level of violence in part because the power of British or English nationalism had been underestimated in the Irish equation. Violence, Irish violence offered rewards to the establishment as well as penalties. Thus the Republican movement could persist but at a level that did not effectively erode the will of the British.

There is no guaranteed tenure in the Irish underground during a campaign, little opportunity to speculate, no time at all. The security forces deny time to speculate, often even the opportunity to meet. When the shooting starts, time for the faith must be snatched and there is no time for analysis. The Irish did not pretend to be strategists in 1970. After a decade in 1980, they needed little further analysis. Thus a great asset for the IRA was that so much evolves from consensus and quick recourse to past experience: the job is done, the structure of analysis like the form of the secret army inherited. The political option can be explored in the 1980s without denying physical force. IRA Rules OK. And those rules are unwritten and so often unread. With an endgame, part of the struggle is over editing the past text, the received history, to fit a novel arena. Some commanders prefer not to make the effort; but those in control have forced the issue, pursued the new directions, shifted for even the most limited gunman the strategic terms of reference.

LIMITS OF CONTROL

The rules work remarkably well, hedge about the commanders with unarticulated restrictions and indicate proper directions. Any commander knows what is permitted and what is not. To err, as did Dublin GHQ in 1969, to lose touch with much of the movement, to make a virtue of the loss assured schism. In 1986 the new generations made sure that the consensus would hold, that only some would be lost, and so entered the General Army Convention after long preparation able to control the IRA and so Sinn Féin and so much of the movement. The new leaders did not impose a new direction but a new focus that would aid the campaign at a cost of some traditional Republicans and the abandonment of what some – and some still loyal to the leadership – had assumed was principle. The transition was relatively smooth because commanders sound in theory and campaign experience could offer old reasons and old habits as rationale for a novel direction that much of the movement suspected. Denying the use of physical force that led to the two ceasefires and the entire endgame was far more difficult. Yet from the first the decision was made by all at the centre that there would be consensus not a split. A split over the role of the IRA would destroy the movement – or the movement as structured in the 1990s.

At the top the consensus is the medium of the movement not a matter of votes. At the bottom the individual IRA volunteer often violates the edges of ideology or the consensus: elects forbidden targets or derives personal advantage from membership or remains truculent on the ceasefire. This is the price paid for command by consensus: the margins may do violence to the faith – and always in any movement there are individuals who merely serve time, collect one reward or another, get a gun, misuse power, fail to accept restraint, fail to deny themselves. Discipline is often slow and halting because control relies on the discipline of the faith. Ill-educated, marginal young men without skills or sophistication, armed, dangerous, often arrogant, easily or too easily step outside control beyond easy reach of commands – it is the price of control through consensus. And it makes imposition of new directions as difficult if as effective when the consensus gels.

STRUCTURE

There are three IRA structures of command and so control. The book version, evolved out of the Irish volunteers and the Tan War codified in 1926, is maintained in attenuated form shaped by the Constitution. Second, the actually informal structure of control: not all Army Council members are equal and local commanders vary in capacity and responsibility as do active-service volunteers, and some who serve only in Sinn Féin have risen to power within the movement. The IRA has always been something of a ruse, not a real army but one so taken by members and opponents. In effect some IRA units are at half-strength, some ghosts, and some hardy and battle tested. What matters is what can be done. All units in action are small whatever the book strength and the operational requirement is more apt to shape the unit than the reverse. Thus the commanders, intimate with their army, adjust structure to reality and rarely reality to structure. Finally, beyond the formal structure and the actual one used to wage the campaign is the actual power structure that drives the movement. The real Republican world of command and responsibility is more diffuse than the IRA Constitution would indicate or the operational needs of the campaign require. And with the endgame the IRA does not as easily command everything within the movement: Sinn Féin exists with its own dynamic, restricted by IRA concerns, but these are the concerns of the Sinn Féin constituency. And all constituents are not equal. No more than can the most political make physical-force people deny themselves without advantages offered, neither can the IRA impose a consensus. The IRA could and did break the truce only to find that without an enthusiastic constituency, the support of all in the movement and all sympathetic, there could be no effective campaign – perhaps in time no campaign at all. So before that happened, the physical-force advocates accepted a new ceasefire and a new direction. So there are all sorts of sacrifices, all sorts of commitments and careers and leaders.

DECISIONS

Someone, sometime, at least on occasion, must make decisions, choose among options. Even in a secret army like the IRA that nearly always agrees on all matters large and even small, someone must decide; but often no one does. The centre is seized on other matters, one man cannot run an entire army, the commanders are busy elsewhere. Decisions are divisive, easy to postpone. So in a campaign the margins decide on many operational matters within the assumed framework. Everyone knows the appropriate targets starting with Margaret Thatcher or her successor – John Major, a less appealing target but still on the IRA's invisible wish list – and on down through the military even to those who deliver bread to the British army or repair bombed police stations. Decision arise from local vulnerabilities noted by the active and at times targets selected for campaign purpose – more bombs this week or no shooting until next week. If the target is appropriate, the necessary assets can be assembled, weapons, car, planning, volunteers, and action taken. Only the disasters, a British army ambush or civilians killed or a great success engender discussion at command centre. Decisions are made by those close to the pointed end of the stick, often at the last possible moment – the target of the car-bomb not picked until the key is turned in the ignition. And at times the operation is set in motion long before the bomb detonates so that the rationale is unrelated to the current climate.

Tactical decisions come without great reflection from the centre: an escalated bomb campaign to emphasize a point, or more action in England now that an active-service unit is in place. The Army Council is as often informed about operations as asked for permission. And permission is hardly necessary to bomb Margaret Thatcher any more than to shoot a part-time, inevitably Protestant, member of the police reserve or to bomb the Dublin–Belfast railway. What is there to decide? There is precedent for nearly everything.

The crucial problem for the IRA and Republican leadership is that in the last decade of the century the precedents are not very comforting without severe editing. The political option has in the past generated co-option for those who gave up on physical force. Some flourished like De Valera and Fianna Fáil and some disappeared like the radicals of the 1930s, Peadar O Donnell, George Gilmore, Republican Congress and so to other 'Republican' initiatives. Thus at the end of a generation the leadership pursuing an endgame had first to convince all that this was not the past replayed as failure, that the past as previously imagined need not be prologue. The result was a novel and extensive effort to convince all, the margins and the militants, the suspicious and the traditional that the new direction was appropriate for the dedicated.

Thus 'political' matters subsumed for greater discussion than had operational ones during the campaign. Then military matters moved without fine-tuning. Without serious analysis, without reflection on the eventual implications – a bomb exploded after months of preparation can hardly be tied to the events of the previous week. In January 1991, the mortar attack on Prime Minister John Major and his cabinet in the midst of the operation in Iraq was in IRA statements linked to Middle East events: Britain has an Irish war as well. Actually the attack had been planned long before without thought of Iraq or consideration of any context but the prospect of success. The attack was 'obvious' – no decision needed – because the IRA people in London discovered means of access to Downing Street and an appropriate weapon. Iraq was simply tied in to the event – and to the delight of Baghdad who made contact if without effect with IRA agents. And the reverse may be true – the enormous cost of the two great bombs in the City led many to assume that British policy had shifted to pursuing contact with the IRA. There is always a desire to make the incoherent cohesive, the IRA a single action. This is true with nearly any complex operation and most tactical events that add to the noise of the armed struggle. It is true in the effort to weight and balance the fate of the new strategy within the Army Council or the movement. It is not that chaos theory runs but that Republican decision making is not amenable to conventional methodologies.

The IRA and the movement do make real decisions and do argue out past precedents, present needs, and future options – especially in the more conventional structures like Sinn Féin. Real operational decisions arose from opportunities at the margins and from reactions to pressure and events that require an Army Council response: an offer of a truce, the need to improve the political posture of Sinn Féin, the collapse of a truce or the offer of a ceasefire, the chance to discuss covertly matters with agents of the British cabinet. Someone has to say yes or no, send an order, take command.

The Army Council does decide but not often and not much, rarely votes and has in a generation suffered only one or two serious defections. Mostly the commanders, conservative and harried, seek to avoid decisions, avoid change. Change is dangerous. Change requires decisions and decisions must be effective, accepted, or imposed. The fewer decisions necessary the better: and so the endgame has been painful.

CHAPTER EIGHT

Maintenance

Those in 1969 who took up the long march toward the Republic knew more than most that much was needed: far more than within their control, far more than had been available to the IRA during the previous generation. The Provisional IRA at least had ample exposure to the problems of the armed struggle; the daily obstacles had become part of Republican life so what came next would be no surprise: one of the few virtues of experience. Mostly rebels are content to begin, fire the first shot: the need for the next bullet would be discovered later. The IRA, on the other hand, felt they first needed bullets to be able to fire at all. To begin, the IRA needed gear if there was to be a defence of the Northern nationalists.

After August 1969, those who would form the core of Provisional IRA began to seek arms. A great many in Ireland mistakenly assumed that they needed *more* arms when in fact there was almost nothing and most of that in the hands of Dublin GHQ. Arms were the key. No one doubted that they could acquire the volunteers if they had the guns. They were assured of the commitment and organization, the leadership and the example; but there was no possibility of an armed struggle unless there were arms.

The lack of gear was, of course, the fault of all the IRA but the responsibility was that of GHQ. A few, like Mick Ryan, appointed quartermaster when matters were already hopeless, saw to the collection of bits and pieces after August 1969; but many of his official colleagues remained focused on political options. The Official IRA never solved the problem of arms. The Provisionals felt a greater sense of urgency: arms were the way into the future, the means to effective events.

Old Republicans had already begun looking beyond GHQ for arms, for arms money. In this they were not alone for some of the more nationalist Dublin politicians, those who could feel history moving, felt that the IRA might be exploited, manipulated to defend the Northern nationalists that the government could not protect and do so at the cost of renouncing their radical ideas. The tender offers to the IRA were, of course, accepted, something for nothing, money that required only a nod since once given the orthodox had no recourse to law and no desire to be exposed.

Between the Belfast pogroms of August 1969 and the end of the year provisional arrangements to take the IRA into a campaign, discard the political people at GHQ, and to find arms were being made by the traditionalists. Contacts with the legitimate politicians were merely an aspect of the confusion and turmoil of the period. In time those who detested the Provisionals would see in these arrangements a Fianna Fáil plot to summon up a secret army out of the ruins of the Republican movement – a call that if not made could not have been answered. Actually the Officials received some funds, bits and pieces, and went on their radical way while the evolving Provos without any interest in politics in any case found more promise than reality in official toleration and complicity. Those in power in Dublin, like those in Belfast, simply overestimated the reality of the Republican movement, accepted the myth of a secret army, trained, eager, organized ready to venture to the barricades once armed.

When the provisional Army Council first met in January 1970, the centre of the circle had little to maintain, little to distribute but enormous potential. Their avowed Irish constituency was active, committed. And already in Northern Ireland many militant young nationalists were seeking entry to the IRA – any IRA, not drawn by faith but by the arms that did not exist. The entire thrust of the Provisionals was to supply these recruits with guns and so create momentum toward a real campaign. All organizations, all assets, all concerns was focused on this process rather than on the validity and nature of the anticipated armed struggle. No one had to consider the broadening of the battleground or non-military options for there was time only to seek arms and money and organize the arriving volunteers.

REQUIREMENTS

In January 1970, the Provisional IRA would have appeared to need everything. There was a provisional structure, an Army Council, there were those already active, in some case before the actual break, a GHQ. There were those who as soon as touched would be active. There was a revitalized movement, partly structured by the loyal Republican organizations that had denied Dublin GHQ's aegis and partly awaiting the imposition of traditional forms. So there was enormous potential but little else.

There was little money but promises. There were few arms but prospects. There was the potential of the American Diaspora. And not written in any account book or much considered by the Army Council was the accumulated experience of running a clandestine movement. Nearly everyone involved was intimate with the obstacles that an underground would present, familiar with the subversive life. Whatever else, the IRA also knew how to make do with very little and do so under the scrutiny of the police. This was an enormous asset for the cost of secrets if not considered were factored into all considerations.

The Army Council foresaw the need to maintain a protracted campaign but little could be done until there was something to maintain. Underground the future is today – and the day of triumph. A secret army would have to be maintained for years. No one foresaw 20 years or 10, but most knew that to defend and to provoke would lead to a protracted campaign – a matter of years perhaps if not a decade. So from the first, the Army Council and the new GHQ sought more since more would always be needed. The shrewd knew that there would never be enough. This is always true for all revolutionaries even when there are tanks and heavy weapons, millions in the bank, sanctuary and diplomatic support. If there were enough, then there would be no need for an armed struggle. For the Republicans there never had been enough and often there had hardly been anything. And suddenly there was the prospect of everything that was really needed, support, mission, and operational opportunities.

RESPONSE

Beginning in August 1969 and without reporting the results to the official GHQ in Dublin, certain Republicans began to seek out arms and money that would be of use if there were to be a break. There was no point in finding money if it were to be used on politics not arms, no point in finding arms if they would not be used. Some local units suddenly brought up to strength after August 1969 began to seek out their own arms. Agents of opportunity left for America or began to circulate in strong Republican territory. Once the break with Dublin GHQ occurred, the Provisionals concentrated on organizing their existing assets in the traditional forms and seeking aid and comfort where it might be found. Everyone in the Provisional movement was tasked in one way or another – almost always in congenial ways.

What was done – and done automatically – was to shape the faithful into purpose. This was not a tidy process. The movement had no department of veterans affairs, no mailing lists beyond those taken away from GHQ, no computer-generated prospects. Many, most Republicans once retired disappeared, led normal lives, often disapproved of present directions. Some of these would remain loyal to GHQ for political and personal reasons. Many others could be found and co-opted. And many Republicans could not be found because they were not known. Organizational chaos was such

– and was to remain so for years – that some towns or parishes had two IRA commanders, often ignorant of the other, not to mention an Official competitor. The movement's components had been driven apart by defeat, recrimination, sloth, indolence, lack of purpose, lack of prospects, and a lack of compelling skills at the core. The Northern events acted to magnetize many of the drifting Republicans, who sought out their own and in time reached the attention of the Provisional organizers who were sweeping back and forth across the island in larger and larger numbers. And mostly those who were attracted to the movement were Republicans – the potential recruits eager to defend existed but the new GHQ relied mainly on their own.

The Republican movement was pulsed and again and again for assets. There was a limit to the money available through contributions so that soon more violent means were deployed if not recognized. Expropriation – armed robbery, theft, extortion – was an early and easy option. Some contributions were not always fully voluntary – the enthusiasm of the collector not without foundation being mistaken as intimidation. In the matter of arms, there was little to find, little to expropriate/steal, and nothing to be bought. Firearms are carefully restricted on the island and even shotguns and .22s in the countryside regulated. The IRA had few real dumps and they contained very old weapons and dubious ammunition.

The Provisionals' QMG and the Army Council knew from the beginning that the army would have to be properly armed with imports – dumps, gifts, confiscations, and theft from the security forces would simply not do and would offer diminishing returns. So from the first, agents were sent to potential suppliers especially in the United States. The GHQ–QMG suffered here from a lack of recent contacts, a lack of serious money, the fact that England no longer had many enemies who might be interested in harming the empire at minimum cost and their own innocence about the covert arms trade.

Thus the major response of the IRA commanders was to rely on their own and to seek, however haltingly, new friends and new alignments that would bring in arms. For some time arms and money so dominated the concerns of QMG that few had time for anything else. The first QMG Jack McCabe was killed in an accidental explosion when he was handling explosives in his garage in North Dublin – an indication that for some time everyone had to do everything, delegation was impossible without competent volunteers waiting for instructions. Those volunteers had to be organized, trained, deployed at the same time that McCabe was trying to fashion materiel for them to use.

In a post-industrial society the threat of a man with a shovel moving chemicals about in his garage seems marginal. But the ensuing bomb, however primitive, may have spectacular effects. What the IRA wanted was not primitive bombs but anything that would escalate a threat. Thus what could be done easily was done first and if effective never discarded: chemicals are still be moved about garage floors, although not often with metal shovels. A generation later bombs not very different from the first attempts did billions and billions of pounds of damage in London. What worked was used not always to effect and what was wanted was sought not always successfully.

As personnel increased and received some training, the level of capacity gradually improved. One could trace the escalation by the arms used; first shotguns and an old Thompson, then Lee-Enfields and next American M-1s. Then came the Armalite and soon more sophisticated European examples and then a full rearmament with the arrival of shipments from Libya in 1985–87. There were by then after two decades weapons of choice for active-service units: the Heckler and Koch, Beretta sub-machine guns, or the Libyan AK-47. As far as such weapons were concerned, there had been a sea change: there were more guns than gunmen, more AK-47s than could be deployed – a rare Irish example of over-supply. The QMGs had also over the years managed a few heavier weapons from various sources if never in great quantity and never a long-cherished effective ground-to-air missile.

Mac Stiofáin had sent an agent abroad who managed in 1972 to acquire RPG-7 rocket-launchers; friends in America shipped over real United States Army machine-guns, and elegant odds and ends were found from time to time. What could not be found was, as in the case of mortars, simply made – along with an entire spectrum of mines and explosive devices. The IRA even unsuccessfully sponsored research-and-development of a missile in America. What proved highly effective was the arrival of Libyan Semtex to complement the existing explosives made or stolen.

Old habits were not discarded. Nothing is thrown away – although some of the used Armalites were auctioned in America – nor was there ever a time when the QMG felt the arms situation was absolutely satisfactory. Persistence had for so long been an Irish necessity and the struggle for the Republic so protracted that long-term maintenance always had a spot on the agenda. Even during the renewed ceasefire, revolvers were imported from America. So many Army Council meetings focused on the paucity of resources, the perpetual needs that neither cunning nor luck seemed to reduce. More was always needed simply to protract the existing level of intensity.

Mostly maintenance was seen as a matter of better arms and more money and only gradually did the Army Council and others realize that a modern armed struggle needs a vast support mechanism that the faithful did not always supply. The leaders were so used to drawing on their own resources that for a time they saw no necessity to organize the process. In many cases the movement produced little technological capacity and offered few with limited professional skills. There were among those of no property and sound views, few engineers or chemists or computer programmers, no investment bankers or social scientists.

Some IRA needs, really most IRA needs, hospitalization, welfare payments, propaganda, internal communications, ritual displays, safe houses, and political contributions, had always been fashioned during previous campaigns. All that need be done was to fill out the skeleton structure, make new telephone lists, new arrangements, adapt to demands that could largely be met in old ways. Those running raids across the border in Tyrone or Armagh knew all about safe houses and safe medical care and keeping active-service people warehoused in the Republic. They knew how to contact GHQ and where to dump the guns and in time how to confuse battlefield radar and avoid SAS patrols, how to run complex single-shot sniper operations. The volunteers adjusted to infrared overflights and electronic sensors just as they did to loyalist gunmen and armoured Landrovers.

From the pointed end at the bottom of the lane with an active-service unit all the way back to a house in Kerry or a dump in Carlow, the war was largely maintained by the old Irish ways. Those responsible sought out the familiar rather than the novel or often even the effective, relying on one's own, waiting and watching and confident that matters would work out, something would turn up. They sought and often found an Irish solution to an Irish problem. And in time the learning curve went up as volunteers survived and acquired experience, the old ways gradually became new means as needs shifted and skills accumulated. Those who maintained the struggle were apt to have a longer free run than the active-service people who engaged in operations so that accumulated wisdom began to come into play as the years passed – of course, as the years passed more skills were needed merely to persist.

For the IRA the really novel challenges were not increased British skills or even the need for new weapons and more money but the escalating demands of an armed struggle waged in a post-industrial world by working-class cadres. The IRA had to seek out advanced technologies, counter advanced counter-insurgency tactics and skills, cope with hi-tech anti-insurgency devices – even if with low-tech response. The GHQ had to learn on the job, had to purchase high-quality electronics to keep their fuses effective despite British countermeasures, had to use import and export facilities without being caught, had to make friends with advanced degrees and friends with elegant arms for sale in the back room of Europe or the Middle East, had to operate in a world far from the estates of West Belfast or the hills of Tyrone.

If they did not manage to do so, the gunman would be caught out, shot down driving the streets of the Ardoyne by a high-rise sniper or killed sitting in a blue Toyota van on the country road in front of the Loughhall RUC station. Over the operational years, the losses could be and were replaced, new guns found and the money to buy more, better techniques and machines were mastered, and all the old ways kept, the fertilizer still went into bombs and messages arrived late on a bike. Agents might negotiate with the Iraqis, move millions about by hand or purchase a .50-calibre sniper rifle to intimidate the security forces in South Armagh, but fertilizer was still purchased in bulk and orders sent by a nod.

CURVE OF REQUIREMENTS

In January 1970, the Provisional IRA Army Council assumed that while they needed everything tangible they had everything that mattered: the legitimacy to wage an armed struggle and the strategy to make sure that such a struggle would be tolerated, the capacity to attract recruits, the contacts and experience to organize, and – the will to counter British assets. They had a plan to win and the energy to find the means. Still, in the beginning, the conventional structure of the IRA was, as always, short on solutions to the problems of maintenance.

The only officer really concerned with acquisitions was the QMG – and the degree of his involvement was indicated by the death of McCabe while making explosives himself. The QMG had in the recent past been a beggar charged with housekeeping – in fact the man who knew where the arms were not buried. Mac Stiofáin began the practice of dispatching special emissaries to arrange for arms shipments: O Conaill's adventures on the continent along with his aide Maria Maguire was the most notorious mission. Two more visible and improbable covert operators would be difficult to imagine, for O Conaill looked like a romantic's idea of a gunman and Maria Maguire a flower child past due date. Other agents then and later were more traditional – tourists or salesmen. Usually GHQ handled procurement and the QMG hewed to traditional tasks.

Finance officers were inclined to hold the money, collect dues, ask for more. There was no department of treasury, no procurement office, no research and development. Much was done on an *ad hoc* basis: money was found so that Mac Stiofáin could dispatch an agent to potentially friendly states – where no contacts existed – to purchase RPG-7 rocket launchers. American faithful mortgaged their houses to produce the funds for an arms purchase. Every Republican at any moment might be legate, fund raiser, always intelligence agent, contributor, or supplier. As the years passed some grew more astute and habit made accountings more accurate but a clandestine movement only rarely hews to sound business practice: the money is spent before acquired, moved before counted, hidden rather than entered in the books. Over a generation only rarely has money been stolen by volunteers – the losses come from failed arms deals and money spent for good cause, operational cause, political cause, because the movement has it to spend.

Any IRA volunteer might take part in raising the money, buying his revolver, finding further bullets, replacing a part, hiding the bits, and not think his actions special. Everyone did anything and continued to do so regardless of their title or responsibilities. Differentiation of function was for grander institutions – the IRA had no airs and graces, only the assets of the movement and the occasional aid and comfort from afar. The lack of differentiation in many matters was not unique to the IRA – everyone does everything because an armed struggle is a process, not war, not peace, not divided up along traditional lines.

By 1972 the IRA was a semi-secret, partly armed militia dug into no-go zones and rural strongholds attacking the security forces both along the fringes of nationalist areas and at vulnerable spots elsewhere. Thereafter no one in the uniform of the Crown could walk unprotected anyplace in Northern Ireland. This situation was stabilized in 1972–73 after the British Motorman Operation that closed down the open no-go zones in Belfast and Derry. Escalation ended – the death total was down to 250 for 1973. From 1974 through to the 1975–76 truce on to the hunger strikes of 1981, the Provisionals' campaign struggled, the British counter-insurgency capacity had increased, the prospect of victory had receded, and the needs of the secret army had gradually shifted to a covert low-intensity insurrection. The Libyan arms and money made maintenance far easier but the expansion of the political option and the growth of Sinn Féin during the 1980s absorbed the fiscal gains.

After 1981 and the hunger strike, the IRA faced eroding popular support, especially in the Republic, which meant difficulties not just at the ballot box or during fund drives but in all aspects of maintenance: fewer helpful doctors, fewer barn doors open, fewer blind eyes or even kind words. In Northern Ireland, the police and army professionals had fulsome support among loyalists and Unionists. After a generation, the IRA had largely lost the support not just of the Irish establishment but most of the middle class in both the Republic and Northern Ireland. Each IRA operation that killed the innocent alienated more – another atrocity in the name of the Irish people. Many young people who abhorred the trinity of Provisional support – country piety, Gaelic parochialism, and Irish patriotism – found the campaign horrid, the IRA evil, their pretensions outrageous, in an era when Europe beckoned. The unexpected prosperity of the 1990s increasingly isolated those of no property from a new successful generation all but untouched by the national issue. For them there was no dream, only a nightmare. The Provisionals found aid and comfort once more only among their own and for the IRA this mattered less because the new direction and the ceasefires meant that less aid and comfort could be deployed for operational purpose.

During the campaign the operational and technological skills of the security forces improved. To counter this the IRA had to improve as well and do so without aid and without tutelage that middle-class friends might have supplied. And the IRA coped, haltingly but in the end effectively. Sometimes it appeared that at last the security forces were reaching the end of the tunnel where each new Northern Irish secretary and each British general reported the presence of light. Then the Provos would find new and soft targets, carry their struggle to England or the continent, deploy a new device, find a way through the latest barrier. As the conflict grew protracted, IRA field skills and tradecraft accumulated. The dividends were ample during the 1990s to maintain a secret army that only the prospect of peace and the erosion of unused capacity diminished.

What made the IRA effective was in part the unconventional solutions necessary, the dependence on the invisible movement, the habits of the Irish, the few cunning devices beyond orthodox imagination – and a regular dosage of the tried and true. Thus from time to time, the poor Paddy, scorned by the elegant and the professional military, deployed elegant bugging equipment, penetrating security secrets at the highest level, and made use of home-made mortars; cunning, guile, and the unorthodox approach for spectacular purpose. Then poor Paddy was seen as a ruthless and effective terrorist – a professional in impact.

Not only did the IRA bring down the Grand Hotel around Prime Minister Thatcher and the Conservative government but then bombarded Downing Street while Prime Minister John Major chaired a war cabinet meeting. The IRA mortars were as good as need be, made on lathes in Ireland and smuggled along with their home-made projectiles into London. There the Provisionals had found that by parking behind Downing Street outside the security ring about the front entrance their weapon was in range, could be fired from a specially adapted truck with ample time for the involved to withdraw. What could not be done was to follow standard operating procedure and zero in each round from the drop of the previous one. The IRA could only fire once. Still, it did not really matter that the mortar shells did little damage, caused no casualties, for the deed was ample reward – more reward than would have been forthcoming from killing results. Mortar shells that did not go off at Heathrow airport had an enormous effect – for precautions had to be taken for fear that the next time the IRA would be lucky or more skilled or more reckless.

In order to operate within London against Downing Street or Heathrow, the Provisionals simply maintained the habits and assets of the past: use what is available, what has worked, and do so when not expected. What choice was there without elegant weapons, skilled volunteers, tangible assets? After years of attrition and stalemate, the IRA has incorporated not wholly but in part a generation of struggle, acquired more weapons than volunteers, acquired effective and complex systems, often made of old pipes and percussion detonators tooled by hand, and acquired the skills to persist. What has not stayed the same is the mission of the secret army during an endgame. The leadership must still maintain the faith that supplies the energy for any new mission.

VOLUNTEERS

The first great assets proffered by the faith is the faithful. Their dedication, determination, their energy and talents and time are crucial for usually any revolutionary movement lacks almost all else, needs money and arms, visibility and skills and luck, and has instead the innocent burnished by their ideals. The Provisional IRA started with a movement in place, a familiarity with the clandestine, the capacities and limitations of their secret army, and the perceived arena. The movement then and subsequently did not represent a profile of the Irish nationalist much less of their avowed Irish constituency. The Republicans were a self-selected segment of those Irish nationalists with no property but great conviction. To them the nationalist issue mattered enormously but the Provisionals acquired those who wanted to use a gun not discuss politics or march against bigotry.

In the beginning the new volunteers had wanted guns to defend not to provoke, not to wage war but to protect the vulnerable. The Provisionals, then, welcomed these recruits who would be predisposed once convinced, once converted, to the necessity of using the gun against the real enemy, deploying physical force not in defence but in an armed struggle. Remark-ably few new recruits were alienated by the concept but only disappointed by the inability of QMG to produce enough guns. Those who could wait, sit through the classes, and – of course – grasp the validity of the Republican dream were soon prepared to commit fully to the struggle as defined by the movement. The defenders went on the offensive by 1971 and internment and thereafter those who arrived volunteered for a campaign, for a role in a secret army. And after a time and the visible cost of such a vocation, none volunteered for adventure, out of romance, to achieve awe and respect. The IRA offered suffering, prison, death, as well as service – and everyone involved knew this.

The new volunteers supplied energy and numbers but little talent – not necessarily a dire matter since recruits to regular armies come without skills, and must be trained before being deployed. Those who volunteered for the Provisionals in the first years entered a movement that was very short on skills at all levels, lacked teachers who often had to attend to operations, lacked a skilled elite, and often lacked those in command who realized the extent of the shortcomings and the necessity for unfamiliar campaign skills. A few of the Provos had regular army experience but not as officers.

Still, no form of war offers more opportunities for those innocent of the curriculum of the military academies or even the requirements of soldiers in regular armies than the campaigns of the guerrilla or the gunman. In time the protracted nature of the campaign and the skills of the security forces reduced the prospect of active service and so recruiting and increased the age and skills of the operational. Maintaining these volunteers, however, is often more complex than deploying them operationally. Then all sorts of talent are needed beyond courage, audacity, and dedication. And if the Provisionals lacked this talent over the years, they either found means to co-opt it or learned or tried something else. And some volunteers at least could learn on the job if the job were not too complex, but none could reproduce the real benefits of proper education, real managerial skills, detailed technological and engineering capacities.

What the Provos faced was for them unconventional, an arena increasingly dominated by an emergent hi-tech society. This new world, only obvious in Ireland over the previous decade, was not fully understood: the impact of television, the intricate transnational economic system, the technological advances not only in counter-insurgency equipment but also in matters of communication or banking or data storage. Even more elusive was the impact of a society changing in wealth and agenda. Some traditional ways even in a complex society had continued validity. And one did not have to be able to build a car to drive one, or to build or even to programme a computer in order to use one – selling it to a sceptical audience was still another matter. In any case, unconventional wars are fought unconventionally often by those with limited assets, narrow vision, and flawed expectations. The Provos, making do with the talent to hand, did not do badly if almost always at great cost.

As always the first focus of Republican resources was on operational matters, the visible and traditional aspect of the campaign. The evolution of Provisional detonators and timers, for example, left behind a trail of dead idealists, 'own goals', murdered and maimed innocents, discarded devices, and primitive options. Each year saw a slowly rising curve of skills. Those skills never equalled that of professionally trained people like the demolitions experts in the service of the state. The old ways traditionally learned often continue to work – matches still light fires – and the acquired experience was such that the Army Council was involved in the instruction of African National Congress cadres – one of the rare examples of international revolutionary co-operation. Over the years the IRA volunteers' unorthodox solutions often compensated for lack of formal skills. And often they did not. Their diplomatic initiatives and propaganda often lacked empathy until the pressures of the peace process generated the necessary skills. To a degree every movement that possesses the absolute truth lacks empathy, tends to believe that faith overcomes all, that fine-tuning is pointless and so preaches to the converted.

What has stayed the same over the years has been the conviction of those who volunteer, those who serve and those who have persisted. If the endgame collapses the impact on such individuals will be enormous.

TRAINING AND TRADECRAFT

Unlike those organizations engaged in irregular wars or dominating liberated zones, the IRA has always depended on volunteers who are self-recruited and may in almost all circumstances withdraw from the movement if the impetus fades. No one is drafted, none attracted by a salary. Anyone can leave. In fact over the years most recruits seldom last the course, or go on active service. Many can simply not be accommodated, particularly true in the years of turmoil and escalation when there was a lack of arms and training and then true again when the arena closed down and there was an overload and so a lack of operational opportunities. Whether there are too many or too few recruits, the formal processes of transforming the recruit into a Republican and so an effective volunteer have remained much the same over the years. What matters is the commitment to the ideal and all the acquired tradecraft and military skills are a bonus. For Mao the *Red Book* was more important than target practice, for communism supplied the energy not the gun. And such revealed truth in Cairo or Kurdistan or Kosovo is more important to an armed struggle than fieldcraft.

Most recruits appear all but openly at the door of a known Republican. Most have to be merged into existing activities until a time of testing has passed or a place in a recruits class opens. So from the beginning, the enthusiastic must wait. Most who wait are shuttled into Sinn Féin or publishing *An Phoblacht* or in matters peripheral to operations. This had been so increasingly after 1976 and during the endgame there has been almost no recruiting – even by the splinter groups of the Continuity Army Council and the Real IRA. In the summer of 1998 the Real IRA sent three young men – aged 26, 21, and 20 – to place small bombs in Fulham Broadway in West London stores – and they were arrested, convicted, and as violators of the ceasefire given harsh sentences, the oldest 25 years and the other two 22. And unlike other Republican prisoners, they had little hope of amnesty. Sacrifice is all very well, and commitment, but service in a splinter without prospects is apt to attract only the rash or the foolish. And in 1998 those without experience were not so much trained as deployed.

Formally, especially in urban areas, the recruit begins with weekly recruits classes that focus as much upon ideology as the rudiments of military drill – the faith always comes first – and are often extended to discourage those without true conviction. At times, especially in the country, association with the secret army is more covert, a gradual initiation into active service with no overt signs, no presence at protests or demonstrations, no Sinn Féin meetings, no visibility. Those who are visible may be in the secret army but much of the IRA in the country is a secret society. The early training varies from time to time and place to place, but in the most typical cases runs from lectures to 10 or 12 recruits for a few months and on to training classes and camps where weapons are used and operational skills introduced. All learn the structure, capacities, and dogma of the IRA and something of weapons and communications and explosives.

Training camps are as much intended to raise morale and steel the faith as teach tactics and weaponry. They are at risk of discovery but have paid sufficient benefits to be maintained. At times firing ranges are constructed in isolated places, abandoned mines or convenient cellars, just so some volunteers can fire in practice. For some years many volunteers fired only shots in anger, had never really practised before their first operation. Still, most recruits are apt to assume that they have been far better trained than is the case which, given the risks of operations, is just as well.

In any case operations often arise from need or opportunity not from the existing skills or assets of the movement: the report of a new electronic device in New York or the combination of a delayed fuse with a predictable presence, as in the case of Margaret Thatcher at Brighton. The operational leadership recognizes an opportunity within the IRA's capacity. And all those cunning operations proposed or feared by those outside the movement are seldom a matter of concern to the leadership seized on the moment, restricted by a limited world vision, confined to the local and dependent on experience not speculation. All the potential horrors of weapons of mass destruction have nothing to do with IRA reality. What can be done is attempted but what is beyond that remains untouched: no assault on British communications, no use of computer-generated sabotage, certainly no atomic bomb in the basement.

Those aspects of operations in the field that form the curriculum of conventional forces' battle schools or intelligence agencies' courses in tradecraft are not taught except on an individual basis. There can be no course for gunmen, only experience gained in the trade. How to maintain cover or communicate secretly, how to plan an ambush or to set up a safe house is a matter of trial and error with those who managed able to continue managing at an increasingly effective level. It is impossible to simulate the impact of driving a live car-bomb: the anxiety generated that determines operational parameters must be experienced not imagined.

Most tradecraft must be learned in action. Admonitions and warnings do not necessarily assure cunning and caution. Despite the evidence around them, despite the advice of the experienced, some persist in habits or behaviour that all but assure failure: they call home when told not to do so, they arrive early or late, forget to check the end of the street, use a dirty weapon or the same route home. Those who do not manage are quickly lost, arrested for loitering, shot at an arms dump, caught at a roadblock. And the security forces are always raising the fences. Some volunteers never learn. Visibly working class they set up housekeeping in middle-class districts of London or Birmingham, loiter on the stoop, appear at the pub with their Irish accents, buy clocks at the corner store, telephone the family back in Belfast, go about armed, move innocently in harm's way.

ARMAMENT

One of the universals for those who pursue the armed struggle is the importance of arms. In some cultures weapons are rare, symbolic of power and glory; in others they are common, an aspect of life, a sign of virility or items in the closet. Many armed struggles in the beginning must scramble for a few shotguns, dynamite from the quarry, a hunting rifle. And the Provisional IRA began with odds and ends, mismatched revolvers, old Lee-

Enfields, a few elderly Thompsons, and began on an island where weapons, even sporting guns, are closely held, licensed, and monitored and where no great war has left the countryside littered with discarded military gear.

To acquire more was the first priority – and 'more arms' is nearly always the very first priority in matters of maintenance for all movements. There will never be enough arms, but the Provisionals knew from the first that there were hardly any arms. Former volunteers had been turned away empty-handed when they appeared at the office of the Officials on Gardiner Street. No one had arms – even the Irish government had a badly armed army. The British army was making do with old NATO equipment to keep the peace and then pursue the gunmen. They, however, had real arms, unlike the secret army with next to none.

All the Republicans and their friends and families scoured the countryside for bits and pieces, collected the odd revolver, the old war souvenir, the shotgun or handful of cartridges in the barn and sent them along to the QMG. The result of the search, which would continue for years, was not at all satisfactory. There were simply not enough military weapons for use and few of those could be used for training and those trained would have nothing. Some explosives could be stolen and others crudely made, but the end product was more a nineteenth-century diabolic device than an effective weapon. Worse still, for several years the haste and innocence of those involved produced a long series of premature explosions – 'own goals' that cost as many lives as did the actions of the security forces. In sum, during 1970–71 the Provisional IRA was, if not unarmed for their campaign, certainly ill prepared.

To find the arms the movement needed talents that did not exist: specialists in import and export regulations, those who could find or make the proper papers, agents who knew trustworthy contacts. The entire world of end-users' certificates, bills of lading, letters of credit, suborned attachés was alien and largely so remained. Those responsible took two paths. They responded to opportunity, mostly offers made by most dubious individuals and often offers known to security officials elsewhere. And, more effectively, they sought supplies in the American Diaspora. The first route even with initial contacts made by IRA people only occasionally bore fruit – for example, the RPG-7 rocket launchers flown into the country and then used somewhat ineffectively in the autumn of 1972 – even a simple weapon is complex without proper training.

The American connection proved more important. The Irish-Americans who responded to Provisional needs, however, rarely were specialists in procurement and knew as little of acquisition and shipment as did the QMG in Dublin. Regularly, small groups of Americans, often in NORAID, were arrested in sting operations, usually attempting to purchase military weapons. A few such purchases were real – the seller criminal, as in the case of United States Army machine-guns stolen from a national guard arsenal in Danvers, Massachusetts, a matter of mutual profit, or sympathy. More effective at first was the dribs and drabs purchased legally in small lots, smuggled boldly in golf bags and coffins and in pieces. Because in many states gun laws were lax and civilian versions of military weapons available – some for hunting and some as 'collectors' items' – this stream, even with very tight control of Irish customs, continued for years. The sum total was substantial. The Provisionals thus added to their front-line Lee-Enfields and Thompsons left over from the olden days and began to get M-1 rifles and a few Garands and whatever else the gun stores stocked.

The major long-lasting American connection, however, came through a well-known radical Irish Republican in Brooklyn, George Harrison – too obvious to attract the law-enforcement people for long. He and a few friends, especially a neighbourhood acquaintance George Meo, bought from gun stores, deceptively packed the results, and shipped to an unknown receiver in Ireland, each step being in theory compartmentalized. Once in Ireland the weapons were moved about, usually not far from Dublin and then turned over to GHQ. It was simple, effective, not especially expensive – money came from the parallel net running alongside of NORAID – and also obvious.

Once the FBI and the Treasury agents had their attention attracted by Meo's purchases in North Carolina, the conduit was closed down. Meo was turned and those involved in the United States arrested when the new man foolishly telephoned an Irish contact. The financiers, including Mick Flannery, a founder and co-chairman of NORAID, insisted they were good Americans who thought the CIA had authorized the operations, were judged innocent by the jury to the horror of the authorities, and the receivers in Ireland went to ground and were never discovered.

Thus for nearly ten years the American connection supplied the QMG with the ideal guerrilla weapon, the civilian version of the military M-16, the Armalite, that could be purchased legally as a deer-rifle. The Armalite was produced under warranty by a Japanese company and then British Sterling so that at the end of the decade the IRA was equipped with a British-made weapon more effective for their purpose than the British army's SLR rifle was for theirs. And the ultimate introduction of the new British-made assault rifle changed little. The Armalite became symbol of the armed struggle, an ideal weapon that when broken down 'would fit in a cereal box' and used on semi-automatic as intended was ideal for poorly trained gunmen. The .223 cartridge, furthermore, could pierce the shell armour on

British personnel carriers which did nothing for military morale. The Armalite arriving regularly became the Provisional standard weapon augmented by small shipments from the continent of elegant first-line equipment like the Beretta sub-machineguns.

As for a technological escalation, other than better fuses, the RPG-7, more a propaganda coup than useful weapon, and the Armalite, there was nothing dramatic – no heavy weapons, no exotic explosives, no hi-tech equipment that could not be bought at Radio Shack. The IRA did prove ingenious in all sorts of explosive devices and traps, in the use of hi-tech monitoring equipment, in adapting their weapons to rural and urban conditions, but they lacked what was wanted most: ground-to-air missiles to counter the increased British use of helicopters. Such missiles remained the dream of the QMG and a steady trickle of agents ended in prison seeking them in bars and through contacts and even by establishing their own research-and-development group in America. There were real prospects with the Palestinians and then with the Libyans, real hopes for the American contacts, but always failure and each failure further alerted authorities everywhere to the IRA quest.

The first really successful contact to be exploited was with Libya, a state run on the simple whims and anti-imperialist ideological assumptions of the leader Colonel Muammar el-Qaddafi. He saw rich but primitive Libya's destiny as a revolutionary catalyst – a guide to the future that should sponsor every one of the faithful, mostly those faithful to Islam but also those opposed to imperial bastions. Those around Colonel el-Qaddafi knew nothing of Ireland except the reputation of the IRA as a liberation movement opposed to Great Britain, not one of Gadaffi's favourite states. In 1972 he and his number two Major Abdul Salam Jalloud agreed to aid the IRA but wanted someone in Libya they knew – and the only person they knew was Joe Cahill, because he had given a public news conference on the morning after the British internment sweep in August 1971. So Cahill flew to Libya and the project moved ahead, probably revealed by local Western agents if not the shipping people involved or even Cahill's own presence.

In any case the failed attempt to bring in Libyan weapons in 1973 on the *Claudia* with Joe Cahill arrested off Waterford, the weapons lost to the Dublin authorities, and only some of the money recovered from the safe dropped overboard. The operation attracted general attention to IRA procurement intentions. The IRA seemed to be mixed up with one of the godfathers of terrorism.

Men with Belfast or Kerry accents seeking timers or missiles or even addresses in Amsterdam or Philadelphia and certainly in London were instant objects of suspicion. The horror of transnational terror, the hi-jackings and hostages and bombs, coupled with the success of the authorities in Dublin and London in including the IRA with the PLO and the Red Brigades and the rest made procurement increasingly difficult. For many the IRA were not freedom fighters, not engaged in a strategy of national liberation but terrorists who placed no-warning bombs in Ireland and England, murdered women and children, left bodies in plastic bags on country roads, shot suspects in the knee – and all the explanations and excuses could not shift the stain. Those who in 1972 were eager to help, even at some risk, in the Republic or America, within a decade could no longer be found. Dumps were harder to place, lorries could not be borrowed, warehouses used, documents crafted.

In America the enthusiasm went up and down as did fund raising but involvement in arms procurement was no longer a patriotic lark, no longer worth the risk for most. And American authorities in particular became astute at frustrating any Irish shipments – the trawler *Valhalla* out of Boston that unloaded arms onto the Irish trawler *Marita Ann* was an elaborate operation that swept up all those involved. America except for bits and drabs was no longer producing for the IRA.

The situation was retrieved unexpectedly with the reopening of the Libya connection because, once again, Colonel el-Qaddafi was embittered with the British who had allowed American military planes to fly from their bases to attack Tripoli in an anti-terrorist foray as well as for other clashes in London. In effect he allowed IRA agents to move what they could from warehouses filled with small arms and even the cherished missiles. Rather than move the weapons with false papers, the QMG with Malta as head-quarters, relied on the classic methods of filling small vessels and sailing illicitly into Irish waters, unloading by lighter, and sailing off undetected. They co-opted a captain in Ireland who was in financial difficulties and prepared to load up a trawler in Tripoli. Malta was filled with watching British eyes, Tripoli was filled with intelligence agents reporting back to Washington or Tel Aviv or even London. Satellites took pictures, maritime agents reported to their handlers, and all electronic communications were monitored. Everyone knew the IRA was looking for arms but no one could imagine a small boat with a travel agent as captain and arms drops off the Irish coast or using Malta or simply loading up in Libya. It was too primitive, too unconventional. And so the IRA brought in the arms in 1986 and 1987, moved what was for them a huge amount of gear into the Republic and on to dumps North and South, Finally the size of the shipment alerted the Western watchers and the *Eksund*'s 150 tons of armament was seized by the French on 1 November 1987. By then the QMG had more AK-47s than volunteers, an enormous amount of Semtex explosives that would allow for

sophisticated bombs, and a variety of other gear including reportedly SAM
ground-to-air missiles that could not be made to work, perhaps so intended
not to work.

Given the level of intensity and the small stream of special shipments from
Europe and the United States, the QMG had for the first time more gear
than needed. The Semtex in particular proved a lethal addition to the
IRA arsenal, but as always the responsible wanted more and so even with
their weaponry problems greatly eased, the QMG still sought more Semtex,
functioning missiles, advanced electronic gear – more. Given the isolation
of the arena, the limited initial resources, the skills of their opponents and
the innocence of the volunteers, the IRA had over a generation managed to
maintain momentum and on occasion escalate the campaign because of, not
in spite of, their efforts at weapons procurement. And even with the ceasefires the IRA continued to pursue sophisticated electronic monitoring projects.

MONEY

There is little doubt that money makes the world go round, allows the armed
struggle to persist, is even more important than arms, for with it can come
arms. Except for bright shining moments – always in the past – there has
never been enough Irish Republican money. Some few underground movements may have been adequately funded, may have had assets to save or
squander; but most live from hand to mouth, from expropriation to a quick
whip around the membership. So too the Provisionals. When matters go
well for Republicans the armed struggle can, is often, run on prospects and
on credit, and when times turn hard the movement must run on empty. No
matter the assets to hand, there are always more bills due than funds. Even
during the endgame with money flowing in from the American Diaspora to
Sinn Féin there was never a surplus: needs emerging to absorb any new
funding. It is always possible, somehow, to find crucial money at critical
moments, to continue to keep up the welfare payments, to pay from time to
time the active-service units, to purchase necessary supplies although a
considerable portion of the arms bought are never received.

At first the faithful contributed to friends or IRA organizers to Sinn Féin,
to special drives, to commemorations and private raffles, to unknown
solicitors who knock on the door late at night, to old comrades who ask just
one more time. The conditions in the arena affected the nature of both these
Irish contributors and at times even those further away. Contributions
tended to rise during spectacular times – the Hunger Strikes – or briefly after
spectaculars, win or lose – Bloody Sunday in Derry on 30 January 1972,

when 13 protesters were shot dead by British paratroopers, or the assassination of Lord Mountbatten and the death of the 18 British paratroopers at Warrenpoint on 27 July 1979. When nothing happens, or rather nothing is reported to be happening, when error is revealed in a flawed operations – the Poppy Day massacre in Enniskillen on 8 November 1987, when 11 civilians were killed by an IRA bomb – when there is public Republican dispute over politics, as was the case with the withdrawal of Republican Sinn Féin at the 1986 Ard Fheis, then, despondent and confused, the movement contracts, grows darker, and the contributions, local and international, dwindle. When the IRA seemed an anti-imperialist organization to Libyan observers money was forthcoming – an eventuality few had foreseen. When there was vast enthusiasm over the peace process money flowed into Sinn Féin if not GHQ – an eventuality all had foreseen.

External funding was often the most visible source of Republican money – some seen and much suspected. The traditional means has been to organize the sympathetic Irish who are apt to imagine Ireland as much as remember it. In America the creation of NORAID provided a legal means to aid the Republican cause although the United States government has always monitored the activity closely. In time NORAID was made to register as a foreign agency. Those involved in NORAID and their contacts also managed a less visible net of support for money sent directly to Provisional GHQ to use essentially for military purposes. More or less the illicit contributions about equalled the legal recorded contributions. Both tended to decline over the long haul although this decay was finally eased by renewed interest and so contribution from some of the illegal immigrants that renewed the Irish-American Diaspora in the 1980s and again for political matters with the initiation of the peace process.

This American money was often cited as the fuel for the armed struggle, blood money sent abroad to be used to kill Irishmen. None of the governments involved doubted its importance for a moment – outside agitators have always had an attraction for those besieged by domestic woes. So the 'innocent' American was blamed – giving money to gunmen not welfare. Few ever understood that the legal, welfare money was the more important. And that many others who gave wanted their money spent on guns, knew exactly where it was going, were not innocent but militant. And the sum total, quite welcome, was never enormous, never crucial. Money, often flown over by tourists carrying it in paper bags and airline totes, was used for guns, often came from the same NORAID people, went through customs and appeared at GHQ.

Washington, London, and Dublin have always overestimated the impact of this Diaspora money which came in bits and drabs, a matter of cake-bake sales and dances in suburban halls, crumpled bills in bars, and almost never great cheques signed with a flourish. The Zionists could raise more in New York over a weekend than NORAID managed in a generation. Still, the money was important and an indicator of distant support for the armed struggle. That support did exist in the Irish Diaspora – except in England where the Irish tended to disappear into ethnic anonymity as quickly as possible – but America was the key.

Internal funding effort was not simply skimming the resources of the faithful but organizing the faith for profit. Gradually, as order collapsed in Northern Ireland, especially in the nationalist areas beyond the reach of the law, the Provisionals moved into various opportunities. Clubs were established, first as protection and then as centres for the followers and ultimately as money-spinners for the movement. There followed the licensing of black taxis that replaced the decaying public transportation system, burned out and intimidated off the streets. As the black economy spread into other areas, Provisional intervention varied from outright extortion – licence to operate – to self-created industries in pirated videos or small businesses. Government programmes were exploited and reluctant private donors intimidated.

It is far more difficult to persuade an idealistic young gunman to steal than it is to kill – a soldier's lot. Necessity made volunteers into armed raiders. Thus at first because they were vulnerable, because they were familiar, and because they were state targets the IRA in the North hit post offices. It was simply the thin edge of the wedge. Armed robbery became a convention in Northern Ireland. In theory the Republic was immune but in practice money was money. The Provos even managed the great train robbery at Sallins that Seámus Costello had been planning first as an Official and then as C/S of the new Irish National Liberation Army. The Provos got the money and watched while the authorities sought to make Costello and the INLA guilty. There was always danger with any operation in the South generating a backlash and so repeated arms raids and kidnappings in the Republic were a risk – and one that did not always pay off. Gárdá and soldiers were killed and nationalist opinion alienated.

GHQ tried to imposed some order with a regulation that expropriation operations were to be undertaken only if there were prospects of at least £3,000; but the audacious and enthusiastic were quite content, often eager, to arrive at the door of a sub-post office with a gun to snatch stamps and £20 or try their hand at a branch bank counter. So too did the self-denying aspects of funding erode with time: kidnapping was countenanced and more armed bank raids in the Republic and extortion. At least GHQ managed to keep the actions as operations, the money within control of the commanders, the volunteers as volunteers.

Any recourse to criminal means by revolutionaries runs risks. The operation must be treated as if it were military. The funds acquired must be returned to command central, no percentage kept for the local unit, no individual rewarded, no others involved as sub-contractors for part of the take. To fail to follow such rules tends to lead to private initiative, criminal involvement, and on revelation disastrous public response as the Officials were to discover. Once the expropriation process had begun, although banks remained an ideal target, hijacking of trucks, thefts from business premises – or payment not to steal from the store or the lorry – became conventional operations and so over the years a vital influx of funds. Even after the first ceasefire some units could not deny themselves although gradually restraint was imposed.

The Provisionals often became involved in all those activities on the fringes of legitimacy: after-hours clubs, smuggling along the border, cut-price appliances, but not drugs. In fact the effort to impose Provisional order in the core areas often focused on ending the drug trade by the use of physical force – beatings and maimings that alienated many people. The Republicans, however, remained fixed on closing the drug trade not exploiting it.

Thus the Provisionals had tolerated, if reluctantly, the pretensions and sectarian murders of the tiny lethal remnants of the Irish National Liberation Front, a few radicals, some criminals, and too many sociopaths, calling them-selves the Irish People's Liberation Army, until autumn 1992 when their use of Republican rhetoric to authorize the drug trade could no longer be tolerated. Naturally the enemies of the Provos were always willing to believe the worst, wanted them mixed in drugs as well as murder and armed robbery, but this was not the case despite opportunities offered by those who could see the IRA as an ideal distributor backed by an awesome protection system.

The Provos' black economy tended to get the best returns from nearly legal businesses like the clubs. Accounting was honest but often not centralized and records scanty. Numbers were hard to discover even for those responsible because documents were a danger. Still there is no doubt that the basis for the campaign, the daily expenses, the welfare cost, and much of the political and publicity cost arose from the combination of contributions and covert capitalism. Even with the new direction after 1994 movement funding was much the same – the new money went into politics, salaries and offices and campaigns.

There was never much help from beyond the island and the Diaspora – Libya being the great exception. The active guerrillas and gunmen were little real help, much the same was true for the state sponsors of revolution. The Russians, who had turned down IRA enquiries back in the 1956–62 campaign, the Chinese, the Czechs, or Algerians could be contacted but little happened – one small shipment of RPG-7 privately managed. Deals with the Palestinians did not work. The Iraqis arrived too late. The radical states, even the crazy states, saw no advantage in an IRA connection, and states whatever their ideological pretensions are run pragmatically. The one exception was Libya. Giving the IRA money was even easier than giving them small arms and even the arms given were easily overlooked. Once the arms contact was made, the Provisionals had a friend who continued to dribble funds into their coffers year after year to mingle with the cake-and-bake cheques and the bundle of banknotes taken at a post office in Tyrone.

The end result was that year after year, good years and bad, the Provisionals spent several million dollars, much wasted on failed arms purchases but little lost or embezzled. No one knows exactly how much comes in or how much goes out, since there is no central office of budget and management. Those with tidy minds, especially outside the loop, have estimates, make lists, put figures to activities that are not inclined to yield quantitative results in practice: money passed about in a speeding car, money snatched from a drawer and handed on, money brought in paper bags and doled out by weight. Even when the tidy demanded an exact, written accounting much came and went that did not reach GHQ notice. The IRA is not a fiscally proper organization. It is internally honest if externally violent but not one to publish annual reports or accountant's audits.

ADMINISTRATIVE MANAGEMENT

Within the Republican movement the various organizations are structured and managed almost as if they were conventional committees and parties. In each case the final word on matters of dispute may come from the Army Council – a Council crafted to represent the consensus of the movement – and in some cases funds may arrive somewhat tainted in acquisition but almost all else is orthodox. As in the case of the secret army, the movement is organized by those with little formal training, Sinn Féin does not rely on media experts, sociologists, polling experts, and political scientists but then these callings still have a limited if expanding place in Irish politics and by the end of the century the Republicans had as many so skilled as conventional parties. The book-keeping of politics, the collection of funds for the National Graves Association, the distribution of newspapers or the filing of legal forms can be done, done effectively, without university degrees. At times Republican management may overestimate their own skills and capacities, but generally they manage adequately. They have managed to ride the current towards conventional politics with great skill. The simultaneous management of the faith and the secret army takes place out of sight and is another matter.

In the IRA armed struggle effective managers are largely determined by tasks. If an operation is possible, a vulnerability suspected, and a weapon to hand, then anyone, anyone sound, may become involved regardless of title or previous experience. There is leadership but often little differentiation in operations: a leader chooses who is needed and they fulfil the needs, the more often successfully the more often chosen. Both politics and war can thus be run by those who move upward in responsibility and usually capacity. More technical matters – finances or law or the details of import–export – often prove less complex than professionals imagine and professionals are often available to offer aid and comfort or simply accept legitimate fees. Essentially, the Republican movement is small, a crusade through time and history, where each volunteer manages because there is no other way, assumes responsibility, seeks guidance from the sound, and so contributes to the movement of the movement. Without the bother of paper credentials the Republicans manage – after all the difficulties faced by an armed struggle are not often managerial but operational. And the movement manages to collect and deploy assets adequately and often more cleverly than any text on business tactics might indicate.

The most unconventional management is the total fiscal structure, for no individual or organization directs a single, united shaped policy – not unlike certain orthodox governments. There are books and accounting and the movement copes but the mix of illicit and/or covert funds, illicit purchases for materials and service, and local control means no coherent economic oversight is possible – or attempted. And there are oddities: the individual responsible for paying the bills at headquarters on Parnell Square knows that the telephone bill can be paid last, run months and months behind time, for it will never be cut off just as the volunteers know better than to use the telephone for real business or use any near-by telephone for that matter. And as the years pass the oddities simply become part of management tactics and assumptions.

Although the Republican movement is seemingly a collection of mostly legal fronts plus a secret army engaged in an insurrection, in fact it is a special ecosystem, a movement, where management of the whole is the result both of intervention from out of the core – often the few key figures are almost in constant motion – and self-regulation by the faithful who touch and communicate and encourage in ways impossible to chart. The visible sign of this world can be the extension of Republican activists into neighbour-hood activities, especially pronounced after 1981, usually through conven-tionally organized activities that seek to involve the people, those not yet committed, in Republican concerns. Thus in core nationalist areas in Northern Ireland and to a far lesser sense in certain areas in the Republic, the movement seeks first a place among competing conventional structures and then to replace such 'illegitimate' authority with their own. This may mean welfare payments from Sinn Féin, intervention in housing or local family disputes, exerting pressure on conventional structures or the punishment of drug sellers or snatch-and-grab thieves by the local IRA unit.

Many areas in Northern Ireland have no real government presence – police arrive in armoured vehicles, street lights have not worked for decades, no public transport exists, census takers are hesitant to ask questions, the only authority is what can be found at the Sinn Féin office. When this authority is imposed with a gun, as must be the case eventually, the Republicans are caught between the need to act, to display power and capacity, and the certainty that such acts alienate because of their barbarity. And simultaneously with such brutality Sinn Féin operates like any democratic, radical political party. So administering the movement is not simply running a collection of orthodox structures. Even the most conventional management has a clandestine side and much that is administered – parades and punishment shooting – falls outside management texts and often even for those involved the concept of management. A lifetime in an underground imposes certain habits of minds, certain adjustments that remain when decisions are to be made or agendas shifted.

The most successful management is that of internal morale. and takes place without administrative consideration. Much that occurs within the movement is shaped to enhance the faith, encourage the faithful. Thus *An Phoblacht* is less a newspaper in the traditional sense than a house-organ of belief and an arena for carefully edited policy discussion.

The movement has developed a set of rituals and ceremonies from past practice, from Irish customs, from foreign example, and from need that enhances belief. There are parades and marches with pipe bands and banners. There are military funerals often with a part for the security forces pencilled into the programme. There are commemorations before the graves of fallen comrades and seminars in country hotels on economic policy and programmes and protest meetings in draughty halls, and collections on the street that may lead to scuffles and arrests and so excitement and demonstration of the faith. After the hunger strikes the new political direction appeared in part in the wall murals in Belfast and elsewhere: public art by a risen people, Republican art to affect those people – work as important for being done as being finished. Everywhere in each activity no matter how administered the improvement of faith and so morale is a factor that would be easily recognized by the gurus of Japanese industry as participatory management.

MORALE

Since all those involved in an armed struggle are incurably, at times criminally, optimistic the leadership begins with a major asset. The converted are convinced of the direction of history, thus need encouragement not conversion. The new recruits must be tested to see that they are of the faith. Although the Irish Republican movement does proselytize, the major propaganda thrust is really to its own: the newspapers are written for the faithful, read by the faithful and the police and few others. The meetings attract the convinced. The commemorations are for members. The rigid divided society in Northern Ireland tends to encourage a focus on the converted – the others are beyond reach or reason even if as Irish, Protestant Irish or Irish nationalists, should be congenial to Republican aspirations. Everyone votes the same way each time, thinks the same way all the time. So effort is best spent where results can be expected: on the convinced.

In maintaining the faith the Republican rituals are perhaps the most original and the most effective: a military burial for a lost IRA volunteer, loss into asset, a martyr made, a name chiselled on a monument and remembered once a year, is the greatest gift within the power of the faithful. The funeral parade down a country lane or up to Milltown cemetery in Belfast, the wail of pipes, the flag-draped coffin with the black beret and folded gloves, the graveside oration – '… the fools the fools, they have left us our patriot dead' – and always validating the sacrifice the circle of sullen police, the clatter of British army helicopters overhead, the men in three-piece suits taking photographs – them. And so too each year at Bodenstown the Republicans gather to celebrate their mentor and founder Wolfe Tone – and so too the splinters and schismatics on different Sunday afternoons seeking too legitimacy, the mandate of heaven.

ALLIES AND ALIGNMENTS

No matter how enthusiastic the faithful, how high morale or successful the war news, no armed struggle is content to labour completely isolated in the revolutionary vineyards. To live underground, to exist within a rebel ecosystem, to hide the faith in the everyday world creates for each a sense of isolation: does no one notice? does anyone care? The maintenance of morale is generally an indigenous matter but is also one of the activities of the struggle that can be assisted by aid and comfort from abroad. Thus the Provincial leadership is aware that arms and money may be found in the Diaspora and an easing of isolation but that the best contacts may be elsewhere. Thus contact with the al Fatah and so the PLO in Beirut was a plus even though efforts to move arms from the Palestinians to Ireland failed. Any friendly contact is a plus. Aid to the African National Congress, a volunteer timely dispatched, may have later returns but even at the moment aligns the struggle with all anti-imperialist movements with all liberation struggles. And so the gable ends of Belfast streets have huge murals proclaiming unity with the ANC and the PLO – and in many parts of the world the single export of Ireland is not poetry or piety but the name IRA. Even in the final years, the Iranians who had named the street after Bobby Sands opened negotiations with the IRA. Nothing happened – the mullahs' agents, shrewd, sophisticated, zealous understood little of Irish aspirations or agenda but knew that the IRA was a world-class organization. If the fame of the IRA is real, most abroad wanted no part of the IRA. In a time of terror no country wanted to support gunmen.

In the 1970s, the IRA was not interested in the Euroterrorists, difficult to contact at best, sought friends among separatists, anti-imperialist struggles, and interested if irrelevant radicals. International contacts were carried out for some time by a special, largely overt, Sinn Féin office under Richard Behal. The effort produced no prime returns, no money, no arms, no publicity but did lessen the sense of isolation and encouraged those who needed little encouragement. Still, interest in Ireland was never high and when Behal left contact became sporadic: those who sought arms did so on special assignment, those who kept political contacts often did so personally, on holidays or through the mail. Beyond the American Diaspora international contact was a sometime thing low on the Army Council's list of priorities. The Provisionals were always parochial, Ireland not in the mainstream and the battle arenas provincial, and grew more so as the struggle limited movement and vision.

As time passed so did international interests: the IRA was not hard news and when the news was hard it was often bad – another atrocity or a spectacular murder. So revolutionaries, particularists in most cases, had no call to reach out to the island and even the radical states could see no advantage. The one great exception was Libya, who aided the movement almost in a fit of absent-mindedness, a penny on the anti-British scales by those who could not find Ireland on a map. There was no lasting alliance, no trust, only ultimate betrayal when to ease the international boycott imposed because Tripoli would not extradite suspects in two airline bombings, the British were told all that the Libyans knew. Data that were not especially useful but may have given the British more details on IRA arms supplies than held by the IRA QMG. The Anglo-Libyan meeting in Switzerland simply indicated that states have interests not friends – and so too is the case with rebels.

For the IRA these interests were seldom mutual except through the ethnic and historical ties of the Diaspora and then only of real advantage in the United States where the Dublin government, the authorities in Washington and British propagandists and diplomats competed successfully for the loyalty of Irish-Americans. In fact in diplomatic and foreign affairs just as Libya was the great and unexpected success so was the failure of the Republican movement in America to control the Irish Diaspora the great and unexpected defeat. The Dublin and London authorities convinced the vast majority of Americans that the IRA struggle was futile, counter-productive, a matter of terror and violence by brutal gunmen who were quite different from the old IRA. They failed to sell the Provisionals as communists but the long series of IRA operational blunders and disasters persuaded many that if the Provos were not communist terrorists then without doubt their armed struggle was terrible, murdering innocent people, contemptible, certainly not worthy of support. Historic Anglo-phobia had eroded, there was a special connection between Washington and London, and most importantly the Dublin government made common cause in damning the Provisionals.

In retrospect it is clear that the Republican movement, self-centred, comfortable with the support organized by NORAID, innocent of the techniques of persuasion and propaganda in America was out-manoeuvred and isolated. Much that went on in America was beyond the control of the leadership – a constant problem in dealing with the Diaspora – but little effort was made to respond to changing American conditions. Again the provinciality of the leadership, their innocence of America where few moved beyond Republican circles, and the pressing demands of an island campaign combined to allow their enemies to control conventional opinion leaving the Provisionals with the hard-core NORAID and the opposition of most other Americans including most other Irish-Americans.

Whether concern and intervention from Ireland would have off-set the lack of American assets, the lack of understanding of American society is problematical. What did occur was the loss of potential assets in America. Not until the peace process and the emergence in America of a new Irish-American generation, sophisticated and allied with the Democratic White House, did the Irish Republicans recoup some of what had been lost. Gerry Adams and company became media celebrities, American political opinion was sympathetic to Republican needs – and with the ceasefires there were no IRA gunmen to complicate matters. When the first ceasefire ended so did American enthusiasm – never to return to the first enthusiasm but present as long as Sinn Féin was seen as dedicated to a peaceful solution. Those not so dedicated in America had been reduced to a fringe – they might favour Republican Sinn Féin and understand the Real IRA but they had neither much money nor influence to offer.

An armed struggle is a matter of maintaining momentum – operational momentum means tactical success that in the long run will work to strategic advantage and the collapse of the enemy's will and capacity. To keep up the pressure is everything and so everything is operational, focused down on this ambush or that active service unit. And everywhere those involved, no matter the front, whether shooting or writing, need more than exists. The Provos have always had to scramble, as did their Republican ancestors, depend upon themselves for money and arms. Aid from outside the movement was rare – Libya was a pleasant surprise and the limits of international revolutionary solidarity a disappointment if not also a surprise. As always the Provos' vision was focused on the immediate, today, tomorrow. How to pay this bill or arm that unit. Their optimism and perception largely off-set the intrusion of reality. Given the immediate past most Provos felt the secret army had never been stronger – and this was true even as momentum ebbed after the first glory years. It was possible for the leadership to accept past error, past problems, but rarely to see the present as desperate. Thus the truce of 1975–76 was later considered a cardinal error but this was really not the case in 1975 nor with most new initiatives or directions – few planned long in advance. The movement was always on the right course and so momentum was anticipated if not visible. There were hard times when the hat had to be passed or a bank raid authorized, when volunteers were killed or captured or frustrated after months of planning and the investment of GHQ's limited assets. There were the blunders, the wrong people shot, a volunteer killing for the wrong reasons, a nun murdered or the faithful shamed. Much could be blamed on the nature of dirty wars or the enemy or the times but never did the leadership lose the conviction that, even at ebb, the long tides of history favoured the Republic.

Momentum could be found despite all because for so long there had been so little hope; persistence may be a virtue but sacrifice for a struggle that is moving forward is far easier. So in a real sense, to maintain the armed struggle after 1972–73 was to maintain the sense of momentum and every decision was so shaped. If new fronts were opened, if gunmen were sent to Gibraltar or Germany, if funds were invested in home-made American missiles, if abstention was discarded, it was in the name of momentum –

escalation was all and if impossible then the existing level of intensity had to be maintained. Momentum is a matter of revolutionary strategy, each penny collected, each cartridge found, every poster pasted maintains momentum and so speeds history. And after 25 years of military operations had not achieved sufficient momentum even with a revitalized Sinn Féin, then the leadership sought a way forward through negotiations, a pan-nationalist front, the power of the American president – entered an endgame that should, but in time did not, offer a sense of rising momentum. By then the process of negotiation seemed little different from the experience of the armed struggle: a constant search for means to maintain momentum when new obstacles constantly appeared. Then, again, maintaining the momentum, the sense of purpose, the coherence of the faithful – like maintaining the armed struggle – absorbed all the energy released by the faith.

CHAPTER NINE

Communications

There is always a cost to communicating underground. Any illicit, clandestine movement suffers in order to maintain secrecy, and so security, denying access at a cost of efficiency. No structure, no arena, no campaign differs greatly in such matters: the more secret the movement the more the cost in efficiency. Yet, maintaining touch is a means and one that most revolutionary movements give little serious thought. The underground copes with obstacles unforeseen or unrecognized or long assumed integral to the arena. The costs of coping are not factored into the equations of struggle nor in many cases recognized. If communication is considered at all it is a matter of forms, a formality, letters and newspapers and access to the media to put across a message or an explanation. Sending orders, reassuring the uncertain, negotiation with the enemy without recourse to direct contact, touching the prisoners or overseeing operations are all aspects of the daily underground grind, not a separate category, not communication at all but the tasking imposed by the armed struggle, familiar and often comfortable tasks. Republicans have always lived partly clandestine lives. The Provisionals are neither inclined to analysis nor especially reflective so that 'communication' means what it implies: keeping in touch, getting out the word, keeping the secrets, the usual.

THE MOVEMENT AS FIELD

The men who established a provisional IRA in 1970 read history and the present as one and so needed no analysis or discussion, only to work through the common agenda. So too after conversion do most within the IRA and those within the movement know without receiving further instruction how to respond, how to target, how to operate, how to react. The endgame made this more complicated, required what was known to be adjusted to existing reality rather than as a basis for persistence. Thus a consensus had to be shaped rather than simply assured and so special contact made that even during a ceasefire posed risks. Until then and still in some part, the IRA must communicate as much by osmosis as through cunning. The various concentrations within the Republican movements often seem to keep their place and direction without touching – Brownian particles in constant motion but giving stability when viewed from a distance. To move the whole movement in a novel direction is no easy matter, but to maintain direction and persistence without investment in communication, as has been the case in the past, is a net asset.

Viewed from a distance few realize how little the IRA resembles a real army, even a secret army. Order, control, even the links between the involved are assumed rather than asserted and, of course, never defined. The IRA command and control is largely determined by the nature of Republican consensus, a factor that mirrors in part Irish society.

In the Republican movement the consensus focuses on certain perceptions and prospects. Most of those on the dangerous edge or isolated in the countryside are so in touch that little guidance is needed. Any stimulus that touches and spreads through the movement tends to do so instantly, the movement is a field that encourages action at a distance. Republicans know what to make – instantly – of electoral defeat or a spectacular operation, the Pope's criticism or a British shoot-to-kill ambush. If the isolated, the margins do not know, then special and unusual – and risky – means must be deployed to maintain the consensus. All reactions to those intimate with the movement tend to be highly predictable.

The movement absorbs external reality but only after adjustment. Data will be grasped, adjusted, and digested instantly by the faithful. This is true for most revolutionary groups possessed of the revealed truth. And this is true for the active-service volunteer on an operation where guidance can be found by looking inward. First principles apply tactically, operationally. It is also true for those out on the fringe who know without explanation what to believe and how to act. They may need, certainly want, contact, reassurance, exhortation, but rarely need it. When they do need guidance, it is when tomorrow is no longer like yesterday – and for a very long time in Ireland tomorrow was determined by yesterday, by perceived history as prologue, by the assumptions of the past. The faithful could thus operate in isolation. Volunteers like the sisters Marian and Doloures Price in an English prison for car-bombings in London may be painfully force-fed day after day, week after week, on a hunger strike without any contact with command central and yet be in touch, know the significance of their sacrifice and the part they play. The lad in the ditch with an Armalite is there through local initiative not a grand plan – in fact most grand and spectacular operations, but not all, come as a surprise, not always a pleasant surprise, to GHQ, often even to the local O/C.

All of this is an enormous obstacle for the security forces, especially in the United Kingdom where the nature of the movement and the faith is less well understood. Even the Northern Unionists and loyalists are of limited help with any insight into the Republican mind because their own perceptions are skewed and their own perspective transforms the motives and intentions of the others. Thus with little local guidance the security forces cannot easily prevent Republican communication that takes place without visible form, instantly, over great distance, without need for conventional message units. Much of the time there are no orthodox channels to find, to cut, to manipulate, rather there is a field with action at a distance assured and protected.

Much of the time rebel communication is instant, self-generating, unavailable. This means in the most meaningful terms that an active-service unit does not need to communicate conventionally because all relevant data is to hand; any 'new' data from command and control are often unnecessary, encouraging but unneeded. Some operations come down from the top, through new intelligence or GHQ ideas, but most, the daily grind, is local. And even new fronts directed by GHQ soon run themselves. In 1990–91 the London active-service mortar group did not have to be told to switch to the new prime minister of the moment when Thatcher resigned – this was obvious – any prime minister will do if not so well. No one in the IRA needed to think about such matters, not in London, not in Dublin. Of course, much IRA military activity followed more conventional patterns with orders from the top arriving daily, plans prepared conventionally, and operations run to form. And so communications had to be covert and offered risk. Consensus greatly assists any underground vulnerable to the centre's power to limit and manipulate communications. The police, the military, all security forces everywhere are apt to assume communications concerns message units to and from the centre and as is their wont attempt to cut or monitor such a stream. Some, the cunning or the sly, seek as well to turn that stream to advantage, to meddle with the messages.

All undergrounds are to some degree immune to manipulation because the dream shapes a world that cannot easily be adjusted by the security forces. The tenets of the faith have real advantage: the fear of schism and apostasy, the belief in conspiracy, the fear of the great terror shape a counter-intelligence barrier. Few of the orthodox understand this; they seek to corrupt with money or to cut contact with techniques. On the other hand because of the need for secrecy all undergrounds find all sorts of communication enormously difficult. The state has all the assets, controls the telephone exchange and the components of hi-tech equipment, has radio cars and spotter planes and taps on every telephone. The underground must first cover its traces and hide its messages before anything else is possible. Sufficient security techniques may offer strategic advantage.

The Provisionals from the first recognized that their campaign would have to have better cover. This was at first difficult because the movement was only slightly covert and because many in Ireland were enthusiastic about the IRA supplying a defence for nationalists in the North. Worse was that in 1970 all militant Republicans were listed, known North and South. Thus the Republicans had to hide what had already been shown. And the old bad habits, open contact, lack of serious cover, ignorance of tradecraft, were passed along as part of the heritage of persistence. GHQ and the Army Council often operated all but openly. Key figures gave press conferences, the media was welcome, visitors came and went, new friends appeared without vetting or raising suspicions. Not until 1973–74 did cover become more conventional although the secret army was never quite secret. What the leaders wanted secret, however, was muddled with the openness of the movement. And the leaders at the centre knew that army matters should be secret and so communications secure. What ultimately occurred unexpectedly was the imposition of secrecy on the process of consensus-building during the endgame so as to avoid any split and deny observers insight into Republican dynamics – the secret army became most secret when it was no longer deployed as an army but as an arena of discussion.

OBSTACLES AND OPTIONS

The Republican movement in all its facets, visible and invisible, legal and covert, has for the relevant governments been considered subversive and, no matter how quiescent, a dangerous, armed conspiracy. Once the Troubles began and the Provos appeared all the governments involved sought first to monitor the movement, partly legal, and then to close down the IRA, wholly illegal. As a matter of course without theory or great planning, communications was an obvious target from the first, and for a generation absorbed the interest of the security forces in Dublin, Belfast, and London. Haltingly new technologies were brought to bear, the lessons of other insurgencies, the traditional skills of the criminal justice system, and those engaged in special operations were deployed as well as the habits of the past. The security forces over the years became highly skilled in causing the Provos trouble, limiting their freedom, cutting, monitoring even manipulating their communications.

This power forces any rebel into a cycle of communications problems as one channel after another becomes vulnerable. Over time the rebels become anxious about the risks but are still inured to some of the dangers in difficult communication that are not as readily apparent. Thus fear of monitoring means no telephone, no cables, no computer net. The rebel trades down, uses notes and memory and public transportation. And few at GHQ realized that narrow and crude message units if safe also encourage schism disguised as tactical or political difference. And the IRA tended at first to suffer least from limited communications because the involved continued to make conventional use of overt institutions and facilities.

Actually communications were not seriously attenuated. It was and is possible to bike a message around Belfast or even out to Armagh, to send a car with a letter up from Dublin. It worked but it was not the same as a real meeting. Real meetings had to be limited to really needed meetings: the regular Army Council meeting, the contact within GHQ, Northern Command inspection tours, conferences if not conventions. Some at GHQ were constantly on the move, but these moves were circumscribed and could seldom be risked purely for morale, simply for appearance's sake. Increasingly only the very necessary contacts were risked although the necessary kept most senior commanders focused on meetings much of the day and most of the night – either talking or waiting or driving or waiting.

Communications are always vulnerable. Haltingly the secret army, nevertheless, grew more secret if still enormously open in contrast to many armed struggles. In Dublin the government and establishment was embittered at the Republican pretensions and then at Republican operations in the Republic. Despite some initial public sympathy for Republican aspirations and from time to time for Republican martyrs, especially during the hunger strikes, there was never a reduction in security concern with the dangers of subversives. In practice this meant that all militant Republicans were suspects, even while the movement retained legal structures like the Sinn Féin party or the Fianna Éireann scouts. The Special Branch detectives maintained a constant watch. This watch was limited by technical capacity and the unknown recruits of a new generation, but in time surveillance made operating and so communications in the Republic troublesome if hardly impossible.

The situation within the United Kingdom was different. Overt organizations were monitored by the police especially after the bombs began in England. Wales and Scotland, as Celtic countries, were not bombed, but used as bases. The British focus was on operational penetration as had always been the case from the Fenian bombers to Brendan Behan – or for that matter Cathal Goulding and Seán Mac Stiofáin, both arrested after an arms raid in 1953. The British responded with traditional police methods enhanced by modern technologies and focused in large part on the links of the active-service units back to Belfast or GHQ. Over time the system grew more coherent, more centralized but in the end no more effective: IRA volunteers were as often caught by luck as by design.

In Northern Ireland, the Stormont system had always maintained pressure on all known Republicans. The IRA and Sinn Féin were banned and in 1967 the cover for Sinn Féin, the Republican clubs, was banned as well. Thus with Belfast disproportionately represented in Provo councils there was an early recognition of the need for secrecy. When Stormont was prorogued in March 1972 there was no change in the agenda of the security forces. The enormous security presence replete with the most advanced equipment could not effectively close down IRA links and nets and contacts. After a decade West Belfast closely resembled a low-security prison but the IRA coped.

Everywhere each Republican except for moments of active service led an above-ground normal life and much Republican activity was so organized – in plain view, legal with open communications. All of these Republicans had practice at communicating on three levels, the everyday, the suspect, and the secret. Since at times there was very little to communicate, no news was bad news, the very act of communicating became important. And this importance was underlined by the continued attention of the authorities – to be followed indicated significance. Thus in the lean years the Republican movement assumed surveillance was a sign of vitality. This meant that most members communicated with care or covertly but just as often in the open or through legal organizations.

The result was peculiarly Irish. A secret organization with no secrets watched through habit by the Special Branch who had no special interest but because of the often unarticulated concern of the establishment of three governments. All this changed after 1970 when much of internal communication focused on organizing the means into the future – not what was to be done but rather how to do it – and the involved governments were, on the other hand, focused on what tomorrow might bring. IRA security and secrecy simply grew more thorough if never total. The years of surveillance meant that if someone on the south side of Dublin wanted to communicate with someone on the north side of the Liffey he drove for 30 minutes and tended to matters personally. Telephone calls were guarded and letters rare. Personal conversations between the involved were easy to arrange – many Republicans lived not only in a movement of the faith but also in close proximity to their own. Contact could take place at Sinn Féin meetings, at commemorations, and funerals, at normal events – hurley matches or the races, at shared pubs and after church. In sum, the members were cautious about their illicit activities relying on contact for serious matters, aware of surveillance – how could they avoid the police car parked in front of the house – and so optimistic about the level of security that existed. Denying access to the underground over the years tended to be more of the same: quick meetings, trips in the country, nods at funerals and the police car at the side of the road. As technological capacity increased on both sides with the IRA always behind but never out; distances from the basics did not vary.

Before the Troubles the Irish police and the RUC wanted to intimidate and display power as much as monitor or interdict IRA communications. The security forces were no more prepared for a modern insurrection than the IRA. One of the early bugging devices put in place by the police in Provisional Sinn Féin headquarters on Kevin Street in Dublin appeared to have been a contemporary of the first mercury vapour light bulb, a large and clumsy apparatus that fell from the bottom of a table during a Sinn Féin meeting to the consternation and delight of those present.

Mostly the IRA could circulate data through legal organizations or conventional meetings. IRA meetings are in any case difficult to understand even with proper transcripts. Most IRA people had known each other for decades, a lifetime, most shared all sorts of special experience, family connections, a singular history, unwritten and unknown outside the move- ment. This was true for each generation. Often taciturn by practice and sometimes by inclination, those involved in IRA meetings spoke shortly, often in parables and allusions, citing precedents beyond easy under- standing. One must live for years within the core of the movement to understand such conversations – especially when now most IRA people at the top prefer to forget as much as possible and discuss little of the remainder.

As with all rebels, communications were noticed by IRA GHQ only when interdicted, producing an operational disaster. Then the first suspect was betrayal and only then flawed communications. Even then the organization and the movement took no special steps in the matter of communication. In the 1970s the movement grew rapidly, stabilized, and then was honed down to pursue a long war without need to focus on 'communication'. The IRA moved deeper under cover and no increase in security skills ever managed to stifle underground communications even if at times it was always difficult to communicate effectively on the island.

The nature of Irish society meant that communication, like much else, was not especially efficient. Republican organizers ran 24 hours late, no one brought the word on time, the telephone calls went astray, if made at all, and the messenger was last seen going the wrong way. For the knowledgeable all the obstacles could be avoided by making contact directly, popping on the bike and going down to the headquarters on Kevin Street or later Parnell Square, driving out to Monaghan to see the man in charge, calling at Falls

Road to talk to someone who would talk to someone. This is the way the country worked, the IRA had always worked, a reliance on consensus, cunning deployed under pressure and necessity, the occasional stroke of innovation, and always the faith retained in muddling through.

TARGETS AND TACTICS

Clandestine Communication of the Secret Army

The IRA is, given all, a small organization on a small island, composed largely of friends and neighbours living in a society attuned to consensus and conspiracy. It is an underground with a very long organizational history, with members who have spent a lifetime under surveillance – first watched, perhaps, while Republican parents pushed the stroller at the Wolfe Tone Commemoration at Bodenstown in Kildare on a June Sunday. Neither the imprecision of society nor the skills and techniques of the various sets of experienced opponents could off-set the IRA's capacity to cope. And coping meant furtive contact, little relevant paper, elliptical conversations, a permanent police mentality, the frustration at the inefficiencies of the underground – and an Irish underground in particular. The organization lacked readily available hi-tech talent, lacked, as do many in the underground, institutionalized tradecraft on matters of communication and stealth, denial and deception – and so lacked a corporate memory. The IRA also lacks the disciplines of more structured cultures but received the advantages of an Irish society shaped by consensus and private conspiracy.

The IRA focuses on immediate obstacles, takes care at times and liberties at others. At the top the Army Council members meet at least once a month to authorize, accept suggestions, contemplate urgencies, oversee the consensus. The Army Executive is there if need be but out of the loop, and the Army Convention is rarely summoned. During the endgame there have been more conferences and conventions but communications are easier as the movement becomes more conventional if in many ways more clandestine.

Paper is dangerous and often ends up in police files rather than safe dumps. Notes are ordinarily taken at Army Council meetings but there are few copies and these are – in theory – to be destroyed. Moving down the operational level sees an erosion of records just as moving out from the core into support and so more conventional areas sees an increase in paper. Individual volunteers, however, *always* seem to keep papers better discarded, papers unneeded but dangerous to carry, papers that should never have been composed, papers that will endanger missions and covert assets, papers that often commanders order destroyed. Too many volunteers are stopped, searched, and found to be carrying 'papers' that lead to a prison sentence. Inevitably the 'papers' – addresses, telephone numbers cunningly hidden by use of initials instead of names, lists and memos – would all be better memorized. Individuals, for various reasons at various levels, are apt to dump material rather than destroy it – the country is pocked with husbanded documentation as well as forgotten weapons, odd lots of ammunition and posters.

The IRA surviving records for some years can be held in one hand and more often even that paper record is lost. The minutes of the Army Council are suppose to be destroyed – although sly secretaries have made copies – but such records are mostly a few names, a hasty agenda, one or two sentences of details. Active-service people in England holed up in shoddy rooms for long periods gradually accumulate heaps of papers, old newspapers, thrillers, reference works, and notebooks filled with potential targets and operational details. Collectors take notes of meetings and hide them in the mother's attic. All the inevitable blunder of the underground, coupled with the natural fecklessness of many and the lack of appropriate training mean that there is a record of communication but much of it is hidden away and forgotten.

Nearly always important matters must be handled personally – except much of prison communication – even when a meeting merely authenticates the present direction. Decisions are seldom formally made and seldom formally communicated. More than most, the Irish like personal contact for serious negotiation, for serious exchanges. Thus the Army Council meets and communicates. The major commanders, the Chief of Staff, the Director of Northern Command, the visible Sinn Féin people, organize their schedule and their security around contacts – this may be secret like those of the Army Council or the Belfast Brigade or overt as a funeral or a political rally. Some commanders are constantly on the road while others prefer to sit and have their contacts drift in to meet quietly, often secretly.

In an emergency urgency must wait until the appropriate response can be made. This time between contact and answer is always an indicator of the health of the movement's communications. Sometimes the centre is under siege; arrests, searches, surveillance all make covert contact difficult. At times the movement is seized on an issue – internal dissent or heavy security pressure – and the centre cannot respond to lesser priorities with alacrity. Generally operational information moves swiftly but in all cases the key is to know how to touch the net. A system with unlisted numbers, no forwarding addresses, receivers on the move and known to only a few frustrated the security forces but seldom the involved. At worst personal contact may take two or three steps of several hours each.

Most messages within the operational pool follow special routes – arteries of convenience rather than appropriate hierarchical channels. Some vital operational messages arise from those not formally within the IRA but are treated in relation to assumed content – the man with a bag of money or a visitor with word of a missile has no trouble getting to the centre and often without explaining either the money or the missile to an intermediary if his – or her – credentials are valid. Like all else, contact is judged by previous experience. Thus a money man may find his point of contact gone – arrested, died off, retired to the country, helping the police with their inquiries, somehow gone. Then there may be some delay until his credentials are recognized by the next in line. Messages from outside the IRA are weighted by the original point of contact as to urgency. Such messages usually seek a personal contact and that for varying reasons may cause delays.

When Sinn Féin, the newspaper *An Phoblacht*, and the Republican Publicity Bureau – anyone available to read an IRA statement called in or carried down from GHQ or the C/S or the Army Council – moved from Kevin Street on the south side of Dublin to larger quarters on Parnell Square there was no change in habits. The technological skills in Dublin had increased, no need of clumsy bugs under the table, and the assumption was that all electronic and perhaps much voice communication within 44 Parnell Square was vulnerable. In fact this is why the movement often allowed months to pass without paying the telephone bill – assured that the state would rather listen into the movement than cancel the service for lack of payment.

Those within 44 Parnell Square realized that some messages might best be hidden. Something had to be done to increase cover for those who wanted to hide the sender and/or the receiver, wanted to talk a little more openly – almost all internal telephone conversation on covert movement matters is cursory, elliptical, and camouflaged – often to the receiver as well. The caller walked down to the south side of Parnell Square and used the telephone in Conway's Pub near the top of Moore Street. Since the Special Branch generally kept a log on those entering and leaving Number 44, this play had a short shelf life. Policemen could drink at Conway's too and the listening devices were easy to adjust. A stop at the more up-market Mooney's pub next door instead of at Conway's was soon ineffective and so too calling from the box on the top of Parnell Street a block away. Finally the sender had to walk down Parnell Street where dozens of telephone points in public boxes, shops and hotels were available. Whether the police ever really listened as the callers moved away to new telephones further from Number 44 or not, these precautions were typical, measured, reluctant, a response to a perceived obstacle, no more. Communications become more difficult and so less frequent: simpler means – the lad on the bike – replaced the more elegant but often the less intimate.

The possibility of police surveillance meant that for the IRA fewer telephone calls were made. And if the receiver were to be hidden no call at all could be made with the message so coded as to reveal there was a message. Along with fewer calls, fewer contacts, there was a reliance again on personal contact. The receiver could adjust a schedule to pick up any messages – pick it up openly or pick it up under cover – or the sender could dispatch a courier with a message – sometimes not even the message only instructions for contact. The IRA had no apparent options. The skills to counteract any police monitor did not exist nor did any viable hi-tech option, burst transmission or transmission beyond the ken of the surveillance teams who could listen to all that the IRA could send.

Even if an effective code could be managed to hide content it tended to reveal its use. At times the message could be coded simply by speaking in Irish: in theory the first national language was in the grasp of everyone in the Republic but in practice only haltingly understood by many and by almost none of the security people in Northern Ireland – at least at first. And the situation grew more difficult for the IRA as the security forces used a growing technological capacity to monitor not just specific telephone contacts but also to apply sophisticated computers to monitor great numbers of calls – all cross-border calls, all calls to known Republicans, all incoming calls from Germany or Holland or the Bronx.

What made the telephone still useful to the IRA was that it could be used for instant if narrow contact, that much of the movement was above ground and could be used as cover, and finally that no matter how sophisticated the monitoring system it was run by those easily bored, apt to miss the obvious, and directed by individuals who were prone to think that those monitored were stupid.

The very fact – the 'Paddy factor' – that the security forces, especially in Northern Ireland, considered the IRA to be low-tech, clumsy, dependent on the obsolete and primitive, tendered to work to the IRA's advantage. Thus an IRA hi-tech move inevitably caught the authorities by surprise. In 1979 the authorities discovered that for six years IRA Belfast Brigade staff countermeasures could eavesdrop on radio traffic of the British army and the RUC. The volunteers had deployed transmitters and monitors and position fixing devices, used taps routed through the British Telecom network – and all this while the authorities rested content at their own skills and the gunmen's lack of them. A similar operation was equally successful during the endgame – and in reverse the British monitored the IRA–Iran contacts at the same time: the same problem, different solutions, and similar results.

What an astute counter-insurgency commander wants is a whole spectrum of intelligence reports that permit the authorities to shape a picture of the normal, the movement of the inhabitants, and so the deviations from the normal. Overlaid are maps of the wanted and suspect, the evidence of past events, and the rumours and indicators of future intentions. Old felons, suspected volunteers, members of the movement or potential recruits to the movement are monitored – daily rounds are logged and car repairs, milk deliveries, telephone calls out and letters in, dry cleaning listed, and visits to relatives. All this goes into a computer data-bank – what comes out is what is wanted and this may not serve security well – or may be operationally rewarding. This constant watch means that the IRA must constantly cover communication – and essentially the means are no different from those used elsewhere and no less effective than those applied in the prisons.

The Prisoners

Those Republicans easiest to monitor should be the prisoners and yet prisons are notoriously porous. Even solitary confinement in the core of a high-security prison in most modern states is no guarantee of isolation – the guards still have children, money still talks. The IRA man may, indeed, be more isolated in British mainland prisons but not if an escape is planned, for even the most isolated and guarded can be reached somehow. Inside, a prisoner has 24 hours a day to contemplate communicating to the outside, and outside the IRA has recourse not only to ingenuity but also to force.

The nature of IRA communication within the prisons is different in that the means is the message, the act operational, the deed defiance. Just to maintain contact, to be a functioning part of the secret army is often ample reward. The Republicans in the Maze outside Belfast called themselves the Fourth Battalion – to go with the other three in the Belfast Brigade. This, while not actually the case, contained a real truth. Service in prison is service to the cause. Some IRA men found a vocation in prison.

The details of communication in and out of prison are traditional. The message written in tiny script on stolen paper with illicit tools, hidden so that even a naked search will not find it, goes out in a kiss. Messages come in through a corrupt warder, a visiting child's touch, hidden under the beans, floating in the tea. Anything that goes in and out of a cell may be conduit, dishes and dirt and books stripped down to bare pages. Any line of sight to the outside world may be used, a wave at the window, a blinking light from afar. Some prisoners have managed to construct radios or arrange for a message to move out in stages, here left, there moved, handed on, and arriving at headquarters the next day. The means are always endless and the easiest is simply to corrupt or to intimidate the prison service. The result has been not only lines of contact but also escapes and policy discussions or even operations – the INLA managed to acquire revolvers and murder a loyalist paramilitary leader, Billy Wright, in prison.

The real difficulty in communication with those in prison arises from perception: the world behind bars is different and different volunteers make different adjustments. Resentment, despair, and disobedience may occur and is often encouraged by the authorities. Thus the IRA volunteer loses all rank in prison where the command structure is created locally. So the IRA people in prison may have no say in policy. They remain within the consensus but often on the margins: central command seldom has time to deploy the prisoners, only to offer aid and comfort in escapes. The prisoners are out of the policy loop. So when the hunger strikes occurred in 1980 and 1981 through prison initiative, the Army Council outside, all too aware of prison conditions and pressures, found the situation novel: the formal leaders could not risk disobedience inside the prisons by exerting authority when no consensus existed. In this particular operational matter command and control shifted to the prisoners – their sacrifice could be exploited by the IRA but not controlled. Communication was reversed because meaning was added by the prisoners. And the hunger strikes, propaganda of the deed, was in itself a form of communication: a message to their own, to their Irish constituency, and to the enemy. Misunderstood by the British, their message was more effective for their own and for many at a distance, international opinion, the media, the liberals abroad. A message need not be a smuggled note – just as in a campaign there need not be secret: meetings with the enemy, symbolic bombs or leaders murdered, informers displayed and riots arranged are message units. The hunger strikers sent a message that had mixed but advantageous results. The intransigence of the authorities who did not understand that their refusal to negotiate, much less concede decently, was a net loss not the net gain they assumed. Even after the strike the British establishment failed to understand quite how being right and reasonable, being strong and correct had produced disaster – how had the weak and criminal shaped communication so that the legitimate and legal lost? The Northern Ireland Unionists, even from within the other tradition, only occasionally sensed that the British authorities had missed the point, had not received the message properly and so had responded to Irish Republican advantage.

In the case of the strikes, the prisoners communicated not simply as an exercise in resistance, not on operational matters, escapes and riots and protest, not even on a mere tactical matter but rather on the most serious matter possible – the direction of the movement. And in so doing they escalated by opening a new battle area. In losing ten lives they won a victory and created assets for the movement that took years to erode.

The Faithful

The Irish invented the contemporary form of a national liberation struggle in 1918–21; the mix of secret army, hidden government, overt institutions all claiming legitimacy while a war evolved that the rebels sought not to win but rather to use to erode the will of the enemy. Thus to communicate within the movement, the rebel leaders developed an entire spectrum of means and channels, orthodox and novel, and rarely, for rebels, contradictory. As the decades passed the IRA, ever smaller, did not so much add to this store of tradecraft, for the IRA had no corporate memory, but retained some and rediscovered other of the necessary skill of subversive communications. The Provisional IRA in January 1970 assumed this legacy. There would have to be a newspaper and a publicity bureau, contact with the Diaspora, organizers to carry the word, party propaganda organs, posters, and press releases, and secret means to reach the active units. Volunteers would be assigned. Matters would go forward as before – this time with more money and more hope. And so it evolved.

Thus, as always, for example, there was a newspaper. In the Republic *An Phoblacht* was published and in Northern Ireland *Republican News*; for America there was *The Irish People*. Ultimately *Republican News* was subsumed into *An Phoblacht* with headquarters first at 44 Parnell Square and then at No. 58, further down the street. As always the newspaper formed a node of power and influence in the movement, less extensive than Sinn Féin but still significant. The newspaper was a base and an internal forum, a nexus of ideas, a poor movement's think tank and often a physical haven for the transients, the visitors, those seeking the word. The production of the newspaper was the overt purpose, but the product was a symbol of the faith as much as a means of communicating.

Much of what was communicated was not news as known to journalists but rather a reworking of the faith around contemporary events. It was a mix of sacred texts, the recent events explained if need be, a house-organ for volunteers and Sinn Féin members, a medium of remembrance, a forum for ideals and explanations that could not find a conventional home. Anyone aware of the divisions and turmoil within the movement, inside Sinn Féin or the IRA at any crisis point, would search the newspapers without result. Even during the endgame the Republican publications do not give a play-by-play of that game or the options open but rather the state of the consensus.

Now and again in the past, there were hints and clues for the knowledge-able – Gerry Adams publicly, as President of Sinn Féin, urging IRA care in choosing targets after a particularly lethal lapse in Enniskillen – the Poppy Day Massacre – gave only a glimpse of the discussions concerning priorities and the often unarticulated rivalries and agenda of the IRA at the time. *An Phoblacht* communicates not facts but the faith reviewed. The facts stay inside the movement beyond the visible spectrum.

The public face of the movement found in *An Phoblacht* is often intended to conceal not to reveal. The potentially very serious schism created by Ivor Bell's alienation from the leadership of Gerry Adams was more fully, if not very accurately, detailed in the conventional newspapers – *An Phoblacht* made but passing mention and that only because of the public disclosures. The purpose of the orthodox means of Republican communication is inspira-tional not informative. Everyone already *knows* the news from the regular media and through the pulsing network of the movement long before *An Phoblacht* appears on Thursday of each week. And the result in form as in function is often pedestrian.

This lack of style and grace is everywhere present. There is no talent nor interest in such talent. No recognition that presentation or image may have a role in communication. The text is what matters – and often the signs and posters are composed of 'text' lettered from a primer from an early art class, stark, direct, unimaginative. The posters combine the most conventional and primitive of typography with cartoon drawings reminiscent of the school cartoonist. Books and magazines are illustrated by the faithful without schooling and talent but obviously great faith and rarely verve. Some of the results are considerably more than pedestrian, like the international journal *IRIS* but nothing to equal the skills of the Cubans or Nicaraguans. If the medium is the message, then seemingly disseminating the truth has a low priority. This is *not* true. Disseminating the truth is a prime priority but since the message goes from and to the faithful it need not be embellished. The act of delivery is what counts, not the costume of the messenger.

Belfast has long been famous for painted murals on loyalist gable walls and even kerbstones painted in patriotic red, white, and blue. The loyalists add to or touch up or begin again traditional subjects during the summer marching season: territorial markers. Thus King Billy or the Union Jack and other patriotic emblems are to be seen in various configurations amid the slogans and murals of the paramilitaries. During the hunger strikes Republicans initiated a continuing series of icons. These wall paintings as image are neither the traditional primitive work of local delegates, attractive because naive, nor the skilled work of an advertising agency nor product of art school. They are instead, huge, almost eerie renditions in style and content of work found on the back covers of school notebooks, work done in a third-form style using the available models of debased religious art and Boy's Own comics. Inevitably they are poorly done but never naive, never very attractive, powerful without being commanding – evidence, not art work. And they are so meant. The crucial factor is that they are done – being done – not finished and so not a means but an end. They, unlike the loyalist paintings, are not territorial but aspirational. Many are never finished, destroyed along the way by the army or the loyalists or changed priorities. And finished, unlike the Protestant icons across town, they have a short half-life, are soon forgotten if not photographed, perhaps recreated later, elsewhere, even on the same wall. There they loom, splattered, painted saints and martyrs of the cause, limned like the figures atop religious calendars, protected by crude silhouettes carrying Armalites, and then some ancient heroes, Connolly and Pearse and new friends the Palestinians or the African National Congress of Nelson Mandela – and always the slogans of the faith, the flag of the Republic, the symbols of the movement.

Because the secret army, the volunteers, are integrated not only into the movement, often within the various overt organizations, but also within Irish society, the many are from time to time in touch with the few activists, the guerrillas and gunmen and organizers. Those on the run stay at a safe house, once this year, maybe last year, and so keep the faithful in touch. The host learns nothing of operations but can visibly feel the faith of the guest, the faith made real, the faith communicated with a taste of cordite. Not all such means are covert.

The need to involve the faithful and so strengthen the bonds of the faith has generated the most striking of Republic institutions and extended meaning to all sorts of borrowed and devised tactics and techniques easily seen by the innocent as 'simply' politics, 'merely' a demonstration or a march. The great, overarching challenge for the Republican movement has been to persist in hard times. Only very, very rarely since 1921 have there been operationally promising times. Even then the reality of the times was often exaggerated by the perception of the Republicans desperate for good news. The Provisionals first expanded rapidly and then gradually contracted but the rituals and rites were never abandoned, proved as vital in good times as bad during an open-ended, 20-year war. The endgame only reduced the casualties, not the commemorations and what they communicated.

Essentially the rituals were involved with the past – commemorations and orations, with present grievance – parades and protests and public meetings and so with communicating solidarity and the faith by different means. The Republican calendar is filled with new grievances, often new deaths, new causes as the struggle moves on. The present is transmuted before Republican eyes, again and again, into the past and the past thus is never past.

The past for Republicans is a clearly defined responsibility, an unfinished legacy, a burden, and a strength. Those who have sacrificed and become part of that past cannot easily be forgotten – those who serve without regard for the cost of sacrifice are not offered medal or pension or promotion but remembrance, a place in the Republican past, a perpetual role however small. Their names are in *An Phoblacht*, their grave in the Republican plot, their day remembered, often by the whole movement, often in a march and an oration. The commemoration for Wolfe Tone in Bodenstown in June brings the entire overt movement to one arena.

Constituency

Like many undergrounds the IRA was loathe to admit the difference between their own and their constituency, the Irish nation that had always seemed so reluctant to rise, so averse to sacrifice, resentful, sullen but rarely rebellious. All risings were small and most opposed by the sensible. This the IRA tends to ignore, blaming instead the political leaders, the local imperialists, the impact of anti-national propaganda. Much Republican political communication is thus directed against those who are not sound on the national issue as much as to those who would be the beneficiaries of the Republic. At election time no matter how Provisional Sinn Féin has stressed local issues, the welfare of the people, the just demands of those of no property, the national issue plays a far greater role in the appeals to the electorate. And when it does not, the voters still identify Sinn Féin with both partition and the gun, rather than with the political agenda of the day. No matter how pressing social and economic issues, the special agenda of election day, the Republicans want to be sure that the people understand that the national issue is primary. And the voters seldom do and elect not a sound man or even a competent one but a satisfactory intermediary with the central powers who have the right to deny or grant entitlements.

In other matters Republican grievance should have an echo in an Irish constituency, one concerned about civil liberties or British security policy or police harassment. Yet most of those in Ireland that did not experience these first hand do not care to learn of them second hand. Thus the only Irish congenial to Republican ideals are those most threatened by the fallout of IRA operations. Such voters have both grievance and a need for defence. In fact most Republican communication directed at the Irish is really directed at Irish Republicans, preaching to the faithful, exhorting the convinced. Those who watch a Republican parade are apt to join the march as the end of the line passes them, spectator and participant. And none of this is easy to adjust because most Republicans believe that the Irish people *ought* to be as one with them. At least in this the Republicans are in good company since most revolutionaries preach to their own and find their declared constituency – the Jews, much less the Zionists, the Italian or German proletariat, the everyday Moslems – less than enthusiastic as did Menachem Begin in Palestine, the Euroterrorists of the 1970s, and the fundamentalist Moslems in Algeria or Egypt.

Enemy

The Republican attitude toward the British enemy is that the anti-imperialist forces within the United Kingdom, those who live in the Celtic heartlands of Scotland and Wales, and the people of no property are not enemies but actual or potential allies: a reading of Great Britain singularly inept and self-serving. Mostly those in Great Britain have no serious interest in Ireland. First choice in the polls has always been withdrawal. None expresses sympathy with the Irish, nationalists or Unionists. Thus almost all Republican propaganda falls on stony ground. Still, what the Provisionals would, in fact, prefer is not to persuade the many that their cause is just but to convince the establishment that it will inevitably be successful. Much of the campaign was focused on the concept that if the IRA can maintain the costs to Britain in all sorts of currency, security and the quality of life, money and convenience, self-esteem and soldiers' lives, eventually, the will in London would give way to the persistence of the Republicans. It is not so much propaganda of the deed as deeds to maintain the visibility of the issue, the integrity of the violence. And what was missed was the power of British – English – nationalism and the psychological benefits that Northern Ireland tutelage paid the establishment. The British would claim that they had no strategic or economic interests in the province – but they did not mention the commitment to transform the province to British standards. The endgame was opened by a Republican movement who felt the currents of time had eroded the British enemy's commitment and a British enemy who sought only to impose an effective, decent, and proper decision by an act of will.

Communicating directly with the British establishment has proven as asymmetrical as the conflict for the IRA. The British establishment, less now that at one time, had long been familiar with the representatives of anti-imperialist forces, few considered admirable or even competent, many assumed to be leaders of darkness and death or simply communist terrorists.

When the mandarins and powers first met the Provisionals directly they found them wanting, innocent, ignorant, limited, without guile or vision – men of no importance – and so treated them and the Provisional movement as beyond serious consideration. In other colonial struggles this posture had to be adjusted, once the costs of staying became too great, so that London magnanimously ceded independence not to a black communist or a Mau Mau murderer but to a new generation of African leaders who along with their other Commonwealth kin could meet, old boys in the rebellion game, for annual photographs with the prime minister of the day. Yet, since the cost of Ireland never grew too great and also offered secondary benefits, psychic returns of the first order, the British establishment scarcely bothered with the Provisionals. Nothing during the truce negotiations changed British opinion – the gunmen could be led at least part way down the garden path to British advantage snapping at unwritten formulation, accepting nods and ambiguities, small men from a small island. After a generation the British decided that given the arena, the IRA could persist forever – better to seek to involve the Republicans in negotiations that would give the prospect of unity on the instalment plan while reassuring the Unionists that this was not the case.

The Provisionals feared that negotiation would lead to accommodation rather than the Republic, feared a repeat of the Anglo-Irish Treaty of 1921, admired but would not admit the skills of Perfidious England. The Army Council was always willing to talk but feared such communication and for a generation nothing happened: the long war continued. Apparently the IRA could persist forever. Apparently the British would not communicate – had nothing to say, believed on good evidence that the IRA could not and should not win, saw no parallel in previous imperial scuffles, no indication that Ireland was worth concession. So there was no continuing IRA communication with Britain – beyond hints and guesses, suggestions and unilateral speculation – except the campaign. Not until the British, after Thatcher, had opened negotiations did the Republicans have to review their image of the enemy.

As for the other Republican enemies on the island, the Army Council for a generation, as had their ancestors for over a century, repeated the appeal to the Unionist community, the Protestants, especially those of no property, to deny their assumptions and faith and merge in the Irish nation. No one listened. A few radical Protestants from Belfast from time to time considered working class ties. Certainly many admired what those of no property on the other side of the divide had accomplished without the aid of the rich or the well-born gentry. The Catholics had shaped the IRA, changed history, manipulated governments and the media. They were, however, still the great threat to Protestant Ulster, to Protestant values. Many Republicans had hope that class unity might have takers or even Irish nationalism have an appeal across the religious divide. Many Irish nationalists in the countryside, intimate with the realities of a divided society, had very little expectation of change. Such hopes were in vain and mostly any communication based on Republican assumptions fell not on deaf ears but never really crossed the divide. No Protestant paid any attention to Republican propaganda assumed to be cover for sectarian aspirations. And there were always those within the IRA who had sectarian motives, whose outlook was as shaped by the priorities of a divided society as the admonitions of Wolfe Tone. Thus to some degree the appeals to the Unionists were evidence that the movement was in practice as in theory non-sectarian, evidence to be read by their own, not efforts to persuade or to communicate. In fact most Republicans knew very little about the Protestant enemy – could not do so in a divided society during the Troubles, where the transfer of populations and the bitterness of loss eliminated contact.

To the south in the Republic, the Provisionals had to communicate with a completely different set of enemies, both politicians and the wilfully reluctant Irish people. Such communication had to take place while support and toleration declined unevenly but inevitably over a generation. The social arena changed in the Republic, pub patriotism disappeared, the costs of unity were judged too great and the IRA increasingly stigmatized as a murder gang. Republican communications, intentionally or not, were adjusted for the reality of the Irish state. For years the Irish politicians were beneath contempt unless they could be manipulated, which was the exact view of those Irish politicians about the Provos. Not until the endgame did the Republicans find a warm welcome in Dublin and even then the country at large wanted peace even if the price was Gerry Adams on the Gaye Byrne Late Night Television show. For most of a new generation – and Ireland was a young country – the Provos were not legitimate descendants of patriots but mad-dog murderers who killed the innocent in the name of all the Irish. Even the exploitation of the wonders of the peace process and the skills of the Sinn Féin spokesmen – in particular Adams, a world-class politician – failed to convince. The Irish people understood what was being communicated, welcomed peace at nearly any price, but had been the recipient of a generation of non-verbal communications that shaped their response.

Propaganda and Publicity

The Republicans had a lot to say but did so by offering the revealed truth rather than shaping images, manipulating the media, deploying the skills of artisans and technicians, and co-opting the talents of the sympathetic among the great and famous. For a generation this meant that the Provisionals' propaganda was directed mainly to the faithful and publicity futilely used to persuaded the unconverted. The truth of their perception seems so simple to those involved – and many, almost all, of those involved dispatching the message are pure in heart. The result was a simplicity of argument, a simplicity often without charm of presentation, that often alienates even the sympathetic and rarely can sway the distant or disinterested. Increasingly the armed struggle has limited those responsible for IRA publicity to their own; hedged in no-go zones or isolated from general Irish society, their perception of reality always at one remove.

Thus it has been hard for many to sell a Republican case to those who find the armed struggle abhorrent, the IRA murderous, and order more important than justice. Often denied legitimate and conventional means of distribution – banned from television, their case ignored by the media, their position twisted and their explanations neglected – the movement had from the start had very serious problems. They were and are often justly blamed for horrors and massacres and could only offer ineffectual explanations. Only the compensating blunders by the security forces tended to offset the damage done by no-warning bombs or charges of sectarian murder. Any dirty war is hard to justify and especially so if the means to explain are withheld: a crucial handicap that in many cases Republicans did not see the need to justify but rather to explain necessity for horror. This had few takers. When the movement had more amenable messages to send during the endgame the audience was more accepting – and the means were more conventional. During the armed struggle, however, the results tended to be mixed.

What has been remarkable is not that Republican efforts were so limited but that from time to time they have been so successful. This has been especially true during the peace process when extensive effort has been made to shape a new image, separate Sinn Féin from the agenda of the IRA, and to deploy sweet reason in front of the television cameras. The efforts have not always been effective but are a radical change from the failures of the campaign years.

The failures are often still easy to see: read *An Phoblacht* or watch the dull signs held aloft at protests, scan the posters for even the skills taught at night school in lettering class much less design, listen to the rationales served as analysis. Yet there was talent. Gerry Adams as President of Sinn Féin, and for a decade member of Westminster, was articulate and effective even in the face of IRA blunder and atrocity. He transformed himself, as did other Sinn Féin people, into a highly effective advocate. Others over the years have been sensible and reasoned, Ruairí O Brádaigh was always present for the media and even in Republican Sinn Féin remained congenial, disarmingly frank, clearly dedicated if in the end opposed by almost all. The Provisional movement learned how to arrange tours of the secret army, even if they do not begin on time, offer access to gunmen, even if not the gunman sought, give briefings and special television interviews. They may lack the polish and skills of London or New York but are better than most of their conventional and certainly more effective than the Unionists of all varieties. The Provos at least while they see British control and influence everywhere believe that the media is an effective and largely neutral medium for their truth. And if the truth is not taken, they do not blame either the message or the medium and so try again.

Over a generation the means used have hardly grown more elegant. *An Phoblacht* is still a house organ, the signs at protest done at best to a printer's skills, the posters and postcards, if still in stock, pedestrian – the faithful make do with rude icons, for it is the dream that matters not the vessel. Digital cameras and portable phones do not assure competence in public relations but by the end of the century the movement was competent and often impressive. A great deal of time and effort was invested in publicity – in large part because appropriate media coverage was seen as vital to produce momentum in the new directions.

The gable-end murals in Belfast and Derry are justly famous, but talking with the United States president as party leaders not gunmen far more vital: a new managed image not divorced from reality valid for the movement as well as the public has to be shaped. And the Republicans had become involved in shaping a new image. The envy of the Unionists and often the dismay of the British establishment indicates the impact of lessons learned.

THE COSTS

Saying nothing is costly. Saying something is a risk. Everything is difficult in a covert organization. Secrecy is very expensive in all sorts of ways including efficiency, especially inefficiency. And beyond the underground an inability to present an effective explanation of the armed struggle, to rationalize a dirty war, to convince their own, their constituency, public opinion in general can be a costly external failure.

Internal

The IRA is hardly aware that being secret is costly – since revelation is a disaster. Closed communications are traditional, managed with seeming ease – and even at the most difficult of times and over great distances. The general and specific costs have often been paid for so long – generations – that the involved imagine them integral to the movement rather than rising in part from a lowly technique like communications.

Every clandestine movement needs cover to deny entry. Every clandestine movement must find a means to command and control secretly. Every movement must counter efforts to manipulate or interdict communications Some problems seem integral to any armed struggle – informers and surveillance and denial of the means to reach the people. Messages must be short and hidden. Those on the run must run silent and run deep. Those under suspicion must appear normal. This means paying costs in time and capacity: but didn't it always. Because there is a heritage of experience, the IRA tends to rationalize costs as no more than to be expected and no more costly than is apparent on first reading.

The greatest impact of difficult communication is not only short messages but little personal contact – and that often limited solely to the business of the moment. This not only causes operational difficulties, sometimes operational confusion, but also loosens the invisible adhesive of the faith within the movement. Distance does not make the clandestine heart grow fonder but suspicious, cold. Minor or operational disagreements and dissent easily adjusted through contact become more serious at a distance. This does not mean that such disagreements can always be so adjusted by contact: Séamus Costello was in constant touch with his colleagues at Official GHQ headquarters but still could not find common ground for his ambitions and analysis and the direction of the more politically minded and so withdrew to found the INLA. Those in Republican Sinn Féin had ample opportunity to put their case to their rivals but to no effect. Often IRA divisions were rarely eased by personal contact, Yet, over the long haul of the Troubles small problems, policy problems, matters of priority, all were apt to grow if there was no contact – and contact in Ireland was always possible but often risky. Faulty communications simply permitted problems to persist – some were always beyond solution, a matter of vision and principle, but many would never have arisen if individuals had met regularly without fear of surveillance. The cost of truncated communication is most likely to be felt in internal strains, schism, tactics discussed as principles, regional dissent as well as operational obstacles. For the IRA most of these difficulties could be alleviated by recourse to old habits, the rules of the arena, and adjustments over time. For the movement – mostly overt – many of the problems could be transmuted and discussed above ground. So operationally there were problems at the covert end, and at the other cusp of the movement the problem was distribution rather than denial.

External

What cost the movement was the lack of an effective means to rationalize the dirty war. The secret army and the core of the believers needed little explanation but many of the faithful, who read patriot history as real, found dead children killed by error, dead Republicans found bagged on the border hard to rationalize with the purity of the past and the hopes for the future. Beyond the movement efforts to explain, to indicate that the British were worse, shot to kill, tortured and lied, did not work as well. So good at communicating the energy and drama of the faith to their own, the movement could not communicate necessity to their constituency much less those further afield who soon labelled them terrorists. The great failing was that the skills and assumptions involved evolved over the decades in preaching to the faithful had made empathy with others difficult, made effective explanation nearly impossible. History has been adjusted to validate the right to resist British pretensions but at a cost in reality that could not easily be made right after the shooting began. The revealed truth repeatedly failed to communicate the cause beyond the core.

Because the campaign lasted so long – a generation and into an endgame with seemingly endless acts – the movement gradually became more flexible, more effective, more astute in communicating aspirations and position that in turn grew increasingly congenial to more and more people. The armed struggle may have been a hard sell by those with flawed means but the peace process had takers and was elegantly presented. Thus instead of costs, there were communications shaped by publicity, appearances and presentations, returned dividends, enormous and tangible benefits.

CHAPTER TEN

Deployment

An armed struggle must deploy the assets of the faith in such a way as to accelerate the course of history. Traditionally the revolutionary says 'no' to history as it is being written. In Ireland the 'no' had been said by Republicans long before and the major thrust was to acquire assets to deploy in pursuing a campaign, most with little but determination and a few guns. Those in *foco* like that of Castro can only act in one way, hide in hopes of generating support. In the Palestine Mandate in 1944, the Stern Group had only one viable option: personal terror. The Provisional IRA in January 1970 had far broader opportunities if not very many visible assets. The Army Council recognized that they would have to deploy in escalating stages in order to convert the nationalists and their own new recruits from defence to offence. Each of these stages would require deploying hoped-for assets in increasingly militant ways.

STRATEGY AND TACTICS

Seldom have the ideas of the leaders so easily flowed into a single strategy congenial to objective reality, to potentials favoured by the rebels. Everyone knew how to deploy. In January 1970, when the Provisional Army Council first met, there was near consensus on what had occurred in the past, the distant past, the last year, the previous month, what the present situation was and what was to be done if there was to be war. What the Army Council, what the IRA, what the entire movement of traditional Irish Republicans wanted was war, not reform or security, and sought the organization, volunteers, and gear that would lead to such a war.

They, like all rebels, knew what was wrong, what was to be done, and what they sought. All Ireland's ills arose from the British presence on the island, not from the divided society of Northern Ireland, not from a paucity of resources or the institutions of the past. The only effective resource was physical force, not the radical politics of the Officials, not the conciliation and delay of the Dublin establishment. The enemy was the British. The only proper outcome of continuing sacrifice, a renewed armed struggle, was the Irish Republic. The key was to seize the moment, transform the turmoil in the North into a real campaign, carry along the uneducated and innocent defenders, provoke the ignorant and arrogant British – wage war.

So there they sat, seven men around a table in a cold room during a cold season, in an everyday house, no place in particular. All were devout Republicans, all had known each other for years. They were men of no property but great commitment. No doctors or lawyers, no former officers, political sophisticates or engineers were present and few were on call. The movement had even with the rise of the civil rights campaign continued to attract only those of no property, the clerks and time-keepers, barmen, the unemployed, the skilled workers, and drifting students, perhaps with a leaving certificate and perhaps not. The seven represented their own, narrow, hard working, conventional in most ways, loyal and true and absolutely without doubts. Their lives had been enhanced and blighted by the revelation of the Republican truth. Prison, misery, death, and condemnation as fanatic and crank had never swayed any of them. What they lacked in formal skills, technological sophistication, elegance and presence, they compensated with faith and so a singleness of purpose that dominated the hours over the table.

There in January they foresaw the three-stage move toward war: defence, provocation, and a campaign. First all within the movement must be organized to expand the IRA – arms and money were wanted, and political support and intelligence. The influx of volunteers had to be accommodated. A defence first in Belfast and then throughout Northern Ireland had to be erected – and seen to be erected immediately. The IRA would rely first on the faithful and always on patriot history. In January 1970, they had no guns, no real money, and as yet no volunteers, only potential recruits seeking a means of defence. They had no organization but the traditional forms of the movement to hand. They had no very useful friends, few friends abroad, and no friends among the establishment in Dublin or in nationalist political circles in the North; but as defenders they would find friends. They had nothing but promises, possibilities, and enormous potential. So in order to effect their chosen strategy, they must simultaneously expand, defend, arm, and organize. They had to deploy on all fronts at once. Everything was possible and everything was needed. What was not needed was a discussion of IRA strategy, IRA assets and assumptions, the reactions and predilections of the enemy and of false friends. All that was known, had been known for years. Now, suddenly, objective reality fit IRA perceptions.

The nationalist population in Northern Ireland had begun to withdraw their consent to be governed by Stormont, by the British. This might not be readily apparent to others, to the nationalists in the North, certainly not to the conventional in Dublin and London, but was to the Army Council. This tendency had to be encouraged and defended by the newly invigorated, newly deployed IRA. The British army, saviour in 1969, had to be transformed into the problem rather than the solution. The nationalist posture must be encouraged, expanded, and tempered during the period of provocation and retaliation so that when the time came to wage war the movement would be ready. Being ready was the first priority.

The entire thrust of the first meeting was to organize the movement, to expand the faithful, to marshal, equip, and deploy the recruits in such a way as to transform them into effective volunteers. The size of the task was enormous, quite beyond tangible assets, but was assumed a matter of time and effort not discussion. Someone must go into the American Diaspora. Someone must organize Dundalk or Strabane. Someone must revive the nets and webs in Munster or Leinster. There was a newspaper to publish, a real Sinn Féin party to structure, staff, and expand. There was a desperate need of money. There were overtures from those in power to probe. There was the animosity of the Officials to deflect. There were command roles to be filled and dumps to be found. There was more to do than could be done and so for the first time in years there was an urgency to go with a real sense of purpose.

What was a curious and mixed asset was that just as in 1969 the IRA during the campaign years was assumed far more powerful, effective, ubiquitous, than in reality. The IRA was an Irish myth, not a few hundred armed zealots. The security forces imagined the IRA sometimes professional – cunning and cruel guerrillas and assassins – and sometimes a conspiracy of the incompetent. Few in Ireland understood the Republican clandestine world, the assets possessed by the leadership, the limitations of the movement imposed by secrecy, and the faith, nor the organizational capacities the faith made possible. The end result was that IRA cover was easy to maintain and that IRA capacities were often misjudged. None of this was noticed by the IRA commanders, not during the final decade when the endgame was dominant nor at the beginning in 1970 when the reality was that there was nothing at ground zero but faith.

By the spring of 1972 the militant Republican movement saw reality conform to assumption. By then the British had repeatedly blundered as expected, culminating with Bloody Sunday in Derry and thus transforming the IRA defenders into guerrillas and gunmen. By then the IRA more closely resembled the force active in the Tan War than the tiny band of the faithful active in January 1970. By then arms and money had been found, recruits transformed into volunteers, operations expanded, publicity generated: the

IRA was engaged in a full-scale campaign. Belfast was burning, the cities had IRA no-go zones, the countryside was bandit country, and the international media ubiquitous. The Army Council felt easy, comfortable without dissent or division. Their strategy had unfolded as planned, as theory demanded, as real life encouraged. Stormont was closed down and the British cabinet in June 1972 offered to talk. The future had appeared as planned.

STRATEGY AS TACTICS

From 1970 to 1974, the Provisional IRA expanded, not without stress, not in a rising line, and not as fast or as far as many assumed, even many of the involved assumed, but still as planned. The old organizational form was never questioned, nor the old routines. The old were deployed as of old and so too the new. All the tasks were assigned, undertaken, and in some part, usually a large part, achieved. The country was organized into a renewed movement, the Diaspora was revived, the IRA units grew experienced and the volunteers faithful. Some of the newly created auxiliary units – home guards in nationalist districts, especially Belfast and Derry, came under IRA direction but mostly growth came from the recruits that sought entry after each British blunder – searches and seizures only for Catholics, harsh word for Paddy at the cross-road, all the inevitable fall-out of an army keeping the peace that some of the people did not want. So the IRA flourished. The steps from defence through provocation to war were taken as all actors played the part as written.

So relying on strong individuals, many of them new recruits, the Provisionals filled out the paper structure. Some IRA companies would fill up and split and others would be little more than a man at a cross-road but the real problem was too many recruits, especially in the Republic, and too few active-service slots. The IRA was in danger of a guerrilla overload. In Belfast, the key arena, the nucleus of a couple of dozen attracted those Republicans of like persuasion and those recruits who understood that a military defence would be stressed. Formally a Belfast brigade with O/C and staff was set up first under Billy McKee and then Joe Cahill and after internment in August 1971 Seámus Twomey. The internment of Republican suspects – all Catholic at the request of the Unionist government – and the revelation that not only did the British army manhandle the prisoners but also selected a few to question by means of sensory-deprivation techniques perfected in previous colonial wars. The alienated and outraged nationalists proved a fruitful base – especially in Belfast. There the IRA Brigade had three battalions: The First Battalion included the Upper Falls and Ballymurphy and west to the council development of Andersontown. The Second operated in the Lower Falls, Clonard, and the Divis Flats, while the Third took in the outposts of the Bone, isolated off Crumlin Road and the Short Strand cut off over the Lagan River to the east. Each district was enthusiastically parochial, as always, and each battalion area became a new reality. The crowds in pubs singing rebel songs and waving one, two, or three fingers in the air to indicate their loyalty. Within the battalion areas the companies varied in size, as always. Within each company area, the recruits were generally well known, vetted by their neighbours, entered an organization to defend and stayed to become Republicans. This process, attraction, enlistment, commitment, persistence, and deployment as a volunteer, remained for years. Only when the campaign evolved into a long war was there adjustment: the recruit knew what the IRA had to offer, the risks and sacrifices, and the IRA adjusting the size and structure of the army knew that very few recruits could be deployed.

Most of the new recruits stayed the course for the first several years because if not the promise of action there often was action and as IRA provocation became more blatant the service more military. By July 1972, all had seemingly changed – changed utterly. Then matters began to shift. The British meeting had no results – no concessions; nor did other contacts. The British army's Operation Motorman in August 1972 closed down the no-go zones. The IRA still kept control of the nationalist areas if not as openly, and still had trouble deploying all the new recruits. So the campaign making use of new weaponry and the flood of volunteers continued: the centres of Belfast, Derry, and the other Northern towns were bombed away, the nationalist countryside was a war zone, aid filtered in from America and the international media was all but resident in the Europa Hotel. When Seán Mac Stiofáin was arrested in November 1972, the secret army had never seemed so strong nor the establishment so vulnerable.

This was not really the case. Mac Stiofáin had been arrested because the Dublin government sensed that with Operation Motorman the tide had turned. The British were not going to make significant concessions. The IRA was vulnerable, had peaked. The IRA still assumed that Britain would not long tolerate losses in Ireland. The will would falter. And all about them was evidence to that effect. The secret army with a variety of weapons and new RPG-7 rockets, with eager volunteers and control of the nationalists areas with important friends on the island and off felt capable of imposing an unacceptable level of violence. The IRA had marshalled their assets, deployed their volunteers, moved to confrontation. They had their war. They had bombed away Stormont. Physical force was vindicated. The

British had come once to the bargaining table. The remaining options dealt with escalation, timing, and persistence. The IRA became an institution integrated into Irish society, for some a career, for many a rite of passage, for all a fact of life.

The war continued. The urban units continued the bombing campaign but not at the same level, as security filters made centre-city demolition risky. The countryside was still bandit country but the IRA 'bandits' had to be more cautious, operate only at night or with increasing care. So the British remained and grew more competent in all aspects of counter-insurgency. Sympathy in the Republic eroded. The cost of a dirty war gradually emerged. And times grew if not hard, then different. What the IRA felt necessary was to make adjustments in the historic form and assets to counter novelty in opposition, to exploit vulnerabilities, and so to continue to exact from Britain a high cost. So the IRA persisted despite the new deployment of their old enemy. The IRA leadership recognized that a war of attrition had begun – they could not lose but could not yet escalate effectively. Thus the Army Council, if not unanimously, entered into negotiation that led to a truce – a tactical initiative by the British who had no intention of withdrawing from Northern Ireland, their Irish responsibility, or a war that did not offer too high a cost.

The IRA of 1972 had by 1976 been scaled down into smaller cells. IRA prisoners using their time as a think-tank had offered a variety of restructuring plans to a leadership ready to adjust the large militia army to a more effective form. There were fewer full-time volunteers, especially in the country. There was a new Northern Command that began meeting in November 1976 to co-ordinate operations in the six-counties leaving the national picture, special operations, military action abroad, and maintenance to GHQ located in the person of the Chief of Staff, often in the Republic of Ireland, for years in Monaghan.

The army was shaped for a long war, Tactical deployment thus became more of the same, more bombs against vulnerable targets – any store or hotel became symbol and reality of the 'artificial economy' of the six-counties – against traditional targets – the security forces and their allies. In any effort to escalate more targets were added to the IRA agenda. In August 1986 the IRA listed people and businesses co-operating with the war machine: contractors: civil servants; fuel, food, and cleaning contractors; British Telecom and Standard Telephones; shipping and bus companies who transported soldiers; members of the part-time Ulster Defence Regiment; and vending machine suppliers. Loyalist paramilitaries were British agents and retirement from the UDR or the RUC did not necessarily remove one from the target list that included nationalists collaborators as well. There were more arenas for action, English cities and then British facilities abroad, more means – specially crafted mortars, letter-bombs to symbolic targets, ambassadors and generals, time-delay fuses, and when possible spectaculars like the attacks on Prime Ministers Thatcher and Major. The limitations imposed by the nature of the assets – working-class volunteers with occasional access to middle class skills – tended to keep the deployment consistent; one year's operations were like the last except for the surprise of location or the skills of the volunteers.

The great strategic decisions had been made in 1970 – options had been explored with the talks in London in 1972 and the negotiations that led to the truce in 1975–76 without effect. After 1976 the IRA sought both militarily and politically to escalate through various means. The military deployment was intended if not to escalate then to maintain pressure: use tactical operations to erode British will and so create concession – the strategic aim of the movement. For over 15 years despite a rising political component strategy was a tactical matter arising from operational considerations.

OPERATIONAL COMMITMENTS

In 1970 the Provisional Army Council could hardly deploy what did not exist but more to the point the members were hardly aware that they lacked certain assets. The necessity of making do with matters to hand, the returns of those self-taught, the narrow vision and parochial assumptions of the involved all protected them from the realization that IRA deployment was limited, could only maintain a level of violence the authorities found undesirable but acceptable. The Army Council for years was hardly aware of the technological vulnerabilities of a post-industrial state much less the psychologically complexities of using force effectively against the British. Over the long run the result was a remarkable consistency in operational desires and choices.

The Provos as a secret army wanted to fight a war, a low-intensity guerrilla war. They wanted military targets although were not averse to deploying against significant or typical figures in the opposition – intelligence operatives, loyalist gunmen, relevant bureaucrats, and symbolic politicians. The IRA, however, preferred to operate against the British military, to kill soldiers first and then members, ideally uniformed, of the security forces – the RUC was in any case a paramilitary force not simply a policing agency. The most congenial operations were those most military, but often the more spectacular were urban bombs or assassinations. On a single day, Monday 27 August 1979, the Provisionals hit double lucky, one of each. At Warrenpoint,

County Down, a typical, regional active-service unit, acting on local observation and intelligence, used a double-trap ambush: one explosive device
was planted in a truck to hit a scheduled British truck convoy and another
in the ground where the survivors would take cover. Both bombs went off
as planned and killed eighteen British soldiers – a rescue helicopter barely
evaded the second blast. This was real war – what the IRA wanted. On the
same day, almost the same time, a few volunteers assassinated Lord
Mountbatten aboard his boat *Shadow V* off Mullaghmore in Sligo on the last
day of his holidays. This was bringing the war home to the English people,
to the establishment. This was surely an unacceptable level of violence –
which was true, but the IRA could rarely repeat such spectaculars for their
deployment largely probed rather than found vulnerabilities, laid rather than
sprung ambushes, and always found the opposition more effective than
imagined. Thus even a series of bombs and shootings in English cities did
not in the end engender English despondency but only disdain and
determination not to concede to terror. If Hitler had not bombed London
into submission, the IRA certainly lacked the capacity to do so – in fact lacked
the capacity to deploy active-service units in England except on occasion.

The operational deployment of the Provos was shaped not just by a desire
to wage war or the vulnerabilities discovered but also by the consensus
assumptions about the campaign and, of course, capacity. Some potential
targets were never considered and others avoided for articulated ideological
reasons – the Celtic regions of the United Kingdom, Scotland and Wales.
No one wanted to cause the United States trouble, but merely exploit the
money and arms shipped illegally by the Irish-Americans. Few were
interested in 'stunts' – revolutionaries are singularly lacking in enthusiasm
for novelty, given the nature of their activities – nor non-violent sabotage. If
the lights of London were to be turned off, the IRA bombed the power
stations rather than tinkered with the computers. Mostly the IRA opted for
familiar operations, sought vulnerabilities close to home, and then if frustrated attempted to escalate capacity or sought softer targets.

The choice of targets, the venues of action, the intention of the Provisional
planners varied from those of their radical competitors. The short-lived Saor
Éire group from the first focused on armed robbery to undermine the
Northern state. Their activists, however, spent much of the money privately.
The Official IRA up until their unilateral withdrawal from the campaign in
1972 avoided bombs. Such devices were ideologically impure according to
their GHQ because they hit Protestant targets and were thus sectarian. GHQ
was in Dublin. In the North without authorization, Officials attempted to
assassinate the Unionist politician John Taylor. In time the Official 'military'
presence was reduced to protecting their part of the black economy and

providing guards for the leadership. In the Republic, a residue GHQ unit carried out a long series of armed robberies but the Official IRA, denied by the Officials, no longer had any military role by the end of the 1970s. By then, those Officials eager to pursue politics with a gun had been organized as the INLA by Seámus Costello. When he was murdered by an Official, the group became subject to schism and feuds but from time to time carried out spectacular operations – the assassination of Margaret Thatcher's Irish adviser Airey Neave with an explosive device under his car in the parking lot at Parliament. INLA operations were more sectarian and less discriminating than those of the IRA. In fact the tiny core of INLA continued to operate for years amid feuds, shoot-outs, arrests, and betrayals culminating in the murder of the Protestant paramilitary Billy Wright inside prison. When the IRA moved in a new direction, the ceasefires and negotiations of the endgame, Republican competition was scant: the Continuity Army Council, supported by Republican Sinn Féin, detonated a few bombs in the North and a faction from South Armagh and the border – the Real IRA – carried out a series of bomb attempts that culminated in the massacre at Omagh in August 1998. In both cases traditional IRA volunteers deployed in traditional ways for traditional purpose even if Ireland, and so the arena, had been transformed over the previous 25 years.

The Provisionals' operational deployment varied from the other paramilitary groups because they were, in fact, a secret army, possessed of a mandate of legitimacy, and drew up a considerable constituency. Deployment, however, was shaped by IRA capacity, not numbers or authenticity or even the shifting social climate. The IRA was a mix of units in the countryside and urban gunmen – all but a few lived conventional lives appearing only for operations and to maintain the campaign. Despite the titles and labels the IRA was never a real army, an army waiting to emerge from underground. In 1972 the IRA was a partly visible force engaged in low-intensity attacks in both town and country that were still treated by the authorities as crimes not military operations. There was no place to hide guerrilla columns or use heavy weapons. None could wear uniforms. All were wanted by the police – as well as the army. That army, the real army, was British.

The security forces were in effect a pattern placed over the Northern Ireland operation grid, shifted to respond to attack and to protect the vulnerable. Such tasking required very considerable resources that even when concentrated, as in Belfast, could not assure tranquillity nor eradicate the Provos without resorting to means denied an open, democratic state. Thus the British army was engaged in a war defined as a criminal act while the IRA engaged in criminal acts defined as war. All low-intensity wars are asymmetrical, not only in assets and assumptions but most importantly in the perception of the combatants.

The Provos, unlike the security forces, were unevenly distributed in number, talent, capacity, and even dedication. Their operations, shaped by the movement consensus as to what was proper and justified, were for the most part left to local units except ventures abroad or those put together for special purpose: the assassination of the British ambassador in Dublin, Christopher Ewart-Briggs on 21 July 1976. Some activities operated out of GHQ, such as the acquisition of missiles in the United States. Then special groups were deployed – again largely composed of the sound and the available. The Provos generally deployed what they had where they had it in ways that engendered no dispute within the movement and that caused turmoil and damage, deployed against security forces that had to provide order to civic society.

ASSETS

Any deployment, especially revolutionary deployment, rests on capacity. And few revolutionaries have many tangible assets – or else there would be little need for an underground; a coup, a civil war, or even electoral victory would achieve the movement's aims. The Republican movements seemingly had nothing in January 1970 but to the knowledgeable great potential. In the beginning and continuing to the endgame, the IRA relied first and mostly on Republicans to supply the necessary assets so that there could be a deployment. In 1970 there were old Republicans while 30 years later there were several generations – not always amenable to being deployed in an endgame but only rarely in splinters or factions.

In January 1970, the sound and the available, the assets to hand, for the Provisional Army Council were the small core of the like-minded who had increasingly separated from the Official GHQ line. These included several 1940s people in Dublin: Joe Collins, who had been imprisoned in England as a result of the bombing campaign; Jack McCabe from Cavan; Charlie McGlade from Belfast; and Harry White, who had been one of the last commanders free when the IRA was all but closed down in 1944–45. There were, of course, others as well outside the central dissenters in Belfast. These were often long isolated or alienated, but who had often kept in touch with the silent opposition. They deployed themselves.

Many undertook to organize what they could reach, raise money in America or call on old veterans. The Provisionals began straightaway to fill the old husks but also almost at once found new people who wanted to do something. The central command found first Belfast and then Dublin easiest to organize simply because there were pools of old volunteers and more appearing daily. Everywhere a historical form existed, but the two cities supplied a foundation for the two great structural needs: a central head-quarters in Dublin and a Northern bastion in Belfast where the threat of pogrom was most pressing.

The campaign key was Belfast where a brigade was established with three battalion areas. Formal IRA titles were given to local reality. Some units with the companies were large and effective, some were tiny, the sound man was made O/C sooner or later. The Northern volunteers had always been prone to military titles for individuals as well but mostly the practice was to give functional titles – GHQ staff or O/C of Derry rather than commission generals and captains – except in time and in only some cases in obituary notices. In conflict the formalities and structure of a secret army were adjusted to local conditions and assets and not really to military titles or proper units. The IRA in South Armagh was structured like a mix of clan, secret conspiracy, and night riders capable of keeping the authorities on the defence, and pursuing operations in Britain. The military surface was a comfortable pretence but crucial to the deployment of assets: guns and money and tangibles are not as vital in an armed struggle as legitimacy, the authorization of history and so the IRA, an army without banners, could not be deployed without ranks and military forms.

By the beginning of 1971, the Provos had a real and growing secret army organized on a 32-county basis with very considerable strength in traditional Republican areas especially in Northern Ireland. Belfast had the brigade with the three battalions, Derry a unit without a charismatic centre – Martin McGuinness would soon supply that – and each town and many nationalist country areas were organized although the full Northern array would not be set for another year. In the South recruitment paralleled the perception of the threat and the prospect of action: for two or three years volunteers in Dublin or Cork or Kerry anticipated a military role. The growing resources were thus deployed as an armed defensive militia stationed in sound neigh-bourhoods with local commanders: Derry leaders for Derry and the Ardoyne in Belfast run by the locals. In Belfast effective parish leaders moved quickly up to staff and brigade positions but almost never in the early years did anyone transfer in talent from the outside.

Ireland, Belfast, even the Falls Road is filled with exclusive neighbour-hood groups, this street, this patch, the Bone, or the Ardoyne. In Derry there was the loyalty to the Bogside down under the old city walls and also the pride of those on the council estates above. Each urban patch was special – and often had a special unit. In the countryside units would cover larger areas and integrate with abutting Republican territory – which might well be over the border in the Irish Republic. Some country areas like North Antrim were like some Belfast areas, cut off and operated on their own. Much the same was true in the countryside. Outsiders come from a few miles away and foreigners from the next county. The assumptions, motivations, experience, and accent of those in Tyrone are at a great distance in time and space and attitudes from the Bone or the Ardoyne or from the North Circular Road in Dublin, much less Kerry. This meant naturally that the IRA was deployed locally. And despite years of turmoil, change, and challenge, the Provisionals have tended to remain operationally very local. On the other hand the British army, even with years of commitment, was foreign – unlike the police North and South – and despite corporate memory would remain so.

By 1973 it was clear that most of the IRA volunteers in the Republic had limited operational opportunities except for those living along the border. A volunteer from Kerry was more alien by accent and attitude on the Bogside than an American tourist who at least could have ostensible business there. So the operational capacity of the IRA in the Republic shifted to maintenance, border units, and those sent on foreign missions. As always the IRA relied on the volunteers they had because they were sound.

When the very incompetent were deployed, blunder and disaster produced not only operational error but also the reputation of organizational incompetence: the Paddy factor. This assumption that the Irish were inept, and so therefore the Provos, tended to be based on British prejudices about the Irish, the assumption of the security forces that only professionals could display competence in an insurrection and the general belief that taught skills and general sophistication were necessary for any endeavour including an armed struggle. The Provos were thus seen as ignorant rather than, as was often the case, innocent. The London talks in 1972 and those in 1975 and 1976 focused on the truth indicated that, despite a profoundly held conviction that the British were duplicitous and perfidious, few of the Republicans involved could recognize duplicity covered by tactic, discussion, discursive initiatives – the rites and formalities of sophisticated diplomacy. Revolutionaries, possessed of the absolute truth and endless grievances, are apt to lack empathy with their chosen enemy.

Provisional volunteers without formal training, given an opportunity, did learn on the job, tap into secure British communications, get elected to the Assembly, find valid passports, make contact with foreign friends, publish a newspaper or keep two sets of books, establish a black economy and – incidentally – run a war. And when it was peace, there was Gerry Adams in the White House, a long way from the Falls – as those on the Falls were apt to notice.

THE CAMPAIGN

Slotting the faithful into the process of an evolving armed struggle was relatively pointless. The new cell-structure was simply a name given to local necessity: the deployment of a great many volunteers on daily bombing missions in Belfast or shooting all night at security bases were discarded after the truce to be replaced by focused attacks – still bombings and shooting out of safe zones using greater cover. The army in the Republic of Ireland was no longer a complex of grand units but small cores of the useful, a great many loyal volunteers on call but seldom called, and the support mechanism. The Republicans so engaged were both visible and invisible, and in a few cases under very deep cover – supposedly known only to a very few on the Army Council. In many ways the IRA in the Republic was deployed, if on a war-time footing, not unlike Republican assets had been distributed in 1969. And the active IRA was deployed as it had been in 1972 but with fewer units, fewer big operations. Mostly it was more of the same.

The major differences was the thrust to escalate by means of new soft targets and arenas and the almost unnoticed rising level of disorder in nationalist areas of Northern Ireland. In the first case there were spectacular assassination attempts, bombing in London, volunteers attacking the British on the European continent. There were over time whole categories of new targets – bureaucrats, those who repaired bombed facilities, retired RUC constables. In the countryside there were hundreds of incidents each week – stones thrown, buildings burnt, shots fired, bomb warnings, roads blocked, dummy bombs to go with the reported active-service attacks. Not only was much of the countryside made ungovernable but also impossible for the security forces to penetrate except as a military operation. These British forays in South Armagh were actually defensive, used to keep the IRA off balance and to lure the IRA into traps, and not to protect people long lost or ground that could not be held. Often the level of turmoil was maintained by individual initiatives, often by those not in the IRA, but still a crucial factor of campaign deployment.

The campaign could be pursued in Northern Ireland – and so the border – by only a few hundred active-service volunteers. And the British assumed that they knew most of the 400 but could not prove complicity in court. The names might not be entirely as imagined but the number of the active was not far off – and what the British did not consider was that sweeping up the suspected would only open opportunities for those in waiting who were often likely to be as ruthless and soon would be as effective. By the 1980s planned operations were limited to an attack force of less than ten with only one or two full-time volunteers. Two or three volunteers in a stolen car was often the attack force. Most of the time most of the urban IRA volunteers, working-class workers without work and relying on the dole as they sought to destroy the state, waited for orders. Commanders might be busy full time but the opportunity to deploy operationally grew limited. In the countryside the full-time organizers and military people on the run were often to be found south of the border except during operations. Many were on the British wanted list of 400. A few were unknown, lived at home, but most played a key role in Northern operations.

The Loughhall attack on an isolated RUC station – a favoured tactical option of Northern Command arising from vulnerabilities as much as tactical rationalizations – was directed by both the local O/C and the GHQ operational officer for the area. The volunteers were those closest to the target. Some might have been included with other locals in a slightly different area but always those on the spot were deployed – it was simply that the spot was no longer one lane or one village and those involved no longer so visible to the security forces or necessarily indigenous to the spot. As time passed and new volunteers were integrated into this structure, some – never all – were suspect only because they were Catholics, nationalists, associates of Republicans, not because the RUC or the army knew them as IRA people.

In the South the number of fully secret Republicans was small: most of the faithful were in Sinn Féin or attended commemorations and parades, signed petitions, made their views known – and those who did not often had police records. They were protected simply because the known Republican universe of some 50,000 to 100,000 was too great to monitor with care. Discretion was often ample cover even for those on a police list. Only a few new recruits were kept secret – secret from the movement, from their family, from all but a few contacts. These were often used abroad or as agents of penetration. Some were not even formal members of the IRA – particularly true with those abroad. Mostly, however, the Provisional IRA in the Republic of Ireland was either involved in operations along the border, dispatched in tiny numbers to foreign operations, engaged in maintaining the struggle or on stand-by. The IRA could only deploy certain assets in the campaign against an increasingly effective counter-insurgency force and did so over and over and often in the same ways.

Beyond Ireland there was little but the occasional active-service unit operating under GHQ for military purposes. Agents and legates were dispatched on special operations but the IRA ran no overseas offices, had no effective foreign office, overtly in Sinn Féin or covertly in the IRA. Often one or two volunteers dispatched to Africa or the Middle East paid very considerable dividends; but there was no continuing deployment of assets abroad – each mission tended to be special. There were always friends in the Diaspora, mostly organized, the odd walk-in assets, and a few contacts elsewhere, but the key deployment was for military purposes – to persist in the armed struggle against the British, first in the six-counties and then, if possible, elsewhere.

The erosion in numbers and military prospects was especially noted in the urban area – not as true in the countryside where the escalation of security capacity still could not overcome IRA ingenuity, the natural assets of the movement in a rural area, or the advantages of the border. The break in 1986 with those who wanted to maintain the abstentionist policy as principle produced an ideological rival in Republican Sinn Féin but almost no IRA losses. One of the cohesive factors was the arrival of the Libyan arms shipments: more AK-47s than could be used as well as Semtex that would assure escalation in the bombing campaign. Who would leave an army with such an enhanced capacity? So the IRA did not split, although many were sympathetic to Republican Sinn Féin. The IRA came first, however, and it was made clear to Republican Sinn Féin that they were to stay out of the army business – which they did but their very presence meant that the more traditional IRA people knew there was an alternative leadership if the armed struggle was seen to be neglected. And the exploitation of the hunger strikes had transformed Sinn Féin into an increasingly visible and effective means to act on events. The party no longer produced only propaganda but electoral support, political, economic, and social control of many nationalists districts, an increasingly subtle and experienced leadership not only within the party but also within the inner circle of the army. In the midst of a long war of attrition the feel of momentum offered by Sinn Féin was important – novel assets to deploy in the campaign – and the reality of the Libyan arms equally so – means to escalate the struggle.

The Provisional leadership, whatever else, was determined to persist and persist largely with the existing military deployment. The AK-47s made no real difference because no one could devise a way to deploy a few thousand assault rifles, but the Semtex increased the bombing campaign just as the security forces had narrowed the number of IRA bombing operations that could be undertaken. In a sense, like all novel IRA assets, the end result was a conservative deployment that did not escalate the level of violence but made defeat even more unlikely. The political option was often played out in a parallel universe, monitored through the Army Council, but rarely impinging on operational matters until the prospect of an end to military matters and a ceasefire. For a decade what was good for the IRA was not always good for Sinn Féin but this was as much a result of operational blunder as varied agenda.

For the IRA the campaign had primacy – and a campaign that always seemed to be thwarted by new enemy assets. In 20 years the urban and especially Belfast military assets and capacity had narrowed and the Northern Ireland countryside IRA presence had remained much the same, oozing over into the Republic where most of the secret army was no longer an operational army but a support mechanism. There had been repeated spectaculars and thousands of aborted operations. Yet the Troubles revealed that the factors determining Provisional deployment were the natural response of an old movement to a reality that largely fit preconceived notions. The enemy was the same, if more competent, the arena was the same if less supportive, and most of all the movement was still the same and more dedicated.

In retrospect most of the adjustments came relatively easily – the Provisional IRA moved from stage to stage, weathered Republican competition from the Officials, IRSP–INLA (Irish Republican Socialists Party–Irish National Liberation Army), and Republican Sinn Féin without having to shift form or function, reacted to the anti-insurgency challenge to good effect by adjusting its deployment to advantage. The result was a protracted armed struggle employing historical assets along with a few novel additions. The operational maps in 1975 and 1985 were little different – that in 1995 was transformed by the endgame.

One year after the August 1994 ceasefire in October 1995, the IRA decided to renew the campaign and discovered a very considerable erosion of capacity. Public support, even among Republicans was thin and so maintenance became a problem. There were few recruits. The low-level violence in nationalists areas in the six-counties could not be generated and operations in England were sporadic and ineffectual. Strategically the operational deployment looked less like a renewed war of attrition than recourse to the familiar – physical force in any form – rather than the reasonable or effective. With declining capacity the IRA then renewed the ceasefire – which meant that for the foreseeable future military deployment, however enticing, was a non-starter. The splinters who advocated physical force simply indicated that military operations engendered only disaster. Tactics as terror was not the same as tactics as strategy and there were no assets to do more. Not only did the Provisional IRA face all the problems of opposing in arms a modern, post-industrial state but the British enemy has special advantages as well as affording the usual vulnerabilities of any open, democratic system. The international system as well as the prime enemy was opposed to the radical changes sought by the IRA. There nationalist constituency was divided, the legitimate Irish government opposed and the majority in Northern Ireland denied their aspirations and logic – and some, the loyalist paramilitaries, use violence to defend British Ulster. The United Kingdom was considered by most to be the fount of democracy, a fair, judicious society amenable to adjustment, no longer burdened with any imperial legacy. Few in the world at large, certainly few in Great Britain, saw the state as tyrannical or at fault. Where once the world was filled with those who saw London as the centre of an evil empire, by 1970 Britain had lost that empire and found no role that seemed to threaten others, create enemies useful to Irish Republican purpose. Thus the IRA campaign would have to deploy force to oppose an apparently benign but skilful modern state admired in civics classes and even by former rebels. The existing international system was not sympathetic to the IRA aspirations and so deployment was even more difficult.

Few in command paid attention for the ideology defined the British as the source of all Irish troubles. Thus the armed struggle had an ideologically congenial enemy and was organized to deploy existing assets to maintain and escalate the campaign, would deploy other means and other methods but only the unarmed strategy of the endgame raised any doubts. For a generation the faith in physical force was ample engine for the campaign. The movement accepts that the dream did not attract sufficient of the Irish people and so had not generated an armed struggle sufficiently intense to force the British enemy either to concede or to revert to form and deploy self-defeating force by closing down their open society and alienating their friends. The international system, the West, NATO, even the new Third World was hardly sympathetic to the IRA campaign. Support was even lost in the Irish Diaspora, with Dublin exploiting the legitimacy of the real Irish Republic and the blunders of a dirty war. Thus the Army Council had to rely more on their own devices and capacities, deploy the increasingly limited resources to keep up the Northern Ireland violence and to undertake other fronts and seek other vulnerabilities. These in turn led to the choice between persistence without prospects or negotiations that might squander the gains of the faith won during the long campaign.

None of their enemies, all stronger and more certain, less prone to blunder each year, could, however, destroy the movement of the faithful, could even restrict the armed struggle to a truly tolerable level of violence. Since what was tolerable grew with exposure and resignation, the IRA's violence became almost institutionalized, the new Troubles convention not anomaly. The arena that had evolved over the generation of the struggle operated with an existing level of violence as the norm. The IRA's campaign was dedicated to changing this norm. Even during initiatives to find other ways forward, the momentum of the campaign continued. The IRA would persist in the campaign with traditional deployment but could not escalate: the monster bombs in the City of London in the 1990s did not change the basic arena any more than had the high incident level in the 1970s.

In a sense the Provisional IRA failed to realize that in the summer of 1972 the direction of events had shifted. When the campaign offered obstacles unlike those of the immediate past, the Provisionals simply responded to the new with the same tactical deployment, the same operational habits but with rising difficulties and few compensating returns. They remained convinced that the British were less likely than the Republicans to pay the cost of an endless armed struggle. Increasingly the kind of deployment that would elsewhere be considered escalation – new target categories, new arenas, new political and policy initiative, new weapons – became instead means to persist.

Before the ceasefire in 1994, the tactical options and necessary deployment were managed without incapacitating pressure or grave losses. The attempt to improve political capacity within the campaign in part led to the schism that produced the Republican Sinn Féin and to real gains. In time the gains for Sinn Féin stabilized and thus innovation became persistence and persistence was still congenial underground to the IRA military focused on deploying physical force, responsible for the campaign, but less welcome to those who could see further gain as Sinn Féin became the more conventional and so less traditional. Effective persistence meant the continuation of the campaign but such protraction no longer offered the prospect of new gains: the IRA did not have the assets to deploy, to impose its agenda on events – but neither did the British have the will and capacity to destroy the IRA. The rules of the arena and the correlation of forces meant tomorrow would be like yesterday. To change the equation, the Republicans deployed other forces during an endgame that many felt was an option with faint prospects, great dangers but worth a trial.

CHAPTER ELEVEN

Intelligence

For the Irish rebel, like all rebels in every underground, data reaching the movement go through the filter of the faith. The more meaningful the incoming data the more they are automatically adjusted – adjusted to the creed, to the consensus, to the perception of the moment. The volunteers of the Provisional IRA only believe what they believe, if need be despite, not because of, the data. They are not so foolish as to deny the evidence of their eyes.

The volunteers live within an Irish political reality as well as their own. This is not always the case for it is not simply African factional guerrillas who believe in magic. The Palestinians issued battle communiqués based on wishful thinking – what should have happened was assumed to have happened. The *Brigate rosse* had faith in a scientific socialist analysis of Italian reality that engendered strategic disaster – the world was not as *Brigate rosse* imagined it and the movement imploded. What events mean, what time can produce, what can be inferred but not touched is adjusted by the faith. In Ireland reality tends to intrude operationally, tactically even on the most committed, the most idealistic, on the optimists who fill the command centre who spent a generation waiting for the British will to erode.

It is the conviction of the Provisionals that in time the British will accept their Republican perception, just as the British have in the past accepted first that of the American and then the Indian nationalists, the Zionists and the Arabs, the Africans, all the other successful rebels. Ulster can be seen as the last colony as Ireland was the first British imperial venture. The British may have tangible assets but these cannot be brought to bear on Provisional perceptions and those perceptions of intangible matters are regularly fed by intelligence from the field that is adjusted as it passes through the movement. The faithful believe that if they cannot win then at least they cannot lose – and this is not true for the British. Hence even very bad news need not be fatal, can be adjusted to expectation. And if one cannot lose it is possible to risk an endgame and acquire the Republic by stages, with a pan-national front and aid from America, from Washington. This perception cannot be proven any more than the asymmetrical struggle between will and tangible power can be predicted.

More than those who operate in the real world, the Provisionals desperately need to adjust all data so as not to despair. Any astute leader might assume that his intelligence data are adjusted by his subordinates to official tastes and expectations. The figures, charts, and graphs, the photographs or the evidence of the assets in place are often made to fit existing desires and so buttress foregone conclusions. When analysis of the present proves faulty – the fault is sought in others not the data or the interpretation. The failure of the British to react within the peace process as the IRA assumed causes painful frustration. The Republicans had found the indicators that they sought in events during the 1990s and tended to assume that London had come to similar conditions. The British establishment, the Northern Irish Office, and even the army sergeant on patrol in Tyrone, all want to discover what they believe about reality.

The British security forces can more easily cope as long as their civil society is not at risk – and few in Northern Ireland or in Whitehall and Westminster identify with British Ulster. So Irish wars do not threaten British vital interests. Hope is not required for most of the security apparatus – the police being a difficult exception – only the competence of professionals -- and even the police never expect to close down crime. Wars are often not won or lost but pursued. This has been especially true in Ireland where the rules of combat, the imperatives of the arena, assure that not only can the IRA not win militarily but neither can the British security forces. The IRA, however, must have hope, for the volunteers are dedicated to changing history not pursuing careers as guerrillas. For the British army the Irish situation is a professional challenge not a matter of hope, not an arena where victory will be won but only an acceptable level of violence achieved.

When the Provisional Army Council met in 1970 with the intent to exploit Northern conditions to begin a campaign, there was no need of confirming intelligence – history supplied the data. What was needed was to begin and so organizational roles were assigned immediately. Once the shooting started, the major effort would be escalation, more of the same, operational matters. And if those operational matters did not prove fruitful then something operationally different would be introduced in a new tactical campaign. So strategy became tactics. And tactics were dominated by operational needs as was IRA intelligence. History would take care of strategy and the IRA would take care of tactics. When a variety of other opportunities appeared – truces, negotiations, popular support, political options, the focus remained much the same. Intelligence focused on military operations rather than on dissecting British diplomatic intentions or the intentions and agenda of the Irish voter. These were and for long remained peripheral to the main thrust of the campaign: the armed struggle When the endgame arrived IRA interests had been shaped not by formal intelligence but the assumed lessons acquired over the long war and the analysis of those who sought to probe new options and those content to persist. The intelligence, other than operational, sought by the IRA during the endgame tended to focus on the internal consensus – who opposed and who favoured – rather than on the intentions and capacities of the other players, all known intimately by the movement but each adjusted by ideology. Essentially the IRA knew what it knew without need of strategic initiatives.

TACTICAL INTELLIGENCE

With strategic intelligence a matter of faith, and tactical analysis one largely of interpretation, the most pressing and realistic need was for information that would permit operations and so protract the struggle. When the struggle was on hold during the two ceasefires, the IRA still accumulated operational information and probed opportunities advantageous to a renewed struggle. During the campaign, the IRA commanders wanted low-grade, operational intelligence – so, indeed, did the security forces. In the case of the IRA, this data passed through the ideological filter in many, in most cases, without need to adjust reality. Too much adjustment means a failed operation, dead volunteers. So in operational matters, always undertaken, however cautiously, in an atmosphere of optimism as is the case with most cavalry charges, the penalties of mistaken analysis are all too clear.

The IRA views in operational matters are short views; today's problems, not even the direction of the campaign nor the returns of a new battle arena, can deflect the necessities of the day. Few commanders spare time to consider either failure or the opinion of the public. If a British army camp is vulnerable only to a truck-bomb driven by a hostage, then such an operation can be authorized without contemplation of the horror it might generate. In any case, war is horrid and the loss inflicted on the security forces vital. None in command are apt to have empathy for those long viewed as opponents – the Unionists, the British, the conventional nationalists, the proper and decent with property.

For the years of the armed struggle, long views are a matter of the faith, analysis almost entirely the province of those outside the movement, and the nature of intelligence never a priority but rather a given. Operations always come first. These make up tactics that are authorized by the use of physical force. How force is used may be determined by local intelligence analysis, by local needs – the search for soft targets or to reassure nationalist victims of sectarian murder or to find use for Semtex. Decisions to withhold force, to delay or to defer operations by command centre has led to schism and can cause serious trouble on the ground. Hence local priorities are often dominant priorities – and especially in the application of fresh data to present needs. And local events are shaped by the general consensus so that the parish tail need not wag the whole diocesan dog.

There is no long-range strategic planning, no central intelligence core, almost no discussion of strategic options beyond re-examining Republican experience laced with reading in the popular political analysis. When the endgame offered strategic challenge, the IRA took some time to cope, to consider matters that heretofore had been taken for granted. Then, just as the movement had coped with other novel challenges, the ideology was reviewed and revised, history often rewritten, and novelty encouraged. During most of the armed struggle, however, tactical intelligence was the primary goal of IRA collection efforts – and often those efforts were so natural as hardly to be noticed by the involved.

The commander's prime concern with operational matters means that much intelligence is so low-grade that the faith need not intrude. Faith may without dictate limit the target list or encourage certain tactical options but rarely intrudes on Army Council meetings. Often substantial tactical decisions shaped by the faith are taken with very little analysis: the exclusion of the 'Celtic' areas of Scotland and Wales in the United Kingdom from targeting seemed logical and natural and has almost never been disputed or even discussed. The focus on softer targets meant that many would see the campaign as sectarian but since the faithful did not, no notice was taken then and little later of such assumptions.

What was needed by the commanders of the IRA in 1970 was not information that would lead to escalation but material things. All actions were focused on the means to war, to a real armed struggle. All intelligence indicated that this was possible so the faith did not have to filter out the bad news. For some years after 1970 almost all the news was good and realistic and useful. The IRA did not need more accurate data but more weapons, more money, more skills to exploit recognized reality. As soon as the security forces were provoked into aggressive responses, the IRA needed operational data to allow effective responses and soon appropriate targets.

Thus the Provisionals' campaign began as planned, as the incoming data had indicated would be the case, and moved on as anticipated. The IRA needed not tactical analysis but operational vulnerabilities and additional resources. Formal IRA intelligence tended to focus on operations, resources were left to special structures and counter-intelligence hardly recognized as a field but rather as a general concern. With the IRA, the two persistent foci of all traditional intelligence activity for the generation beginning in 1970 have been potential target vulnerabilities sought by intelligence officers and the informer sought by everyone. External focus was first on the acquisition of resources, a matter assigned to various individuals operating out of GHQ and not seen as an intelligence matter other than that the movement would report on such resources – but to GHQ not to GHQ intelligence. IRA intelligence officers, IRA volunteers, the entire movement tended to focus only on the enemy, the armed enemy – clearly visible and vulnerable once conditions were ripe. Operational intelligence was needed and often found, analysed, and used without recourse to any formal GHQ I/O staff. To a degree every IRA O/C, even and especially those commanding very small units, was also doing intelligence as an integral aspects of their operations. Every and any Republican was apt to pass along material informally. Some reached the proper operational commanders and some did not, some was useful and acquired by the GHQ I/O QMG and much data drifted away unnoted.

As for counter-intelligence, in the beginning internal concerns tended to be focused on the fallout of the split with the Officials – who was going to go with whom. As the split faded and the occasional armed confrontation ended especially after the spring of 1972, the Officials tended to be mostly irrelevant to IRA concerns. This was also true with Costello's INLA where cordial contacts were maintained. As is always the case in an underground arising from the revealed truth, the threat of informers, paid, co-opted, or worse converted to heresy, was the major concern of all. The apostate was an unarmed and invisible enemy. This was even more the case when the authorities began mass trials based on the testimony of professional informers, often unsavoury and untrustworthy witnesses – supergrasses.

Yet counter-intelligence was not seen as an aspect of intelligence, that was a matter of operations; or even seen much of the time as a matter that should engender a particular institutional response. Betrayal remained a matter for all. Fear of heresy was a strategic matter while most reactions to betrayal were hurried, *ad hoc* investigations, rumours, courts-martial and on occasion execution. As in the beginning with operations, every volunteer, every member of the movement, was involved in discovering those who would betray the dream. There was no real counter-intelligence apparatus but a very real movement focus on the most feared vulnerability of all – betrayal from within. Inexplicable IRA operational failure would produce efforts to trace a leak or discover a betrayal, often not by a special unit but rather by those who remained.

The number of informers revealed and often punished in a generation creeps toward 100, exact numbers are difficult to establish. The visible indications of IRA counter-intelligence could also be found in the repeated public calls for repentance with a promise of pardon, the threat of vengeance for those who might or have been tempted, and finally the tangible evidence of justice done in the form of suspects shot and maimed, tortured, or discovered with their hands tied, eyes covered with electrical tape, and a bullet hole in the skull. A few informers simply vanished not to re-emerge until May 1999 when the IRA began to indicate secret burial sites.

For the IRA commanders, 'intelligence' consisted of tactical, often technical, operational material more often than not acquired by random observation, by friends and allies in general, and as the result of requests for particulars of some sort. The major intelligence thrust was to organize proper intelligence officers, set up lines of communication, allow the IRA to operate as had always been the case. Often anyone available is tasked, at times for intelligence duties and at other times for whatever need be done. And many appear with data as to what can be done. Much of this intelligence had a very short shelf-life, a use-by date of a month or two, but some could be stowed away, added to from time to time, and unearthed eventually for an operation. Mountbatten was surveyed as a target for ten years, the attacks on Margaret Thatcher at Brighton and John Major on Downing Street indicated a considerable level of tactical intelligence gathering.

The various I/O officers, chosen for inclination and interests rather than the slightest training, can often call on all sorts of secret assets. And from time to time, the IRA is capable of moving up technologically and constructing a complex and continuing operation for other than immediate purposes, to have recognized tactical impact. There is no parallel capacity for analysing non-operational data although Sinn Féin and various local structures supply an uncertain means to estimate reality, political reality, general morale, the capacities of allies and potential enemies. Much of this non-military data is simply accumulated by the movement because everyone is involved within a small compass. Much of the data are shaped by wishful thinking, limited tools, a parochial vision and the faith; for example, the expectation of votes in the Republic once Sinn Féin had given up abstentionism, an expectation criticized by those familiar with the 26-counties, failed to materialize. In fact the importance of the pan-national front within the peace process has become problematical.

Still, the capacity to acquire useful and realistic political data increased over the last decade. Since those involved – unlike the gunmen – remain active within the movement, their skills gradually accumulate even when not institutionalized. Those in the IRA leadership unsympathetic to the cost and prospects of the new direction are apt to draw their data, like their support, by traditional means.

OPERATIONAL INTELLIGENCE

In curious contrast to the agenda of most undergrounds, the IRA operational commanders do not want more intelligence but only what is needed. There is no place in the IRA for more, no storage facilities, no time to consider options, no prospect of any long-term demand, and no reason to shift resources to build such a database. What exists is what the IRA can remember individually. What IRA operations need is ripe data good for the present – tomorrow can wait.

At times the IRA initiates intelligence operations far beyond the search for operational data. Then an opportunity is taken that requires, investment in time, planning, readjustment of structure, and the co-option in or out of the movement of the necessary skills. In Belfast in the early part of 1979, the RUC undertook *Operation Hawk*, a major surveillance effort relying on sophisticated electronic equipment, covert operations, and existing files to track leading IRA suspects. In March 1979 an RUC checkpoint stopped a car to find they had scooped up the key IRA GHQ operational officer Brian Keenan – and as bonus his coded address book. London informed the RUC that his notes suggested a raid on three houses. On 15 June 300 police and another 100 soldiers swooped and discovered that the Provisionals had been running a highly sophisticated intelligence operation – running their own surveillance, keeping a watching brief on *Hawk* and tapping into many other covert security forces activities – and doing so unnoted, unsuspected for over six years.

The Belfast IRA had set up telephone taps in the British Telecom network that included a tap on the private line on the Dunmurry residence of the general commanding the army garrison. Components had come from the Ulster Polytechnic, and the Grundig and Strathearn Audio factories. And there were the IRA files, real files just as any professional intelligence operations would generate: details of the houses, cars, lifestyles of civil servants and judges and security people. There were photographs, endless pages of transcripts of secret transmission of the security forces. And they had used their skills and the electronic equipment from Grundig and Strathearn Audio to set up a modern factory producing elegant electronic and radio detonation devices for the IRA bombs: research and development underground as well as intelligence.

Once the IRA had cracked the codes for the RUC's *Operation Hawk* – the volunteers watched the watchers. One early ploy was to move their own people around so that the authorities would track them thus revealing the police code word – one gunman was disgruntled to discover he had been named 'Chicken' and another 'Budgie'. The IRA had also followed much that the security force assumed was beyond reach. At least the British also found data that allowed them to thwart another helicopter rescue to get Keenan out of Brixton Prison in London, but this was scant comfort. The 'incompetent' Paddies had for six years been watching the watchers, bugging the bugs, calling off risky operations, moving out of unsafe locations, refining their bombs, and the authorities never the wiser. The Provos had, in fact, engaged in one of the most highly sophisticated, long-lived surveillance operations by an underground on record – indicating that learning-on-the-job and a lack of certificates need not deter the determined.

The bulk of IRA operational intelligence remained focused on tomorrow's target. Local operations from across the border or out of the parish might require more data. Sometimes the information is wrong or limited or misused. Sometimes the volunteers are fed deceptive data – the IRA rarely has the time, skills, or opportunity to put together complex counter-deception policies relying on cunning and a sense of the arena. While the security forces invest considerable effort in planting agents, planting rumours, running up false flags, using deception and counter-deception ploys, the IRA is apt to wait for walk-in informers, local reports, and occasionally on volunteers directed specifically to gather operational data – Lord Mountbatten's schedule or details of the IRA counter-measures in London.

Very little hard data is really needed for most operations. The information on Mountbatten had been accumulated by the local I/O for years, kept up to date by observation each summer. There was always the possibility to exploit the existing vulnerability: an assumption on Mountbatten's part that he was safe, even admired, in his summer residence, and by the local Gárdá that the IRA would not make an attempt on his life. Access was relatively easy once GHQ decided on the operation. In general, on the island, the campaign arena was small, the routines of all – English royals, RUC or Gárdá patrols, British army habits and the homes of many of the involved – known. Britain was hardly as small but in an open society much intelligence was easily acquired.

The attacks on the British prime ministers in Brighton and London required very limited investment in time and effort. Downing Street could hardly be moved nor could Thatcher's reservations at the Grand Hotel be hidden. In both cases, the problem was not one of intelligence but access that allowed withdrawal: and in both cases technological adaption to existing conditions – a time-phase detonator in Brighton and a disguised mortar truck in London. These put the IRA within reach of the targets – a bomb hidden in the wall of the hotel by a 'guest' and a place to park a 'truck' in range of Downing Street. Observation, a close reading of open sources, a bit of logic and the operations were viable.

Those under threat are apt to exaggerate the complexity of acquiring such intelligence and the details needed and thus the skills of the IRA. The bold and ruthless, those dedicated to risk and violence, can make do with very little. Those who operated in England did so with reasonable success until bad luck, lack of craft, routine police work, or British technological capacity caught up with them. As for most IRA operations – routine ambushes along Irish country roads or a murder done not from a ditch but in the midst of a shopping centre or even in Germany or Holland – the IRA gunmen needs only the most immediate operational data. What is wanted is arrogance, audacity, good luck, and an escape route back into the underground. Most targets are soft and any target can be vulnerable the first time or for those willing to take great risks.

Sometimes operational intelligence is personal knowledge, sometimes the data drifts in from the neighbourhood. Rarely is information sought out as in Brighton or Downing Street and even more rarely the output of a continuing surveillance operation like that in Belfast. Often special needs like those of the prisoners or the requirements of the GHQ for arms and money generate special focus. These are seldom considered intelligence needs but rather special tasks to be filled by those sound and available and capable – and these may well include those involved in intelligence but mostly likely not. Most volunteers selected for data collection will be those available rather than those specifically involved in underground intelligence gathering. In such matters diversification is rampant. Intelligence is rarely compartmentalized but everywhere an aspect of life within the movement, for the volunteer, for GHQ, for the woman in Sinn Féin or the old man on the way home from Crossmaglen. Each is not only faithful but a source of data, sometimes sought, often volunteered, always a natural act and one hard to chart or to counter.

COUNTER-INTELLIGENCE

For the IRA counter-intelligence as a special province of the underground hardly exists as a concept. Keeping the secrets is natural, not a matter that needs form. The less said the better. The closer one is to the centre the fewer secrets one wants to know, the fewer names. And everyone recognizes the need to say nothing, to keep the secret as a secret even when the dogs in the street know. Ireland is filled with those who know secrets, some imagined, some not. Again the closer an individual to the violence of the campaign, the less attractive is the possession of data – say nothing, see nothing. Safety is thought to come with ignorance just as for those more distant power arises from the revelation of an imagined secret. In point of fact denial of access by the IRA is special, some things all know and some matters are closely held – few know even at the centre of the circle.

Any non-military activity is apt to reveal those who also are on active service. Not too many operational volunteers can retain anonymity for too long. Yet knowing the names is not the same as understanding the movement. Even if the 'names' were arrested – the 400 suspects – little would change.

The result has been that many people outside the movement know something about the movement and some of these are professional watchers – police agents, loyalist paramilitaries, plainclothes soldiers. Because of the nature of Irish society, garrulous but secretive, while everyone may know something or everyone within the movement may know something, the watchers may not. And what is known, names and behaviour patterns, the ownership of automobiles, and the meetings of commanders, may be of limited use. The movement remains a conspiracy and its nature remains elusive even to those living next door, those who know names, those whose careers have been to gather data despite the cover.

Cover in the form that has evolved over the years is a given, not a matter that counters active measures but merely the way matters proceed. All undergrounds are composed of the faithful with their special language and priorities, with a vision and the faith and one cannot enter without conviction or conversion. Beyond this underground is the conspiracy, the operational world of the campaign that is vulnerable to penetration. The foolish volunteer takes risks, the inept talk too much, the feckless, wanted by the authorities, appear at home or at the pub, make telephone calls back to Belfast from abroad, break the obvious rules, get caught, and are replaced. None of this is considered by the IRA leadership a matter of intelligence, a matter that can be countered but rather a condition that must be endured and a condition that may be ignored only at risk. Over the years many volunteers took such risks and many paid for so doing. And those who did not, who combined luck, audacity, and cunning, have often remained unknown and active year after year. Even those suspected may keep under-cover beyond reach of formal charges.

Security is maintained not by organizational rules but common sense and habit. Some without common sense are apt to acquire information that might better be closely held. Rumour and revelation are everywhere and there may be evidence that the authorities are seeking to suborn volunteers. Informing is a fact of life and in Ireland a long-lived danger for any conspiracy.

Within the IRA underground there is always free-floating suspicion about any volunteers just as there is great trust in all volunteers. So there is a range of possible leaks from the agent-in-place, most feared and mostly rare, to the gossip of grannies, the background music to any local operation and least considered by the IRA if not always by the authorities who must find the right tune amid the clamour. And after a generation the authorities, despite the welter of technological devices, programmes, and systems, despite the filters, watchers, and active measures, want more than all else a way into the movement – and the best way is always the informer.

When an operation like the failed raid on the Loughall RUC station that cost the lives of eight volunteers occurs, a complete shambles, a walk-in ambush, the assumption is that not only had cover been lost, secrecy violated, information leaked out, unwittingly perhaps, but also that someone may have betrayed all. Many operations abort in ambiguity or as a result of obvious blunder. Sometimes subsequent discovery indicates how cover was lost: a security source is tapped, a constable talks unwisely, an informer caught recants past sins. Sometimes it is clear that simple ineptitude or Irish luck was at work: Keenan arrested at a chance roadblock while carrying his 'coded' address book. Sometimes the authorities plant rumours, sow distrust, and sometimes everyone is too busy to investigate

Loughall was typical of those examples where suspicion had to be raised, directed, investigated. The loss was too great to blame solely on Irish luck or British competence. Usually each such case is taken on its merits. Those most concerned are those most proximate to the event and they seek as a matter of course the informer as a possible explanation for disaster. And if such betrayal then or later is discovered, an institutional response is to hand within the procedures of the IRA military structure. The informant is either a spy and so treated or a traitor and so tried. Such trials are often less than fair despite the apparent formalities resting on assumed evidence and quickly gathered suspicion. All of this pretrial activity would above ground in the world of the orthodox be counter-intelligence, but for the IRA it is a mix of *ad hoc* investigation and military forms.

It has become apparent from the record that at times agents, British soldiers disguised, police spies as potential allies, individuals on the make or in the pay of the security forces, may penetrate cover and so do specific damage. This can be contained. Penetration is in any case difficult in a small country where so much is known about everyone: no legend for a British soldier can last long if suspected, few Protestants can long pass in Catholic areas. Moreover such penetration is considered by the IRA a serious but conventional danger – an act of the dirty war.

Much worse is when penetration is not from the outside but through the corruption of the faithful. For a volunteer no cover is necessary, the legend is real, only hiding the connection with the security forces. Family history and past service become cover to treason. A volunteer, a friend, may be co-opted, intimidated, purchased, may not be sufficiently faithful. To counter such a prospect, a reality none likes to face and all assume inevitable during a dirty war, everyone must be alert. None, however, wants to articulate any general suspicions; for all are committed to the ideal, possess the revealed truth as sound Republicans. Each depends on the faith of all. Still each must have some doubt about all so not to allow the heretic free play. All the Republican faithful are one but all must remember the prospect that one is no longer faithful.

So there is a real but unrecognized anxiety to counter any signs of faith-lessness. At worst in bad times, the movement is driven by paranoia, trusts no one. By and large this suspicion is the obverse of the faith, comes with the original commitment, plays no formal role in any underground counter-intelligence but forms a barrier to the success of the informer. Within this atmosphere the IRA specifically seeks information on those who might have penetrated that cover or may have betrayed the organization. There is no formal counter-intelligence, only the suspicions of the underground and the quickly organized pursuit of those involved in failure. What the IRA does about betrayal is necessary, prudent, and natural, not a special case requiring a special permanent structure or even much consideration.

STRUCTURE AND INSTITUTIONS

IRA intelligence is, for example, most general in accepting the faith as a means of security from betrayal and the most particular in seeking evidence to such betrayal. Mostly intelligence is special: the hunt for targets, the open door, the loose window, the unarmed guards. It is practical intelligence. The kind of special and general intelligence, scenarios, tactical options, cultural, economic, and social backgrounds, vertical files and data stacked in computers is mostly beyond the capacity and the concern of the organization. It is difficult enough being a secret army staffed by the self-taught under constant pressure without reproducing the luxuries of a state security apparatus. And such an apparatus is vulnerable to loss, as the IRA found in Belfast after six years, difficult both to use and to hide unless focused on narrow operational matters: what the British army intends next, what the RUC knows. Then the data grows stale, need not be kept, filed, and analysed. Analysis for future use is a luxury the gunmen cannot often afford.

The texts of Republican dogma supply much of what might pass as strategic information – present reality is filtered through historically valid prescriptive spectacles. IRA Rules OK and a return to a tactical focus: a sensible allotment of priorities since most strategic analysis would be depressing and most long-range planning pointless. When the basic dogma comes into question, as has been the case with the peace process, intelligence like all other IRA functions must undergo a sea change: no targets, no operations, no tomorrow. During a campaign the IRA needs tactical, really operational, information and in order to escalate talent that cannot be found by research. As in the case of reality, too much intelligence may be an obstacle not an asset. And if there is no campaign the need is less but still real – Sinn Féin can gather political, economic, and social intelligence but the IRA even during a ceasefire or a truce is apt to continue to seek targets for tomorrow.

Although called an army, the IRA has been more the armed and central core of a movement. The formal structure of the IRA is not that of a real army but that of the armed underground of 1922–23 with military titles. These titles indicated roles and so missions. There were in 1990 as there had been in 1970, titles for intelligence: GHQ, usually if not always, has an intelligence officer, I/O, as does Northern Command and certainly Belfast brigade and sometimes other 'brigade' formations. Each battalion or operating sector has one as well. Before 1993, most of the intelligence officers oversaw collections, collated and passed the interesting along. Some played more active roles. And, of course, none stopped in 1993 – and when the ceasefire was ended the data played a part in the renewed campaign.

Mostly the individual in control of operations under whatever title is also the prime collator of intelligence data. Mostly the data is collected on targets, occasionally sought by order – a means to reach Thatcher or the vulnerable British bases in Germany or to renew the campaign with a strike at Canary Wharf – and sometimes arises directly or indirectly from the movement. Certain intelligence officers have imposed their capacity on the position, but more often than not operations officers are the most important in the process. When there is a need or an opportunity, special intelligence groups may actually be created, as has been the case in Belfast at times on a large scale and other places to a lesser extent. Often IRA intelligence is assumed extensive because every operation must use denial in order to be a surprise – and every IRA operation is a surprise to the target or victim. Such surprise is assumed to arise from a considerable net of spies, informants, agents, and associates – a vast intelligence net in Ireland and at times abroad. This is both not the case and not without reality: the IRA does rely on many who are haphazardly maintained and cursorily organized but always sufficient for the purpose.

What the IRA lacks and has always lacked – without missing it – has been a central analytical capacity, a core intelligence group with institutional memory and proper files and the future as priority approached not solely as a time for more operations like the ones of yesterday. At times intelligence officers may accumulate files – a danger to possess – especially on individuals; but much of IRA intelligence comes not out of a database but personal experience – and such experience is regularly depleted by time, arrests, and negligence. There is no real corporate memory, rarely relevant files and so no extensive intelligence structure.

There is little political or economic intelligence that cannot be found in the overt assumptions of Sinn Féin. Sometimes IRA records do exist but they are often beyond reach in dumps. There are photographs, lists, addresses, hard data; but often such material is beyond the reach or interest of those engaged in the daily struggle. The IRA does, indeed, have an intelligence capacity, often so labelled on the chart, often discovered to the amazement and horror of the authorities; but the IRA intelligence establishment is never the flip side of the conventional. The intelligence analytical tail is small, the records scant, non-military matters largely ignored, and the impact of corporate memory at times almost negligible. And counter-intelligence is focused on informers and the failure of cover. As in most matters the IRA must make do, like all others engaged in an armed struggle.

Everything underground is difficult including intelligence that seems to flow to command central so easily. Keeping files is no easy matter underground and always risky. A poster has sent the owner to jail in the Republic and any IRA 'paper' found by the authorities is time in a cell in Northern Ireland. The less paper the better. And so a cunning activist can hold a year's paper in one hand without strain. While a revolution, just like a political party or a real government, seemingly moves ahead on reams of paper, programmes for the future, lists of grievances for posters and protests, sheaves of printout and now floppy disks, all these contain the exegeses of the faith, the text of belief. Paper is for the pure, for politics, for the periphery. The gunman wants whispered instructions that will get him to the target on time and back home in safety.

Those on active service, if effective, try to avoid paper; but there is no IRA class in tradecraft, no mid-career IRA review of the state of the art in covert affairs, no form, no book to read, no experience to absorb in a seminar. At best there is on-the-job training expanded by conversation and example. And even then some volunteers forget, are feckless, arrive at a meeting with a written agenda, talk over a pint. The searching and seizing are regular, the monitoring constant, the raids regular. Nothing is secure for long or forever. Obviously 'Keep No Written Data' should be a cardinal rule of rebel trade-craft but it is not, certainly not with the IRA. Over and over even the most experienced volunteers keep dangerous paper. At best they hide paper in the flower pot or the hollow bed post but more often they hide it not at all as the first search reveals when they empty their pockets. In a sense to hide paper is to imply personal vulnerability and all those underground remain criminally optimistic about their chances. No one who believes in the law of averages should volunteer as gunman. The active-service volunteer may be cunning in most things but rarely can afford to plan for failure, the arrival of the police. The more cautious keep operational data in mind and even then such storage is easy to lose. Thus IRA intelligence is not only finding but hiding where retrieval is possible – the former is easier than the latter. So there is no central archive and so no central analysis agency underground but means in place to cope.

THE PRACTICE OF REBEL INTELLIGENCE, OPERATIONAL FACTORS

Since the IRA has relegated strategic intelligence to the rituals of the faith and most tactical intelligence to a focus on the day-to-day campaign, practice is centred on operations. There is little else to practise on but the search for traitors and the needs of GHQ which are usually defined as special operations rather than intelligence matters. Finding money, acquiring arms, ferreting out the intentions of Irish politicians are not considered intelligence matters.

Target Data

The IRA focuses its resources, much of the movement's resources, on persisting in the armed struggle. Even in the rare pauses the maintenance of capacity has first priority. As for the campaign, protraction requires operations and these require target data. For most within the secret army, intelligence is entirely a matter of targets: the data needed for every operation and by each operations officer, by the secret army involved in an army's business. And even during a ceasefire the secret army must remain in the army business, wants intelligence about targets even if the targets are now irrelevant.

After a generation much of this data arrives with the regularity of the daily newspaper and without any greater cost. No real investment is needed by the IRA, by the movement, to track soldiers, to find a way into Belfast central, to number the staff at a police station or to map the way home of a prison guard. Many in the movement in the combat arena report as a matter of course. Constant repetition has produced craft and militants always open to the main chance. The chances are taken, the operations follow the conventions, and the lethal muzak of culvert bombs, sniping, arson, sabotage, and ambush runs on with preparation, planning, commitment, and with-drawal all but blended into one. Each facet contains an intelligence com-ponent but this is rarely considered separately. For a few special cases those in command must step back, see the matter in parts, seek, often by novel means, specific intelligence rather than the usual.

These novel targets often require more craft than is available and often more sophistication than can be found among those volunteers so dis-patched for the operations. Being sound and eager, veterans of mid-Tyrone or a tour in England, does not help much to operate in Spain or find sophisticated military equipment in Chicago or New York. Sometimes talent can be co-opted, often unexpectedly, and often unexpectedly talent appears; but if not those involved must cope anyway. They must find the novel target unprotected, the necessary data somewhere. If at times they do not and when they do not, GHQ most often learns about it from the evening news: terrorists shot in Gibraltar or Irish suspects arrested in London. The innocents abroad have been swept up or shot down, lost their cover, gone missing, their mission aborted, if lucky escaped but returned without data, without arms, and often without any lessons learned for GHQ to apply, to ponder. And others who may or may not be more crafty are sent.

In general, operational data sought by the IRA falls into the categories of targets of old, targets of opportunity, and targets novel. Only in the last case is a very special effort made. At one time all targets were novel, all opportunities a surprise and welcome, and the only experience that of old campaigns haltingly remembered. Now, after a generation, much of the action on the island is almost conventional by IRA standards – only from time to time does an unexpected opportunity appear and rarely does GHQ construct a really novel direction. Elsewhere in England, on the European continent, and in the United States the IRA has fewer assets and often less received wisdom. Special efforts to find ground-to-air missiles, especially in the United States, have indicated no learning curve and no real results. Even commissioning sympathetic engineers to build from scratch, for the IRA a novel if time-consuming and costly procedure, failed.

Much of the failure of IRA covert intelligence remains covert, hidden from the authorities, the public, and often even GHQ. Cover and the necessity for covert operations means at least that disaster does not always appear in the newspapers. This is because most failure is quiet, aborted probes, false rumour checked at great length, informers without informa-tion, leaks without value, observations discarded because of new priorities. And the security forces may in turn hide IRA failures for their purposes. In a sense the peace process eroded secrecy everywhere – the British were pleased to learn the fact that the IRA had been in contact with Iranians during the negotiations thus doing harm to Sinn Féin credibility at low cost. Still, just as most IRA operations never last to break cover so most intelligence failures pass unnoted – often unnoted by the Army Council or GHQ. And when there are failures, the enemy makes every effort to exploit the opportunity to engender suspicion, lay false trails, damage reputations, and so further perceived interests.

Within intelligence, as within the IRA in general, the many spend most of their time waiting, waiting for events, for data, for messages, for contact, for tomorrow, and often waiting without result. Those involved, however, at times do not wait in vain, for even the long hours in the railway station, on the side streets of Birmingham, in seedy hotel lobbies, in the bus station in Dublin also serves the dream. So, if much is futile, much can be reinvested in ways not apparent to those who focus solely on results, on craft, and on the conventions of the operatives. The conventional, the orthodox in offices and on missions can, do, learn to wait. They are paid to wait and pensioned for waiting but that is craft rewarded.

Security Data

To protect the underground, to deny penetration, the IRA needs data about its own. No one arrives within the secret army, at least since the early helter-skelter days of mass volunteers, without passing through an informal clearance sieve – family, friends, watchers, and the locals know everyone and so, too, the IRA. Volunteers are taken through recruits class, live among their own, rarely surprise their associates: a few may filter through with limited talents or personal weakness but mostly the IRA need not worry about entry at the bottom. In difficult times with lax control over isolated volunteers, the faith can erode but then GHQ knows this.

Those who approach the movement to sell information, proffer resources, involve the faithful are always suspected, often not sufficiently so, for the IRA rarely has the time or the resources to make sure. The *Claudia* was lost despite warnings because needs outweighed caution. And besides there is no institutional means, no databank to check for loyalty or past history, no central records to clear the contact; moreover, no one wants to let slip a grand chance or to contemplate the obstacles. The vast conventional technological assets of the security forces do not intimidate because often the IRA remains innocent of their existence or finds unconventional means to avoid the orthodox. And as for informers – no one wants to think about such matters until too late. What matters is that the faithful remain true. Within the movement the weak, the fearful, the limited, may betray all; so this concern is always present if unarticulated, not a matter of counter-intelligence but a given in the community of any revealed faith.

When betrayal is suspected, then the suspects may be questioned – formal groups often exist to debrief prisoners and active-service volunteers, just in case. After a generation the toll of those caught, questioned, and tried and often executed by the IRA indicates that the clandestine effort at penetration is a constant.

Operational officers, intelligence officers, those on active service as a matter of course check the suspicious, check failure: an active-service unit walking into a trap, an ambush at an arms dump or an arrest in a safe house automatically produces a review. The review is not allotted to special volunteers but often to those close to the event, those trusted and proven. This can be the intelligence officer, often involves those operationally responsible or involved, and may be those sent specifically into the area to investigate.

There is always the additional problem that the authorities are apt to complicate matters by deceit. And, too, the security forces often succeed not because of information given but simply army or police intelligence that rests on gossip, Unionists' co-operation, hi-tech surveillance equipment, good luck and shrewd estimates or a meld of means and sources. Rarely do the authorities detail their sources and at times imply that their success comes from penetration of the secret army.

IRA counter-intelligence, to prevent penetration, to monitor the attempts, to control the damage, to turn the agents, are all subsumed into a response to a problem shaped by a secret military court or the concerned operational officers. If the agent is a plant, a spy is executed. If the plant is an avowed Republican, a heretic is executed. In both cases, damage control is part of the investigation of those so assigned – assigned because of rank or responsibility because of proximity or experience but not as counter-intelligence officer. Within the secret army everyone is a counter-intelligence specialist without assignment but with responsibility. This means that penetration is more difficult. It means that a constant covert battle is waged involving not only the real agents, the greedy on a string, the frightened paid in threats, but also perception, deception, shadows, and mirrors. And in this covert world of suspicion and betrayal, the IRA is always more likely to react than to initiate.

SPECIAL CASES AND SPECIAL OPERATIONS

Not unlike many states in the West, the central command of the Republican movement has some difficulty in finding an appropriate structure and a satisfactory institutional base for certain operations – they are special and at times hardly considered intelligence matters at all, since most operations of a secret army like the IRA have no real parallel in the orthodox world. Basically these IRA actions require the techniques of underground intelligence operations applied to needs that have arisen during the protraction of the armed struggle, especially in two major areas.

The first is to organize, encourage, and deploy prison assets where communication and command is difficult, and the second is to acquire resources that are denied by the authorities and beyond reach without recourse to special operations. In the beginning there were no prisoners; but even before the formal beginning of the Provisionals arms and money were being sought – there is *always* a need for arms and money and inevitably the former and mostly the latter must be acquired covertly. And almost as soon as this process starts there are prisoners.

Prisoners

The IRA inherited a variety of policies and assumptions related to prisoners. Since 1916 except for a few years, there had always been Republicans imprisoned for their actions or potential so that the leadership was aware of this responsibility from the first. And prisoners play a far greater role in an armed struggle than in orthodox organizations because they are still assets, often greater assets in a cell than out. An orthodox army feels the captured are lost – at best a small drain on enemy resources; but a secret army merely sees volunteers arrayed on a different front.

There was an IRA code of prison conduct, rules for prison organization – all rank was lost on arrival in prison. There has been in IRA history an inclination to view with suspicion advice and admonition arriving from those isolated in prison. In the case of the Provisional IRA, however, those imprisoned in the 1970s established think-tanks and seminars, mid-career courses for guerrilla command, that would have been impossible if the same volunteers had been free and engaged in the campaign. Within prison the IRA volunteers accepted unit discipline, voted on the leadership – prison units were more democratic than the movement in general – and obeyed the guidelines and rules on matters like escape, degrees of co-operation with the authorities, and acts of defiance. Some prisoners in British jails remained isolated, one or two in a large prison population. As soon as there were sufficient prisoners, a formal structure arose along with the traditional classes and protests and secret, usually subversive, activities.

All of this required communication with GHQ, often easily arranged on the island but only possible, for the most part, for those outside Ireland at times and on special matters like escapes. Those few isolated in prisons on the British mainland had only fragile links with GHQ and at times were dependent on their own. No contact was often sufficient since the faith indicated conduct. Those more conveniently place in the prisons of Northern Ireland or the Republic were more closely integrated into the movement, relied on external aid and comfort and constant contact. The volunteers in Long Kesh, entitled the Maze prison by the British, and then when the new buildings were erected the H-Blocks by the nationalists, were not so much prisoners of war but prisoners still at war.

The evolution of the Republican prisoners into net asset and during the hunger strikes of 1980–81 arrayed in a major new battle front was, like most Provisional successes, achieved naturally: experience, habit, and the challenges of the moment met kept those in cells in action. Some Republicans found that as gunmen without guns they could still be effective. Bobby Sands was the best known of all IRA volunteers but not for being a gunman. Joe Doherty, isolated in America fighting extradition, was more effective in a cell for the movement than he had been in an active-service unit in Belfast.

The most special prison operations were those dealing with communication and command – control has always been a lesser matter within the secret army loathe to discipline the bold or even the brutal. In the case of the prisoners, those operations under their control – the level of defiance that evolved into a hunger strike that posed many awkward questions for the Army Council outside – produced in 1980–81 not a prison unit maintaining the faith but a prison unit leading the battle. Since this evolution came within Republican prison practice, awkward or not, the Army Council outside coped. What caused almost no difficulties was the matter of communication: the prisoners in Northern Ireland were never out of touch, never felt isolated or ignored, never beyond reach, always integrated into the struggle.

This integration was in considerable part made possible by the daily effectiveness of special means of communications arising from precedent, ingenuity, and cunning, and – when needed – recourse to ruthless brutality. The techniques of communicating, moving tiny bits of illegally acquired paper covered with densely packed data written with illicit implements despite the guards, despite the isolation of the cells and blocks, and despite the constant counter-measures taken by the authorities, were successful because the prisoners had 24 hours a day to invest in the operation, no qualms about means and ends, and help on the outside from those willing to take great risks. Those in the H-Blocks were also driven by a sense of urgency and need so that merely to succeed in communication, to keep the link with the movement and GHQ regardless of the message was a triumph. The meaning was the transmission.

The operational details, revealed when the authorities cut a link or the

Republicans revealed one, were largely traditional: a kiss in the visiting room, a message screwed into a tiny ball and moved through a strip search twisted into a nostril or hidden in a tooth, a bribe or a threat someplace down the fragile line to the outside. All of the skills of generations of prisoners were deployed or rediscovered, invisible ink or garbage to be sifted by allies, a wink, a nod, a warder blackmailed. Any physical link with the outside was exploited, every means of coercion was at one time or another used: during and after the hunger strike there was a steady toll taken on the prison authorities. Officers, warders, superintendents, anyone involved, became target and so was open to threat. The result over a generation has been that GHQ has a line in and out of all Irish prisons more effective than the post and often more effective than communication with various parts of the movement. This could never be exactly the case with British prisons and certainly nor those on the European continent or in the United States where contact took a little longer if initiated at all. Yet the physical distance between GHQ and the prison may actually increase the commitment of those inside – better involved in protest than simply serving time. IRA command concern for an individual is apt to decline with time and with distance if there is no action. One prisoner rarely is worth the investment necessary to keep in the net through covert communication unless a spectacular escape is planned. Escapes, because external force is available, are easier for IRA prisoners than simple criminals; but violent escape from an American or German prison may be counter-productive and a secret escape impossible to manage at a distance. And large escapes generally fail. Many prisoners prefer to focus on spending their time effectively rather than hoping to go over the wall.

In any case the IRA prisoners in Irish and even British jails have over years perfected and maintained communications through special operations – the communication has always been into GHQ and so the Army Council, but there has rarely been an institutionalization of these operations within the command structure. The local units near the prison often become involved, the individuals with access to the prison – relatives or friends become involved, those ready and sound and concerned at GHQ become involved. Those once in and now out become involved. Few have even considered an IRA special operations bureau for prison affairs or prison communications. Since these very special prison operations work effectively no one has tinkered by imposing structure where none is needed and few consider such matters the province of 'intelligence' in any case.

Resource Acquisition

Those with access to a gun are apt to see the gun as a first option in most matters. Thus when money is needed for arms, theft or extortion or, more often than not violence, guns are the prime options in acquiring the needed assets. And such options become active-service operations so that intelligence operates in the same way as moves directed against assets. An attack on an arms dump or an armed raid on a bank, the latter always more difficult to rationalize than the former, is treated as a military operation with the usual procedures in place.

Some assets, however, must be acquired by covert means, illicit purchases, secret diplomacy, coercion at a distance, special matters where the gun is rare even as a last option. Then intelligence is needed about everything and everyone involved: which houses are safe, which agents are real, who is trustworthy, who vulnerable, which car to buy or boat to rent, what time to make contact.

Mostly any general picture of the situation – states or movements that might be friendly, the attitude of police in this country or that, even the techniques of border control in the United States or the effectiveness of Western European airport security, comes, if at all, from reading the newspaper, watching television, and the tales of friends and the faithful. There is no office filled with data that indicates the likely response of al Fatah to a request for aid and comfort: that is the result of the evening news, a few telephone calls, and perhaps a special flight or a request sent by a friend. There is no big picture for special operations There is also no aid at GHQ for moves that require a mix of diplomacy and gunman guile, international sophistication and covert tradecraft.

As always, the sound and available are sent and are often remarkably successful. Sleepers can be found and used, those with no Republican connections and familiarity with international travel or the right language. And sometimes a sound volunteer is thought adequate, well known to the authorities, innocent of abroad, speaking with the recognizable accent of Belfast. And many opportunities are lost not simply because of a lack of an intelligence base, a central command with broad horizons, but also because those horizons for GHQ are very limited. Even when opportunities might be obvious, as was the case during the Falklands War, the movement may not grasp the obvious. And in the case of the Falklands, with no friends in Argentina, no contacts, no money, no experience and no certainty of any return, the obvious may not seem worth the risks. Still, over time the IRA has attained funding and arms from strange places, dispatched successfully all sorts of agents, some innocent and some not, coped if not flourished.

In their small closed Northern Ireland world, asset acquisition for fiscal purposes has been traditional, managed either by IRA operations, almost entirely on the island, or by illicit collections from the Diaspora. The Libyan contact was the only effective and productive arrangement with a government, and those contacts with congenial revolutionary organizations other than al Fatah and the African National Congress have been oblique or unrewarding in material matters – that Nelson Mandela and the ANC would not deny the Provisional IRA in public indicates that some of the returns need not be tangible.

The IRA search for arms, especially sophisticated arms, has left a highly visible trail of aborted attempts, some a result of innocence, others caused by the blunders of local friends equally innocent. Some failed because of bad luck and other disasters were provoked by enemies. And the search assured that the IRA would make new enemies. Contact with al Fatah and ANC meant new enemies. The Libyan connection was taken as the final evidence by conservatives that the IRA was a terrorist organization. The IRA simply has neither the time nor the funds, much less in most cases the skills, to operate abroad without taking grave risks. GHQ has never managed to institutionalize a foreign department except in matters of press and publicity. Each case is treated separately and often there is no corporate memory, no prospect of late briefing, no intelligence in place. The intelligence needed in each case must be acquired operationally – and often this has not been done. The fact that the IRA in 2000 has an excess of weapons, stocks of sophisticated explosives and detonating devices, has paid the bills or at least, like governments, run on credit for a generation, indicates that, despite limited intelligence and a lack of an analytical capacity or great tradecraft skills, the Army Council has coped.

EVOLUTION OF IMPERATIVES

What the leadership of the Provisional IRA wanted in the beginning was information that would allow a campaign to begin – who had guns, who would volunteer, which targets were vulnerable. All of this flowed into GHQ almost for the asking. After 1971–72 the key needs were continued target data and increasingly the means to acquire further resources – most found in the American Diaspora. After 20 years the IRA's perceived needs had scarcely altered: how to persist, perhaps by opening new fronts, how to find vulnerabilities and money and arms. Nothing has changed. In the end-game the mission is narrower, the necessity to persist as a secret army and to do so without deploying the gun from time to time to keep up morale not as urgent. Some still imported revolvers but times had changed.

The IRA means to acquire assets stayed much the same over the course of the Troubles. The same individuals had the same titles, the operations were planned the same way. For example, the saga of the ground-to-air missiles continued year after year without resolution. And it seems likely that not until there is a united, free Irish Republic to negotiate such purchases will the IRA QMG priorities change. The search has all but become institutionalized in all those within the movement, ever eager for any hint or guess that could produce the desired end: an engineer with sound views on the national issue, a traveller from some distant and disturbed land with news of an arms bazaar, a man met in a bar in Hamburg or Baltimore. There is no reason at the start of a new century to imagine whatever the state of play in the endgame that the Army Council would easily deny itself missiles even as the prospect of decommissioning existing arms is argued out in private and public.

Skills and experience have improved but seldom as fast as those of the British – always far more sophisticated if not always far more effective. It is in fact the reality of British counter-insurgency that has kept IRA intelligence consistent: the security forces have eroded IRA options, raised IRA costs, and imposed limits on IRA capacities. In order to cope, the IRA has perforce relied on more of the same, even when the same is taken overseas to England or Holland. To persist, the IRA has had to persist in the congenial for the involved have had neither the time nor resources to try novelty, to try more than to keep up. Yet in keeping up, the unorthodox, the make-do, has often done well enough. The IRA special operations have not been without success or without a return of assets. In the next century with a new mission and a new role the shifting imperatives of the IRA may enhance Republican intelligence – until at last the Republic is achieved or the road to the future opened and the army disbanded.

UNDERGROUND INTELLIGENCE ADVANTAGES

If so much of the operational world of the Provisionals is without recognized structure, has evolved without master plan and is deployed by the self-taught and limited, the results have seemingly been miraculously effective. The fact is that any underground, while it must pay for advantage with the inherent inefficiency of all illicit covert movements, receives certain benefits as well. The ecosystem in place is not simply a community of believers but is also a huge and effective intelligence organization. It may not be as effective as the analytical would wish but the system does work. As the countryside or a city street has unseen watchers, so too does the IRA.

More to the operational point all intelligence activities and much communication – and these are tactical and operational matters – for generations have been secret: the means secret as the contents. The movement is comfortable with secrecy, and resigned to the resulting inefficiency that is seen not as a by-product of secrecy but the natural condition of unconventional war. The long war is convention not aberration, and secrecy a necessary price not a romantic indicator of conviction. If there is to be an endgame, then it is assumed these conventions will simply continue.

After all, despite all the skills of British counter-insurgency in Northern Ireland, all the assets of London and Dublin, all the talent and skills involved by the orthodox in the endgame, the IRA, secret and violent, persists. And the intelligence to do so always seems available to IRA GHQ, available for operational purpose, to counter penetration, to undertake special operations, to maintain communications, to enrich the political options of the peace process – and to keep the faith.

CHAPTER TWELVE

Campaign

The campaign of the Provisional IRA, a classic, has followed a generally agreed pattern, recognized by all concerned. Except for the imputation of unpleasant motives – wicked, evil men – and the perception of future events – the direction of history – there is a remarkable agreement on the evolution of the IRA's armed struggle. The campaign has been a low-intensity, nationalist insurgency in a post-industrial, democratic state with limits imposed by law, self-interest, the unavowed rules of engagement, and by the morality of the involved leading to an endgame. All observers, as well as the participants, most of the time, tend to agree on the stages, the intensity levels, and even the reasons for the shifting tactics and strategy of all. The disagreements deal with the application of theories, first causes, the nature of the clandestine.

The first phases of the IRA campaign were those planned by the Army Council in January 1970: defence merging into provocation and then war in 1971 once internment had alienated many nationalists. There are still those who would like to see the involvement of Irish politicians as crucial in the 1969–70 stage but usually for obvious purposes. There is no doubt, however, that the intensity level of the turmoil rose – any list of indicators shows a rising number of bombings or fatalities or bomb incidents. As the violence escalated in 1972, quite beyond even the expectations of those at IRA command central, expectations rose as well; so that by mid-1972, there was hope that the British could be coerced into accommodation. The talks in London in July 1972 confirmed that more pain would have to be inflicted by the IRA. For the next year or so, the IRA assumed that the level of intensity, even if somewhat down in raw numbers, would be sufficient: the British would give an intent to withdraw, more or less replaying the events of 1921.

The British establishment, of course, could not imagine that the IRA presumed to win in the field, could not imagine discarding responsibilities and legal commitments because of provincial disorder, chose, if possible, to view Northern Ireland as a political problem, not the site of an insurrection. The Republican leadership were considered limited, fanatics, crude, and perhaps beyond co-option if not corruption. The Irish politicians in Dublin were ineffectual, romantic, and irrelevant. What was needed was the establishment of order so that reforms could be effected and devolved government restored. Thus, the British counter-campaign was to reduce the intensity of the violence, ameliorate grievances, devise effective provincial institutions, and so return Ireland to a minor matter on Westminster's agenda. None of this was easy – perceived grievances cannot be eroded by legislation and all Northern Ireland political initiatives engendered a zero-sum game: nationalist gain, Unionist loss, Unionist gain, nationalist loss. So year by year the turmoil continued. Limited success at curbing the IRA was insufficient to keep Ireland out of the headlines and on the road to stability.

Thus 1975 – after five campaign years – marked a time for reappraisal for all. The IRA foresaw a long war. With an acceptable level of violence, the British still foresaw some sort of accommodation. As is always the case in an unconventional campaign, reality as well as nearly all else was asymmetrical. The IRA sought to escalate so that the British will would erode, and the British sought to close down the IRA campaign by superior military and political skills and greater operational assets. Neither were encouraged by events. The British opened negotiations to involve the IRA in politics, managed a truce, and when time ran out were content with the pause and again pursued a policy of counter-insurgency and political initiatives. The IRA persisted, renewed the long war, their view of British perfidy vindicated.

By the end of 1976, all agreed that a speedy end to the Irish problem was unlikely. The British could not win and the IRA could not lose. The IRA not only failed to escalate but could not maintain the intensity of 1974. The British not only could not stifle the IRA campaign but also recognized that fanaticism is not so easily ignored – Irish Republicans as always were difficult to corrupt or coerce. The Irish Troubles had become a constant, beyond significant accommodation, a tragedy in endless acts. The IRA continued their campaign, grew more experienced, more cunning, often more brutal but no more effective. The British security forces grew more experienced, more cunning, often more ruthless, and not effective enough to end the insurgency. The British continued the series of political, economic, and social institutions constructed to erode grievance, create middle ground, and deny the Republicans support. No matter, Republican support remained stable – to pursue an effective anti-insurgency campaign the British continued to alienate the nationalist population without reassuring the Unionists – in fact, the fearful loyalists sporadically resorted to sectarian murder. And all non-military policies, programmes and initiatives hardly changed the zero-sum game. The IRA campaign grew protracted, a classic, a media stop, an academic case study, analytical foci. The British response too became a classic if not the success the security forces sought.

From time to time the focus of concern of each side shifted – the struggle over the prisons, British dirty tricks, IRA contacts abroad, the conflict over British political initiatives, the obstacles to pursuing an unconventional war treated as crime, the operational blunders of both sides exploited, the rise of Sinn Féin as a conventional and successful political party, the cyclical outrages of the loyalist sectarian paramilitaries, IRA operations in the Republic, the intervention of the good and powerful – but the balance remained remarkably stable. The IRA could not win but could not be defeated.

The IRA sought a means to create an intolerable level of violence by the use of force and if need be by use of other means – politics or propaganda or social services. At the very least, the IRA wanted to keep British cost high – cost paid in lives, in sterling, in pride, even in concern. As far as the armed struggle was concerned, this campaign of attrition proved operationally difficult. Novelty, new directions, IRA technological advances barely kept pace with British capacities. On the other hand, the security forces, no matter the gains in technology, organization, experience, unity, and political credit, could not prohibit the IRA from maintaining the struggle at a high and unpleasant level.

The IRA learned on the job. Money was found, weapons were shipped in from abroad, new bombs were constructed, new tactics devised, and despite the losses, those killed, those imprisoned, those no longer available, the accumulating experience was put to operational use. The level of violence in 1979 or ten years later in 1989 could not have been imagined in 1970. Certainly no one on the Army Council could have imagined how difficult creating such a level of violence would be. As years passed, however, such violence became the norm – an armed struggle institutionalized.

When the focus shifted to the peace process in 1991–92, the IRA was placed on hold by the ceasefire in August 1994, and Sinn Féin was permitted to seek advantage. The IRA assumed that the mission was the same but that the secret army had accepted a new and not necessarily permanent role as silent enabler and protector. The IRA waited until Republican frustration with the pace of negotiations permitted a renewed struggle in February 1996 with the huge bomb placed in Canary Wharf, London. The new campaign did not escalate but rather cost the Republican movement dearly even among friends. There was little support for the renewed campaign and less capacity than the Army Council had foreseen. The ceasefire was renewed and the major thrust into the future was ceded to Sinn Féin. The IRA had not fully realized that the endgame imposed not only different roles and missions but a different arena and different imperative. Bombing and talking was neither novel nor necessarily fruitless in an endgame, but in the Irish case proved ineffectual. The traditional IRA response had suddenly turned out to be viewed as a novel and unpleasant surprise to all but the physical force advocates who had been driven by frustration, were seeking vengeance as much as advantage, and so misjudged their own capacity, the enemy and their impact.

Changing roles and missions simultaneously after a century of stability was not easy, no matter the logic or accepted imperatives. A few refused, the Continuity Army Council, and dissenters along the border organized as the Real IRA; but most Republicans placed their eroding hopes within the ambit of the endgame. Thus the period from 1991 to the end of the century was distinct, the IRA was involved in neither pursuing a campaign nor dominating options but rather shaped by the priorities of the endgame undertaken by the movement leadership now visible at the centre of Sinn Féin.

The British, resigned to the fact that the IRA campaign could not be closed down, had soldiered on for years deploying all sorts of tactical and technological assets to erode the appeal of the IRA, reassure the loyal, while the politicians found institutional means to achieve stability. All this occurred with some if not great success. The IRA was confined to Republican zones, the incident level was down if not low, and soft targets had been hardened – the security forces coped. Assemblies and conventions were proposed, established and collapsed. An effort was made to Ulsterize the Troubles – give priorities to the RUC and provincial authorities thus transforming the IRA–British conflict. A formal agreement was made to bringing the Dublin government, long suspected of nationalist sympathies, into an accommodation that alienated the Unionists and was ignored by the Republicans. The Hillsborough Agreement changed nothing. The protracted IRA campaign continued, the loyalists pursued sectarian murder, the security forces remained active, deployed, occasionally successful. Politics went on. Most of Ireland went on. The Troubles had become a given with accepted rules of engagement. Only a few in London – although many loyalists – wanted greater force deployed against the IRA but the British government was never so inclined. Dublin in this and many matters agreed with London. And the IRA eager to deploy greater force could not do so.

The IRA with wasting assets, faltering political and social returns, and fading prospects remained convinced, year after year, in 1990 as in 1970, that persistence would pay, the will of the risen Republican people would ask a price that ultimately the British establishment would not pay. Revolutionary strategy elsewhere is also based on the conviction that will can triumph over tangible assets and so the IRA campaign was simply a matter of bringing what force existed against the British until their will to persist failed. Time would tell, toll out the last of the British empire and welcome at last the

Republic. So the military campaign can easily be read in a chronicle of events, in the incidents tables and kill counts, in assassinations, show trials, country ambushes, in informers murdered and hunger strikers dying. There are spectaculars and horrors, blunders and murders and new means sought to solve the same problems. There were increasingly effective IRA mortars, bombs made with Semtex, hi-tech fuses and the same old fertilizer factories refining home-made explosives. There were British shoot-to-kill ambushes, the use of paid informers – supergrasses – to convict suspected IRA volunteers, and the introduction of a new generation of battlefield sensors and computer-based intelligence programmes.

The campaign then, stripped of special tactics, had become a long war within an arena where from time to time novelty or calculated horror was introduced as technique in a struggle for tactical advantage. Strategy waited on the will of the involved. The Republican policy to move toward power with the Armalite in one hand and the ballot box in the other evolved into seeking political power to aid the military campaign rather than a major shift in priorities. Sinn Féin did, indeed, acquire political assets but insufficient to change the course of events: a military stalemate and a political impasse.

NATURE OF THE STRUGGLE

The Provisional IRA's campaign has been typical of all armed struggles even in its singularities. What was Irish was very special but what was specially Irish was hardly alien to other movements, other campaigns. The Irish Republican cause, like so many causes, was flawed in that the avowed constituency tended to deny first the means and then, if not too loudly, the aims of the movement. Even those most closely concerned, the nationalists of Northern Ireland, often voted against Sinn Féin, criticized IRA excesses and error, showed little gratitude and much venom even if they still would rarely countenance informing and betrayal. And the longer the war the more fragile the support, the less enthusiasm for the too visible dirty war and the protraction of hope. The need for a defence kept many in line; not an aspiration for a Republic. And to the South in the Republic the graph of support dipped year by year, nationalism grew unfashionable and the IRA detestable. Pub patriots disappeared, rebel songs had a minority audience, few voted for Sinn Féin. Not only the established and comfortable abhorred the pretensions of the gunmen but also increasingly the Irish people.

The combat arena was a mix, not simply a national liberation struggle within a nation occupied by aliens or ruled by proxy, not a matter of unredeemed nationalism, a campaign to achieve a nation once again by seizing a lost province; but rather it was a struggle against the Dublin government that claimed to represent the liberated nation as well as against the British who controlled part of that nation in the North. The campaign was also entangled in the historic bitterness of a divided Northern society. To complicate matters still further, a considerable majority of the Irish in that unredeemed North wanted nothing but union with the British, preferred their Protestant way of life, their own traditions rather than the nationalism of the Republicans that they saw, not unreasonably, as aggressive Celtic-Catholic triumphalism with no place for them. And many, especially in the Republic, agreed, preferred to let matters rest, express vague hopes for union someday and get on with daily life.

Thus the IRA was opposed by most of the Irish nation and adamantly opposed by most in Northern Ireland. To operate in such an uncongenial arena, especially when its reality was often fudged for ideologically reasons, was no easy matter. It was also not a novel matter for rebels and revolutionaries: in the Palestine Mandate Menachem Begin's Irgun Zvai Leumi represented if haltingly the Revisionist Zionists, a minority of the Zionists who in turn were a minority in the Mandate. In Cyprus Grivas and EOKA represented neither the Turkish minority nor the large Cypriot communist movement AKEL. *Brigate rosse* or ETA in the Basque country had no electoral mandate, the Italians a tiny violent conspiracy far beyond the Communist Party and ETA a tiny underground faction in two Spanish provinces drawing support from some resident in France. Few undergrounds – Egyptian military officers, Latin American radicals, ethnic zealots, and religious fundamentalists are elected to revolt. Few revolts fail to inspire peaceful and political alternatives. The IRA recognized this by representing the patriot dead and Irish history but reality still isolated the movement. And had done so for so long that the faithful had few tangible assets: a working-class movement, provincial, pious, persistent, and willing to sacrifice but limited in proficiency and resources.

To wage their campaign against the British and British allies, the IRA had to juxtapose weakness, especially military weakness, against British power, especially the power of the security forces, and so rely on their faith, their commitment and their historical legitimacy. The result was a typical asymmetrical campaign that required the weak to resort to unconventional means and the strong to waver between peace with all its legal restraints and war that offered order but imposed internal violence. Such a confrontation, as always, was shaped by the perception of the involved. What the IRA Army Council perceived was not at all what London imagined in Ireland or for that matter what many of the Irish, Protestant and Catholic, North or South, radical or conservative, imagined when exposed to events. All agreed on the events of the campaign, even on the stages, the level of intensity, but not on what it all meant any more than did the Marxists or realists, those who focused on religious differences and those who stressed social justice. What had happened was an IRA campaign – why was another matter and one that grew increasingly irrelevant after 20 years of violence.

IRA ANALYSIS OF THE CAMPAIGN

As in all armed struggles, the grand strategy requires little elaboration once the long process of beginning has finished – and for the IRA this 'beginning' had taken place a century before. To begin the campaign they used their role as defender to provoke the British army into responding in such a way that a campaign could begin. After 1971 and internment, their tactics were hardly novel, a matter of increasing the intensity of provocation wherever possible, finding the means to escalate. The parallel process to spread the battlefield – use politics or publicity or social means – evolved naturally without great planning: persist, raise the pressure, spread the arena. Sometimes the IRA had trouble adjusting to opportunity: the role of Sinn Féin after the hunger strikes was novel and all had to adjust to political priorities being considered during a military campaign. Opportunities were taken and until late in 1972 escalation was impressive, even to the British security forces. An increasing number of Provisionals for some years assumed that IRA force could coerce a British withdrawal. With the agreement on a long war, the campaign focused on persistence as much as escalation, widening the battlefield as much as expanding operations in Northern Ireland.

Until 1973–74, however, the entire thrust of the IRA campaign was for more of what was available and congenial: more recruits were needed and more gear and more money and so more operations, and largely this was sufficient. The bombs on non-military targets were rationalized as strikes against the artificial economy of the six-counties and the civilian casualties as the unavoidable cost of a just war. Basically the secret army was simply still doing what came naturally, what had been done sporadically and on a far lower level in each of the previous campaigns. Bombers had been sent to England before so they were sent again. Ambushes in the country had worked before and so were used again. Operational novelty tended to arise from those operating rather than any tactical plan. And the more effective the British so too the more novel responses by the IRA.

The pressures to escalate were such that for some time the campaign proceeded with very little planning, quite cursory training, a great number of operations and ample evidence of IRA incompetence, murdered civilians, blundered warnings, bomb factories demolished and self-inflicted disasters. This lack of skill was owed only in part to the penalties of the cover required for an unconventional war. The need for haste, that lack of precision in many Irish matters, the lack of trained talent on call, all hampered the campaign but not – except in the case of volunteers killed by their own bombs – visibly. The competence level over time improved but error was integral to the entire campaign imposed by the needs of secrecy, the turn-over in personnel, private failure, and ethnic shortcomings – each nationality shapes campaign error in a special way, for German punctuality or Italian cunning can be liability as well as asset.

The level of IRA competence might have been low, the bombs clumsy, the killing coarse, but the intensity was high thus hiding much. Yet because of an effective British response the level of intensity began to go down. What was maintained was the danger of violence throughout much of the province, the level of constant harassment and low-level incidents – many that did not appear on published lists. If there were not as many ambushes, the fear level and the security commitment level did not go down. Bandit country still required a massive commitment of British force even if there were fewer bandits operating. The IRA made organizational changes and accepted a revised agenda, both more fitting for a protracted campaign. To persist a high price had been paid, would have to be paid. The movement, however, was used to persisting without support or prospects: the Republicans were members of the oldest unsuccessful revolutionary organization in the world, over a century of failure and renewal.

After the failure of the 1975 truce and as the years passed, it became clear, even and especially to Provisional leadership, that IRA military means were limited. They were limited by British and Irish security successes; limited by the exhaustion of will within their avowed constituency; limited by the paucity of IRA assets. The IRA simply persisted. They sought and often found new tactics, new weapons, a new battle arena or new means. And yet all the running barely kept them standing still.

So none of the old ways were discarded unless advantage could be gained – as was the case in the move from Lee-Enfields, to M-1s and on to Armalites and then in 1985–86 to the AK-47s. The new weapons were deployed in the old country ambush – but that ambush was no longer easy, no longer a daily matter but one of serious planning and grave risk, one shot and a scurry to keep ahead of the technical monitors and army patrols. The habits of the nightriders had to be adjusted to infrared sensors. The weapons could at least be used in ways congenial to the IRA volunteers and ways that would have been familiar to those who fought in the border campaign a generation before or for that matter to the heroes of the Tan War. Tom Barry or Dan

Breen would have known how to use an Armalite or a Barrett 90 rifle. And the old ways permitted a basic level of intensity, made the countryside unsafe except in Unionist areas and the cities dangerous if less so in middle-class and hard-core loyalist areas. The old ways provided a base line of campaign persistence. The old ways alone, however, were insufficient for much was needed that Tom Barry did not have and much could be achieved that the Army Council had not foreseen in 1970. Times changed and so did the IRA, traditional, persistent but avid for advantage.

The new directions evolved from opportunities: new grievances, unpalatable British initiatives in technologies, the hunger strikes, Sinn Féin as a political tool, a concern with local social and economic conditions, and reliance on the new military possibilities that the gradual adoption and adaption of techniques and technologies by the active-service units. And all the while, the old assets were kept. There were commemorations and parades and car-bombs. The new initiatives – often reactions – revealed a pattern of ups and downs in impact that ran along in time with the continued refusal of the British establishment to consider withdrawal or even at times the IRA as a serious part of any future accommodation. This refusal was based on a distaste no less strong in the Irish Republic where the movement, in one way or another, alienated not only the Dublin establishment but also much of the Irish constituency. The IRA after a generation had few friends even if the Irish had not become advocates of partition or often even friends of Britain.

And few but friends saw the IRA as freedom fighters; many as terrorists, bombers, and gunmen. On this front the IRA could not reverse the trend by finding new targets or opening a new battle area – they lacked the skills, they lacked experience and even understanding of world opinion – much less British opinion. At least the British with sophisticated assets found their own difficulties in appearing as a crusader in Ireland. What the British did manage over a generation was to persuade the many that the problem was a divided society, an ethnic quarrel, not that they, as the Republicans insisted, were the problem. Yet, given British experience and skill, the reality of an era of terrorism, the predilections of both the public and many politicians, the IRA did not do badly, and certainly outraged the British, who felt the media, even the British media, too sympathetic to the gunmen.

The Army Council, as the years passed, oversaw a wide variety of novel campaign initiatives, no easy matter for any underground. And such initiatives were no easy matter for an Irish underground, always reluctant to experiment or to risk any move away from reliance on physical force as practised in previous campaigns. While all undergrounds are directed by revolutionaries, in tactical matters all revolutionaries are apt to be conservative, reluctant to risk their very few assets, driven to the unconventional by desperation not guile. The IRA campaign could only continue at the expense of tradition, the Republicans' greatest love and a major asset, only continue if there were a consensus shaped on new means, even new targets. In fact it was the nature of the targets, the tactical options, that seemingly gave direction to the campaign although new targets, new weapons, new means were all incorporated into the original thrust toward an armed struggle – once begun the Provos had no intention of reducing their reliance on physical force even when other factors seemed to predominate.

In fact, ever so gradually, as the years passed, the aspirations of the movement narrowed. Many traditional Republicans began to see the long war as all but a permanent phenomenon – worthy of sacrifice even as the goal came no closer. The British were not, as they had in Palestine or Kenya or the Suez Canal Zone, going to pack up and leave. Ireland was special not only to the Irish but also to the English – the British – offered mission. And even an intent to withdraw was forthcoming – what would be the response of the Irish Unionist, the Irish Protestants. Converting them was not a matter that could be left to guns. Irish unity was not simply a geographical expression or even a matter of justice but an aspiration that had to be shared. These were matters some chose not to consider. The pursuit of operational matters was an immediate concern. All Republicans and still many Irish nationalists agreed that the Brits must go. 'Brits Out'. How to use the gun effectively or at all was the day-to-day challenge of the campaign – was the campaign, operations as strategy. No one in the movement for two decades seriously questioned the reliance on physical force as the major means to assure a desirable future for the island.

THE CAMPAIGN AS INSURGENCY

The Provisionals' campaign has followed an easily traced intensity pattern: count has been kept of incidents or armed robberies or explosives captured, not to mention security casualties; books of campaign statistics have been published, every fatality listed, operations costed out and chronologies available. Some data are more difficult – the movement income or the number of IRA volunteers wounded; but generally a more revealing indication of the nature of the campaign is not a narrative of the war but the division of IRA targets into categories, for once the period of provocation ended in 1971, the entire campaign became a mix of chosen options – and the choices were from a self-selected, seldom seriously considered spectrum. Those targets on the margins – Protestant paramilitary locations or even loyalists and

Unionists chosen informally to intimidate or for vengeance's sake – were considered by all, even those operationally involved, as ideologically unsound. The movement knew, as did the active-service units, where to draw lines. No one was killed because of religion; but, of course, some were. No innocents were to be put at risk; but often some were. So little care was taken at times in Manchester or London that most observers assumed that the IRA was deploying no-warning bombs as terrorist tactics. The IRA always had rationales – not Protestants but loyal agents of the Crown were killed, civilian deaths were accidental – and internally had difficulties first in penalizing audacity and second ignoring the pressures for a response to sectarian murders focused on the Catholics. Anyway, the British had no compunction about carpet bombing German cities or the loyalists about murdering old men and boys – any Catholic would do – and the security forces deployed for war while pretending to be engaged in policing. In any case, the unwanted and unintended targets along with those in violation of ideology if not irrelevant, to the IRA's plan of campaign were not formally an aspect of operations.

IRA TACTICS

Despite the military titles and overt command structures, most revolutionary organizations spend relatively little time on target selection. Targets seem obvious – American embassies, the governor general, the tank park, or the police force. This is especially true with the IRA. The organization fashioned by consensus and a shared institutional history has ample precedent, accepts – much of the time – ideological and tactical strictures without need of discussion. Most discussion is focused on details, for in an armed struggle most events are tactical. What the IRA had wanted was the opportunity to attack traditional targets that would further legitimize the secret army – attack the British army and, perhaps, the British political leadership. In Ireland the RUC as a paramilitary force, deployed after 1970 not to pursue crime or direct traffic, was generally accepted as an appropriate IRA target. Such desirable targets often proved wary, prepared, and hard to hit. And many less compelling targets were vulnerable to IRA capacity – physical targets in particular. The target list grew.

A target may later be rationalized as a facet of a special campaign: against businessmen or the Dublin–Belfast railway link, but the first operation was most often selected because a vulnerability was discovered. First comes the opportunity, then the sound and available are dispatched, often by local commanders, and then, if need be, explanation is offered. The pressing need is always to maintain pressure, seeking targets that can be attacked to advantage and without exceptional risks. The IRA in 1971 had access to explosives and the security forces could hardly defend every building, so bombing was initiated almost without discussion by Joe Cahill in Belfast. The sophistication and complexities of explosive devices improved because of necessity, varied means of delivery were initiated because of necessity, and the potential sites for detonation widen because of necessity: to keep bombing, the IRA had to expand operations – until expansion no longer was possible, the targets too hard, and so bombing reduced to the occasional spectacular penetration of security. Then the IRA had to look elsewhere.

Categories of targets were not always chosen because they were convenient or possible but simply because they were ideologically attractive and possible: British critics, symbolic British buildings, British politicians, suspected loyalist spies, informers. More often than not, IRA operations that are targeted on particular enemies – such as Margaret Thatcher – or particular categories – Protestant loyalist pubs or retired RUC constables – contain the professed ideologically sound motives adjusted to reality and convenient operational consideration but also less savoury indicators. In a divided society vengeance and resentment encouraged certain attacks – certainly Margaret Thatcher, no friend to Ireland, was targeted not simply as the prime minister but also as the prime minister who had a hard word for the Irish. Prime Minister Major offered only his office as symbol, so the mortar attack on Downing Street arose from a slightly different target mix – one more ideologically sound and personally less appealing. And there are always volunteers who opt for appealing targets over valid ones: vengeance done or provocation punished. The movement makes every effort to see that volunteers do not act out of a sense of personal grievance, however valid, or for vengeance's sake. If they do so, there is seldom penalty anymore than there is for operations that risk civilian deaths – at times assure civilian deaths. And over time with the increase in soft targets, the institutionalization of calculated ruthlessness, the accumulation of grievances against the enemy, the IRA grew less discriminating: murdered the member of parliament Ian Gow because he criticized the movement, shot reserved and retired constables at home in border areas where Protestants and Catholics had long clashed over the land – shooting a neighbour off a tractor might put the farm on the market, intimidate the others even if the IRA explanation insisted that the only motive of the volunteer was to strike at the forces of the Crown. These 'forces' often were elderly farmers, construction workers, post office workers, not especially symbolic or operational targets but convenient, congenial, and soft.

There were targets chosen for even less appealing reasons. Those driven by unsavoury desires or by personal grievance exist in any armed struggle as do those who seek personal, usually criminal, benefit as a primary return for participation. With turmoil and chaos, the criminal can see advantage to armed robbery for the cause with the returns spent for personal pleasure: seemingly a predilection of some of those in the early Saor Éire group when the difference between criminal and revolutionary was blurred. The use of IRA authority not only for monetary gain but also to express personal power, to impose on the innocent, to threaten the obstinate, to seek gain or to punish personal rivals has long been a troublesome disciplinary problem. The suspected 'informer', or 'criminal', may be guilty of no more than going with the wrong girl or failing to show appropriate respect to an arrogant volunteer. Thus IRA, like all such secret armies, is apt to correct such situations covertly, punish secretly those who would use the IRA name or would act for discredited motives and so leave no record that some acts were not authorized.

Some operations are in fact a result not of impure motives by unsatis-factory volunteers but rather are aspects of what often in Northern Ireland has been endemic violence: the constant round of arson, sabotage, bullets fired, rocks tossed, cars tipped over, barns burnt, or individuals beaten. Just as no one, no unknown car, no strange man on a bike, moves through hard-core Republican areas without being watched, certainly tracked, often stopped, and not necessarily by authorized volunteers or even members of the Republican movement, so too do volunteers, Republicans, and many nationalists seize any opportunity to disrupt order. Sometimes destruction is reasoned – the smashing of street lamps to aid the IRA gunmen at work; but often the destruction is a sign of authority denied. No one orders every riot, although some are on call. Not every sniper who takes a shot when the chance offers does so because ordered. Many false warnings are telephoned in by those who in other times would find less costly amusements. Some units punish provocation to pretensions, knee-cap dissent in the name of the revolution – and many do not. Such violence and lawlessness is endemic at times and at certain places in Northern Ireland, undirected, spontaneous, often useful as grist to the mill of the armed struggle but indicator of the nature of the times rather than the tactical direction of the campaign.

IRA targets then tend to follow a curve of opportunity noted, operations expanded and refined, and then the defence denying access. At times the result is either not sufficient to persist or not sufficiently attractive to the constituency. And sometimes for insurgency is not as orderly as the text might suggest – attention is distracted, the volunteers are bored, something else appeals; and so the bombs on the Belfast–Dublin railway end not because of criticism or reappraisal of advantage but because those in South

Armagh are interested in other matters, other targets. And those targets are likely to follow the pattern – be alternatives to more difficult operations, be novel at the time, be rationalized as military and exist only until a new defence is constructed and the IRA denied.

TACTICAL TARGETS

Since tactics have been strategy in the IRA's campaign, the tactics are operations that can first be divided as to target audience: those within the movement, the constituency without, and finally, if most importantly, the enemy. Any successful operation encourages the movement, confounds the enemy and should impress the distant. Most operations are undertaken not with cunning rationales but simply because they are possible – and each makes governance more difficult and the faithful more assured.

Unlike other armed struggles, the IRA have almost never used violence to organize either the movement or the avowed constituency. The secret army has in the past, however, been deployed in large part to act, to persist rather than win on the ground: the bombing campaign in England, 1938–40, and the border campaign, 1954–62. These kept the faith, offered example, and so were not in vain even if militarily failures. What is on offer with membership in the secret army is an ideal, an opportunity. No one is shot simply because they will not help – may be killed as betrayer, by mistake, in arrogance, or through confusion but not shot because commitment has gone. The active-service volunteer must be sent out to kill for cause within the perimeters of conviction, must be given order to attack not only certain targets but also often in certain ways. Some operations are not denied because in violation of the imposed restraints and some because the option never occurs to the command. The IRA does not hijack airplanes: armies do not do so. The IRA has kidnapped individuals, but rarely and even then often at local initiative. What is desirable for each volunteer is an operation against the British military: Warrenpoint. What is often offered is a newly discovered vulnerability – soldiers jogging, a Poppy Day ceremony, a nightclub filled with off-duty RUC: the potential for massacre as well as success. So every operation becomes an expression of the faith as much as a model of military planning. And the targets are determined by conviction: the historic enemy, friends of that enemy, and most of all what is available. The volunteers tend to see all operations as functional, undertaken to erode the will of the British. Any secondary motive is less important.

First, there is the necessary defence of the vulnerable nationalist people, almost all Catholics, almost all in Northern Ireland – the Irish in Cork or in Liverpool need no such protection and those Irish actively opposed to IRA aspirations, mostly all Protestants, mostly all in Northern Ireland, clearly have been the problem not the solution. The IRA professes to defend not Catholics but nationalists even as some of the volunteers in a divided society find attacks against loyalists congenial as well as necessary, find aggressive response to provocation of the centuries congenial.

Second, there has always been provocation as operations drive the authorities into a desired response. From 1970–71 the campaign was dominated by such initiatives – in fact almost any IRA operation was then perceived as provocative. And so every operation does in some way provoke a response from the authorities – some advantageous like the initiation of internment in August 1971 and some less so like the improvement in counter-insurgency tactics and techniques. Provocation is the IRA's operational escalation, raising costs and assuring British response. That response often as not makes further provocation necessary but also costly. Nothing is easy underground. The authorities are aware that what they do must balance affront and response, must balance the anguish of the threatened with the investment in more repression. Repression is often to IRA advantage. The more troops or police needed, the more obvious the threat and the more difficult any pretence of normality; the more brutal the counter-insurgency operation, the more sympathy for the volunteers.

Often the IRA provocation is shaped to shift the public concerns of the authorities so that the first car-bombs detonated on 8 March 1973 in London would not only carry the war to the English heartland, spread security forces thinner, raise the financial costs to Britain, but also and especially draw attention away from a plebiscite on the border, thus indicating how 'unreal' such a political exercise was in fact. The target was not the buildings endangered but British opinion and the expectation that such opinion provoked by the IRA bombs would be made manifest in such a way as to overshadow the border poll. The bombs went off but the bombers were arrested, tried, convicted, and sentenced and there unlike the real world the operation did not end.

Many Irish events persist as does the campaign generating new grievances, opportunities, and disappointments. And in English prisons the IRA volunteers went on hunger strikes. The Price sisters from Belfast suffered force-feeding for so long that the distinction between torture and dinner had no meaning. Prisoners are no longer force-fed in British prisons – the hunger strikers deployed on the advantage won in the British prisons. The Price sisters were moved back to Northern Ireland prisons and released early for medical reasons.

Any significant or spectacular IRA operation is apt to have a provocative component. GHQ tended to see the campaign as a constant, bombs every day, ambushes every day, a steady toll of British soldiers killed and wounded, more headlines, more television coverage, more of everything. The targets were largely conventional, the people, places, and systems that had long been the target of any armed struggle: soldiers on patrol, army camps and police stations, airports and bridges, the commercial centre of towns and cities, and the symbols of authority. When this offensive peaked by 1975, the campaign was no longer escalating, the number of incidents went down, the international media went home, and the struggle became protracted.

Once the IRA recognized that there was to be no swift or easy British concession, then targets had to be chosen more selectively: what was vulnerable, what could not be easily protected, what was for the moment not protected at all, what was outside the assumed boundaries of the arena. Novelty in targeting was needed, novelty in intelligence, planning, novelty in techniques and technologies, novelty in concepts. And no underground has either the time or inclination for much novelty: simply maintaining momentum with the old targets and the old tactics was difficult enough for most of the IRA commanders in Northern Ireland. Maintaining the capacity to do so was more and more difficult for the commanders everywhere on the island. Running in order to stand still, running harder each month, leaves little time for reflection and novelty.

The result tended to be that once a vulnerability was discovered or announced the available IRA resources were focused on the opportunity – notorious loyalists, those who repaired damaged police stations, the railway line between Dublin and Belfast, the major London tourist attractions. The first time was always easiest and so often wasted through haste and necessity – then the security forces hardened that target or the vulnerable took precautions. Some targets simply could not be made absolutely secure: for example, there was a constant competition between the security forces to make the centre of Belfast safe and the IRA to bomb in the middle of town. With such a static goal, a hardened defence in the end became not impenetrable but too secure except for the increasingly rare bomb attack. The IRA, in fact, during the 1980s found Belfast operations very difficult, the room for manoeuvre narrow, but targets of various sorts still available. On the other hand, sometimes, in the case of the Dublin–Belfast railway, the target was simply beyond the capacity of the security forces although they could increase the risks. In fact the security forces so effectively hardened some targets, monitored access and exit routes, canvassed by one means or another IRA intentions, that the intensity level drifted downward all over Northern Ireland despite IRA initiative and innovation. The drift was never sufficient for order to be restored or the IRA to despair. In fact the IRA compensated for the daily operational problems by choosing soft targets and from time to time structuring operations that had enormously spectacular results often at marginal costs. And GHQ found other British vulnerabilities outside Ireland.

The difficulties of operating in England using active-service people with limited tradecraft and limited capacity who often failed to achieve very impressive results were never made good. Yet, even with the blunders, the no-warning bombs, the massacres, the captured cells, and lost equipment, such tactics were effective. The war was brought home to Britain – Christmas was not only a time to be jolly but in London often a time to beware of the IRA's annual bombing campaign. And a sense of escalation could be obtained not only by escalating but also by displaying action. The IRA campaign in Britain was attractive to the media – hard news with good film to be sent by satellite feed to New York or Bonn. Thus bombs in Britain often had an all but strategic effect raising the visibility of the struggle, encouraging the faithful and horrifying many but to useful purpose.

In a sense any bomb in England would do and often this is the kind of bomb within the capacity of those who were deployed: three or four men, the odd woman as courier, sitting about hired rooms making up target lists on lined notebooks to pass the hours before setting an incendiary device in a museum book shop or shooting out the windows of an elegant West End restaurant. Some of the targets were beyond protection because unimaginable to the authorities: Ross McWhirter of *The Guinness Book of Records*, who offered a reward for IRA bombers – felon setting – was murdered. Any violence in English cities tended to be magnified, tended to be effective, and tended to risk only a few – and over the years rarely gave indication that the volunteers were more competent or for that matter despite all their efforts that the authorities were more effective. Operations moved to the European continent repeated the pattern of inefficiency, great effect, increased security presence, and a widening of the arena.

In time the IRA acquired insight into the factors necessary to bomb in England. Technically the most desirable targets were those that permitted both access and withdrawal. In the case of car-bombs, all that was needed was a place to park next to the target and time to walk to safety, the get-away car, the crowd in the next street, the nearest underground. Even intense protective rings could be penetrated, as the big City of London bombs proved. Car-bombs were a constant; they were nearly as easy to construct in Britain as in Tyrone. Explosives slipped into England – some bomb factories made their own and inserted Semtex smuggled across from Ireland. Fuses and detonators, timers, all could be fashioned from legally purchased items and were; others were made, in South Armagh, and sent over on the ferries. Volunteers unknown to the police were sent over as sleepers until the time for action. Car-bombs could, if cunningly placed, cause enormous physical damage – the bomb in a truck at the Baltic Exchange in the financial district in April 1992 ran up a total of 800 million pounds sterling in claims and forced serious reconsideration of insurance practices. This cost was achieved with a 20-year-old technology, audacity, and British over-confidence. The most symbolic targets of all were always people and not places – the Tower, the Waxworks, five-star restaurants, Pall Mall clubs – and over the years the IRA made special efforts for special people: spectacular operations crafted for general effect.

The people that the IRA targeted tended to come first in categories: all uniform members of the security forces, their leaders and auxiliaries, their political overlords, their suppliers, and loyalists, those who would act in the Crown's name without authorization. Thus the IRA wanted to target armed and uniformed soldiers first and the tea boy passing around cups to the men pointing the mortar on the rebuilt RUC station last; wanted to hit prime ministers, not Protestants who repaired an RUC station. All, however, were targets: the loyalist gunman, the off-duty police constable, the soldier playing his flute in Regent's Park or resplendent in ceremonial dress riding his horse alongside Hyde Park were killed as soldiers, just as were soldiers in Armagh or Derry. And if IRA targets were elusive in Northern Ireland and then England, if the police grew more cunning and the informers more prevalent, then the IRA moved across to the European continent and shot British soldiers in Germany and Holland and shot by error women and children – as well as two Australian lawyers who happened into a fatal ambush.

Just as there were categories of people targets and special individuals, so too were there places and systems and things that were targeted by the IRA. These, too, fell into tangible military targets, British army facilities or police barracks, or resources, airports, the London underground, the Dublin–Belfast railway line, power facilities, and symbolic targets, the Tower in London or even the National Gallery and the Walker monument that towered over Derry's Bogside. What was more apparent, however, were the targets that were in theory chosen as part of the campaign against the economy of the six-counties: stores, the centres of country market towns, hotels – the Europa Hotel in Belfast bombed nearly 30 times, and whatever lay within the vacinity of a parked car-bomb. In the English campaign the stores on London's Oxford Street were hit as well as a variety of civilian facilities, office buildings with offices that played no part in governance – targets of opportunity that would cause damage and dismay.

The IRA was not averse to striking out at any functional targets. With the ceasefire of August 1994 almost in place, a two-man IRA active-service unit shot and killed one of Dublin's premier criminals Martin Cahill – 'The General' – for uncertain purpose and to mixed reviews. The IRA expressed no regrets. The Belfast Brigade also hit certain loyalist paramilitary leaders in the last days in order to intimidate the others and to reassure the nationalists concerned about the rising number of sectarian killings. There were no regrets, no admission that such operations were not reasoned and reasonable.

There had been no regrets for those forced to drive proxy car-bombs, those punished for stealing cars or secrets, for the loyalist paramilitaries or for retired Ulster Defence Regiment members who might report what the IRA did not wanted reported, or no regrets for two elderly Protestants shot and killed for repairing an RUC station. No underground can afford regrets or any general too much compassion. War generates casualties, cruelty, mistakes, blunders – and all of these were especially associated with the IRA in Northern Ireland, in Britain; in turn, the IRA saw the security forces as cruel, oppressive, brutal, and hypocritical. In the operational period between ceasefires nothing changed operationally although the messages sent by the bombs were different and as poorly received by many. For a generation what IRA bombs had done was basically what the IRA intended: expanded the campaign, raised the cost if in nothing more than horror, maintained the campaign and so the ideal. What the bombs did in the midst of the endgame was to indicate that the process towards peace could not be deployed by London as a mask for stability as had been the case in 1975–76. The IRA could not and so did not resume the campaign in Northern Ireland after Canary Wharf, could not operate easily or at times to any effect in England, but could pursue bombing – next time lucky – until a new seriousness of purpose emerged within the London establishment. Thus a very limited and technically flawed bombing campaign was in part for strategic purpose, in part simply congenial, and in construction tactically limited.

In the midst of all the turmoil of operations, the IRA continued to muddle maintenance with action. Volunteers in England, as in Ireland, played many operational roles – intelligence officer and planner, bomb maker, driver and director of a safe-house. The IRA had to run operations but often to make operations possible. Both might in turn lead to escalated violence. Guns to be acquired and money, guns to be hidden and money spent wisely. Doctors found and volunteers hidden – and all overseen by IRA command. The black economy required organizations and administration: licence fees were paid, taxes were not paid, grants were engineered, stolen goods sold, or export duties evaded. Some on active service had no part in maintenance and others specialized in armed robbery or economic protection. The very necessities of maintenance skewed the economy of Northern Ireland. The British government, through the dole, welfare programmes, and social initiatives, was in considerable part funding the IRA campaign. At times IRA maintenance had no violent content but even on the most trivial level the gun might be required – to defend against a raid, to intimidate, to protect. IRA operations always have blurred edges – no quick, sharp commando raid, no simple truck exploding in the City.

In the Republic IRA efforts even when successful tended to erode public support and even the enthusiasm of the committed: kidnappings, armed robberies, and shoot-outs did produce funds but also problems. The tactics required to maintain the struggle assured that the struggle was harder to maintain. Still the system of control suffered. And to make matters worse for the system, the Protestant paramilitaries had become deeply involved in crime and corruption, established their own black economy, so that a parallel world was created that drained away far more sterling than did government payments for bomb repairs. And the parallel world of the IRA black economy often led to the deployment of the gun – often the first resort not the last to pursue the campaign. And as long as the campaign was pursued, the faith was secure so that the arrival of an endgame shifted the direction and meaning of physical force.

THE MILITARY CAMPAIGN REVIEWED

The IRA campaign targets, ambassadors on the European continent or money from the till of a country post office, are chosen not out of a set list, not as a result of special priorities, but because they are convenient, historically valid, and often the only possibility, given the commanders' resources. Many means and many targets have been standard for a generation – the destruction of buildings, the country ambush, the sniping, the bombs in England. From time to time there were target-initiatives, a wave of letter bombs or the trucks driven by proxy bombers. These were introduced, deployed, and for a variety of reasons, including the response of the authorities, often discarded. Like all else in the campaign, the dynamic is a cycle of challenge and response, provocation and reaction. There is the contingent and unforeseen. Essentially the IRA wants change and so must make the military running – the British want order and so must defend the system. The peace process entangles the IRA into the system and so over time makes recourse to physical force less likely, a closed option. In the meantime the IRA focuses on maintaining capacity underground.

What the IRA used during the campaign was what was available. Early on the IRA sent explosive devices through the mail in England; unsophisticated but potentially deadly, the letters were thick if anonymous. The British found the most effective response was not to close down the mail, monitor every letter, alarm every potential victim but simply to narrow the slots on pillar boxes: either the IRA had to upgrade their technique or move on to something else. And as was usually the case the IRA moved on – to return to letter bombs later, a convention used and forgotten and remembered and used again over the entire generation.

When targets are hardened and resources strained the movement looks elsewhere – targets police at home in civilian clothes having tea in the kitchen, targets those who do business with the army, targets elegant restaurants in London. The effort is to move out where the target is vulnerable but familiar – same kind of people, same type of buildings, same category of resource. And once again as the authorities respond and harden the new targets, gather new intelligence, monitor access, then the tendency is to extend the bounds of the battle arena where there is not yet a response: shoot the familiar soldier in Germany, bomb the band in Gibraltar instead of the band in Kent. Since the Provisionals are in every way a provincial movement, operations abroad are a complex undertaking, require volunteers who must learn the craft on the job, and few do, require a leap of imagination in the first case. The result is that the net returns of expanding the battle arena are not as great as they might have been.

Yet the means remain remarkably stable: the British bombs during the endgame were no advance on the first car-bombs in 1973 except in size. There was a 'ring of steel' around the City in London, a huge security investment, and no ultimate defence. The target was more vulnerable and more costly than a military target but for a secret army not as appealing. The IRA always wanted military targets. The dream of the campaign were missiles to strike at British army helicopters and so to raise the military costs of the campaign to the military. So IRA military targets have remained conventional, comfortable. That secondary targets may be more effective – all the money lost to one truck-bomb in the City – does not alone make a case. The IRA commanders choose secondary targets not for strategic purpose but out of necessity and secondary considerations – for the money, to punish the arrogant, to intimidate dissent. Symbolic targets, targets in England have had enormous impact. The results at the Grand Hotel at Brighton or the shambles on Baltic Place in London have not been inconsequential for the British. Che Guevara and Black September are gone, Carlos the Jackal in a French jail and Euroterrorism largely a memory; but the IRA was still in business in the 1990s and could be again if the endgame shifts. In time this IRA will be neutered by politics, concession, lack of options, become part of the solution instead of the problem to be solved – and in so doing may open the way to the Republic. If not, then even to start again at ground zero any next and future IRA would emerge as much the same: targeting the usual, blundering on, leaving mistakes and ruin and chaos and turmoil behind largely as intended.

The Evolution of Military Strategy

Not even a movement as traditional as the Irish Republican fails to move with time and reality. And times have changed more than campaign tactics or the dynamics of the IRA. The original strategic decisions were no longer especially relevant by the 1990s. Persistence was possible but no longer paid very well. Costs of all sorts were high and prospects narrow. The no-lose and no-win posture, in fact, punished the movement more than the British. And certain assets were eroding.

A persistent problem grown more severe had been that the Irish people largely disavowed any action to achieve the ideal Republic. This might not have mattered but many publicly opposed force, the existence of the IRA – and even at times the advantages of unity. What the government, the establishment, and the man at the cross-road wants is peace and quiet and so hope, peace at nearly any price. In the Irish Republic they want the North, British Ulster, the security forces, and the IRA to go away. They want the peace process to bring peace whether it brings an end to the national issue or not. They want an end to the IRA, to the gun in politics and the North on the television. And so they vote and so they say. Some will not inform but none but the faithful believes in patriot history.

This has been increasingly the case for years as Ireland changes: unexpected and enormous prosperity, the charms of Europe, the end of provincialism, the power of the Church, the old pieties, have become convention. At the end of the century the IRA was out of step with the times. The national issue is not an issue. For decades, only the arrogance of the British establishment or the reality of brutality in the North awakened general concern, fleeting, emotional, open to some exploitation, but not for the long haul. For the long haul the Irish public, many of the nationalists in the North – and, of course, all those others in the United Kingdom – wanted politics not war. Sinn Féin might have political prospects but not as a war party.

Few in the 1980s could easily imagine gain that did not relate to the IRA military capacity, to the legitimacy to pursue the Republic with the means to hand. That the gun contaminated conventional politics, that the Armalite and the ballot box were not partners but might be opposing poles, was not really apparent. What was wanted was escalation through other means, gains made in society and votes and loyalties. The more power of any sort the better. The basic nature of the military campaign simply did not change. The same process of running faster to stay in place continued not only for the IRA but soon also for Sinn Féin. The new political options generated problems and obstacles as well as benefits – but did not greatly affect the campaign. Sinn Féin produced diminishing returns because there was a military campaign. There had been, however, a net gain in power. The campaign disasters – no-warning bombs and public distaste – were balanced by the disproportionate impact of Sinn Féin because the IRA existed – an impact conventional politicians chose to ignore. Yet the gains, as always, were limited, eaten up by time, brought the Republic no closer. The military campaign continued. The same cost accounting was in use in 1990 as in 1970. In effect the IRA was not a tool to move history but waited on history.

Most IRA operations were not crafted to have a desired effect on their avowed Irish national constituency or for that matter potential friends and support. Spectaculars reassured the loyal but often alienated all others. Most IRA operations were assumed to erode British will. Most were necessary to maintain morale, capacity, and so the organization. And most IRA operations were not crafted to send complex messages to the enemy – raising the cost was the prime motive. Taking the war home to England raised the cost and so, it was hoped even after 20 years, would erode British will. When the first ceasefire ended it ended with a bomb in London. History had not so much repeated itself but not yet begun: the IRA was going back to the future.

Each violent IRA operation had several targets – the movement to reassure the faithful that the struggle continues, the enemy and their friends to show the cost of their persistence, and to the others, friendly or no, to generate pressure for a culmination satisfactory to the dream. The particular target may be worth a set amount, may be a soldier or an ambassador, a subway terminal or market street, must be paid for by the enemy, may intimidate or dishearten a specific group as well as all the involved. The deed, however, is perceived by the involved as a military action in a long, low-intensity warfare that might best be terminated, if not by concession on the part of the British, then by escalation in intensity by the secret army. The IRA was engaged in a war and war does, indeed, have a component concerned with images and messages, punishment and intimidation; but for the IRA the real conflict is asymmetrical, the will of the Irish nation against the interests of the British.

The will of British nationalism was underestimated and that of the Irish nationalists exaggerated. Yet for decades it remained the belief of all that sooner or later the IRA would raise the cost past paying. And when this did not happen, there was an agonizing reappraisal by those who had lived their lives within the movement dedicated to the campaign, faithful to the dream. To open negotiations to explore what might be achieved without the gun required the IRA to accept a new role and a new mission and so close the campaign – at least for a time and then with the second ceasefire perhaps for good. This strategic decision to be effective must arrive from a consensus – and that consensus remained at the end of the 1990s fragile. The militant accepted that a military campaign brought limited returns but doubted the prospects of the new direction. Those committed to the new direction had to wait for the consensus to gel sufficiently to allow further pursuit of the negotiated option. Thus the decision had been made not to continue the campaign but not to dismantle – for the time being – the structure that would allow a next and future campaign. Such a strategic decision, taken slowly and incrementally over years, had as by-product that process toward agreement by consensus of the new direction which would assure that the IRA as composed would become irrelevant. What generated anguish for the IRA core was that every step forward assured that less could be done if the road to the Republic could not be found. Someplace in the next decade, there would no longer be a possibility for the faithful as organized to begin again or to start over. The campaign would, as had all others, end short of the Republic, end in songs and myths, victims soon forgotten, commemorations. History would move on, the Republicans could grow irrelevant, the national issue an artefact, the ideals forgotten. Out of sight, beyond the everyday there might be those planning a new campaign, there always had been, but then in time the slow erosion of history has often abraded valid dreams and so the necessary engine of any new recourse to the gun.

CHAPTER THIRTEEN

The Enemy

In an armed struggle one is often known by the enemies one makes. Opposition determines not simply the prospects but also the arena, the cast, and often much of the scenario. And while all enemies are by rebel definition inherently doomed by history, outwardly potent but inwardly flawed, the foe holds the centre of the stage, has the tangible assets and recognized legitimacy. If not, then no struggle would be needed. Thus the Irish rebels in general and the IRA in particular are in considerable part shaped by their perceptions of the imperial opponent, the United Kingdom, Great Britain, the English, as well as the reality of that enemy. The campaign, the armed struggle is shaped to erode the will of the British, a campaign based on Irish perceptions and analysis. Previous campaigns had deployed varying strategies: Wolfe Tone sought a general rising in conjunction with French aims, the Fenians bombed in Britain and invaded Canada from the United States, and the Irish Volunteers rose at Easter Week 1916 hoping to seize much of the country before Britain, engaged in a great war, could respond. After the establishment of the Irish Free State, recognized by the entry of Eamon De Valera into the Dáil, the Republican movement could no longer aspire to more than a limited campaign until the brief moment of intense optimism in 1972. In all cases the British, from 1798 to the end of the twentieth century, remained remarkably stable in Republican analysis. Class-based analysis simply gave other language to perceived oppression, late imperial capitalism little different from Hanoverian monarchy.

Thus the founding father of the Republican movement, Wolfe Tone – a Protestant, an English officer, and a failure as a revolutionary – defined the necessity that arose from recognizing the enemy: '... to break the connection with England, the never-failing sources of all our political evils ...'. He sought to mingle the divisive elements on the island, Catholic, Protestant, dissenter, for all shared oppression, all had mutual non-sectarian interests, all shared the common enemy. For two centuries the English, now defined as British, have been the prime, the only enemy for the traditional Irish Republican. All other opponents are facets of the Crown. Protestant para-militaries or Irish political parties are merely, if not always wittingly, playing the British game. The Irish rebels in varying forms under various titles have opposed the Crown, the London centre that has always been dominated by the English. They have often opposed the loyalist backlash at nationalist – Catholic – aspirations. They have opposed until recently the government in Dublin as illegitimate just as they opposed until recently any devolved institution in the six-counties.

The Irish Republican may even look far back beyond Tone and the United Irishmen to a history shaped around resistance to the political and cultural hegemony of the great isle. For them Irish history is the struggle of the special and particular to repel the alien oppressor, powerful, efficient, effective, dominant, recognized as legitimate, innately arrogant – all the things the Irish Republicans are not. What makes one Irish is not a passport or birth, an island granny or an act of will, but not to be English. The Protestants of the North are thus Irish but also British, offer loyalty to British Ulster, a creation of the imagination no more vivid than the Irish Republic. The divisive nature of the Protestant community, Irish and not Irish, is eased by the passionate loyalty to the Crown, to a United Kingdom that includes British Ulster – visible as the six-counties of Northern Ireland. Thus for traditional Republicans, the island with two illegitimate governments, neither representing history nor the patriot dead, with six counties controlled by British security forces, is not free, not Gaelic, not united, is occupied. The votes and flags and laws do not make British reality legitimate, offer instead rationale and legitimacy to rebellion. That rebellion is not about Catholic grievances, does not arise from a divided society, cannot be explained by Marx, but is in response to the British control over the island, often over the tastes and habits, the economy, the social mores – certainly over six Irish counties and the minds of the Protestants.

The whole historic struggle has been waged on the principle of Irish separatism and English illegitimacy to rule on the island, to rule over the Irish, to force them if not to be English then to be obedient. The issue is a matter of sovereignty but also a matter of a nation denied, often denied as an afterthought – a charming people but feckless, amusing, and creative, but prone to violence. The fact that the British – the English – found on the island a mission to impose righteous behaviour, civic standards, proper manners and airs, to impose their alien standards and society has generated more support for recourse to rebellion than all the economic exploitation, cruelty, or imposed governance. Any Irish struggle, any rising or insurrection, every assassination, the IRA's long campaign after 1970, arises from past humiliation.

The English with their alien ways and alien logic, their exploitation and awful influence, through sheer size – not to mention self-interest and justified confidence – have posed enormous obstacles to all on the island. British magnetism for two centuries has often dominated island events, island culture, the island's economy. Northern Ireland has always been a remittance state and the Irish Republic a market for British goods and services and habits, a source of labour, a vacation land for the rich and disliked by the poor. Those who admire power, prospects, the achievements of centuries, civic order and social creativity have had difficulty in resisting British power and domination. Many have found fame and fortune in London or Liverpool within imperial service or by the use of the English language. And Ireland offered only narrow compass, frugal comfort, and intellectual penury. For centuries London has arrayed against the Irish the English language, the law, the land, the established church, the armed forces, the state, culture both elegant and popular. Often the very Irish people acquiesced in their own oppression, were co-opted and corrupted or bought and sold with the land, with the power of the pound and the pleasures of the penny press. And when the English relinquished any visible grip, made any accommodation with Irish interests, it was because compromise or concession served a greater purpose, corrupted the lesser, let the Irish feel free or prosperous when they were only less Irish. In the last decade with prosperity, the prospects of Europe and the British empire a memory, the sense of urgency is, if anything, greater in the faithful: their children root for Manchester United and weep for Princess Diana and see no contradiction in their pride in Ireland. For Republicans this pride has always been goad to break the connection. No one is sure if such a goad can generate a new generation, if the new direction of the Republicans will prove ample, if the British enemy is no longer worthy of opposition. In a new global order, there are Irish who care less about the national issue and see no need to sacrifice for patriots long dead, peripheral to present interests, irrelevant.

Those who have tangible grievances linked to the national issue, the poor farmers of Tyrone and Fermanagh, the workers along the Falls Road, and those open to historic aspirations, are a wasting asset. Even the rock of South Armagh may erode. Reality and prosperity may yet drain the national issue of meaning. In the meantime, however, the enemy remains England, Britain, the present United Kingdom and all its ancestors, Perfidious, cunning, arrogant, and ruthless. The enemy was not and is not, however, drawn as simple monster.

The Irish tend not to hate the English so much as they hate England more – and focus hardly at all on the others within the Kingdom except for those who should be Irish but are not. The Irish have lived by and in England for centuries, recognize the imperial virtues, the virtues of the people, even the assets that flow to the smaller island; but militant nationalists always have opposed the centre that would have all be the same and Ireland reduced to one more cross on the Union Jack. The enemy has been and is England, Britain now, the establishment, the power brokers, barons of influence, the clubmen and the colonels, the media, the system that has sought to break the inchoate Irish nation. The everyday English, who are in reality, in the results of polls, in conversation, no friend of the Irish, are assumed misled by the establishment who seek the advantages, material and psychological, in the domination of the island. In no small part the purpose of much politics, certainly nationalist politics, in Ireland is to oppose the process of domination and so absorption. Many small nations and former colonial nations have such a problem although the Irish have had to cope for a millennium – and one defence has been physical force, just as others have been cunning, deceit, literature, and a search for concession and reform. The Republic is not so much an institutional alternative as the obverse of the Crown.

While the generations of struggle have created a rich historical legacy, the vision of Irish Republicans has tended to narrow: only so much could be carried into conflict as one campaign follows the next by those of no property and scant prospects. The British have always been the single obstacle to Ireland rising as a nation once again. Once Britain is no longer a factor in the Irish equation all matter of complexities tend to emerge: there is no longer a single cause for failure, incompetence, the failure of the language or the persistence of poverty. Britain for centuries supplied explanation and rationalization. The optimists – and almost all rebels are criminally optimistic – assumed that Ireland on its own would generate its own rich rewards, prosper and flourish, absorb the diverse, the Protestant and dissenter into the meld. This for the faithful is reality – England has set a bound to the nation that must be removed. And the Irish constituency must be made to see that operations are directed to that end – and that physical force is deployed not so much against the British as against the security forces, the system. Physical force has been the ultimate means to defeat the enemy; for some the only means. That the Irish Republic after a decade of prosperity has generated the fruits of victory without a united nation and without the defeat of Britain has seriously disturbed Republican analysis.

No matter the cars and highways, new buildings, expensive houses, and European connection, for the many Republicans, for some militant nationalists, the essential reality has not changed since Wolfe Tone laid down his dictum. Until the British withdraw from the island, Ireland will not be free and so never at peace. The British have been and still are the alien occupier, the direct and indirect exploiter of the Irish people. British interests in Ireland are inevitably defined as exploitative and illicit. All British means to retain control by moderation, co-option, integration, or devolution are considered as illicit as is the use of force. The paramilitary police, the British army, the Dublin government, the giant companies with headquarters in London, the habits of the bureaucrats, the wigs on the judges, are all means to an end. The London Sunday newspapers, football and rugby and English-made Bass ale have been seen as means to control and certainly as symbols of oppression. Everything English should be burned but their coal – and much that is Western or modern or radical, if advocated by the English, should be suspect to the Irish, the real Irish. These are a people summoned up in the nineteenth century by the nationalists, romanticized by the writers, given history and substance, and role. Awash in English influence for centuries, the Irish had to reinvent themselves from an imagined past, from a heritage of resistance, from differences raised to principles.

Bobby Sands sealed in the H-Blocks shouted out to those in his cell block the memorized chapters of Leon Uris' popular *Trinity*, history as novel but without novelty. The previous generations had reinvented Irish sport with Gaelic football and hurling, decorated their proclamations with Irish greyhounds and round towers, learned Irish as a foreign language. The Irish Free State if not free taught the native language, taught Irish history not that of Britain or even Europe, printed stamps with Celtic designs, painted the pillar boxes green. The great energizer was the presence of the English, the alien, always across the sea and still in the six-counties of Ulster where the stamps were imprinted with monarchs and the pillar boxes red.

And in contemporary times, this British presence was most painful and most adamant in that province of Northern Ireland because there the Protestants, a minority on the island but not in the North, fearful of their isolation, reassured themselves by their loyalty to the Crown, became more oppressive than the English and so generated even more sullen resentment. Fearful as a minority on the island, fearful for all sorts of reasons of the Catholic Church, the Unionists transmuted anguish into arrogance, fearing domination they institutionalized injustice as a means of protection. For most Northern nationalists resentment and grievance after 1923 gave way to resignation – what could be done but look south to the Free State and wait out history? And in the 26-counties of the Free State, renamed Éire–Ireland and at last the Irish Republic, the establishment were aggrieved but unable to imagine an effective policy beyond waiting for history, waiting on others to assure justice and a united Ireland.

For Irish Republicans, the small core, bitter, persistent, lethal, waiting was betrayal. Although careful not to be provocative in ways that might release a dreadful pogrom, the IRA in Northern Ireland always sought a way to deploy physical force against the Crown even when it was the loyal Irish

Protestants who pounded the drums of domination, and flaunted their privileges. They were Irish but misguided. And in denial the Unionists, loyal Protestants all, tossed pennies down on the Catholics – the Fenians – from Londonderry's walls, their Protestant walls, their loyalist Londonderry. The native Irish, the Catholics of Derry were left with the slums of the Bogside and a secret army. And so too in Belfast or the farms of Tyrone and Armagh, the nationalists, Catholics almost all, were pushed from the centre, marginalized, neglected by Dublin and humiliated by the Stormont system or Orange bigotry. The Irish option was rebellion when, which was seldom, general nationalist opinion would tolerate the risks – risks in civil stability and order, risk of loyalist pogroms, fiscal risks and the risk of real revolution in a conservative country.

Irish Republicans accepted that force at the end can only be met by force: no other means will in the end prove sufficient, adequate to the needs of the Irish people. Unlike some rebels they did not believe that force would transform the Irish but only serve as means for a risen nation. The nation showed little inclination to rise against the historic enemy so that the Republicans proposed a limited campaign, a protracted campaign that the nationalists would tolerate and eventually the British would not. Such campaigns failed. The image of the oppressor remained the same. The analysis of the arena and so prospects remained the same. Complications and contradictions, new means of analysis, new opponents and a faltering constituency were all adjusted so that the enemy was still the British and the most appropriate means were still physical force. Adjustments, extensions, variations were introduced but the enemy was the same, an enemy to Ireland and all the Irish.

In theory, if not always in practice, Republicans defined the Irish geographically, those on the island who chose to be on the island were Irish and so should support the aspirations of the movement. Those who did not were aliens or English surrogates like the Orangemen or misguided or apostates or, perhaps, even innocents. All who would not support the struggle for the Republic were acting in British interests. Those who chose to live on the island were or should be Irish. And given the opportunity those who lived on the island, Protestant or Catholic, would become Irish once British sovereignty had gone. Political concession was futile, for British interests were too compelling. Each time a nationalist entered the political arena to see the Republic on the instalment plan they were corrupted. Not so the real Republicans, who cherished physical force as the ultimate means.

When class analysis arose in Europe, the Irish nationalists without much direct experience of an industrial society and still traumatized by the impact of the great famine only slightly adjusted their views on the essence of British nature. Where and when useful, the ideas and analysis of Marx and later Lenin could be incorporated into Republican concepts by those attracted to such ideas. In large part, however, class oppression was simply another aspect of British exploitation of the island. The Irish Republican concept of the British as enemy was thus enriched by the spin-off benefits of over a century of continental revolutionary analysis. Republicans, mostly Catholics, were – like Irish Protestants – men of no property. From the first Tone had put his trust in those with no property. And so those with radical views found the movement congenial; however, if class or politics came to dominate their strategies rather than force, the IRA was apt no longer to offer a comfortable home. The movement was dominated for two centuries by reliance on physical force – the socialist James Connolly in 1916 became a nationalist icon after his execution – a late Republican vocation. So as each new ideological wind swept Europe, Irish Republicans were likely to find that their own heritage of analysis was adequate, might be enriched by new ideas but remained as always sufficient.

The British, powerful, arrogant, hypocritical, held the island as asset. This asset was still in 1969 protected by varying means: the threat of coercion, special laws, a standing army, compromises, a surrogate provincial system in Northern Ireland, a continuing policy of promises and bribes coupled with draconian security measures. After 1969 the creativity of the British establishment was on display in Northern Ireland as an assortment of initiatives were proposed, deployed, withdrawn or imposed to assure London's interests. All this was done in time grudgingly given from more pressing matters, for Ireland was rarely high on the British agenda. The fact that what Britain wanted most from Ireland was peace and quiet, was not clear to Irish radicals seized on their own agenda. What the British did not want was to be coerced by anyone especially and particularly the Irish, ineffectual, and irrelevant to great interests. Those interests, daily politics, the economy, the change in class structure, had nothing to do with Ireland but generate the dynamics of a changing British society. The Irish Republicans saw no change but the array of techniques and tactics to retain – as always – control over Ireland, control over the six-counties. If Britain was basically the same then Irish strategy need not be adjusted – and so after 1970 was not.

The IRA could and did make Northern Ireland ungovernable. Every means to impose order, from royal visits to writing local ordinances, was used. These initiatives were rarely as an aspect of a coherent strategy but reflected British skills and traditions. On every front from new sports facilities in Belfast to quiet negotiations in the United Nations, the British pursued their interests. Constitutions and constitutional conferences met and assemblies were established and removed, the SAS was sent in and the

B-Specials phased out, the royals and cabinet ministers continued to come on visits and peace on British terms was sponsored as concession. Mostly what the British still wanted was for the Irish to act like the English, give no trouble, allow the United Kingdom to pursue more important matters without having to worry about massacres in Belfast or bombs in Birmingham. And so IRA tactics were to make complacency impossible, concession irrelevant. The times and the tactics might shift but the essential confrontation remained unchanged, unchangeable as long as the British were on the island unchanged in IRA perceptions.

After 1970 for the Republicans nothing had changed at all except the realization that many in Ireland would not pay the cost for them to continue. So the futile talks in London in 1972 came as a disappointment – no evidence of any intent to withdraw. The 1975–76 ceasefire was accepted in the hope that the process of British withdrawal could begin – unity on the instalment plan – not because a compromise on principles was possible.

What the Republicans continued to claim was that for Ireland to be free the British would have to be forced to withdraw – that Britain might withdraw out of magnanimity was not a consideration as it had been in some British colonies. All the British concessions were for the Republicans no more than cover for exploitation. There was no evidence in the long history of Anglo-Irish confrontation that the British had ever denied themselves in Irish matters: compromises had been forced, concessions had been part of a holding action, even and especially the Anglo-Irish Treaty of 1921 had been a tactic to maintain control not a free offer to a free people. The enemy was the same and so the means was the same: physical force. If Britain chose to negotiate a withdrawal it would be because they no longer would pay the price to wage an endless campaign, because Irish Republican will had proven stronger. Justice would be done but a justice taken not given.

During the campaign years after 1970, the Republican commanders and leaders felt that this historical means, shaped to contemporary conditions, still had the capacity not only to raise the cost to the British for staying beyond a willingness to pay but also to inspire the reluctant people to support the freedom struggle. The traditionalists who coalesced into the Provisional IRA during 1970–71 saw the enemy still as Britain, the Northern Ireland establishment as imperial surrogate, the Dublin government as unwitting puppet. By 1990 almost nothing had changed except that the long war had eroded much nationalist enthusiasm and British ingenuity and Republican analysis was more complex and nuanced. But what had changed was that Irish reality could not be denied: the British would not concede and the Irish did not have the assets to force concession. The IRA could not lose but could not win and the ensuing stalemate was really more costly for the Irish than the British. Irish Republican assets – military capacity, nationalist support – were wasting and novel IRA opportunities and British vulnerabilities were not apparent. It might, as always, be possible to persist but such persistence offered very little. In 1991 the prospect existed that the British would offer something – and what was wanted in 1991 was not everything, and that achieved by physical force, and not something to show for the long years of struggle, but a means to move toward the Republic bit by bit. If the ceasefire of 1994 was but one more cunning British manoeuvre, the faithful could be expected to resort once again to force. The leadership might change within the movement, the names, the core of command but the faithful would co-alesce around those who wanted to continue, if not now then later. The end-game continued to unfold and in the process very slowly a more complicated enemy emerged for some – for others Britain was Britain and so the endgame dangerous.

THE BRITISH FOCUS

The real British on the other island, those who lived in other rooms, spoke with other voices, existed beyond the shaping of the Irish imagination or Irish Republican needs, were not only little understood by the Irish but little understood the Irish. Few asymmetrical conflicts have been as visible as the incomprehension of these two cultures, the two traditions often living amid each other on the smaller island and not always as master and mastered. On the greater island the Irish either became English or were buried back home in Mayo or Donegal as Irish. There were no Anglo-Irish in Britain, only immigrants disappearing into the main and the Irish working for wages in a foreign country, always foreign.

The Republicans in theory avowed secularists, rationalists in the community of the pious and superstitious, nationalists in a Europe dominated by class concerns, made the complex simple, the enemy a monster, but one without a religious component. They chose to ignore the Irish Protestant reality that few Irish Catholics understood in any case, and focus on the British enemy. The Irish people who would not sacrifice for the nation were misguided. The Protestants were misguided. The British were exploitive, greedy, arrogant. This made negotiations as difficult for the Irish Republicans as they were for a British establishment that saw the IRA as ruthless, brutal terrorists, wicked and evil, not real nationalists at all and quite without polish or sophistication or competence.

The Republicans possessed the revealed truth. The British relied on law and order, legitimacy – and in the heel of the hunt the arrogance of centuries of triumph. Until the endgame, complexities and other insights were unwanted, ignored, or adjusted to the original visions. Republicans knew what they knew even if the others on the island did not believe them or their truth. The British knew their Irish and especially the IRA. One of the IRA assets was that their image of Britain was not only closer to objective reality in Ireland but also useful to the campaign. When the time came to probe Republican reality, the British, as always, adjusted to advantage. The Republicans moved more slowly. With the revealed truth any interpretation can risk heresy so that the first decision of the Army Council when faced with substantive discussions was to maintain the consensus: no splits. This meant that not simply those exposed to discussions but most Republicans had to adjust their analysis of the enemy.

The English, the British, only played the game when they could make the rules that assured their victory. The Irish, people of no property, did not know the British establishment first hand. They lived in rooms the Irish could not imagine, lived lives the Irish could not imagine. No Republican had ever eaten at the Reform Club or been invited for a week-end in the country, knew names at Lloyd's or was greatly moved by cricket. The Irish, however, knew the British as oppressor, as enemy, and if not a subtle and sophisticated image one useful to an armed struggle. The Irish knew the hard face of British nationalism and British order. They had long been the loser in the British game, the English game. The English historically made rules that the Irish knew only too well. This was not a matter of perception, summoning up wishfully a monster, was not the fantasies of a few, but the experience of generations. The British as enemy was the reality off the Falls, in mid-Tyrone or inside an English prison. Hypocrisy was as English as Westminster and the Queen; often enough when in Ireland civility, law, decency, and elegance was left behind as the British played out the game for advantage.

British rules shaped to English establishment interests might appeal to Northern Unionists, to the Dublin establishment, to the conservative and comfortable anywhere, everywhere, but not to those in Ireland who dreamed of a Republic. They would not, had not played an English game that guaranteed an English outcome; for it was not who won or lost, received concession or promise, as Dublin assumed, but the name of the game that mattered.

The enemy as far as the IRA was concerned must be met with appropriate means if for no other reason than to maintain the faith. That faith is at the end the real last great hope of the Irish for without it the island will be province, marginal to the magnet at London, a green and fruitless land. For the core of the faithful to offer that faith to risk by means of treating with the historical enemy was bold – required a reinterpretation of British interests and, incidentally, a more realistic acceptance of the aspirations of Irish nationalists rather than the responsibilities due to the patriot dead.

For generations the IRA was focused against the stereotype – the ruthless and cunning enemy not the good and the decent. In an endgame the IRA suspects that accommodation, decency, and compromise are merely extensions of the old cunning deployed while brutality awaits. Either the IRA must counter such traditional attributes to advantage or revise the old image to allow greater flexibility in negotiations – or, of course, both, which is the process underway since 1991. If Britain can be brought to an endgame, to serious negotiations, then physical force has accomplished its primary purpose – the open road to the Republic. Victory in the field, even vengeance, has charms but the IRA has long recognized the campaign cannot win militarily just as it is hoped London has recognized that it cannot be defeated militarily. Hence the IRA, the Republicans, excluding the traditionalists, have come to accept different priorities, a different strategic arena, and a different Britain, a more reasoned, more flexible Britain. And when, as is often the case, that Britain cannot be found during negotiations there is renewed anxiety and frustration.

For the Republicans there is another problem in that the enemy, the British, are not as uncompromising as the Ulster Unionists, who should in theory be more Irish than Protestant and will, with the British presence eroded, be absorbed into Irish society. Such a fate at the expected expense of Irish Protestant values and beliefs is what makes them an enemy to concession, to any move toward the Republic on the instalment plan. For Northern Irish Protestants an Irish Republic would be dominated by an oppressive and authoritarian society submissive to the Roman Catholic Church – a disaster. And so they are the announced enemy of Republican aspirations. And the Republicans refuse, still, to make them an enemy, misguided not malignant. Thus as the endgame moves on the Republicans have warily responded to the prime enemy the British, dubious of motives, suspicious of good faith At the same time, the movement continues to ignore the declared enemy – the Protestants, the Unionist establishment, the loyalists, the paramilitaries, and the pacifists, all resident in British Ulster and all dedicated to the preservation of the British connection that has for Republicans been 'the never-failing sources of all our political evils'. While the nationalist–Unionist dilemma at the end of the century need not be a zero-sum, the perception of reality and the asymmetrical goals – an Irish Republic and a British Ulster – complicate the endgame.

The dream, the goal, remains a united Ireland that contains not simply 32 counties but also all the Irish. What a united Ireland needs is a united people determined to make an effective nation – not simply an island called Ireland, but the Irish however they rule themselves. Such an eventuality might well come over time, on the instalment plan, if the Republicans accepted the Unionists as enemies, if the British were more committed to the ultimate end of partition if reality were adjusted and perceptions changed, if the enemy in London was not as once imagined.

CHAPTER FOURTEEN

Endgame

As in most armed struggles, the Irish Republican focus was on beginning not ending. Unlike others, the strategic beginning decision that had been made for generations. The IRA mostly waited for an appropriate correlation of forces to wage an armed struggle. It was not that those involved could not imagine an endgame, a time of concession. Irish history was filled with the faithful who had played an endgame too soon, too eagerly, and so were co-opted into a system that they had intended to destroy. For Irish Republicans Irish history was a long tale of confrontation eased by British concession and accommodation that brought not a free Ireland but a contented people unwilling to sacrifice further. The Irish Free State, De Valera's Éire–Ireland, the 26-county Irish Republic, were illusions purchased by a people too rarely committed to their avowed ideals.

And too many had sought to end war by employing negotiations, by accepting less than the ideal. The most dedicated had been seduced: Michael Collins and De Valera and Seán MacBride and then all those in Dublin GHQ in 1969, the Officials, Goulding, Garland, Ryan, and the rest. Endgames were always very much in the minds of the Provisional Army Council, in the minds of most veteran Republicans. Endgames that were not about defining the terms of British withdrawal were futile. The Provisionals *knew* that once a campaign was tolerated by the Irish people in time, this time or at worst next time, the British would withdraw. They knew the British. They knew their own, their history, had decades of their own experience and the wisdom of their elders as text. They knew the game. And they knew that at the end the real dangers would emerge – not death but dishonour would be the great danger. In 1969–70 none of this needed be sifted again. For once objective reality and Republican analysis proved identical, so that by 1971 the IRA had what they had always wanted: an escalating armed struggle supported or tolerated not simply by those with pressing grievances but also apparently by most of the nationalists on the island.

In 1972 the British cabinet was merely exploring possibilities. Not the IRA – they saw the Treaty of 1921 being replayed, felt the winds of history, assumed that the stage was large and the play far more important than the

British government could imagine. They, a handful of working-class felons and fanatics, were suddenly part of patriot history. They knew their duty: to lay down the requirements of the Irish people, a declaration of withdrawal, the release of the prisoners, the other details of the last chapter. They felt they had opened the last chapter. The endgame was merely negotiating how fast the dream would become reality. Other matters, from loyalist opposition to British pride and perception, were simply not factored into their world. They saw themselves as legates to history.

The British opposite them in a Chelsea drawing room, suave, sophisticated, clever, and wry, saw them as crude, ignorant gunmen, indeed felons and fanatics, who had to be tolerated for the moment; Adams might have seemed sensible but he had an unpleasant accent, was too young, irrelevant. The others made a dreadful impression, ill-spoken, ill-at-ease, arrogant in delivery without grace or charm and quite beyond serious consideration: hopeless.

The British, not for the first time, would take tea with traitors but in 1972 without trading even the formalities of negotiation. The British establishment had often had trouble with others who fit no proper mould: the imperial rebels, Zionist socialists from obscure Polish villages, Arab tribesmen from the Radfan in South Yemen, African nationalists who had spent years in London bedsitters. The Irish were to remain, as in the past, a mystery to the British in many ways – and an open book in others. The British, however, had not even imagined an endgame – the end in Ireland would come with the restoration of order and civil discipline under the guidance of London.

These IRA leaders in London were irrelevant to statecraft, to British intention, to the future. The Irish in shoddy suits and twisted ties, with harsh accents and no polish were there as a result of British gambit not as delegation. There could be no endgame with them, no need of further formalities. The British were not replaying the Treaty negotiations but merely playing a game, seeking a tactical pause. How could a group of low-level fanatics from the margin of events be taken seriously? They were barmen and clerks, construction foremen, an unknown solicitor, little people, parochial and foolish, inflated by pretensions of grandeur. More elegance and taste, more visible sophistication might have led to more complex bargaining; but the British saw innocence as ignorance and commitment as fanaticism, and the Irishmen as gunmen.

There was to be no endgame except their isolation and so elimination from any future accommodation. For a generation the British would not seriously readjust this perception. The Republicans might be the focus of tactical manoeuvre but an effective accommodation could be, would be, achieved without their consent. The IRA was merely a factor in the Irish formula. Somehow the British clung to this conviction despite the IRA campaign, the bombs in Britain, the attacks on politicians, the assassinations, and turmoil, despite the fact that the IRA depleted British fiscal resources, skewed the posture and posting of British security forces. None cared to recognize that the criminal justice system had to be corrupted, the City in London ringed with steel, Downing Street guarded, and that no servant of the Crown in uniform or out was safe from the gunman, not on any street in Ulster, not on a bandstand in Regent's Park or a hotel in Brighton, not even in Number Ten Downing Street or the Westminster car park. Just as the IRA feared that an endgame would bring co-option, so too did the British establishment seem to feel that treating with the IRA would betray the nation. In 1972 London could still aspire to order imposed in large part by the deployment of power and fixed by political accommodation. At some future date Republicans might have to be included in any devolved system but even then under proper banners of the political Sinn Féin and only to validate an agreement that would have been achieved by others for other purposes. No more than this: the last Republican survivors dragged aboard some future raft of accommodation – and those who would not board would be put down, put down by the gun, by the times, by history.

So after Chelsea the game rules changed, a British specialty: there would be no real concession, no withdrawal, hardly even recognition that the IRA were rebels but merely criminals. To be acceptable at a bargaining table the rebel – and so the Irish – has to be adjusted by British perception into a recipient of patronage, the beneficiary of tutelage or else – as was the case in Aden or Kenya or the Suez Canal Zone – a counter not worth the price, no longer a responsibility but a discard. Rebels are either candidates for the Commonwealth club, grateful new boys in the British establishment, or discards. The Irish wanted neither charity nor concession, denied the need of tutelage, wanted to raise their price so that the British would perforce have to adjust the game to allow room for the Irish rebel to dictate the terms of any endgame. The British thus persisted in an effort to impose order and governance that would allow an end to IRA violence. And the IRA persisted with an armed struggle that would assure an Irish Republic. And endgame continued to mean different things, a basic dynamic of such asymmetrical conflicts: the perceptions of the future and the players were at odds, as was the assumed direction of history or even the assets to hand. The IRA, no matter the obstacles, found means to persist with the armed struggle. The British displayed an enormous talent in seeking a way out of the Ulster maze – but almost always without involving the militant Republicans. The British could and did try to co-opt the Republican's movement and erode

Republican faith, even involve Republican leadership in negotiations, but never considered the prospect of a game that would end without British sovereignty in place in Ireland. On this they could count on the majority in Northern Ireland, the limits of Dublin power, and the lack of IRA capacity. The IRA relied on the principle that the ultimate winner would be not the stronger but the one who was willing to suffer the most. Sacrifice was a component of the Irish psyche so that the game continued to be played with no end in sight.

The British assumed that they possessed both justice and the big battalions. The Northern Ireland Office could manage to deploy a variety of accommodating policies and counter-insurgency techniques often without much guidance from Whitehall or Westminster. The Irish game was not worth the playing in London – the Irish gunmen at most could shape horrid spectaculars, bombs in Manchester or mortar shells on Downing Street; but mostly British matters moved apace without undue trouble. There was no need to consider an end to the Troubles as long as there was an acceptable level of violence and some slight motion toward an accommodation to keep the liberals still and Dublin on the string. So the Troubles became institutionalized and the armed struggle protracted.

The result was a postponed endgame. The IRA, often embedded into a dirty war of attrition with no immediate prospects of military triumph or even escalation, opened other battle fronts: operations in England, local welfare, politics, gunmen on the European continent, and Sinn Féin discussions of options. The end sought by the IRA – the beginning of British withdrawal – was seemingly always the same and always beyond the willingness of the British establishment to consider. This is often the case: the ideal of the underground may be beyond conceding, even beyond imagining. What would *Brigate rosse* have done with Italy? What could Mao have been offered or Ho and Giap? One either won or lost in most cases. The few insurgences with a negotiated end were rare – some obscure as in Yemen, some unexpected as in South Africa, and some still uncertain as in Palestine. Experience and history indicated that negotiated endgames were thus rare, uncertain, unexpected, and unlikely. And for a generation nothing in Ireland contradicted such assumptions.

The lesson learned by the IRA was that only tangible concessions mattered: goodwill, regular contact, the exchange of confidence building initiative, the enthusiasm of the public had led nowhere and so would lead nowhere.

When the 1975 truce failed, never observed by either side with any great scruples, the IRA soon had to respond to the emergence of the women's peace movement – the Peace People – that swept through the province in

1976 on a high tide of emotion. The movement had the intensity of a religious revival. There were monster rallies, media frenzy, a Nobel Prize, and nothing tangible. The IRA was threatened by this countervailing force for peace – however feeble in reality. The Peace People did not want justice but an end to violence – and so, wittingly or not, supported the restoration of order without addressing the root cause – the British presence. Republicans condemned the movement as a British ruse, demanded peace with justice, indicated again that the armed struggle led toward a free Ireland not simply an Ireland free of violence and still dominated by London interests. British enthusiasm for the peace movement did, in fact, persuade many nationalists in Northern Ireland that their interests could not be served simply by an end to the killing.

Irish reality could not be adjusted by more demonstrations and petitions of decency. Crowds went home at the end of the day to the same reality. And the many mobilized for the moment also went home to their same prejudices and perceptions, went home without addressing how justice could be achieved by accommodation. Although the Republicans were apt to appear truculent and unfeeling in their public opposition amid the media circus, their position was rooted in Irish reality and common sense. Peace arose from agreed verities, from victory, from compromise, not from desire and decency. When the Peace People faltered by 1978, as the emotion evaporated to reveal once again the intractable disputes, the Republicans pushed on with their protracted struggle.

For more than a decade the campaign continued. The movement took heart with spectaculars like the 1979 Warrenpoint ambush and the assassination of Mountbatten, from each military success, from perseverance as British counter-insurgency capacity rose. For three years in the early 1980s, the hunger strikes and the new politics of Sinn Féin dominated the movement. Then came the hope that a strategy of the Armalite and the ballot box would escalate support and thus British minds. This aspiration lay behind the effort to move Sinn Féin political power south into the Irish Republic. And this led to pressure to end the policy of abstentionism that produced schism but no gains in the Republic. So at the end of 1986, the Provisionals saw the withdrawal of the traditionalists into Republican Sinn Féin and the failure of the party to attract the southern electorate.

The war went on and on and the British persisted in initiating political options, counter-insurgency skills, and patience. British nationalism had a will as well as tangible assets and the IRA lacked the capacity to change matters. London brought Dublin aboard with the Anglo-Irish pact but could find no way to establish devolved government or impose order – neither informers, primacy of the police, or harsh coercion worked any more than had the assemblies and conventions. So matters did not change. The Troubles, despite the ingenuity and zealotry of all, remained institutionalized.

By 1990 the new generation of a far more sophisticated educated Sinn Féin had begun probing future options and old assumptions. Some within the command structure of the IRA did so as well and many did not, content to focus on their existing mission. An underground takes short views so that the IRA was apt to focus on the excitements of the moment – new military fronts, the new Libyan weapons, and new techniques. All of these were deployed for the same purposes: persistence and escalation. Yet by the end of the decade, there was nothing positive on the operational horizon.

In 1990 the Northern Ireland Secretary Peter Brooke claimed that the British state had no strategic or economic interests in staying. They had to consider the majority Protestants their duty, but if asked to go by all would do so. The majority Protestants, despite an unfriendly media, a declining population base, and an opportunity to impose their terms on any accommodation, preferred no change – a mix of nostalgia, sense, and expectation that in the end London would not abandon them. So the British wanted nothing, for the Protestants nothing changed, and the IRA seemingly wanted the unattainable but lacked appropriate power.

To the sensible, the Republicans appeared increasingly isolated – responsible for provoking the loyalists, unwilling to accept majority rule, dependent upon the gun that prevented any serious negotiations. Indeed to an increasing number of the commanders, members of a generation that had never known peace or quiet, protraction was no longer its own reward. The leadership of Sinn Féin and many sound IRA people wanted a viable option that would end the endless, endless funerals, the sacrifice to no purpose. The traditionalists felt past sacrifices required persistence and present sacrifice was vital to maintain the faith for the future. Everyone perceived reality much alike but drew different conclusions. Those underground who wanted change began to accumulate advocates – and they soon controlled Sinn Féin and the terms of debate.

Increasingly the Republicans and in time the nationalists realized that even if the British were to withdraw, there was still an Irish Protestant problem. They might not find any Irish roots or find them any time soon. They might not run amuck in a great Irish Armageddon as many Unionists North and South anticipated, mostly wishful thinking. Strategically the Republicans were wedded to the proposition that given the opportunity the Unionists would become more Irish than Protestant. This might be possible over time instead of the reaction to British withdrawal. And conditions in Northern Ireland had changed, not all to Republican disadvantage. Fear and sense had produced a population shift that divided the province into secure religious enclaves. The RUC had become a disciplined police force unlikely to engage in pogroms, and the Royal Irish Regiment if more parochial in loyalty was still a regiment, part of an army. Most Unionists were decent even if often understanding of sectarian violence by the loyalist paramilitaries. These loyalist gunmen might cause havoc if abandoned but could not wage war – poorly armed sectarian killers were not a strategic matter in any future accommodation. More dangerous was the prospect that the entire Protestant community, as had been the case with the nationalists after 1971, might withdraw their consent to be governed. Then no devolved, regional assembly and certainly no all-Irish entity, even one supported by London, could govern. Worse would be if the Protestants simply withdrew from British Ulster and emigrated to the mainland. The IRA campaign might have arisen because of a struggle over sovereignty but had long been entangled in the dynamics of a divided society – and now the Republicans recognized some of the implications. The Protestants had to be reassured, the Republican ideal could not be allowed to ruin prospects of moving forward in stages. The strategy of the armed struggle had foreseen a British withdrawal but by 1990 many Republicans doubted that this was to anyone's advantage. In fact the same old answers to the basic questions were not as clear in the Ireland of 1990.

In a sense the Republicans readjusted their definition of a united Ireland to indicate not a geographical term but a united people. And such an Ireland could not be achieved with the gun even if the gun could assist in concentrating British minds, accelerating concessions that over time would lead to a British withdrawal and so peace with justice for all. With such a withdrawal Republicans were convinced that ultimately a united Ireland was inevitable. And so too were the Protestants who saw unity in terms of absorption into a tradition feared and loathed. The shift in Republican perception only intensified Protestant anguish – made clear by the increase in sectarian killing in the 1990s. If the IRA could consider unity on the instalment plan, then the loyalists were fearful that Dublin would seize the initiative and London might see advantage in pursuing such a formula in order to square the circle, co-opt the Republicans into a process that foresaw Irish unity. And the British could see that such co-option would be open ended: the longer the negotiation, the more effective concessions that did not determine a final solution, the less value the gun for the Republicans.

Yet for both the British and the IRA to be involved in an endgame there would have to be an end to the armed struggle, either as triumph delayed or defeat disguised, whatever the involved chose to believe. In the latter case the Provisionals were neither innocent of British intentions nor ignorant of their cherished means. Perfidious Albion had left behind a trail of broken hopes, broken promises, sly imperial manoeuvres, left Ireland in 1921 to civil war and successor states controlled from London. British contacts with the IRA had for over a generation been duplicitous. For many, there was ample evidence that British cunning had not been lost and little that the British were willing to make real concession. The IRA, the Republicans, had to adjust the image of the enemy in order to talk.

At the beginning of the 1990s, outwardly the British seemed content to pursue talks about talks. No one, including the IRA, would admit that Republican power came from a gun. What was at issue was how much this power would bring before the gun was taken out of politics. London and Dublin had always insisted the IRA would have to end the campaign in order to join talks about talks, in effect give up the only real card Republicans held. This mantra had been repeated so often that any endgame had to be adjusted to the requirement. This meant that the Republicans had to be given lots to enter talks – and this was only worthwhile if the campaign were to end – first, simultaneously, soon thereafter. And with a change in British priorities, an effort was made to indicate that there was a real offer on the Irish board.

Thus the very first British effort to talk was made by British intelligence: here the IRA had no doubts about the attitudes and assets of those involved. British intelligence was cored into the British establishment. The secret and personal approach to Martin McGuinness suggested that at the core of the British establishment there was a seriousness of purpose in pursuing nego-tiations. That nothing came of this channel was not as important as the impact it had on Republican thinking. The ensuing secret negotiations were taken more seriously because they were in secret, in violation of announced British policy and denied by the Northern Ireland Office.

In point of fact, the IRA was quite willing to explore any avenue that did not betray the central purpose of the movement which was to turn the dream into reality. This central purpose had for a generation, however, seemed beyond reach of accommodation, for the British establishment would not accept even staged withdrawal as a real option: to withdraw would be to accept the Irish reading of history and their own failure as exemplar of political virtue. So London recognized, if many in Ireland did not, that Irish Republican moderation was a matter of tone not substance. In London after Thatcher left, with few political prospects, few opportunities abroad, the new Prime Minister John Major was willing to consider Ireland for the costs were enormous – the City bombs had cost over a billion pounds and changed life for the financial community. Many, even among Conservative friends in Ulster, accepted with Major that something should be done, could be done.

In the greater world beyond Ulster, there had been solutions, seemingly effective endgames, accommodations reached in South Africa and Palestine. There were the enticing prospects of a new Europe that might engender ambivalence in Great Britain but not in the Irish Republic. Everyone was all too aware of the dangers of militant nationalism as revealed in the implosion of the Soviet Union and the turmoil in Yugoslavia. Why couldn't something be done about Ireland? And anyone who could do so would end in the history books, a prospect that had a certain appeal for Major and later the new Irish Taoiseach, Albert Reynolds.

Seemingly nothing had changed. The aspirations of the IRA were beyond compromise; the British would not cede sovereignty and responsibilities to gunmen, the gunmen would take nothing less. The nationalists and Unionists seemed engaged in a zero-sum game. Dublin had good will but no power. Some had always sought a way out of the maze, did not accept that the problem was that there was no solution. For over 20 years, John Hume had tried to talk an accommodation into reality. And there were others and so no one – not even the most cynical, not even the loyalist paramilitaries often tempted by politics or the IRA commanders engaged in a long war, could give up completely on a general arrangement that might satisfy the involved sufficiently to take the gun out of politics.

Over a generation there were enormous numbers of constitutional arrangements proposed –and often put into place, a thousand books written, endless papers drafted, conferences convened and careers made. John Hume was hardly alone if often isolated. And so Brooke's initiative and the secret British contact with the IRA seemed minor matters. If there was a serious British decision to explore an accommodation by addressing Republican concerns, there might be a formulation that would reconcile opposites, permit the convergence of parallels at some future date, and in the meantime narrow the differences. And British intelligence indicated to the IRA that the due date might have arrived.

For an endgame all had to adjust their perception of the nature of the enemy, shape an agenda – what they wanted, what they said they wanted and what they would take. Such an agenda could not simply be answered by 'Brits out and the Republic in'. And such an agenda could not be the IRA disarmed, Sinn Féin marginalized, Unionists reassured, and Dublin compliant – law and order and the security of British Ulster. And the Unionists and loyalists of British Ulster, and the Protestant Irish had to be persuaded that change was inevitable and need not be a threat. Some had to find a formula that did not simply blur differences but amalgamated them. If the British were willing to try, so too were many Republicans supported by all Irish nationalists.

Such a formula might have had an attraction to those in an exhausted secret army. Certainly many in the movement had sacrificed for years, decades, some a lifetime without tangible returns. Many had withdrawn daunted. Others wanted not formula but the peace and quiet of private life. The movement remained, however, much the same size as before, still capable of expansion, still a powerful attractive force despite the long dirty war – but no longer because of that war. Many involved, volunteers and commanders, did not see great hope of military action but neither did they see negotiations as a very promising option. But after a generation, however fanatical about the Republic and zealous in waging the campaign, they were not averse to exploring other options. A pause would be expensive but not irreversible. This time, it appeared, the British were serious and so the IRA took the prospects of negotiations seriously.

Almost from the first, the Republicans involved recognized the dangers – a split, the traditional Republican response to change. This time the movement agreed that there would be no split – if there were to be change, then all would accept the necessity. The movement rested on consensus, often achieved without discussion or division. This time there would be discussion to prevent division. The prime focus would be to shape a consensus to changing opportunities, to cast change in a different context. What the advocates of negotiations did not do was to explain how conditions were different and so it was time for different priorities. That is what De Valera had said, and Republican Congress, *Clann na Phoblachta*, and the Officials. This time present conditions could be exploited to achieve the same priorities if in different ways. The aspiration was the same, only the means adjusted.

For the first time since 1970 a strategic decision was under discussion and for the first time since 1921 there was a conscious effort to maintain a consensus even at the expense of change. The majority would not break with the others merely to snatch all that was on offer. The movement would go forward as one or not move. There was to be no De Valera option and so no charm in Republican Sinn Féin. There could be no advantage taken unless all agreed that there was advantage. So Sinn Féin was prepared to talk but not to deny the parallel benefits of physical force.

It was a process eagerly supported in Dublin and most visible in the discussions held by Gerry Adams as president of Sinn Féin and John Hume of the SDLP. What Hume and Adams sought, if often haltingly, was a Northern nationalist front that would involve Sinn Féin in a conventional strategy that could be supported by Dublin, by all Irish nationalists – as the Unionist said, a pan-nationalist front – and so welcomed by Major and the British establishment. However, the Republicans had to accept that they had already shot their way to the bargaining table: the gun was no longer needed and could be denied to advantage but not right away. What was happening was the emergence of an endgame where the most vital discussions were and would remain secret and shifts in response not easily polled – a consensus is difficult to quantify.

In fact the endgame did not begin at any single moment but in the long general process of changed perceptions and priorities that made the British gestures relevant to the Republicans and the Republicans open to discussion – if most of such discussion was secret. An unarmed strategy offered – might offer – a way forward while, as the IRA recognized, a military strategy simply guaranteed no defeat. Certainly the direct contacts with the British were an indication that the new strategy would be deployed at the highest level.

The Republicans had far more assets than in the past. They had talent. The president of Sinn Féin, Gerry Adams, was a felon, a former barman, lived on the dole off the Falls; but as well as being a hard man, a volunteer, he was a natural politician, a world-class politician, who if born in Manchester might well have been a Labour prime minister. He understood consensus and symbols, the construction of posture and position. His colleagues, if perhaps less talented, were skilful and increasingly practised politicians. Politics, like war, offers opportunity to inherent capacity, dedication, creativity, hard work, and experience. Adams and Sinn Féin in alliance with Hume and Reynolds might have created a formidable Irish team. Adams, Martin McGuinness in Derry, and much of the Republican leadership, grew convinced that if Ireland were not to continue as a tragedy in endless acts then risks would have to be taken. The movement would have to shift not just priorities but assumptions. As time passed, the new direction convinced many and was reluctantly accepted by the militant for lack of options. And as negotiations continued this slowly emerging consensus lagged behind events but far ahead of what had been Republican assumptions in the past.

Sinn Féin was a player in an endgame that required the Republican movement to accept the logic of changed events: history need not be replayed even if the scenario appeared all too familiar. The movement, cored in the hard men of physical force, never saw Adams and McGuinness as political operators – how could they, given the careers of the two? The IRA commanders did see that a long war was not very attractive : their children would be engaged in it as had their fathers. They could reluctantly see the possible advantages of an unarmed strategy: but they could also see the risks. And most of all they found it difficult to come to terms with physical force as a secondary rather than primary consideration. The goal had always been the Republic, the enemy the British and the means physical force. Now the leadership was suggesting that there could be no united Ireland, no Republic, without Protestant participation – and who could deny this? The leadership was seeking more complex answers than the old verities. In Ireland over a generation the involved were almost always denied what they really wanted, what they claimed to want, and so got process not tangibles. The Troubles, however, offered secondary benefits to all. Nearly everyone gets something, something useful and desirable, vengeance or power, a job replacing broken windows, a specialty in knee surgery, a meaning to a drab life or a chance to appear on television. Over the years, the way of life for many of the involved became addictive; even the gunman might fashion a career in an armed struggle difficult to forgo – what does one do after a decade on the run, being intimate with ambush, innocent of finance or craft? To counter such advantage, real movement toward an end to the long war had to be tangible. After all, secondary benefits are secondary – the charm of the gunman's life is short-lived.

So the Republicans slowly redefined reality, shifted their perceptions of reality. This did not mean that if nothing really changed – the British do not seek a means out of the maze, the Protestants give not an inch, the other Irish fail to pursue the dream so many have denied – the IRA would be content to talk on and on as capacity declined. When in 1994 and 1995 progress toward resolution created frustration the gun reappeared, the bomb detonated on Canary Wharf in London. The IRA – a different, less capable, uncertain IRA – was again engaged in an armed struggle but one configured by the realities of an endgame, a different IRA.

There have been many IRAs, all essentially the same, all heirs to Tone and history and the legitimacy of the gun and so no ceasefire can be permanent if it is merely cover for an Ireland unfree rather than a route toward freedom. The peace process – the endgame – is complex, takes place on many levels, moves at no programme's pace, is not a matter of policies and politics alone but above all else is a matter of perception.

In 1967 an IRA volunteer who shot a member of the Royal Ulster Constabulary on a Belfast street would have been thought mad or criminal, thought so by his commander, his parents, and his community, would have been so treated by the system. In 1972 such an act was an operation, mad and criminal only by definition of the oppressor, and everyone knew this: the volunteer's commander, his parents, his community, and of course the system that would treat him specially not as mad or criminal but subversive. What had changed was everyone's perception and what changes in an endgame is perception. This is as hard to weigh as was the toleration of the Irish people for physical force: the Provisionals in 1969–70 recognized at once that there was a new tide in Ireland. In 1993 and 1994 a new tide was noted, but how strong, how deep, how inclusive, and persistent was not clear. The IRA's renewed campaign indicated just how much had changed: toleration low, enthusiasm nil, capacity inadequate, prospects disastrous.

Thus a renewed ceasefire was indicated and the break in the ceasefire emerged as part of the endgame, not the end of the game. The Republicans were willing to run the risk without a gun – the other options were scant – but not so far the Unionists, who without their veto or the loyalists with recourse to riot and sectarian murder have combined to refuse to become engaged in what is perceived as the dissolution of British Ulster. The guardians of Ulster feel that do nothing is the best policy. Acceptance of new prospects, a new assembly, even if accepted by a scant majority, had little charm. And increasingly it appeared that the British, too, felt no great urgency to move on – to accelerate the process. As long as nothing much happened, the Unionist and loyalist could display truculence, London patience, Dublin and nationalist opinion enthusiasm, leaving the Republicans caught between war and peace, prospects and disaster – just what Republican Sinn Féin suggested and just where the traditionalists feared. The orthodox – and most adamantly the Unionists – insist that the IRA give up their arms – no talks with gunmen – and yet no one else has had to give up anything of substance. True, prisoners have been released – Protestants and Catholics, IRA and UVF, North and South – and praise and money have flooded in for the Irish in general and the involved in particular – a Nobel Prize for Hume and Trimble and Gerry Adams at the White House – but very little progress toward a united Ireland, even an Ireland open to unity. And so traditional Republicans are not only frustrated but also fearful that the new direction has led to nothing new, to one more assembly albeit with Sinn Féin ministers. The cherished consensus still holds, the mandate of heaven has not passed to Republican Sinn Féin, the Real IRA was really not the IRA; but the future is no longer as promising and the options fewer – whatever the conventional want the IRA can at the beginning of the century no longer have recourse to the gun – or not in existing conditions.

Endgames need not lead to conclusion, to victory or conciliation, may end in stalemate, may in the real world, not chess, create new pieces, new rules and aspirations, new conflicts, even a broader board. What cannot be predicted is the medium that will then exist – the nature of the board and so the rules of the game. No one can be sure of the future: the level of toleration by the Irish, the shape of history yet to come, the perceptions of tomorrow. The endgame makes the old game obsolete without assuring the players their heart's desire, without in fact assuring the players even relevance.

The first problem for the IRA throughout the peace process has been to maintain the internal consensus – keep the faith and in so doing deny the mandate of legitimacy to any competition. And this has been done through a complex of constant meetings, conferences, discourse on all levels, discussions, tea seminars, contact both formal and informal. The discussion and often dispute over the viability of the new direction has evolved over time, shifting conditions and the impact of the process. The great attraction of the new direction is that the old direction had proven futile, comfortable but futile. The effort to return to these conditions to effect events, attract attention, satisfy the militancy of the IRA indicated that conditions had changed. There was still a lack of alternatives. This reluctant discovery gave strength to those who sought some advance through novelty if at some risk. Novelty had become orthodoxy and recourse to traditional physical force counter-productive. All during the 1990s. the great risk was schism and so avoided. The zealots were still zealous, still doubtful of the new direction but once again recognizing reality declared another ceasefire. The consensus around the new direction was thus extensive.

The Republican Sinn Féin might be congenial in ideology but not sufficiently so, hence the Continuity Army Council had greater pretensions than prospects. Those still in the IRA who had opposed the second ceasefire had demonstrated the futility of any armed struggle when operations in 1998–99 attracted few, made no useful impact on events and led to another massacre – at Omagh by the Real IRA in August 1998. The IRA had shifted roles and missions for the first time since 1923. If there were to be an unarmed strategy to seek concession in alliance with other nationalists and supported by the American president and much of world opinion, then there could no longer be an armed struggle. The IRA could not act, but also was not able simply to persist waiting for the next opportunity. The conventional wanted to make this reality visible by forcing the IRA to decommission their arms. The Republicans sensibly indicated that if an accommodation worked there would be no next time, no need of arms. And, the shrewd knew that if such an accommodation did not emerge the IRA would not have the capacity to act – military capacity declines steadily from the beginning of any ceasefire and precipitously after a year. Yet, it is not capacity that energizes an armed struggle but the revealed truth that offers answers to the vital questions. And in the 1990s revealed truth no longer revealed a familiar Ireland or a way into the future. No one wanted to pursue an armed struggle with limited assets and no compelling purpose – no incandescent aspiration nor evil opponent. Few wanted to sacrifice merely to protect a capacity that the leadership could no longer deploy or maintain. The will and the means had gone if not the secret army, underground coping with a new role and an uncertain mission.

No one was more interested in the erosion of the underground as the movement and individuals became more conventional. Gunmen ran for office and volunteers quarrelled over the assembly. What the secret army had to hide were not plans and guns and operations but the disputes over the

future. Thus the IRA had no easily defined mission and so played an uncertain role in the Republican movement. And that movement was engaged
in novel and complex negotiations that entangled all in conventional politics
and did not return the tangible benefits expected. The IRA might proceed
truculently but had no other choice. The traditional leadership often made
flexibility difficult by maintaining old attitudes, assumptions and postures
Yet only the few could truly see a return to an armed struggle. So the military
people let Sinn Féin continue to wage politics and the secret army waited
on events. The Army Executive, the Army Council, had a majority dedicated
to an unarmed strategy – often composed of hard men, not Sinn Féin
careerists.

Events indicated that the British could not imagine withdrawal if the
Protestant Irish in the six-counties, the Unionists and loyalists, held them
responsible for maintaining the union. This was as true for the new Labour
Party elected by an enormous mandate as it had been for previous government. This meant that those most opposed to a united Ireland were offered
reassurance not by safeguards in such an Ireland but by a continued British
presence. It seemed that instead of an intent to withdraw that would focus
Unionist minds on adjusting advantageously to an Ireland moving toward
unity, the British sought under different banners what they had always
sought: order, the imposition of law, the protection of the Protestants,
devolution not evacuation. The pan-national front made no difference –
Irish nationalists were quick to compromise and unable to impose on British
priorities. The United States would support what was agreed, not impose
agreement. Thus Sinn Féin had to shape a strategy that would encourage
significant concession to placate their own, to appeal to the nationalists, and
at the same time to shape policies that would create conditions to ease the
Irish Protestants into a more conciliatory mood, into recognizing their
destiny as Irish. Neither exercise proved particularly fruitful.

As always, the British were content to shape their policies around devo-
lution under the banner of peace: a devolved assembly that allowed Sinn
Féin to participate if the IRA admitted defeat by giving up their arms. An
assembly a few years before would have been a concession of a resurgent
Republican movement instead of a promised prize to a Sinn Féin desperate
for tangible benefits once the prisoners had all been released. Times changed.
Yet there was no option, and this, above all else, kept the leadership, Sinn
Féin, much of the movement, and a reluctant majority of the Army Council,
involved in the endgame – and the longer involvement, the more difficult
became other options.

Thus at the beginning of the century, the endgame, as redefined by the
leadership of Sinn Féin offered the only hope forward – a futile hope

according to the traditionalists. Sinn Féin assets and capacity might increase but unlike those dedicated to physical force such power increasingly arose from a narrow constituency not the patriot dead or historical legitimacy. The great asset of the IRA and so the Republicans had been this legitimacy – and for the foreseeable future the movement apparently would have to make do with the election returns and the occasional fears of the hidden gunmen. These were not enormously potent assets.

The armed struggle had begun without assets but with great prospects and potential that filled all Republicans with optimism. The armed struggle by 2000 was closed down because of lack of popular demand, closed down, the traditionalist felt, for the time being – and for good if the endgame paid sufficient dividends. The IRA had no mission but to exist for some uncertain future use and in the meantime act as a balance to the more enthusiastic advocates of political action – not a traditional role, not a welcome role, and not a role with great prospects. Only some at command centre shaped by consensus faced the new century with great enthusiasm but all did so with dedication – there was no choice. Whatever else, however, the Irish, the Republicans, the IRA have been indomitable – the dream has persisted despite failure, defeat, narrowing support, blunders, and schism and so seemed likely to persist well into the next millennium, still incandescent for some, still guide and goad, a clearly defined responsibility.

Epilogue

The IRA, organized in the nineteenth century, adjusted over time and deployed most of the variants of physical force. In 1918–21 the IRA shaped the national liberation struggle, the archetype for the aggrieved for the rest of the century. By 1923 Ireland also indicated the dynamics and dangers of an endgame. After 1923, classic or not, the IRA declined year by year; declined in numbers, capacity and influence, and the volunteers grew less representative of the nation as a whole. The achievements of the government in Dublin eroded grievance. The power of those in London and Belfast was too great to challenge seriously, yet the IRA remained as myth and reality, pursued the grail with further campaigns, kept the faith and a place in the revolutionary text. They bombed in London and Northern Ireland, smuggled arms, nourished their ecosystem, kept the faith even when only a few could be active.

The Irish dream generated a secret army not only no longer secret but also celebrated. 'IRA' can be found scrawled on walls in Soweto and Naples, can be found in the curriculum of the military academies of the orthodox and the guerrilla primers in the outback. The IRA, persistent, romantic, notorious, and lethal, composed of Celtic gunmen with a dream, is a constant in the global arena, a player in all revolutionary circles, a model and a menace. And in the new role accepted during the endgame a source of speculation from those far from the island dedicated to their own armed struggle.

THE NATURE OF THE ARMED STRUGGLE

The key underground is the intensity of the faith and only incidentally the assets and even capacity of the underground. What matters is the dream that makes the struggle possible, supplies the energy. Thus the practical are apt to ask the wrong questions. What assets do they have, arms, money, contacts, explosives, safehouses, or trained volunteers? How many Republicans are they? No one knows, certainly not the IRA. Often no one is sure about the arms and money. What matters, certainly to the IRA, is whether there are sound people available – how many, how sound? What can be done is what matters. And these matters are often not articulated – few in reflection understand why this volunteer was sent or what was expected next month or the month after. The Irish and so the IRA are driven by consensus and unarticulated assumptions, operate within a national ethos. They trust their own, send out the sound, scramble for assets, persist even during an endgame, especially during an endgame, where the faith is at risk. Processes are fluid, shifting, held in place by consensus, habit, and experience, natural to the involved underground. The IRA commanders are not prone to intro-spection. They seek other answers: Who do we have? What do we have? What can be done now? The consensus offers agenda, not the Army Council focused on tactics and techniques, the paucity of resources and the clash of individuals. And after 30 years, the IRA has a new mission and must pursue new roles – but never at the expense of the faith, which more than votes or guns or money empowers the movement.

Ireland for many was a revolutionary text. It was, however, the Irish Republican Army as much as any one campaign that was classic, an arche-type, a lesson in winning and losing and most of all in persistence. Bobby Sands and the hunger strike took the measure of persistence world wide. The most famous IRA volunteer of his generation was not a gunman but a prisoner. And his experience indicated the ingenuity and capacity of the Irish underground. Admiration came to the movement as much as to Sands or the attack on Thatcher or even the classic Black and Tan War of 1918–21. The secret army was the ideal not the tactics and targets of the struggle.

The IRA has a history longer than any other such revolutionary movement, an institutional history rivalled by a few old monarchies, some democratic parties, one or two private clubs and religious orders. The Masons or the Jesuits, the Dukes of Norfolk and the British army have longer histories: but Irish Republicans have gone on generation after gener-ation largely organized as a conspiracy, covert, illicit, underground dedicated to the dream and to physical force. It has been an organization that co-opts each new patriot levy into a form remarkably stable: the IRA constitution was written 70 years ago, the volunteers' structure established before World War I, the Irish Republican Brotherhood – the Fenians, the ancestor of the present secret army – was founded in 1858. The Irish Republican movement has an agenda with roots in the European nationalist rebellions of 1848, and holds to ideals arising from the Age of Reason and the example of Wolfe Tone in the eighteenth century. Before that, before the Republic, there were the centuries of resistance shaped by the times against the British.

While others imagine an Irish history as an aspect of British or a matter of conciliation and compromise, the IRA finds in patriot history a millennium of resistance to oppression. Their dream is no more intense, no more effective in transforming the everyday into the incandescent than the ones that inspired the new martyrs of Hamas in Gaza or the struggle for a nation in the Balkans or Caucasus but is a great deal older.

Most important, then, the Irish experience is not simply a long national dream like the Serbs or a new revolutionary society like that sought by Baader-Meinhof in Germany but example of a dream that for two centuries has empowered a tangible underground, a secret army, a persistent conspiracy. The movement shares with all the basic dynamics of the underground. The revealed truth generates the energy necessary for a classical armed struggle that must be hidden by a congenial ecosystem – the underground – that offers security at the price of competence. All such constructs are special and each is different. Many undergrounds are not truly classic, rely on resentments or tribal mores, narrow convictions, envy, greed or simple practicality; but most are touched with an ideal – to deny the contemporary world or to return to the golden past, to punish the wicked or pursue honour.

All undergrounds oppose visible and legitimate enemies with tangible assets and a similar range of means of response to provocation. And these enemies, mostly states, too impose uniformity on armed struggles, on the dynamics of the underground. The motives, capacity, perception, and reality of the challenged may vary enormously but strategy and tactics of response are similar. Special factors impose shape and direction, intensity and agenda, make each case distinctive but no case unique, no underground and no target without significant comparative qualities.

Some aspects of the militant Republican movement are very special indeed or at least more clearly visible than in other struggles. Campaigns can be parsed in different patterns, location and intent, intensity and opponent. The patterns offer categories: rural communist insurgences or urban millenarian terrorism, ethnic war, or national separatism. Each underground feels that their ideal is so special that no other movement parallels their experience, their ecosystem, their campaign. Begin could see no parallel with the Irgun's struggle and that of the Palestinians. The Marxist-Leninists' reading of history is declared scientific and unique no matter how various those who run up the red flag. Since the faith makes all possible, the assumption is that it also makes all undergrounds different rather than possible, And rebellion, insurgency and internal war, transnational terror are, indeed, driven by different aspirations at different paces and so appear various – the Zapatistas in Chiapas in Mexico and the Tamil Tigers in Sri Lanka hardly appear to fit into a single category. They do, however, share similar dynamics.

The most import special factor in Ireland has been the impact of the perceived history of a struggle that traces IRA organizational origins to 1858, the Republican movement to 1798 and Irish resistance to the twelfth century. The habits of resistance existed in Armagh and Tyrone long before Tone and the French landed. After that the Republic became the goal for most Irish nationalists – the Republic as defined by the French and Americans and as sought under tricolour banners by the radicals in the revolutions of 1848. The IRB bombed over a century ago when dynamite was still awesome and neither Italy nor German united. And when the Fenians failed the few faithful waited until 1916 to rise against the British. Only the Tan War brought tangible gains – an Irish Free State – and a civil war. Then came the long years of marginality, small campaigns, declining prospects sputtering away at last in the political agenda of GHQ after 1962.

When the present Irish Troubles began with the civil rights campaign in 1968, all the camp followers of crisis, the media, the analysts, the commentators, and academics, descended in droves to note, to shape to models and assumptions, to broadcast or to capture on film, the Irish experience. In time they would be followed by others, more serious academics, more knowledgeable journalists with years in the province, analysts or practitioners of one art of conflict or another. The television producer fresh from a Japanese film studio or the scholar who had dedicated generations to Irish matters were as one on the fact that the Troubles arose from a long and often dreadful history. Few noted that Ireland had often been at peace, and accommodation and compromise alleviated many grievances. For most, Ireland's past appeared a tale of grievance and blood, hopes frustrated, virtue denied, the ruin of reputation and the slaughter of innocents. In fact this past summoned up by the concerned appeared to be prologue. The Troubles and the IRA, thus, came in the train of history.

If the Irish have been special because of the weight of history, they have also been special in the contemporary world because the faithful are the working class, men of no property, which made for cohesion but not for competence. Even with practice and talent that did not arise from formal credentials, the IRA had problems exploiting the vulnerabilities of a post-industrial society. Doing so was no guarantee of success – as the Palestinians with extensive professional assets discovered – but certainly compounded the difficulties of IRA escalation. Any extended and effective struggle is apt to be guided by middle class talent. In the outback or on the margins, in Somalia or Burma, once in Beirut, often in West Africa insurgency and rebellion was ethnic or the province of warlords – but often the secret army was commanded by the middle class: but not the IRA. And this reliance on those of no property offer special gains. What has been clear, however, has been that the background and capacities of the volunteers in the Republican movement are different, no obstacle in acquiring the skills of war and politics but a problem in technological matters and a sophisticating reading of the larger arena.

Republicans had for generations in certain matters been content with their own reading of reality. Since most campaigns force the faithful to hide, to evade reality, to close down contact, isolation from events is also not novel. The *Brigate rosse* after the Moro kidnapping was so deep underground that not only could friends not find the activists but also those activists were isolated from reality and common sense. They could not recruit, could not strike at the heart of a state without a heart, could not persist. The IRA never disappeared underground during the Troubles but as the years passed accepted persistence as sufficient reward. This had often been the case in the past: some campaigns were protracted because the underground lacked assets, which was true with the IRA after 1974, but the Irish have for generations found in persistence adequate rewards. So the momentum within the movement was focused on reaching tomorrow with the assets to hand. And there was none to argue and none to offer a valid option until 1990. What partially alleviated the isolation was the very intimacy of the island and the need for most of those involved in the underground to live visible lives. When the time came to move toward the conventional, the obstacles were real but not necessarily insurmountable: an endgame was possible. The revealed truth did not encourage negotiations, it never does, but in Ireland did not deny the prospect.

The ethos of the movement, like much else, was a special Irish factor adjusted to the universal. Each underground is shaped by a special society. In Ireland the impact of the Irish Catholic Church on a supposedly secular movement was real, imposed assumptions, habits of thought, priorities, and restrictions of volunteers, mostly pious, almost all Catholic. All movements are so influenced by existing institutions and assumptions – even when the leadership aspires to Marx but does so in a special Italian or Chinese way. Thus even the inefficiencies imposed on all movements are not simply universal categories of incompetence: the feckless Irish and the wishful Arabs are penalized for those sins just as the Germans are punished by punctuality. The special merely adjust the more general strictures.

Some aspects of the Irish situation are, then, not only relevant to the dynamics of the struggle but also shape the special Irish experience. The Irish Troubles are specifically Irish. The dream exists in an ethos shaped by particular aspects of the past that strengthen the volunteers' will to continue a tradition of sacrifice and service. A volunteer empowered by the revealed truth entered a secular vocation, an order of idealistic gunmen, some cruel, some pious, all dedicated to the cause. The Irish Republic requires first sacrifice and commitment, not talent, not a detailed tactical agenda, and not a world view brought down to mean streets.

The long war has allowed natural talent to emerge – Sinn Féin by the end of the century had not only talent but experience, no longer went innocently in harm's way in negotiation or electoral politics. Sophistication and analytical capacity may have come slowly but flourished as the role and mission of the party and those engaged in the endgame shifted. Everything in Ireland runs slow in any case but the Republican movement tends to parse history, consider the risks before risking any movement, especially any novel considerations, any move is weighted by precedent. Any consensus is slow to form and so slow to change. History as received is thus buttress and obstacle, power and privation. Anyone who has dealt with the Republicans, especially those who engaged in formal negotiations, have found that a movement driven by consensus, driven by recourse to history is often driven slowly. Thus as the new century began, to many within the IRA there was a sense of urgency about major matters instead of the managerial details of an armed struggle institutionalized. History seemed on the move and the direction not sure.

The long Irish effort to remain Irish by juxtaposing the concerns of the island against, always against, those of Britain has established a dynamic of struggle with the nation often defined negatively. Ireland is defined as not British but Irish, not English but Gaelic, not for the most part Protestant but Catholic, not neat and tidy and proper but feckless and romantic and garrulous. The stage Irishman is not only a face to hide resistance but also a counter to the English image. Thus the nature of Irish history, especially patriot history and from that Republican history, has been a protracted conflict against all things British. The problems of a divided Ireland, the reality of British Ulster, their uncertain mandate are for Republicans imposed by the unfailing source of Irish ills across the sea. This forms the integrity of the quarrel. At times this integrity must be fashioned anew to oppose further British inroads but always the integrity requires struggle, resistance, renewed commitment and so ensures persistence. Always that persistence has been betrayed by those willing to find an accommodation with the reality of the British centre or with the Irish state. And that persistence has been eroded by the emergence of a new generation of the Irish and a new kind of Irish, prosperous, sophisticated, international, no longer willing to tolerate murder done in their name. Always there have been those who would compromise, accept less than the nation, Castle Catholics, West Britons, converts to the established church, Fianna Fáil, and the Officials, advocates of the partial, of politics as usual.

Many of these who chose some rather than all were once Republicans who found physical force outdated, Republican politics too confining, the dream too improbable. Thus the real Republic found in the hearts of the faithful took on a special significance for everyone within the movement became responsible for its protection – and the Republic was synonymous with Ireland and Ireland unique, special and opposed to the power and legitimacy of the British establishment, to the reality of the government in Dublin or power, and a career. The 1994 ceasefire had to be sold as a means to everything not a move toward something. If the gun could not win, as seemed to be the case for the next generation, then perhaps an alternative and unconventional front could be opened – but not to seek concession, rather to find a way into the future, perhaps a way that could be taken in stages: a Republic on the instalment plan.

In a real sense the Republican movement is structured to defend as well as achieve the ideal Republic, the heart of the nation, however defined. The movement must oppose the single source of all ills: the influence and the power of the other island. And this opposition must be protected from betrayal and denial. Victory thus comes in large part from persisting rather than in control and power. Those with legitimate and recognized control and power, certainly in Dublin, have, as far as the Provisionals are concerned, hardly proved effective defenders within the 26-counties and quite unable to effect events, even defend their own, in the six-counties. And the Irish people, who have in De Valera's words '... no right to do wrong ...', must be shown that compromise and practicality may pay immediate dividends but are betrayals of the nation. The enthusiasm for the peace process of the Dublin establishment had to be weighed not only to the value of a pan-national front but also in light of past sins. The armed struggle maintained the nation despite the power of the oppressor and the frailty of the people. An endgame could hardly do this. The endgame thus would assure a gradual end to the commitment to preserve in an armed struggle and so close the traditional outward reality of the Republic. It is a Republic visible only rarely on death beds, during a volley fired over a funeral, in an inner vision – and in the armed struggle; but it is no less real for that and more real for those with no other assets.

The IRA was thus shaped for a long, long war since British power appeared a given no matter what the future structural configuration of the two islands. Few movements can find so much reward from denial, from tactical failure, from generations of seeming frustration, for few arise from a history that assures protraction is, if not all, much. Persistence, the struggle *per se*, is an ample if not absolute. And this dream Republic has appealed to those who can expect few rewards from society. To move this struggle ahead without a gun, without indication that the British are going to withdraw is no easy matter – even when the leadership sought to build on history, Republican history, rather than seek concession, seek to show a return on novelty. The militant Republican regards novelty and compromise as clear and present dangers.

The two most particular aspects of the Provisionals are, first, that persistence in a so far futile armed struggle has returned disproportionate rewards for the faithful and, second, that for several generations the faithful attracted to such a reward have lacked the talent, the capacity, the general support necessary to assure an absolute victory but received enormous returns for making the attempt. In failing to lose, the IRA wins, the volunteers win, the movement wins – and in so winning sooner or later the faithful assume that the British will lose the will to persist. Then the movement will win the actual Republic. This did not happen. British nationalism was underestimated and the rewards paid to the British establishment not understood – no economic or strategic interests but an enormously satisfying role as mentor to the troublesome Irish unable to create a civil society and thus in need of tutelage. This was transmuted into a British responsibility, one that appeared open ended since what the British wanted was the Irish to be like them which was, in fact, the opposite of what made the Irish Irish. So the British establishment persisted as did the IRA. The long war paid everyone involved, offered appealing secondary benefits, but even the persistent Republicans were open to a more satisfactory way into the future. Many commanders and leaders suspected that in a different world at the end of the century the movement no longer need rely on physical force as the prime way forward. History began to shift even if the ultimate aspiration had not. This did not make the Irish unique – the PLO, ETA for a time, and the Tamil Tigers, the ANC all entered an endgame but few did so after two centuries of historical satisfaction with the pursuit of the ideal.

Twenty-five years on after a long journey down the road of dead informers, murdered innocents, sectarian slaughter, car-bombs, and hunger strikes with thousands upon thousands passing through the prisons, there is little romance left in the armed struggle and so much attraction in a nationalist front, an unarmed strategy, another means into the future other than killing one more RUC reservist in his shop or detonating one more bomb in a Manchester street.

One special aspect of the Irish struggle is not found in Ireland at all but across the Irish Sea in Britain. Every underground gets the enemy it deserves because most enemies are shaped to the perception of the rebel. And often this is the case with the regime, the target, the victim. In a curious mirror image, the legitimate enemy, the centre in London, shares with the

Republican movement assumptions and attitudes that assure rewards from protraction without prospect of accommodation much less solution. The problem thus becomes not that there is no solution but that without a solution Ireland pays secondary benefits to both the IRA and the British establishment. The British tend to deny these benefits, see London as part of the solution not part of the problem, but whatever is said in public the historical record has shown a long patriot history written on Irish matters by British politicians and generals. So whatever prime minister or party seeks to disengage the process is halting, uncertain, often bad-tempered, pursued at times with the lack of magnanimity and always without great urgency. Even the Labour Party under Tony Blair cannot really imagine politics without an Irish problem even while as always seeking to find an accommodation that will accommodate them as well.

Just how the dynamic of an armed struggle on hold works is uncertain: endgames are difficult, even and especially transitory ones. And the present IRA has had little practice at shaping the struggle solely to conventional ends, playing a conventional game. As that game begins, the secret army cannot remain static, must become more secret and so more divorced from events or more open and so more driven by an orthodox agenda. In effect the IRA leadership must as in the armed phase find means to escalate and so placate the faithful or else means to persist without returns, without movement, enthusiasm, or visible prospects. As commanders their role has changed as has the mission of the movement. The new role of the IRA is a return to the past – to exist as myth and reality – without real prospects of deploying physical force.

This generation of Republicans wants something more than persistence, and apparently will take something less than the dream, perhaps far less, certainly at first far less. The hard men are not going gently into a promised future so that the leadership, however legitimate, however intensely applied the new direction, however hopeful the signs are read, must produce and so maintain the consensus. They are committed, cannot simply go back underground but must see that the parade moves on, that the faithful are fed, that the dream is safe if not yet transformed into power. And so they moved into the new century.

The dynamics of a quiescent army are familiar to the older volunteers – nothing about secret armies in Ireland is all new – but in the past the waiting was for opportunity to act rather than for orders to disband. A volunteer dumped arms until the next chance but the present leadership aspires to change history without using the gun again. When the gun goes so goes the IRA, the legitimacy of history, past experience, and so the reluctance to decommission even a single item. In a sense the IRA is quite explicable – no messianic aspirations, no terror technique turned into strategy, and no long march to victory, escalation, and triumph but rather ups and downs, twists and always the capacity to persist, persist even at the end. And with a new century the focus within the secret army has been on adjusting the dream to events.

The factors that have encouraged Republican dreamers in Ireland have varied, institutions have varied, life has changed, the lure of absolutes has been adjusted and institutionalized. The Irish are not the same this year as last or this century as last so that the factors encouraging the emergency of a lay order of night riders and gunmen in 1970 and their experience over a generation, varied – as did that experience, the response of the threatened and even and especially the perception of all. Whatever else, however, the movement, marginal or grand, isolated at times, spectacular at others persisted. Elsewhere the last French Bourbon newspaper closes or the centre fails in the Balkans, Che is long dead and so too the *focos*, and revolutionary anarchism is with Bakunin in history books. In Ireland because of special Irish reasons, the Republicans have persisted. They have been assigned a role in a divided society – made part of an Irish problem – when they have mostly sought to oppose British sovereignty. They have cherished at times radical ideas and ideals but always within the context of the Republic. The Republic has been the grail for two centuries. The movement has longevity denied others with all the advantages and disadvantages so offered, offered to the movement and its enemies, to the Irish and the British, to any observer. History may not be destiny, written anew each generation, but the IRA offers generation after generation of tangible experience. This is special, not very special but still more special than their working-class composition, their tactical innovations, or their legitimacy.

What has made this experience necessary has been a commitment to an ultimate ideal – the Republic – that requires sacrifice and service. When the volunteer on his way to a cell for life, fist raised, cried 'Tiócfaidh Af Lá' – 'Our Day Will Come' – he did not mean tomorrow, did not mean a day one might watch filter through an hourglass but a time of judgement when the dream would be tangible, justice done, history served and so at an end. Such days can, indeed, be made real, have been made real elsewhere, if at enormous cost, but not yet in Ireland. No Free State, no reforms to a divided society, no concessions on cross-border institutions are likely to satisfy the dreamers who see the end of history as prospect. History has no final act but men and institutions do. So the Irish Republican dream may, as often promised, lead to a Republic if not *the* Republic. A new Irish generation may deny the remaining faithful the legitimacy to use physical force. And so the last gunmen will die out, a species without nourishment in a new and different Ireland. There would no longer be role or mission for a secret army, no volunteers. And then again, the IRA in the past has been declared surplus – often by recent members – so prediction is difficult – especially about the future. The past may this time not be prologue. If not, then much of the past may be readjusted and replayed, the faithful will again shape a secret army to wait or to pursue the ideal, to persist and sacrifice. If the endgame does lead to peace, to adequate progress toward the Republic then there will no longer be the residue of toleration for the Republicans, and so even prospects of persevering. Everything changes and in Ireland things change as well, at times for the good. The prospect of the new century being truly new exists – but then on the island there have always been those who have preferred to wait for their day to come, seek vindication, triumph, at times vengeance, and always the incandescent Republic denied them by the powerful and the weak, by the duplicitous, by history, always by the British and seemingly so far by fate. And they are still there as the new century opens. Perhaps their day will come, perhaps not.

Sources

Although every contemporary crisis generates an enormous literature, a wealth of conventional primary and secondary sources as well as the still available testimony of many of the involved, often in conjunction with extensive and available photographic, tape, and film coverage, there is much that does not emerge. Secret armies are apt to want to remain secret, special operations stay covert, governments engaged in secrets keep, if possible, such secrets. And for Irish Republicans the efforts to establish a concensus during the peace process have been even more secret: peace rather than war being a greater risk for secret armies.

And all these secrets are relevant to understanding reality. Historians wrote and rewrote the history of World War II without knowing that the Allied generals could read vital German code traffic with the Enigma device and so skewed their accounts. Accounts are always skewed since perfect knowledge is not possible but more so when the major factors are covert: motives and operations and the dynamics of organizations. Even after 25 or 50 years many governments are chary about granting access to previously classified documentation. Private files are often closed or lost or destroyed – and by then, of course, the attrition rate for witnesses has reduced recourse to those present at the event. In covert matters beyond governmental policy what is secret is apt to become more secret with time – there were few records and soon there are none, there were few witnesses and soon there are fewer. It is, of course, the involved and their actions and assumptions that matter: not so much what they did, not why they assumed such action was taken, but rather why they actually did as they did.

The most effective source, then, and not one closed to investigation, remains the involved. Talking to Albert Reynolds certainly gives a flavour to subsequent analysis and may offer an odd detail; so too Gerry Adams or the victims of a mistake. Gunmen, even if not particularly gunmen, are apt to talk from time to time; in court, in evidence, across the kitchen table to journalists or friends. There are stories and rumours and words to the wise, often sought and used by journalists if less often by scholars. Mainly the sources of this analysis are people and the method is political ethnography.

This text is based on a generation of association with the Republicans and their friends and enemies, chats with Albert Reynold and Gerry Adams as well as from time to time the victims. Mostly, however, in Ireland, I have been concerned with the Republicans, of all flavours.

Research by osmosis is difficult to document. There are rarely notes, never tapes. At times recollections have been written down but often simply accumulated. It takes a long time to accumulate data without asking and often without any certainty as to what is wanted and what in time may be useful. Always there is the problem of the question leading the source, the query shaping the response. Often the involved never consider those aspects of the armed struggle that concern this text: decisions occur and informers are shot and reason and introspection play a small role.

Over the years the Republicans have been forthcoming but often only on marginal matters, the distant past, or by error. And there is always the value of what is not said, what is assumed or ignored or never considered. The blanks may be as telling as the descriptions. So years of conversation without specific direction have supplied hints and directions but often no firm answers. In fact those within the galaxy may not recognize their processes and responses in the text: their real world is not mine, their world is shaped by a dream I do not share and so any analysis will for the faithful tend to miss the point. In any case the points those involved want stressed are the grievances and the end, and assume those with queries are concerned with operations, details, names, and dates best not mentioned rather than the nature of the system engaged in a struggle. The dynamics of the struggle are part of a necessary but accepted process that leads from a past detailed at length into a future that absorbs all the concern. The Republicans are not very interested in the nature of process except as irritant and necessity.

To investigate that process – not history, not anatomy, but rather physiology shaped not by form and nature but by perception – I have drifted within the Irish Republican galaxy with a visitor's pass. A generation of impressions, filtered, weighted, rearranged, is the true source of the text – a source buttressed by the more formal returns of proper interviews with the conventional and the analytical as well as exposure to the enormous published literature. The latter, the books and articles and papers, by now can be found in bibliographies of bibliographies. The primary sources are scant, as is often true with contemporary history, and access to manuscripts or letters or documents rare and then of marginal worth. The individuals, most of them, are still about and still chary of all but general discussion. Yet, it is the live sources, the participants, that have been the key to the text.

Coupled with the problem of access to the concerned has been the nature of the arena. Early on I discovered a far more complex and impenetrable island culture than might be supposed – the use of English disguises most alien processes. If all spoke in strange tongues, then the special nature of the cultural arena would have been apparent sooner. The Irish, then, are difficult enough for the alien – seemingly so congenial and conventional, cheery and bright and yet so secretive, a society shaped by conspiracy – not unlike the Republican galaxy – rules unarticulated, motives unmentioned, roles without name and names that shift with usage. And if Ireland in general is complex and arcane, then the Republican galaxy is still more so. How does the Army Council make decisions and how can one discover this without altering the results? How does operational intelligence evolve when such matters are closely held secrets long after the term has relevance? What happens when consensus reigns – no one decides and everyone knows?

Some investigators have used comparable methodology – little different from the means of any resident journalists even if the product is shaped for different ends. Few analysts, however, can invest the time, find the patience or the resources – and few have the luck to have access. In that luck, persistence and the investment of time have given limited access and so the text.

Ultimately those without access, the analyst, the scholar, will be left with the available vast public or private literature, special collections, and the work of previous scholars – the traditional ore of the historian. And the traditional sources pay ample dividends: history can be written about Napoleon without speaking to the man. Documents and overt data will often do wonders. There is already access to some of the early archival material. At last a few relevant government documents are appearing. Some papers in both London and Belfast are now at least in part open although the more interesting dealing with security matters are likely to remain closed or inaccessible for some time. Still, many of the involved – including Republicans – are willing to give interviews, a primary source to substitute for the lack of official documentation and the often scanty private papers. As for some of the interviews, they look more relevant in the citation than in content for IRA commanders – or even famous politicians – may talk for the record but censor the content. And also the private papers of many of the involved, the manuscript, letters, diaries, proposals, and notes that are already being used by scholars have yet to indicate substantial change in the accepted plain tale of events.

To a degree much of the Northern Irish past never reaches paper and this is especially true of illicit covert organizations that keep few if any records. The paucity of official records and private documentation has never deterred the bold, the curious, the determined, the ambitious, or committed; rather the reverse. On Irish matters the years since 1967 have seen waves of investigation by all sorts and all disciplines despite the difficulties in the arena, despite the paucity of some sources, and despite the classical problems of contemporary analysis of perspective and access. Thus for the Irish Troubles it is the best of times and the worst of times in the matter of sources: some official documentation, enormous amounts of paper, and most of the relevant actors.

A generation ago a detailed analysis of the sources for the entire history of Ireland after the 1916–22 period would have made a short article. Now a thick book can only make a beginning on the published works. The contemporary Troubles have generated so many published sources that there are separately published bibliographies, always out of date by the time published. For example, *A Social Science Bibliography of Northern Ireland, 1945–1983*, compiled by Bill Rolston, Mike Tomlinson, Liam O'Dowd, Bob Miller, and Jim Smyth (Belfast, Queen's University, 1983) contains 270 pages, counting the index, and lists 5,000 items. For Ireland in general there is the even more substantial *Modern Ireland: A Bibliography on Politics, Planning, Research and Development* (Westport, CT, Greenwood, 1981), compiled by Michael Owen Shannon and now, like the social-science bibliography, a decade out of date. In fact for a discussion of the sources for the Troubles in general, it is possible to consult my *The Irish Troubles: A Generation of Political Violence* (New York, St Martin's, 1993; and Dublin, Gill & Macmillan, 1993); but for the IRA there is a smaller shelf but still a daunting one.

Even a small party like those descended from the Official IRA – Official Sinn Féin, Sinn Féin–the Workers' Party, the Irish Republican and Socialist Party, the Workers' Party, the Democratic Left, and finally absorption into Labour have left a thick paper trail; sufficient in fact that Philip Beresford found enough material up to the year 1974 to write a PhD dissertation at the University of Exeter in 1979. The Provisionals are only different in that their paper is less apt to be theoretical. All of this party publication varies enormously in content, of course, but also in style and impact. Some are elegant, slick, annuals with photographs, some run off on a mimeograph in 50 copies, distributed on a few streets and mostly lost by the next day – if it were not for the Linenhall Library repository of even the most ephemeral scrap. In fact some newsletters may exist only as a single handwritten issue of a prison newspaper.

These publications may have narrow interest, few readers, and limited impact, but that may be vital for those with a special interest in the IRA. Some local history can be very local, making Ciarán De Baróid's *Ballymurphy and the Irish War* (Dublin, Aisling, 1989), seem vast in scope. Some works, many works have a relation to Republican concerns but hardly would be rich sources. A typical example might be the Political Vetting of Community

Work Working Group's, *The Political Vetting of Community Work in Northern Ireland* (Belfast, Northern Ireland Council for Voluntary Action, October 1990), a publication that arose from the concern of some that the British government was exceeding the bounds in deciding which community organizations were assisting paramilitary organizations – in this case the denial of a grant to an Irish-language group. This concern led to a general conference and on to the publication, slick, bright red cover, small circulation even in Ireland and almost none abroad. It is one more of the thousands upon thousands of organizational documents on the shelves.

What the professional seeks first is *primary sources*, documents and letters and memoirs – and the shelves groan with documents in ink, in copies, and in covers, in books. Many of these documents are generated by the Republicans: newspapers and party programmes and studies and press releases – even autobiographies and personal histories produced outside the movement. Some of these 'documents' are not so primary, slip over into commentary, are secondary, not part of the problem but part of the analysis. The Éire Nua programme of Provisional Sinn Féin, party funded, party printed, has had a long life, revived by Republican Sinn Féin, but like many published party documents gives only slight insight into the galaxy. For a study of the movement Republican analysis is a means of analysis if not a very rich lode. The same is true for the newspapers, house journals of the faith not of record or of insight, for the statements of Sinn Féin or the secret army, often intended to hide or rationalize or disguise – like all political documentation – not to reveal.

Reading Republican sources the innocent would assume a movement without dissent, without confusion or despair, a movement assured of the future that somehow continues to recede. For the real action within the galaxy, the core of the galaxy, little can be found on paper and little in public discussion. In this the Republicans are conventional, one with all others engaged in unconventional struggles.

Far more conventional are the published works of those Republicans involved in the politics of the Troubles, the individuals not the organizations. These range from the childhood memoirs of Gerry Adams, *Falls Memories* (Dingle, County Kerry, Brandon, 1982), or the more conventional *Before the Dawn: The Autobiography of Gerry Adams* (also by Brandon but issued by a major American publisher, Morrow, New York, 1996) to the novels of Danny Morrison, the last written in prison, or the poems of Bobby Sands. Seán Mac Stíofáin's *Revolutionary in Ireland* (Edinburgh, Cremonesi, 1975), is as interesting for what it does not contain as for any IRA revelations – details, yes, Republican analysis, yes, revelations, indications of dissent, errors, no. Many of the latter – the errors as well as the gossip – for a brief period in 1971–72 – can be found in Maria McGuire's *To Take Up Arms* (New York, Viking, 1973), based on her time with the Provisional movement. Mostly, like most active rebels, the gunmen seemingly intend to wait until the shooting is over to publish on the armed struggle. Few others have shown such restraint. The views of the involved outside the Republican galaxy hardly reveal novel perspectives and are little different, except for proximity, from scholarly analysis or the reports of journalists.

There are those observers who have come, often, usually, innocently, to Northern Ireland and after what seemed adequate exposure withdrawn to report their time amid the Troubles. Most, if not all, transform the time into history (Kevin Kelley, *The Longest War*, London, Zed Books, 1984) or the product of their discipline (Frank Burton, *The Politics of Legitimacy: Struggles in a Belfast Community*, London, Routledge & Kegan Paul, 1978), and so become secondary, analytical sources. The scholar may become part of the problem or may take away from the problem data that can be cut to a different pattern and purpose. And there are a few who arrive in Ireland and write their memoirs, a genre not unlike travel books, stylists abroad in strange places, the curious among the exotic. And a remarkable number of the involved, Irish and British, the politicians and generals and activists, have written their life stories, sometimes as autobiography and sometimes as history. Mostly such primary sources are more primary than source, certainly as far as the IRA is concerned.

Some of the best accounts by those involved cannot easily be accounted in a list of sources. The elusive give interviews, often taped, that then appear for varying purposes: Cathal Goulding's views may be found in Italian in an ephemeral tract of the radical Left, or Republican views on this or that appear in German or Spanish and published in newspapers or magazines seldom read by those most concerned with Ireland. And few concerned with Ireland are aware that there is a European literature of sorts that at times can be mined for useful nuggets. It hardly seems worthwhile, in any case, worrying about interviews in Swedish when the involved are willing to talk in English to most of the interested.

Many of those who turn their time in Ireland into secondary analysis include large chunks of verbatim interviews, thanks to the tape recorder, in the final result. These memoirs-at-one-remove are often contained in curious cartons or shipped back to assure tenure or promotion. Over the years a goodly number of scholars in many fields have come to Ireland to examine the IRA or at least Sinn Féin for academic purpose and for academic audiences. However the findings are shaped, the content is readily available in more general works on the Troubles.

These, the *secondary sources*, focus on what happened, to whom, perhaps why. The first printed sources for the contemporary historians are thus the newspapers of the day, a narrative chronology of the moment that others will later winnow down and print. For Ireland there are essentially the great newspapers of record that detail all, the more general newspapers of the time, dailies or weeklies, that indicate the nature of the news being disseminated, and the product of the involved, the party papers, the journals of special opinion, the committed papers. Some neighbourhood newsletters have a short half-life, most small papers are the province of specialists. Only the dedicated read student newspapers or ideological journals, seek out the true word published only in Irish. And the Republican papers, the regular and the local and the erratic, rarely very revealing, appear on time.

It is the real newspapers that provide most analysts with the plain tale. In Ireland this has been for much of the period the *Irish Times*, the nation's elite journal of record. The general exhaustion of the population of the Republic with the Troubles shifted prime coverage over the last decade of the century to the *Independent* in London. To find out the day-to-day story, to find out the insight of the security correspondents, to follow the plain tale of events the good newspapers are vital – not the party press or the occasional primary source. In Ireland the political journals, once a week, every two weeks, each month, regularly had analysis or revelation. The best for Northern Ireland and the only one to stay the course is *Fortnight* in Belfast, the last survivor and always the vital journal for the Troubles. Reading 25 years of any newspaper is a more than sufficient chore even for the specialist determined to watch the Irish tale unfold on the page. For the elusive general read what is wanted for the IRA is a plain tale of events, not primary sources or microfilm.

My *The Irish Troubles* gives a general view of the generation while *The Secret Army: The IRA Since 1916* (first published by Antony Blond, London, 1970, and now by Poolbeg, Dublin, 1997), brings the story up to 1997, while Tim Pat Coogan's *The IRA* (also originally published in 1970 by Pall Mall) has had new editions, the latest adding bits into the 1990s (Robert & Rinehart, New York, 1994). Neither IRA book presents a coherent, smooth history to date: mine ends in the midst of the peace process and Coogan's is composed of tacked-on sections. Both have had to deal with the problems presented by a continuing armed struggle where publication may be felon-setting or undertaken despite lack of certain detail.

Historians are prone to want time to pass before beginning; but as the years passed and the Troubles persisted, even the historians joined with the social scientists in treating Irish events as a proper arena for study, more than just contemporary example to add weight to theories or models. The result has been a growing literature, sound, often profound, sometimes comparatives, but nearly always grounded in conventional academic approaches and means. When the peace process began the academics were attracted because Irish events were congenial, more conventional, encouraging – and so did not wait to begin. Much had to be recast after the collapse of the first ceasefire and much postponed; but the appeal of the endgame persisted and work appeared on the heels of events.

There has been detailed work done on divided societies, children and violence, community mobilization, conflict resolution as well as scholars who pursue their interest in political parties or administrative practice despite, not because of, special Northern Irish conditions. Some of these works have focused on Republicans, the scholars found from time to time off the Falls or on the Shankill doing interviews – and the journalists meanwhile turning their sources into prose. Steve Bruce of the University of Aberdeen writes on the Irish Protestants with skill and academic rigour while Martin Dillon, mostly of BBC, has addressed the same subject in a series of works – that includes one foray into the career of the IRA prisoner in the United States Joseph Doherty.

In fact those writing or reporting on the Troubles were at times apt to become involved because of their coverage. Thus the killing of three IRA volunteers on Gibraltar engendered concern on the island by the majority Catholics about civil rights issues, a concern reflected in certain British quarters, and by the Protestant majority in Northern Ireland with the special operation's success, a concern reflected in certain British quarters: but in Great Britain the key was the acrimonious dispute over the television coverage and real or imagined state intervention. The problem of censorship led to a second cycle of television coverage, a subject that fascinated the industry if not all viewers (cf. Nicholas Eckert, *Fatal Encounter: The Story of the Gibraltar Killings*, Dublin, Poolbeg, 1999).

In fact, the journalists often transformed coverage into books and the books became an aspect of the evolving Troubles. The culmination of the IRA English bombers court cases in reversals, scandal, and acrimony everywhere produced works – that of Chris Mullin, *Error of Judgment* (London, Chatto & Windus, 1986), had more than any other factor accelerated the move toward review. Once freed the prisoners added to the literature (Paul Hill, *Stolen Years: Before and After Guildford*, London, Doubleday, 1990, and Gerry Conlon, *Proved Innocent: The Story of Gerry Conlon of the Guildford Four*, London, Hamish Hamilton, 1990) even before the legal scholars and political concern were well underway analysing the implications for the judicial system. The former prisoners became transmuted into celebrities and their everyday lives after years in prison grist for the British and Irish journalists.

The same focus on any spectacular aspect of the Troubles by journalists has engendered a great general secondary literature that addresses directly the actions of the IRA if not the history of the galaxy: James Adams, Robin Morgan and Anthony Bambridge, *Ambush, The War Between the SAS and the IRA* (London, Pan, 1988), or Toby Harnden, *Bandit Country: The IRA and South Armagh* (London, Hodder & Stoughton, 1999), by participants, John Stalker's *Stalker* (London, Harrap, 1988), or their biographers, Colm Kenna, *A Biography of Gerry Adams* (Cork, Mercier Press, 1990). There is something for everyone. Nearly everything is covered if not well at least for the time being: the impact of violence on the family, the nature of peace keeping, the plight of victims, the evolution of Republican ideas, the symbols of the ghettos, the nature of Irish terrorism or simply the latest report, the last atrocity. There is a score of books on Irish 'terrorism', usually collections, often useful to the scholar but rarely to the general reader.

There are new genres such as the bomb-and-tell works, descendants of Maria McGuire's original revelations, by informers, police agents, and the born again – for example, the highest placed IRA betrayer has had a second career informing the public about his first as an informer – Seán O'Callaghan, *The Informer* (London and New York, Bantam, 1998).

A reader concerned solely with the tribulations of the British army in Northern Ireland has not only the conventional sources of all contemporary history and in particular the specialized British military journals but the results distilled. There are regimental histories (Michael Barthorp, *Crater to the Creggan: The History of the Royal Anglian Regiment, 1964–1974*, London, Leo Cooper, 1976), or military memoirs (Peter Morton, *Emergency Tour, 3 PARA in South Armagh*, London, Kimber, 1989) and often some unconventional works as well like A. F. N. Clarke's *Contact* (London, Secker & Warburg, 1983), that gives a most unvarnished account of the brutality of a dirty war followed up by a similar exercise by Michael Asher in *Shoot to Kill: A Soldier's Journey Through Violence* (London, Viking, 1990). There are specialized books on bombs: George Styles, *Bombs Have No Pity* (London, Luscombe, 1975), or Derrick Patrick's *Fetch Felix: The Fight against the Ulster Bombers, 1976–1977* (London, Hamish Hamilton, 1981). There are books composed of memoirs; Max Arthur's *Northern Ireland Soldiers Talking: 1969 to Today* (London, Sidgwick & Jackson, 1987) is especially useful.

There are the detailed four volumes on the British army compiled by David Barzilay, journalist, Scotland Yard spokesman, and public relations consultant, that end in 1980 and the more concentrated and conventional histories by former officers, Michael Dewar, *The British Army in Northern Ireland* (London, Arms and Armour Press, 1985), or Desmond Hamill, *The Pig in the Middle: The Army in Northern Ireland, 1969–1984* (London, Methuen, 1985). There is Chris Ryder's *The Ulster Defence Regiment: An Instrument of Peace?* (London Methuen, 1991) to go with his earlier study, *The RUC: A*

Force Under Fire (London, Methuen, 1989), and the slightly more recent John D. Brewer with Kathleen Magee, *Inside the RUC: Routine Policing in a Divided Society* (Oxford, Clarendon, 1991).

The IRA's operational enemy is amply covered and the works on the political systems that oppose the Republicans are if not endless at least substantial. Almost all such work, including that focused on the threat of the IRA found in the analysis of terror, lacks both empathy and an understanding of underground reality. Those very close to the dangerous edge in Ireland, like conventional operators everywhere, are apt to mistake the means as the message, the underground as the obverse of the orthodox, a mirror image. For those on the ground, the IRA volunteer, the gunman or the bombers, seems real enough not a matter of perception, and for those more distant in policy-making positions a stereotype will often do or actions can be judged to orthodox rationalizations.

The best single work on the Provisional Irish Republican Army, is that of the journalists Patrick Bishop and Eamonn Mallie, *The Provisional IRA* (London, Heinemann, 1987). Mallie's career has been in Belfast and he is intimate with many of the involved, has good sources, as is inevitable in a parochial perspective. Journalists want the spectacular and the plain tale of events – not the details of the dynamics – and this the *Provisional IRA* supplies. Jack Holland and Henry McDonald have done a similar service in the *INLA, Deadly Divisions* (Dublin, Torc, 1994). The Official IRA that dribbled away into armed robbery and extortion in the early 1980s awaits a similar effort. Brendan O'Brien of RTE has concentrated on more recent events in *The Long War: The IRA and Sinn Féin 1985 to Today* (Dublin, O'Brien, 1993). And the journalist Peter Taylor returned to produce a television show and *Behind the Mask: The IRA and Sinn Féin* (New York, TV Books, 1997). Not readily available but most useful has, in fact, been television coverage usually of the spectacular or scandalous from the IRA trials in England to the bombs placed in Dublin and Monaghan in 1974. For the curious the place to begin is the big books – the histories of the Troubles or the gunmen.

Thus nearly any point of focus has been covered for the Troubles in general – the more specialized or those open to comparative analysis by scholars and those more spectacular or conventional to the involved, the individual, the simply interested. There in a text on *Violence and the Social Services in Northern Ireland*, edited by John Darby and Arthur Williamson (London, Heinemann, 1978), and one on *Northern Ireland: A Psychological Analysis* (Dublin, Gill & Macmillan 1980). And as the list of examples in this discipline or that area extends it becomes clear that there is too much even if only the scholarly, the recent, the most useful were to be included. Thus

John White worked on Provisional Sinn Féin in Belfast for his dissertation in sociology, the first printed results appeared in journals – for example: Robert W. White and Terry Falkenberg White, 'Revolution in the City: On the Resources of Urban Guerrillas', *Terrorism and Political Violence*, Vol. 3, No. 4, Winter 1991, pp. 100–32 – and emerged as a book published by Greenwood, a formal text entered into the enormous literature of the Troubles. Ten years later, he was back to see what had happened, what had changed. There is now a library of good history and turgid social science, dreadful history and rigorous social science, a specialist's library of the general and particular, the good and the bad, as well as the few good, conventional works for everyone, for anyone.

The first general books on the Republicans have appeared dedicated to historical narrative – and the seemingly ceaseless flow of analysis continues, shifting, one assumes, to the peace process as viewed from outside, as subject for a special methodology as in the past have been the hunger strikers or the peace people or the Sinn Féin activists. The analysis, in the meantime, continues apace out of sight of not only the general reader but the average scholar. At the September 1992 meeting of the American Political Science Association convention, for example, Cynthia Irvin, who has done field research in Northern Ireland and the Basque country in Spain, turns up in a panel on Media and Conflict as well as a panel on expressing political opposition, while Robert F. Mulvihill, Rosemont College, has a paper on 'The Center Doesn't Hold: Political Violence in Northern Ireland', Mary E. Kazmierczak, Wisconsin, Madison, on 'The Anglo-Irish Agreement and the Conflict in Northern Ireland', and Nathalie J. Frensley, Texas, on 'Rhetorical Transitions across Conflict Stages: Propaganda Content and Style in the Northern Ireland Troubles'. There are also analytical reports done for various agencies, various governments, for banks and corporations, for foundations on Northern Ireland, or that include Northern Ireland as a key example. In the late summer of 1995 there was one more panel of specialists at the American Sociological Association convention. The decade closed with more conferences planned, more papers being prepared. There exists more paper than can possibly be acquired and read for particular or general profit. The peace process has simply increased the analytical product and so the problem.

All this has allowed a new generation of secondary analysis that is not necessarily part of the problem, often undertaken by those who have spent decades on that problem, such as Charles Townshend (editor), *Consensus in Ireland: Approaches and Recessions* (Oxford, Clarendon, 1988) or Bob Rowthorn and Naomi Wayne, *Northern Ireland: The Political Economy of Conflict* (Boulder, CO, Westview, 1988), or Frank Gaffikin and Mike Morrissey, *Northern Ireland:*

The Thatcher Years (London, Zed, 1990). Some work is on one aspect of the IRA like Joanne Wright, *Terrorist Propaganda: The Red Army Faction and the Provisional IRA* (New York, St Martin's, 1990), and others far more general – Michael J. Cunningham, *British Government Policy in Northern Ireland 1969–1989: Its Nature and Execution* (Manchester, Manchester University Press, 1991).

The peace process and the tribulations of the endgame have followed the pattern. The journalists are still rushing their works into print, David McKittrick, *Endgame: The Search for Peace in Northern Ireland* (Belfast, The Blackstaff Press, 1994) or Toby Harnden, *Bandit Country: The IRA and South Armagh* (London, Hodder & Stoughton, 1999), to beat the scholars – David Bloomfield, *Political Dialogue in Northern Ireland: The Brooke Initiative, 1989–1992* (London, Macmillan; New York, St Martin's, 1998).

In sum there is both too much to read but too little that provides concise and coherent analysis, much less explanation, for the general reader. Much published is part of the Troubles, much is done to academic formulae or for special purpose What has not emerged in a rigorous history of the Republicans so that Bishop and Mallie and Holland and McDonald, O'Brien and Harnden offer the proper place to begin. And in the end there is Malcolm Sutton's *An Index of Death from the Conflict in Ireland, 1969–1993* (Belfast, Beyond the Pale Publications, 1994), which if the past is prologue will need a new edition in time.

Index

abstention, 58, 68, 74, 76, 305

Adams, Gerry: background, 81, 100, 120; and conference with British (1972), 67, 302; dominates IRA, 103, 121–2, 123, 141, 153, 154, 158, 162; and endgame, 310, 311; as leader of Sinn Féin, 122, 135, 212, 217, 218, 310, 311; world-class politician, 124, 311; mentioned, xiii, 31, 35, 128, 131, 151, 155, 156, 159, 195, 233, 313

Adare, 37

Addis Ababa, 16

Aden, vii, 303

administrative management, 190–2

Africa, 11, 35, 42, 216, 235, 240, 302, 320; see also names of countries

African National Congress (ANC), 87, 179, 194, 213, 262, 324

AK-47s, 139, 143, 172, 185, 236, 272

AKEL, 270

Aldergrove Airport, Belfast, 110

Algeria, 2, 11, 16, 189, 215

allies and alignments, 193–6

America/United States: Adams allowed entry, 121; and arena, 35–6; and arms supply, 77, 172, 175, 182–3, 184, 185, 186, 231, 255; attitudes to IRA, 195–6; money from, 77, 145, 187–8; mentioned, 11, 12, 43, 120, 130, 170, 211, 219, 226, 229, 240, 259, 260, 289, 315; see also American Diaspora/Irish-Americans

American Diaspora/Irish-Americans, 35, 68, 75, 169, 182, 186, 187, 195, 229, 262; see also Diaspora

ANC see African National Congress

Andersonstown, Belfast, 66, 110, 226

Anglo-Irish pact, 305

Anglo-Irish Treaty (1921), 64, 67, 216, 296, 301

Angola, 4

An Phoblacht, xvi, 36, 63, 104, 124, 145, 180, 192, 207, 211, 212, 214, 218, 219

Anti-Terrorist Squad, 111

Antrim, 30

Arabs, 43, 240, 302

Arafat, Yasser, 15, 97

Ard Fheis, 58, 68, 127, 187

Ardoyne, the (Belfast), 34, 50, 63, 232, 233

arena, Irish, 17–40

Argentina, 12, 261

Armagh, 63, 173, 202, 294, 320; see also South Armagh

Armalites, 143, 172, 183–4, 272, 273

armed struggle, nature of, 1–16, 317–27

Armenia, 3

arms, 137, 168, 170, 171, 172, 174, 181–6, 262

Arms Trial, 118

Army Convention, 58, 68, 73, 78, 114, 126, 127, 128, 129, 142, 144, 148, 149, 162, 164, 205, 206, 207

Army Council: and abstention, 68; and ANC, 179; appointment of Mac Stiofáin as Chief of Staff, 114; and campaign, 80, 82, 265, 267, 270, 273; and command and control, 148, 149, 150, 151–2, 153, 154, 155, 156, 158, 159–60, 162, 165; and communications, 201, 202, 205, 210, 216; and decommissioning, 263; and deployment, 222, 224, 225, 227, 228, 231, 234, 238; and endgame, 301, 315; and intelligence, 241, 243, 256, 259, 260, 262; and maintenance, 169, 170, 171, 172, 174, 190; and organization, 126, 128, 129, 130, 131, 133, 134, 135, 140, 141, 142, 143, 144, 145, 146; and Provisional Sinn Féin, 102; and recruitment, 80, 86; seven men chosen for, 78, 114; similarity between followers and members of, 125, 150; mentioned, 22, 23, 38, 41, 51, 52, 53, 54, 60, 64, 67, 76, 82, 107, 113, 116, 122, 123, 194, 236, 298, 318

Army Executive, 114, 129, 142, 149, 158, 159, 162, 205, 315

Asia, 3

assets, 145–6, 231–3

Baader-Meinhof, 319

Baghdad, 167

Balkans, 15, 319

Ballymore Eustace, Kildare, 113

Ballymurphy, 120, 226

Ballyshannon, Donegal, 115

Baltic Place/Baltic Exchange, London, 282, 285

Baltic states, 42

Baltimore, 35

Bann (river), 36

Barrett 90 rifles, 273

Barry, Tom, 106, 108, 272–3

Basques, xiv, 2, 42, 270

Batista, Fulgencio, 11

Bavarians, 43

Begin, Menachem, x, 96, 97, 132, 215, 270, 319

Behal, Richard, 194

Behan, Brendan, 103, 202

Beirut, xi, 194, 320

Belfast; and arena, 17, 25, 36, 37, 39; and British army, 79–80; and campaign, 276, 280, 282; and communications, 201, 202, 203, 212–13, 219; and deployment, 223, 225, 226, 230, 232, 234; funerals, 61, 106, 193; and

intelligence, 246, 248, 251, 252; and leaders, 114, 117, 118, 119, 121, 123, 124, 125, 128, 143, 150–1, 152, 153, 154, 158, 159, 231; murals, 62, 192, 194, 212–13, 219; and opposition to Dublin GHQ, 76–7, 114, 116–17; and organization, 131, 136, 137, 138, 140; recruitment, 81, 82, 86, 87; mentioned, 45, 60, 61, 91, 100, 103, 110, 115, 120, 136, 148, 155, 169, 175, 216, 237, 279, 294, 295, 296, 312, 317; *see also* Belfast Brigade

Belfast Brigade, 131, 206, 208, 209, 225–6, 232, 252, 283

Belfast–Dublin railway, 137, 161, 166, 275, 277–8, 280, 282, 323

Bell, Ivor, 67, 118, 123, 143, 148, 151, 153, 154, 156, 158, 159, 212

Bellaghy, Derry, 107

Beretta sub-machine guns, 172, 184

betrayal, 69–70, 244, 250, 256–7; *see also* informers

Birmingham, 181, 296

Bishop, Patrick, xvii

Black and Tan War *see* Tan War

Black September, 4, 285

Blair, Tony, 325

Bloody Sunday, 99, 186–7, 224

Bodenstown, xv, 47, 60, 193, 205, 214

Bodie, William, xviii

Bogside, Derry, 99, 120, 232, 233, 282, 294

Bolivia, 90, 132

Bone, the (Belfast), 81, 226, 232, 233

Bosnia, 1, 4

Boston, 185

Brady, Rory *see* O Brádaigh, Ruarí

Breen, Daniel, 106, 108, 272–3

Brigate rosse, xiv, 16, 50, 78, 97, 114, 240, 270, 304, 321

Brighton: Grand Hotel bombing, 139, 145, 176, 181, 245, 247, 248, 285, 303

Britain/British: and arena, 35; army, 62, 79–80, 99, 166, 182, 224, 230, 241, 242, 271, 275; and communications, 200, 202–3, 208–9, 210, 215–16; and

endgame, 299, 301–15; as enemy, 19, 42, 47, 48, 51–2, 56, 58, 75, 108, 133, 215–16, 222–3, 237–8, 289–300, 322, 323; and Hughes, 108, 109; IRA campaign against, 265–88; and IRA intelligence, 242, 247, 252, 263, 264; and Libya, 184, 185, 194; policy in Ireland, 31, 33, 67, 134, 135, 158, 163–4, 216, 226, 227, 234, 241, 265, 266, 268, 295–6, 301–15, 324, 325; and Provisional perceptions, 240; and recruitment, 84–5, 99; security forces, 241, 263, 266, 267; mentioned, 12, 28, 38, 40, 43, 44, 46, 53, 66, 83, 102, 105, 106, 107, 121, 122, 127, 146, 155, 175, 187, 195, 219, 221, 225, 228, 229, 232, 233, 236, 239, 248, 255, 258, 259, 260, 286, 318, 326; *see also* London
British Telecom, 208, 227, 246
Brittany, xi
Brixton Prison, 28
Brooke, Peter, 306, 309
Browne, Nora, xx
Browne family, xx
B-Specials, 296
Bulgaria, 41
Burma, 320

Cahill, Joe, 117, 120, 123, 151, 152, 153, 158, 159, 184, 225, 276
Cahill, Martin, 283
campaign, 234–9, 265–8
Campbell, Bobby, 111
Canada, 289
Canary Wharf, London, 252, 267, 283, 312
Carlos the Jackal, 285
Cassidy, Barney, 108
Castro, Fidel, 3, 11, 12, 16, 97, 139, 222
Catholics, 26, 27, 28, 29, 30, 31, 32, 42, 43, 44, 49, 57, 78, 82, 95, 96, 107, 119, 125, 216–17, 225, 276, 278, 294, 295, 297, 321
Caucasus, 319
Cavan, 231

Chiapas, 319
Chicago, 35
Chief of Staff (C/S): Adams, 122, 153; Bell, 143, 153; Brady, 115; Cahill, 153; and command, 162; and communication, 207; McGuinness, 122, 153; McKenna, 122–3; Mac Stiofáin, 114–15, 142, 152; O'Doherty, 153; and organization, 129, 136, 142; Twomey, 151, 153; mentioned, 38, 97, 153, 207, 227
China, 3, 12, 98, 140, 189
CIA (Central Intelligence Agency), 183
City of London, 37, 157, 167, 238, 281, 285, 303, 308; *see also* London
Clann na Phoblachta, 64, 310
Clare, 37
Claudia, 184, 256
Clonard, Belfast, 226
Coagh, Tyrone, 109
Cold War, 1
Collins, Joe, 231
Collins, Michael, 66, 301
Colraine, 45
Colombia, 1
Columbia, xiii, xviii
Colvard, Karen, xviii
command and control, 141–4, 148–67
communications, 198–221
communists/communism, 74–5, 140, 179–80
Connolly, James, 75, 213, 295
Conservative government, 139, 145, 176
constituency, 214–15
Constitution, 149, 165
Continuity Army Council, 156, 180, 230, 268, 314
Convery, Seán, 154
Conway's Pub, Dublin, 207
Cork, 34, 232, 278–9
Cornish, the, 43
Costello, Seámus, 67, 70, 100, 133, 188, 220, 230, 244
counter-intelligence, 244–5, 248–51, 257
Creggan, the, 34, 50
Croatia, 2

Cross, Devon Gaffney, xviii
Crossmaglen, Armagh, 26, 34, 36, 84,
    103, 119
Crown, the, 43, 57, 108, 289, 290, 292,
    293
Crumlin Road, Belfast, 226
Crumlin Road Prison, Belfast, 115
Cuba, 3, 11, 14, 139, 140, 212
culture and roles, 26–9
Cumann na mBan, 130
Cyprus, xi, 90, 141, 270
Czechs, 189

Dáil, 30, 44, 64, 97, 102, 115, 289
Danvers, Massachusetts, 183
decisions, 166–7
deployment, 222–39
Derry: Bloody Sunday, 99, 186–7, 224;
    and deployment, 225, 226, 232;
    McGuinness in, 87, 120–1, 122, 131,
    154, 232; Protestants and Catholics in,
    294; and recruitment, 81, 87;
    mentioned, 30, 34, 36, 99, 107, 109,
    112, 122, 128, 137, 140, 143, 161, 175,
    219, 282
De Valera, Eamon, 3, 64, 66, 97, 166, 289,
    301, 310, 323
Devlin, Bernadette, 83
Diaspora, 20, 35, 68, 75, 131, 132, 169,
    182, 186, 187, 188, 193, 195, 211, 224,
    225, 236, 238, 261, 262
Diplock courts judicial system, 69
Divis Flats, Belfast, 226
Doherty, Joe, 259
Donegal, 37, 115, 151
Down, 30
Downing Street, London, 33, 139, 167,
    176–7, 245, 247, 248, 276, 303, 304
Downing Street Declarations, 72
Driver, Frank, 113, 115
Drumm, Maire, 124
Dublin, xi, xii, 20, 21, 25, 30, 31, 35, 37,
    44, 45, 46, 48–9, 53, 56, 58–9, 76, 80,
    81, 84, 91, 99, 100, 113, 116, 117, 118,
    119, 123, 128, 129, 134, 152, 153, 159,
    161, 168, 169, 171, 182, 183, 185, 187,

195, 201, 202, 204, 207, 217, 222, 223,
    224, 226, 231, 232, 233, 238, 264,
    265–6, 268, 270, 273, 283, 290, 293,
    294, 296, 298, 304, 305, 307, 308, 309,
    310, 313, 317; *see also* Dublin GHQ
Dublin–Belfast railway, 137, 161, 166,
    275, 277–8, 280, 282, 323
Dublin GHQ: divisions leading to split
    from, 73, 74, 75; and events in 1969,
    21, 47, 75, 76, 77, 168; Leftist views,
    64, 75, 83; split from, 58, 70, 73, 77,
    78, 169, 170; mentioned, 66, 79, 113,
    114, 116, 129, 151, 164, 229, 301, 320
Dundalk, 224
Dunmurry, 246

Eastern Europe, 11
Easter Week, 1916, xv, 51, 289
Egypt, 15, 215, 270
Eksund, 185
endgame, xi, xviii, 148, 149, 162, 198,
    201, 217, 267–8, 299, 301–16, 323;
    see also peace process
enemy, 215–17, 289–300; *see also*
    Britain/British
England/English, 35, 42, 43, 51, 66,
    138–9, 171, 188, 202, 206, 228, 229,
    231, 237, 248, 255, 263, 278, 279,
    281–2, 283, 284, 285, 287, 289, 290,
    291, 292, 293, 298, 304; *see also*
    Britain/British
Enniskillen, 161, 187, 212
EOKA, 78, 90, 140, 141, 270
Eritrea, vii, 16
ETA, xiv, 270, 324
Ethiopia, vii, 10, 14
Europa Hotel, Belfast, 226, 282
Europe, 4, 21, 35, 41, 45, 174, 186, 255,
    260, 281, 282, 291, 304, 309; *see also*
    names of countries
Euroterrorists, xi, 4, 97, 194, 215, 285
Ewart-Briggs, Christopher, 37, 161, 231
Executive *see* Army Executive

faithful, the, 101–3, 211–14
Falklands War, 261

Falls Road, Belfast, 17, 26, 36, 37, 60, 61, 62, 84, 117, 120, 121, 140, 204–5, 226, 232, 233, 291, 298, 311
Fallylea, 108
Fatah, 78, 114, 194, 261, 262
FBI (Federal Bureau of Investigation), 183
Fenians, 41, 42, 45, 51, 54, 71, 100, 103, 104, 118, 140, 202, 289, 294, 318, 320; *see also* Irish Republican Brotherhood
Fermanagh, 99, 291
Fianna Éireann, 82, 202, 322
Fianna Fáil, 64, 66, 118, 166, 169
Fitt, Gerry, 121
Flannery, Mick, 183
France, 12, 96
Fulham Broadway, London, 180
funds *see* money
funerals, 60–2, 147, 193

Gandhi, 11
Gárdá, 113, 247
Garland, Seán, 64, 115, 301
Gaza, xi, 4, 11, 319
General Army Convention *see* Army Convention
Georgians, 11
Germany, xi, 12, 35, 43, 97, 215, 248, 252, 282, 285, 319
GHQ: and campaign, 280, 281; and communications, 199, 200, 201, 202, 203, 204, 207; and deployment, 231, 235; and intelligence, 244, 248, 252, 254, 255, 256, 258, 259, 260, 261, 262, 264; and maintenance, 170, 171, 173, 174, 183, 187, 188, 196, 227; and organization, 126, 128, 130, 136, 137, 141, 142, 143; staff chosen by Mac Stiofáin, 114; mentioned, 37, 79, 153, 154, 169, 246, 247
Giap, 10, 304
Gibraltar, 35, 136, 255, 285
Gilmore, George, 166
Glenholmes, Dickie, 111
Gloucestershires, 109
Goulding, Cathal, 64, 75, 99–100, 115, 126, 128, 129, 202, 301
Gow, Ian, 276
Green Book, 59
Grivas, Colonel George, 90, 97, 132, 139–40, 270
Grundig and Strathearn Audio factories, 246
guerillas, Provisional, 106–9
guerilla warfare, 4, 5, 139–40
Guevara, Che, 4, 11, 15, 16, 62, 90, 97, 132, 139, 285
gunmen, Provisional, 110–13
Guzmán Reynoso, Abimael, 97

Habash, George, 97
Haiti, 42
Hamas, 319
Harrison, George, 183
Harrods, 161
Harry Guggenheim Foundation, xviii
H-Blocks, 16, 50, 105, 106, 134, 259, 293
Heathrow, 20, 177
heresy, 66, 67, 68
Hillsborough Agreement, 268
Ho Chi Minh, 14, 304
Holland, 35, 136, 248, 263, 282
Hughes, Bernard, 154
Hughes, Francis, 107–9, 112
Hume, John, 309, 310, 311, 313
hunger strikes, 28, 50, 54, 68, 105, 106, 147, 186, 199, 210–11, 259, 279, 318
Hyde Park, London, 282

Ibo, 9
ideology, 56–72
India, 240
individuals, 95–125
informers, 69–70, 157–8, 244–5, 250
Inistioge, xiv
INLA *see* Irish National Liberation Army
intelligence, 240–64
Iran, 13, 14, 16, 194, 209, 255
Iraq, 13, 167, 190
IRB (Irish Republican Brotherhood), 42, 58, 59, 64, 318; *see also* Fenians

Irgun Zvai Leumi, xiv, 96, 141, 270, 319
IRIS, 212
Irish-Americans *see* American
    Diaspora/Irish-Americans
Irish arena, 17–40
Irish Free State, 44, 46, 47, 64, 289, 293,
    301, 320; *see also* Irish Republic
Irish National Liberation Army (INLA),
    107, 188, 210, 220, 230, 237, 244
Irish National Liberation Front, 67,
    189
Irish People's Liberation Army, 189
Irish People, The, 211
Irish Republic, 30, 34, 36, 37–8, 42, 44,
    85, 91, 98, 175, 188, 234, 235, 269,
    286, 291, 293, 301; *see also* Dublin;
    Irish Free State
Irish Republican Brotherhood (IRB), 42,
    58, 59, 64, 318; *see also* Fenians
Irish Republican Socialist Party (IRSP),
    67, 100, 237
Irish Times, xi
Irish Volunteers (*Oglaigh na h-Éireann*),
    58–9, 104, 165, 289
IRSP (Irish Republican Socialist Party),
    67, 100, 237
Islam, 14, 184; *see also* Moslems
Israel, 4
Italy, xi, 10, 12–13, 16, 41, 42, 50, 97, 215,
    240, 270, 304

Jalloud, Major Abdul Salam, 184
Japan, 12
Jericho, 4
Jews, 43, 215
Johnston, Roy, 64, 75
Jones, Corporal David, 108

Kashmir, 2
Keenan, Brian, 111, 118, 120, 123, 154,
    159, 246, 247, 250
Keenan, Seán, 120
Kelly, John, 118, 123, 151, 159
Kenya, 274, 303
Kerry, 34, 232, 233
Kildare, 113

Kilrea, 109
Kosovo, 3, 4, 13
Kurds, 1, 13

Labour, 33, 315, 325
Latin America, 15, 42, 90, 97, 139, 270;
    see also names of countries
leaders, 113–25; *see also* names of leaders
Lebanon, 3, 4, 15, 35
Lee-Enfields, 172, 181–2, 183, 272
Left, the, 4, 41, 42, 51, 64, 121
Leinster, 224
Leinster House, 44, 45, 74
Leitrim, 151
Leix, 152
Lemass, Seán, 21
Lenin, V. I., 47, 64, 67, 295
Letts, 11
Libya, 68, 123, 143, 172, 175, 184, 185,
    187, 189, 190, 194, 195, 196, 236, 261,
    262
Limerick, 60, 151, 152
Liverpool, 279, 291
London: bombs/mortars in, 37, 136, 157,
    167, 172, 176–7, 180, 199, 229, 234,
    238, 247, 267, 275, 279, 280, 281, 282,
    285, 287, 312, 317; and Irish affairs,
    20, 21, 33, 45, 158, 195, 215, 246, 268,
    283, 291, 293, 295, 299, 303, 304, 305,
    306, 307, 308, 313, 324–5; Storey
    arrested in, 111; talks in, 66–7, 121,
    228, 233, 265 296; mentioned, 35, 43,
    44, 48, 91, 110, 135, 145, 151, 163,
    181, 185, 187, 200, 201, 216, 224, 241,
    255, 264, 290, 298, 300; *see also* City of
    London
Londonderry *see* Derry
Longford, 116
Long Kesh, 16, 109, 259; *see also* Maze
    prison
Long March, 13
Loughall RUC station, 235, 250
Louth, 34, 37
loyalists, xix, 20, 21, 23, 47, 48, 175, 200,
    313, 315
Lurgan, 119, 123

M-1s, 172, 183, 272
McAteer, Hugh, 117
McBride, Seán, 64, 66, 301
McCabe, Jack, 171, 174, 231
McCabe, Detective Gárdá Jerry, 37
Macedonia, 41
McGirl, John Joe, 151
McGlade, Charlie, 119, 152, 159, 231
McGlinchey, Dominic, 107
McGuinness, Martin: at Columbia
    University, xiii, xviii; and conference
    with British (1972), 67, 121; and
    Derry unit, 81, 87, 120–1, 131, 232;
    dominates IRA, 103, 122, 123, 141,
    153, 154, 158, 162; and endgame, 308,
    311; and Sinn Féin, 135; mentioned,
    35, 128, 155
McKee, Billy, 117, 123, 151, 152, 159,
    225
McKenna, Kevin, 122–3
McMillen, Billy, 76, 77, 117
Mac Stiofáin, Seán (John Stephenson),
    66–7, 114–15, 116, 117, 118, 120–1,
    123, 142, 151, 152, 153, 158, 159, 162,
    172, 174, 202, 226
MacSwiney, Lord Mayor Terence, 28
McWhirter, Ross, 281
Maghera, 107, 108
Magherafelt, 109
Maguire, Maria, 174
maintenance, 168–97
Major, Prime Minister John, 166, 167,
    176, 228, 245, 276, 308, 309, 310
Malaya, 132
Mallie, Eamonn, xvii
Mallon, Kevin, 119, 123
Malta, 185
management, administrative, 190–2
Manchester, 275, 304
Mandela, Nelson, 15, 16, 213, 262
Mao Tse-tung, 3, 11, 12, 13, 19, 59, 93,
    98, 179, 304
Marita Ann, 185
Martin, Leo, 152, 154
Marx, Karl, 42, 295, 321
Marxist-Leninists, 4, 53, 59, 319

Mater Hospital, 124
Maze prison, 112, 134, 209, 259; *see also*
    Long Kesh
Meath, 116
Meo, George, 183
Mexico, 319
Middle East, 35, 167, 174, 235; *see also*
    names of countries
Mid-Tyrone Brigade, 25
Milan, 4
Milltown cemetery, Belfast, 61, 193
momentum, 196–7
Monaghan, 37, 204, 227
money, 168, 170, 171, 174–5, 186–90,
    260–1
Mooney's pub, Dublin, 207
morale, 192, 193
Morrison, Danny, xi
Moslems, 215; *see also* Islam
Motorman Operation, 175, 226
Mountbatten, Lord, 37, 187, 229, 245,
    247, 305
Mozambique, 2
Mulcahy, Paddy, 151, 152
Mullaghmore, 229
Mullingar, 117
Munster, 224
murals, 62, 192, 194, 212–13, 219

National Gallery, London, 282
nationalism, 13, 42, 43, 44, 51, 97, 214,
    217; *see also* nationalists
nationalists, 30, 31, 43, 53, 54, 56, 57, 80,
    95, 217, 223–4, 269, 278–9, 294–5,
    315; *see also* nationalism
National Library, 26
Navan, 116
Neave, Airey, 230
Negri, Tony, 97
New Democratic Left, 47
New York, xii, xvii, 36, 121, 123, 188
Newry, 36
newspapers, 211–12; *see also* names of
    newspapers
Nicaragua, 14, 16, 139, 140, 212
Nigeria, 9

NORAID, 145, 182–3, 187, 188, 195

North Antrim, 233

North Carolina, 183

Northern Command, 118, 122, 128, 136, 137, 141, 142, 143, 153, 154, 162, 202, 206, 227, 235, 252

Northern Ireland, armed struggle for *see* Britain/British; Provisional IRA

Northern Ireland Assembly, 72

Northern Ireland Office, 304, 308

O Brádaigh, Ruairí (Rory Brady), 67, 84, 115, 116, 118–19, 120, 122, 123, 130, 131, 151, 152, 156, 159, 218–19

O'Brien, Brendan, xvii

O'Brien, Conor Cruise, 51

O Conaill, Daithi (Dave O'Connell), 67, 115–16, 117, 118–19, 120, 122, 123, 151, 152, 156, 159, 174

O'Doherty, Eamon, 123, 153, 154, 158

O Donnell, Peadar, 166

Official IRA: and arms, 168, 182; and army, 63; Army Convention, 148; and counter-intelligence, 244; features distinguishing Provisionals from, 78; name, 127; operations, 229–30; organization, 129; as political party, 47; split by withdrawal of Costello, 67, 70, 133, 220; units, 66, 81; mentioned, 22, 53, 56, 65, 68, 79, 99, 114, 115, 121, 148, 151, 152, 169, 171, 188, 189, 222, 224, 231, 237, 301, 310, 322

O'Hagan, J.B., 119, 123

O'Hare, Rita, 124

Oklahoma City, 12

Old Bailey, 112

Omagh bomb, 37, 55, 70, 148, 156, 160, 230, 314

O'Malley, Ernie, 106

O'Neill, Captain Terrance, 21

Operation Hawk, 246

Operation Motorman, 175, 226

operational commitments, 228–31

operational intelligence, 246–8

Orange order, 79, 80, 83, 97, 294

organization, 58–63, 126–47

Orr, William, 60

O Snodaigh, Padraig, xx

Palestine, xiv, 2, 4, 5, 8, 11, 41, 43, 97, 132, 141, 215, 222, 270, 274, 304, 309

Palestinians, 3, 11, 15, 16, 87, 98, 184, 190, 194, 213, 240, 319, 320

Paris, 121

Parnell, Charles Stewart, 3

Parnell Square, Dublin, 207, 211

Parnell Street, Dublin, 207

Peace People, 304–5

peace process, xi, xii, xiii, 21, 33, 35, 48, 52, 64, 68, 72, 143, 218, 313–14; *see also* endgame

Pearse, Padraig, 66, 213

People's Will, xiv

perception, 6, 17, 18, 19, 20, 25–6, 51–2, 312

Peron, Juan, 12

Peru, 2, 15, 97

PLO (Palestine Liberation Organization), 185, 194, 324

Poland, 11, 42

politics, 63–4, 65, 68, 74, 134, 135, 159, 286, 315

Pomeroy, Tyrone, 66, 119

Poppy Day massacre, 187, 212

Popular Front for the Liberation of Palestine, 4

Portlaoise, 123

Portuguese African empire, 11

Price, Marian and Doloures, 199, 279

prison/prisoners, 50, 105, 109, 209–11, 258–60; *see also* H-Blocks; Long Kesh; Maze prison

probationers, 99–104

propaganda and publicity, 217–19

Protestants, 26, 28, 29, 30, 31, 32, 35, 42, 43, 44, 45, 47, 48, 53, 56, 57, 78, 95, 96, 107, 124, 142, 155, 157, 216, 217, 229, 270, 274, 276, 279, 283, 284, 290, 293, 294, 295, 297, 299, 306, 307, 309, 311, 312, 315

prototypes, 104–13

Provisional Army Council *see* Army
Council
Provisional IRA: analysis and reality,
41–55; arena, 17–40; campaign,
265–88; command and control,
148–67; communications, 198–221;
deployment, 222–39; endgame,
301–16; enemy, 289–300; ideology,
56–72; individuals, 95–125;
intelligence, 240–64; maintenance,
168–97; nature of armed struggle,
317–27; organization, 126–47;
recruitment, 73–94
Provisional Sinn Féin, 64, 72, 102, 122,
134, 135, 146–7, 152, 159, 204, 214; *see
also* Sinn Féin
publicity *see* propaganda and publicity

el-Qaddafi, Colonel Muammar, 184, 185
QMG, 171, 172, 174, 178, 182, 183, 184,
185, 186, 263
Quick Reaction Force, 109

Real IRA, 70, 120, 148, 156, 159, 180,
196, 230, 268, 313, 314
rebels, 103–4
recruitment, 73–94; *see also* volunteers
Red Brigades, 185
Regent's Park, London, 282, 303
Republican Congress, 63, 64, 166, 310
Republican News, 117, 211
Republican Publicity Bureau, 207
Republican Sinn Féin: isolation of, 68;
split leading to formation of, 68, 70,
72, 134, 143, 149, 150, 187, 236, 239,
305; mentioned, 57, 65, 66, 120, 123,
135, 145, 156, 159, 196, 219, 220, 230,
237, 310, 313, 315; *see also* Sinn Féin
requirements, 169–70
resource acquisition, intelligence for,
260–2
Revisionist Zionists, 270
Reynolds, Albert, 309, 311
Rhodesia, 140
Right, the, 42
rituals, 213–14

Roman Catholic Church, 28, 31, 43, 44,
49, 57, 293, 299, 321; *see also* Catholics
Rome, 4, 10
Roscommon, 116, 123, 159
Royal Irish Regiment, 307
Royal Ulster Constabulary *see* RUC
RPG-7, 172, 174, 182, 184, 190, 226
RUC (Royal Ulster Constabulary), 26,
29, 99, 107, 108, 119, 204, 208, 227,
228, 234, 235, 246, 247, 250, 268, 275,
276, 282, 283, 307, 312
Russell, Seán, 149
Russia/Russians, xiv, 189; *see also* Soviet
Union
Rwanda, 1, 2
Ryan, Mick, 168, 301

Sallins train robbery, 37, 188
SAM missiles, 186
Sands, Bobby, xiii, 16, 105–6, 194, 259,
293, 318
Saor Éire, 133, 229, 277
SAS, 108, 109, 173, 295
Scandinavia, 12
schism, 70–1, 72
Scotland/Scots, 43, 202, 215, 229, 243
Scotland Yard, 111
SDLP (Social and Democratic Labour
Party), 310
Second Dáil, 129
security data, 256–7
Semtex, 143, 172, 185–6, 236, 269, 281
Serbs/Serbia, 13, 319
Shankill, the, 37
Shevlin, Myles, 67
Shi'ites, xiii
Short Strand, Belfast, 25, 99, 226
Sinn Féin: Adams as leader of, 122, 135,
212, 218, 310, 311; Ard Fheis, 58, 68,
127, 187; banned, 203; and
communications, 206, 207, 211, 217,
218; co-opted as political vehicle in
1950s, 126, 128; desire to enhance
political appeal of, 134; dissent about,
67–8; and endgame, 165, 304, 306,
310, 311, 313, 315–6; increasing

importance of, 165, 236, 267, 287; and intelligence, 245, 248, 253; and international contacts, 194; lack of support for, 30, 38, 49, 65, 269; money for, 175, 186, 187; O Brádaigh involved in, 67, 84, 115, 116, 130; and Official IRA, 47; and recruits, 84, 85, 180; role of, 39, 64, 128, 129, 135, 271; tensions between military and, 130, 135; mentioned, xvi, 21, 36, 39, 45, 54, 59, 79, 100, 106, 113, 115, 121, 123, 124, 125, 131, 136, 145, 146, 150, 154, 155, 156, 159, 160, 164, 167, 190, 192, 195, 197, 202, 224, 235, 239, 255, 268, 273, 286, 303, 305, 309, 322; *see also* Provisional Sinn Féin; Republican Sinn Féin

Sinn Féin–the Workers' Party, 47
Skyways Hotel, Belfast, 110
Sligo, 37, 229
Slovenes, 11
Smith-Richardson Foundation, xviii
socialism, 74
Somalia, 4, 15, 320
South Africa, 2, 5, 304, 309
South Armagh, 36, 39, 50, 82, 119, 137, 142, 156, 157, 160, 174, 230, 232, 234, 277–8, 281, 291
Southern Command, 37, 128, 136, 142, 153
South, Seán, 60
South Yemen, 302
Soviet Union, 309; *see also* Russia/Russians
Spain, 2, 10
Special Branch, 35, 85, 92, 113, 202, 203, 207
Sri Lanka, 10, 319
Stalin, Joseph, 12
Standard Telephones, 227
states, 14, 15
statistics, 29–31
Steele, Jimmy, 75, 117, 123, 151, 152, 159
Stephenson John *see* Mac Stiofáin, Seán
Stern Group, 8, 222
Storey, Bobby, 110–12
Stormont, 21, 74, 75, 77, 119, 203, 223, 225, 226, 294

Strabane, 36, 99, 224
strategy, 222–8, 286–8
Suez Canal Zone, 274, 303
Sweden, 13
Switzerland, 194
Syria, 13

tactical intelligence, 242–5
tactical targets, 278–84
tactics, 222–8, 275–8
Tamil Tigers, 319, 324
Tan War, 65, 100, 106, 107, 108, 129, 165, 224, 272, 318, 320
targets, 227–8, 234, 254–6, 274–84, 285, 287
Taylor, John, 229
Teheran, 14, 16
Tel Aviv, 185
terrorism, 4–5
Thatcher, Prime Minister Margaret, 139, 145, 161, 166, 176, 181, 200, 228, 230, 245, 252, 276, 318
Third World, 41, 87
Thompson (machine-gun), 172, 182, 183
Tipperary, 25, 123, 153
Tone, Wolfe, 52, 64, 96, 119, 217, 289, 290, 292, 295, 312, 318; commemorated in Bodenstown, xv, 60, 193, 205, 214
Toronto, 35
Tower of London, 282
Tracy, Seán, 152
training and tradecraft, 179–81
Trimble, David, 313
Tripoli, 35, 185, 194
Tuite, Gerard, 111
Turkey, 13, 15
Twomey, Seámus, 67, 117–18, 123, 151, 153, 154, 158–9, 225
Tyrone, 25, 30, 37, 50, 82, 109, 119, 122, 137, 151, 173, 233, 291, 294, 298, 320

Ulster Defence Regiment, 107, 227, 283
Ulster Polytechnic, 246
Ulster Volunteer Force, 20

Unionists, xix, 20, 21, 23, 26, 27, 30, 31, 37, 39, 40, 43, 44, 45, 46, 47, 48, 53, 56, 59, 75, 80, 96, 121, 175, 200, 210, 216, 217, 219, 225, 229, 242, 266, 268, 274, 293, 294, 298, 299, 300, 306, 307, 309, 313, 315
United Irishman, 47, 117
United Irishmen, 119, 290
United Nations, 295
United States *see* America/United States
Unity Flats, 34
University College Dublin, 116
Uris, Leon, 293

Valhalla, 185
Vietnam/Vietnamese, 10, 16, 98, 121, 135
Virginians, 43
volunteers, 95–125, 177–9; *see also* recruitment; training and tradecraft
Wales/Welsh, 43, 202, 215, 229, 243

Walker monument, Derry, 282
Warrenpoint, 187, 228–9, 278, 305
Warsaw Pact, 11
Washington, 31, 163, 185, 187, 195, 240
West Africa, 320; *see also* Africa
West Bank, 11
Westminster, 20, 74, 83, 121, 134, 135, 159, 218, 266, 303
White, Harry, 119, 152, 159, 231
Wolfe Tone Society, 126
Workers' Party, 47
Wright, Billy, 210, 230

Yemen, 13, 304
Yugoslavia, 309

Zambezi valley, xi
Zapatistas, 319
Zionists, 42, 43, 96, 188, 215, 240, 270, 302